Essentials
of **Psychological Assessment** Series

ORDER FORM

Please send this order form with your payment (credit card or check) to:
Wiley, Attn: Customer Care, 10475 Crosspoint Blvd., Indianapolis, IN 46256

QUANTITY	TITLE	ISBN	PRICE
_____	_____	_____	_____
_____	_____	_____	_____
_____	_____	_____	_____
_____	_____	_____	_____
_____	_____	_____	_____

Shipping Charges:	Surface	2-Day	1-Day
First item	$5.00	$10.50	$17.50
Each additional item	$3.00	$3.00	$4.00

For orders greater than 15 items,
please contact Customer Care at 1-877-762-2974.

ORDER AMOUNT _____

SHIPPING CHARGES _____

SALES TAX _____

TOTAL ENCLOSED _____

NAME_____

AFFILIATION_____

ADDRESS_____

CITY/STATE/ZIP _____

TELEPHONE _____

EMAIL_____

❑ Please add me to your e-mailing list

PAYMENT METHOD:

❑ Check/Money Order   ❑ Visa   ❑ Mastercard   ❑ AmEx

Card Number _____ Exp. Date _____

Cardholder Name *(Please print)* _____

Signature _____

*Make checks payable to **John Wiley & Sons.** Credit card orders invalid if not signed.*
All orders subject to credit approval. • Prices subject to change.

To order by phone, call toll free 1-877-762-2974
To order online: www.wiley.com/essentials

WILEY

Essentials of WJ IV® Tests of Achievement

Essentials of Psychological Assessment Series

Series Editors, Alan S. Kaufman and Nadeen L. Kaufman

Essentials of Temperament Assessment by Diana Joyce

Essentials of WAIS®-IV Assessment, Second Edition by Elizabeth O. Lichtenberger and Alan S. Kaufman

Essentials of WIAT®-III and KTEA-II Assessment by Elizabeth O. Lichtenberger and Kristina C. Breaux

Essentials of WISC®-IV Assessment, Second Edition by Dawn P. Flanagan and Alan S. Kaufman

Essentials of WJ III™ Cognitive Abilities Assessment, Second Edition by Fredrick A. Schrank, Daniel C. Miller, Barbara J. Wendling, and Richard W. Woodcock

Essentials of WJ IV® Tests of Achievement by Nancy Mather and Barbara J. Wendling

Essentials of WMS®-IV Assessment by Lisa Whipple Drozdick, James A. Holdnack, and Robin C. Hilsabeck

Essentials of WNV™ Assessment by Kimberly A. Brunnert, Jack A. Naglieri, and Steven T. Hardy-Braz

Essentials of WPPSI™-IV Assessment by Susan Engi Raiford and Diane Coalson

Essentials of WRAML2 and TOMAL-2 Assessment by Wayne Adams and Cecil R. Reynolds

Essentials

of WJ IV® Tests of Achievement

Nancy Mather and
Barbara J. Wendling

WILEY

Library of Congress Cataloging-in-Publication Data:
Mather, Nancy.
   Essentials of WJ IV© tests of achievement / by Nancy Mather and Barbara J. Wendling.
      pages cm. — (Essentials of psychological assessment series)
   Includes bibliographical references and index.
   ISBN 978-1-118-79915-4 (print)
   ISBN 978-1-118-79916-1 (ePub)
   ISBN 978-1-118-79910-9 (ePDF)
1. Woodcock-Johnson Psycho-Educational Battery.   I. Wendling, Barbara J.   II. Title.   III. Title: Essentials of WJ 4 tests of achievement.   IV. Title: Essentials of WJ four tests of achievement.
   LB1131.75.W66M373 2015
   371.26–dc23   2014028494

Printed in the United States of America
SKY10026612_042621

CONTENTS

SERIES PREFACE

I n the *Essentials of Psychological Assessment* series, we have attempted to provide the reader with books that will deliver key practical information in the most efficient and accessible style. The series features instruments in a variety of domains, such as cognition, personality, education, and neuropsychology. For the experienced clinician, books in the series will offer a concise yet thorough way to master utilization of the continuously evolving supply of new and revised instruments, as well as a convenient method for keeping up to date on the tried-and-true measures. The novice will find here a prioritized assembly of all the information and techniques that must be at one's fingertips to begin the complicated process of individual psychological diagnosis.

Wherever feasible, visual shortcuts to highlight key points are utilized alongside systematic, step-by-step guidelines. Chapters are focused and succinct. Topics are targeted for an easy understanding of the essentials of administration, scoring, interpretation, and clinical application. Theory and research are continually woven into the fabric of each book, but always to enhance clinical inference, never to sidetrack or overwhelm. We have long been advocates of "intelligent" testing—the notion that a profile of test scores is meaningless unless it is brought to life by the clinical observations and astute detective work of knowledgeable examiners. Test profiles must be used to make a difference in the child's or adult's life, or why bother to test? We want this series to help our readers become the best intelligent testers they can be.

The *Essentials of WJ IV® Tests of Achievement* is designed to be a helpful reference to all examiners, whether they are experienced with the WJ III or just learning the WJ IV. The internationally renowned authors have incorporated fine points of administration, scoring, and interpretation to assist examiners in building their competency with the WJ IV Tests of Achievement and the WJ IV Tests of Oral Language. The authors weave expert guidance throughout to help the reader avoid common examiner errors. Appendix B includes answers to frequently asked questions.

Too often the focus of testing is on getting a score or establishing a numeric discrepancy. Much more information can be derived from an achievement or oral language test than just a score. In this book, the authors provide access to the rich, interpretive information available when using the WJ IV ACH or the WJ IV OL.

Alan S. Kaufman, PhD, and Nadeen L. Kaufman, EdD, Series Editors
Yale Child Study Center, Yale University School of Medicine

ACKNOWLEDGMENTS

We would like to express our sincere appreciation to the numerous dedicated assessment professionals who help children and adults understand their unique strengths and weaknesses and prescribe targeted interventions designed to foster their success.

Dr. Richard Woodcock has had a profound effect on our professional lives and we are grateful for his influence, inspiration, and mentorship. We acknowledge his many contributions that have led to diagnostic and practical tools for assessment professionals. Additionally, we acknowledge the leadership and support of Dr. Fredrick Schrank in the development of the WJ IV.

Finally, we are grateful for the contributions of Marquita Flemming, Sherry Wasserman, and the rest of the staff at John Wiley & Sons.

One

Although many standardized instruments exist for measuring academic performance, the Woodcock-Johnson Tests of Achievement (WJ ACH) is often cited as one of the most widely used and respected individual achievement tests since its original publication in 1977 (Gregory, 1996). The latest revision, the Woodcock-Johnson IV® Tests of Achievement (WJ IV ACH) (Schrank, Mather, & McGrew, 2014a), provides examiners with an even more comprehensive and useful instrument. The WJ IV ACH is a companion instrument to the Woodcock-Johnson IV Tests of Cognitive Abilities (WJ IV COG) (Schrank, McGrew, & Mather, 2014b) and the new Woodcock-Johnson Tests of Oral Language (WJ IV OL) (Schrank, Mather, & McGrew, 2014b). These three instruments form the Woodcock-Johnson IV (WJ IV) (Schrank, McGrew, & Mather, 2014a), a comprehensive battery of individually administered tests that are designed to measure general intellectual ability, specific cognitive abilities, oral language abilities, and achievement. Depending upon the purpose of the assessment, these instruments may be used independently, in conjunction with each other, or with other assessment instruments.

Essentials of WJ IV® Tests of Achievement provides an easy-to-use guide and reference for professionals and practitioners who wish to learn the key features of this instrument. This guide is appropriate for a wide array of professionals, whether their goal is to learn how to administer the test or simply to increase familiarity with the instrument. The topics covered include administration, scoring, interpretation, and application of the WJ IV ACH. In addition, one chapter is dedicated to the use and application of the WJ IV OL. All chapters include "Rapid Reference," "Caution," and "Don't Forget" boxes that highlight important points. At the end of each chapter is a "Test Yourself" section designed to help examiners review and reinforce the key information presented. These features make the guide an ideal resource for both in-service and graduate training in the application and interpretation of the WJ IV ACH. Examiners may wish to

≡ *Rapid Reference 1.1*

Woodcock-Johnson IV Tests of Achievement

Authors: Fredrick A. Schrank, Nancy Mather, and Kevin S. McGrew

Publication date: 2014

Curricular areas the test measures: Reading, written language, mathematics, and academic knowledge

Age range: 2 to 95+ years

Grade range: K.0 through 17.9

Administration Time: Standard Battery, 40 to 50 minutes; with Extended Battery, approximately another 45 minutes; selective testing, 5 to 10 minutes per test

Qualifications of Examiners: Undergraduate, graduate, or professional-level training and background in test administration and interpretation

Publisher:

Riverside Publishing Company

3800 Golf Road, Suite 200

Rolling Meadows, IL 60008

Customer service: 800.323.9540

Fax: 630.467.7192

www.riversidepublishing.com

Price: WJ IV ACH complete test price (for any one Form A, B, or C) without case is $629 (as of 2014)

read the book from cover to cover or turn to individual chapters to find specific information. Rapid Reference 1.1 provides basic information about the WJ IV ACH and its publisher.

HISTORY AND DEVELOPMENT

The original Woodcock-Johnson Tests of Achievement was published in 1977 as part of the Woodcock-Johnson Psycho-Educational Battery (WJ) (Woodcock & Johnson, 1977). The WJ provided the first comprehensive, co-normed battery of cognitive abilities, achievement, and interests. The battery of tests measured a continuum of human abilities across a wide age range and provided common norms for interpretation. The Tests of Achievement consisted of 10 tests organized into four areas: reading, mathematics, written language, and knowledge.

The Woodcock-Johnson-Revised (WJ-R®) (Woodcock & Johnson, 1989) was designed to expand and increase the diagnostic capabilities of the WJ. The tests were divided into two main batteries, the Tests of Cognitive Ability (WJ-R COG) and the Tests of Achievement (WJ-R ACH). The WJ-R COG and WJ-R ACH each had two easel test books, the Standard Battery and the Supplemental Battery. The WJ-R Tests of Achievement consisted of 14 tests organized into four curricular areas: reading, mathematics, written language, and knowledge. Several new tests were added to the reading and written language areas. To facilitate pre- and posttesting, parallel, alternate forms of the Tests of Achievement, Forms A and B, were published.

Like its predecessor, the Woodcock-Johnson III had two distinct batteries, the Tests of Cognitive Abilities and the Tests of Achievement (Woodcock, McGrew, & Mather, 2001). Together these batteries comprised a comprehensive system for measuring general intellectual ability (g), specific cognitive abilities, predicted achievement, oral language, and achievement across a wide age range. As with the original WJ, one of the most important features of the WJ III system was that norms for the WJ III COG and WJ III ACH were based on data from the same sample of individuals. This co-norming provided greater accuracy and validity when making comparisons among and between an individual's obtained scores and provided new options for various discrepancy and variation procedures.

The latest edition, the WJ IV, is composed of three parts: the WJ IV Tests of Cognitive Abilities (WJ IV COG), the WJ IV Tests of Achievement (WJ IV ACH), and the WJ IV Tests of Oral Language (WJ IV OL). Together these three assessment instruments provide a comprehensive set of individually administered, norm-referenced tests for measuring intellectual abilities, academic achievement, and oral language. As with prior versions, the normative data are based on a single sample that was administered the cognitive, the oral language, and the achievement tests. This comprehensive assessment system facilitates exploring and identifying individual strengths and weaknesses across cognitive, oral language, and academic abilities.

ORGANIZATION OF THE WJ IV ACH

As noted, the WJ IV ACH is a revised and expanded version of the WJ III Tests of Achievement. The WJ IV ACH has 20 tests that are organized into five main areas: reading, mathematics, written language, academic knowledge, and cross-domain clusters. The cross-domain clusters include tests from three different curricular areas (reading, mathematics, and writing). For example, the Academic Fluency cluster includes Sentence Reading Fluency, Math Facts Fluency, and Sentence Writing Fluency.

Table 1.1 Organization of the WJ IV ACH Tests

Academic Area	Standard Battery (Forms A, B, and C)	Extended Battery
Reading	Test 1: Letter-Word Identification Test 4: Passage Comprehension Test 7: Word Attack Test 8: Oral Reading Test 9: Sentence Reading Fluency	Test 12: Reading Recall Test 15: Word Reading Fluency Test 17: Reading Vocabulary
Mathematics	Test 2: Applied Problems Test 5. Calculation Test 10: Math Facts Fluency	Test 13: Number Matrices
Writing	Test 3: Spelling Test 6: Writing Samples Test 11: Sentence Writing Fluency	Test 14: Editing Test 16: Spelling of Sounds
Academic Knowledge		Test 18: Science Test 19: Social Studies Test 20: Humanities

All of the tests are contained in two easel test books, the Standard Battery and the Extended Battery. The Standard Battery has three forms (Forms A, B, and C) with one form of the Extended Battery. The Standard Batteries include the most commonly administered tests, so having three forms provides alternate and equivalent tests to facilitate retesting. The Extended Battery, which can be used with any of the three forms of the Standard Battery, includes tests that provide greater depth of coverage in each academic area. Table 1.1 shows the organization of the WJ IV ACH, which applies to Forms A, B, and C; the tests are presented by academic area rather than by numeric sequence.

Although many of the basic features have been retained, the extensive renorming and addition of new tests and interpretive procedures improve and increase the diagnostic capabilities. The areas of reading, mathematics, and written language each include measures of basic skills, fluency or automaticity, and application or higher-level skills. The Academic Knowledge cluster includes individual tests of Science, Social Studies, and Humanities that sample an individual's knowledge of the biological and physical sciences; history, geography, government, and economics; and art, music, and literature. Table 1.2 provides an overview of the content and task demands of each of the 20 achievement tests. Figure 1.1 illustrates item types for each of the achievement tests. The sample items shown are not actual test items.

Table 1.2 Content and Task Demands of the 20 WJ IV ACH Tests

Area	Test Name	Description	Task Demands
Reading	Test 1: Letter-Word Identification	Measures an aspect of reading decoding.	Requires identifying and pronouncing isolated letters and words.
	Test 4: Passage Comprehension	Measures reading comprehension of contextual information.	Requires reading a short passage and supplying a key missing word.
	Test 7: Word Attack	Measures aspects of phonological and orthographic coding.	Requires applying phonic and structural analysis skills to pronounce phonically regular nonsense words.
	Test 8: Oral Reading	Measures word reading accuracy and prosody.	Requires reading sentences aloud that gradually increase in difficulty.
	Test 9: Sentence Reading Fluency	Measures reading rate.	Requires reading and comprehending simple sentences and then deciding if the statement is true or false by marking yes or no (3-minute time limit).
	Test 12: Reading Recall	Measures reading comprehension and meaningful memory.	Requires reading a passage silently one time and then retelling the story orally.
	Test 15: Word Reading Fluency	Measures vocabulary knowledge and semantic fluency.	Requires marking two words that go together in a row of four words (3-minute time limit).
	Test 17: Reading Vocabulary	Measures reading vocabulary and comprehension.	Requires reading and providing synonyms or antonyms.
Mathematics	Test 2: Applied Problems	Measures the ability to analyze and solve practical math problems, mathematical reasoning.	Requires comprehending the nature of the problem, identifying relevant information, performing calculations, and providing solutions.

(continued)

Table 1.2 (Continued)

Area	Test Name	Description	Task Demands
	Test 5: Calculation	Measures the ability to perform mathematical computations.	Requires calculation of simple to complex mathematical facts and equations.
	Test 10: Math Facts Fluency	Measures aspects of number facility and math achievement.	Requires rapid calculation of single-digit addition, subtraction, and multiplication facts (3-minute time limit).
	Test 13: Number Matrices	Measures quantitative reasoning.	Requires providing the missing number from a matrix.
Written Language	Test 3: Spelling	Measures the ability to spell dictated words.	Requires writing the correct spelling of words presented orally.
	Test 6: Writing Samples	Measures quality of meaningful written expression and ability to convey ideas.	Requires writing sentences in response to a series of demands that increase in difficulty.
	Test 11: Sentence Writing Fluency	Measures aspects of automaticity with syntactic components of written expression.	Requires formulating and writing simple sentences rapidly (5-minute time limit).
	Test 14: Editing	Measures the ability to identify and correct errors in spelling, usage, punctuation, and capitalization.	Requires identifying errors in short written passages and correcting them orally.
	Test 16: Spelling of Sounds	Measures aspects of phonological/orthographic coding.	Requires spelling nonsense words that conform to conventional English spelling rules.
Academic Knowledge	Test 18: Science	Measures specialized knowledge in science, including biology, chemistry, geology, and physics.	Requires providing an oral response to orally presented questions; many items provide visual stimuli and early items require a pointing response only.

Table 1.2 (Continued)

Area	Test Name	Description	Task Demands
	Test 19: Social Studies	Measures specialized knowledge in social studies, including history, geography, government, and economics.	Requires providing an oral response to orally presented questions; many items provide visual stimuli and early items require a pointing response only.
	Test 20: Humanities	Measures specialized knowledge in humanities, including art, music, and literature.	Requires providing an oral response to orally presented questions; many items provide visual stimuli and early items require a pointing response only.

Standard Battery
Test 1: Letter-Word Identification
The task requires identifying and pronouncing isolated letters and words.

   g   r   cat   palm   officiate

Test 2: Applied Problems
The task involves analyzing and solving practical mathematical problems.

Bill had $7.00. He bought a ball for $3.95 and a comb for $1.20. How much money did he have left?

Test 3: Spelling
The task involves written spellings of words presented orally.

Spell the word *horn*. She played the *horn* in the band. *Horn.*

Test 4: Passage Comprehension
The task requires reading a short passage silently and then supplying a key missing word.

The boy _____ off his bike. (Correct: fell, jumped, etc.)
The book is one of a series of over eighty volumes. Each volume is designed to provide convenient _____ to a wide range of carefully selected articles. (Correct: access)

Test 5: Calculation
The task includes mathematical computations from simple addition facts to complex equations.

$2 + 4 =$
$3x + 3y = 15, 2x - y = 1,$
$x =$
$y =$

Figure 1.1 WJ IV ACH-Like Sample Items

Test 6: Writing Samples

The task requires writing sentences in response to a variety of demands that are then evaluated based on the quality of expression.

Write a good sentence to describe the picture.

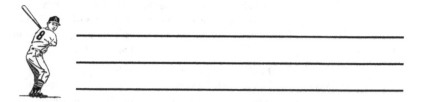

Test 7: Word Attack

The task requires pronouncing nonwords that conform to English spelling rules.

flib
bungicality

Test 8: Oral Reading

The task requires the oral reading of sentences that increase in complexity and are evaluated for accuracy and expression.

The dog ate the bone.
The philanthropist provided the botanical society with a new greenhouse.

Test 9: Sentence Reading Fluency (timed)

The task requires rapidly reading and comprehending simple sentences.

People can swim in pools.   yes   no

Test 10: Math Facts Fluency (timed)

The task requires rapid calculation of simple, single-digit addition, subtraction, and multiplication facts.

$$
\begin{array}{cccc}
2 & 10 & 1 & 3 \\
\underline{\times 3} & \underline{-5} & \underline{\times 2} & \underline{+2}
\end{array}
$$

Test 11: Sentence Writing Fluency (timed)

The task requires formulating and writing simple sentences quickly when given three words and a picture.

books
likes
read

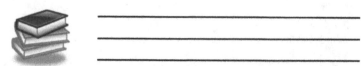

Figure 1.1 *Continued*

Extended Battery
Test 12: Reading Recall
The task requires reading passages of gradually increasing length and complexity and then recalling the story elements.

> Martha went to the store to buy groceries. When she got there, she discovered that she had forgotten her shopping list. She bought milk, eggs, and flour. When she got home she discovered that she had remembered to buy everything except the butter.

Test 13: Number Matrices
This task involves identifying the missing number in a numerical matrix.

2	4
6	

Test 14: Editing
The task requires identifying and correcting mistakes in spelling, punctuation, capitalization, or word usage in written passages.

> Bobby's face was so sunburned, it looked like he had fell into a bucket of red paint.
> (Correct: fallen)

Test 15: Word Reading Fluency (timed)
This test requires reading a set of four words and marking the two words that go together.

> street   horse   pencil   road

Test 16: Spelling of Sounds (audio recording)
The task requires spelling nonwords that conform to English spelling rules.

> larches
> shuff

Task 17: Reading Vocabulary
The test involves reading stimulus words for two different tasks: providing synonyms and providing antonyms.

> Read this word out loud and tell me another word that means the same.
>   big
> Read this word out loud and tell me another word that means the opposite.
>   yes

Test 18: Science
The task involves answering questions about curricular knowledge in various areas of the biological and physical sciences.

> How many eyes do most spiders have?

Figure 1.1 *Continued*

Test 19: Social Studies
The task involves answering questions about curricular knowledge in various areas of history, geography, government, and economics.

What is excise tax?

Test 20: Humanities
The task involves answering questions about curricular knowledge in art, music, and literature.

On a musical scale, how many notes are in an octave?

Figure 1.1 *Continued*

Item content was selected to provide a broad sampling of achievement rather than an in-depth assessment of any one area. Each broad area was designed to measure a hierarchy of abilities ranging from lower-order, less complex tasks, such as the Spelling test, to higher-level, more complex tasks, such as Applied Problems, a measure of math problem solving. Broad measurement of these important achievement areas assists examiners in identifying present performance levels, strengths and weaknesses, and an individual's present instructional needs. In addition, once an area of need has been identified, more in-depth testing can be performed to identify specific instructional objectives using additional norm-referenced, curriculum-based, or informal assessments. Table 1.3 shows the clusters available in the WJ IV ACH.

Table 1.3 Clusters Available in the WJ IV ACH

Curricular Area	Clusters in the Standard Battery	Clusters Requiring a Test From Extended Battery
Reading	Reading Broad Reading Basic Reading Skills Reading Fluency	Reading Comprehension Reading Comprehension–Extended Reading Rate
Math	Mathematics Broad Mathematics Math Calculation Skills	Math Problem Solving
Writing	Written Language Broad Written Language Written Expression	Basic Writing Skills
Cross-Domain Clusters	Academic Skills Academic Fluency Academic Applications Brief Achievement Broad Achievement	Academic Knowledge Phoneme-Grapheme Knowledge

CHANGES FROM THE WJ III ACH TO WJ IV ACH

Examiners who are familiar with the WJ III ACH will find it easy to learn the overall structure and organization of the WJ IV ACH. Rapid Reference 1.2 provides a summary of the major differences between the WJ III ACH and WJ IV ACH. Rapid Reference 1.3 lists the new tests and clusters available in the WJ IV ACH.

≡ Rapid Reference 1.2

WJ IV ACH Major Changes From WJ III ACH

- Provides updated norms.
- The Standard Battery has three parallel forms (Forms A, B, and C) with one form of the Extended Battery that is designed to be used with any of the Standard Batteries.
- There are 20 tests, 11 in the Standard Battery and 9 in the Extended Battery.
- The WJ IV ACH has seven new or expanded tests: Test 8: Oral Reading, Test 12: Reading Recall, Test 13: Number Matrices, Test 15: Word Reading Fluency, Test 18: Science, Test 19: Social Studies, and Test 20: Humanities.
- There are 22 clusters, including 8 new clusters: Reading, Reading Comprehension-Extended, Reading Fluency, Reading Rate, Written Language, Mathematics, Brief Achievement, and Broad Achievement.
- Fifteen clusters are available from the Standard Battery tests and seven additional clusters are available when using the Extended Battery.
- The oral language tests (Picture Vocabulary, Oral Comprehension, Understanding Directions, and Sound Awareness) have been moved into the WJ IV OL. Story Recall has been moved into the WJ IV COG.
- There is one audio-recorded test in the WJ IV ACH (Test 16: Spelling of Sounds).
- Three test names were changed to more accurately reflect the task: Reading Fluency is now Sentence Reading Fluency, Writing Fluency is now Sentence Writing Fluency, and Math Fluency is now Math Facts Fluency.
- The procedures for evaluating ability/achievement comparisons and intra-ability variations have been simplified with increased flexibility for the examiner. Within the WJ IV ACH, two types of intra-ability variations are available: intra-achievement and academic skills/academic fluency/academic applications. One type of ability/achievement comparison is available: a comparison of the Academic Knowledge Cluster to other academic domains. Additional options are available when also administering tests from the WJ IV COG and/or the WJ IV OL.

Rapid Reference 1.3

New WJ IV ACH Tests and Clusters

Seven New or Expanded Tests

- Oral Reading
- Reading Recall
- Number Matrices
- Word Reading Fluency
- Science
- Social Studies
- Humanities

Eight New Clusters

- Reading
- Reading Comprehension–Extended
- Reading Fluency
- Reading Rate
- Written Language
- Mathematics
- Brief Achievement
- Broad Achievement

DON'T FORGET

Reminders to Examiners

- The Standard Battery has three forms and the Extended Battery has one form.
- The oral language tests are now included in the WJ IV OL.
- The Academic Knowledge cluster may be used to predict achievement.
- Important additional diagnostic information can be obtained by using the co-normed WJ IV COG and WJ IV OL.
- It is not necessary to administer all of the WJ IV ACH tests.

THEORETICAL FOUNDATIONS

The WJ IV is based on current theory and research on the structure of human cognitive abilities. The theoretical foundation is derived from the Cattell–Horn–Carroll theory of cognitive abilities (CHC theory). Although this is most commonly discussed in relation to the WJ IV Tests of Cognitive Abilities, applying CHC theory to the WJ IV Tests of Achievement provides a common framework for describing performance and interpreting results. This creates a powerful tool for measuring human performance across the continuum of cognitive abilities, oral language, and achievement.

CHC theory is a combination of two research-based theories: *Gf-Gc* theory, based on the work of Drs. Raymond Cattell and John Horn, and three-stratum theory, based on the work of Dr. John Carroll. Both theoretical models focus on multiple broad abilities, each of which subsumes several narrow cognitive abilities. For more information about these theories, consult the *WJ IV COG Examiner's Manual* (Mather & Wendling, 2014b), the *Technical Manual* (McGrew, LaForte, & Schrank, 2014), Schneider and McGrew (2012), and McGrew and Wendling (2010). The WJ IV measures nine broad abilities: comprehension-knowledge (*Gc*), fluid reasoning (*Gf*), visual processing (*Gv*), short-term working memory (*Gwm*), long-term retrieval (*Glr*), cognitive processing speed (*Gs*), auditory processing (*Ga*), reading/writing (*Grw*), and quantitative knowledge (*Gq*). (See Rapid Reference 4.6 in Chapter 4 for definitions of these broad abilities.) The WJ IV ACH includes several different measures of these broad abilities. Table 1.4 shows the broad and narrow abilities that are measured by each of the 20 WJ IV ACH tests.

Table 1.4 Broad and Narrow Abilities Measured by the WJ IV ACH

Broad CHC Ability	Standard Battery Tests *(Primary Narrow Abilities)*	Extended Battery Tests *(Primary Narrow Abilities)*
Reading/Writing: Reading (*Grw*)	Test 1: Letter-Word Identification (Reading decoding)	Test 12: Reading Recall (Reading comprehension)
	Test 4: Passage Comprehension (Reading comprehension, Verbal [printed] language comprehension	Test 15: Word Reading Fluency (Lexical knowledge, Semantic fluency)
	Test 7: Word Attack (Reading decoding, Phonetic coding)	Test 17: Reading Vocabulary (Verbal [printed] language comprehension, Lexical knowledge)
	Test 8: Oral Reading (Reading accuracy, Prosody)	
	Test 9: Sentence Reading Fluency (Reading speed, Reading comprehension)	

(continued)

Table 1.4 (Continued)

Broad CHC Ability	Standard Battery Tests (Primary Narrow Abilities)	Extended Battery Tests (Primary Narrow Abilities)
Reading/Writing: Writing (Grw)	Test 3: Spelling (Spelling ability) Test 6: Writing Samples (Writing ability) Test 11: Sentence Writing Fluency (Writing speed, Writing ability)	Test 14: Editing (Language development/English usage) Test 16: Spelling of Sounds (Spelling ability, Phonetic coding)
Quantitative Knowledge (Gq)	Test 2: Applied Problems (Quantitative reasoning, Math achievement, Math knowledge) Test 5: Calculation (Math achievement) Test 10: Math Facts Fluency (Math achievement, Numerical facility)	Test 13: Number Matrices (Quantitative reasoning)
Comprehension-Knowledge (Gc)		Test 18: Science (General information/science) Test 19: Social Studies (General information/geography achievement) Test 20: Humanities (General information/cultural information)
Auditory Processing (Ga)	Test 7: Word Attack (Phonetic coding)	Test 16: Spelling of Sounds (Phonetic coding)
Long-term Retrieval (Glr)		Test 12: Reading Recall (Meaningful memory)
Fluid reasoning (Gf)		Test 13: Number Matrices (Inductive, Deductive)
Cognitive Processing Speed (Gs)	Test 9: Sentence Reading Fluency Test 10: Math Facts Fluency Test 11: Sentence Writing Fluency	Test 15: Word Reading Fluency

STANDARDIZATION AND PSYCHOMETRIC PROPERTIES

Intended to be broadly applicable from the preschool to the geriatric levels for either comprehensive or focused assessments, the WJ IV ACH was developed with a special emphasis on technical quality. Normative data were based on a single sample that was administered the cognitive, oral language, and achievement tests. The national standardization included 7,416 individuals between the ages of 24 months and 95+ years, as well as college and university undergraduate and graduate students from geographically diverse U.S. communities representing 46 states and the District of Columbia. The sample was selected to be representative of the United States population from age 24 months to age 95 years and older. The preschool sample (2 to 5 years of age and not enrolled in kindergarten) was composed of 664 individuals. The kindergarten to 12th grade sample was composed of 3,891 individuals. The college/university sample was composed of 775 individuals. The adult nonschool sample (14 to 95+ years of age and not enrolled in secondary school or college) was composed of 2,086 individuals. Individuals were randomly selected with a stratified sampling design that controlled for 12 specific community and subject variables: census region, country of birth, community type, sex, race, ethnicity, parent education (preschool and K–12 sample only), type of school (K–12 sample only), type of college, educational attainment (adult sample only), employment status (adult sample only), and occupational level of adults in the labor force.

For the school-age sample, the continuous-year procedure was used to gather data rather than gathering data at one or two points in the year, such as occurs with fall and spring norms. This produces continuous-year norms that meet the reporting requirements for educational programs such as Title I. The grade norms are reported for each tenth of a year from grades K.0 through 17.9. The age norms are reported for each month from ages 2-0 through 18-11 and then by one-year intervals from 19 through 95+ years of age.

Complete technical information can be found in the *WJ IV Technical Manual* (McGrew et al., 2014). The number of items and average item density in each test were set so that a reliability of .80 or higher would usually be obtained. The goal for cluster score reliabilities was set at .90 or higher. The median split-half reliabilities for the tests and composite reliabilities for the clusters are provided in Rapid References 1.4 and 1.5, respectively.

PURPOSES

Because it is a comprehensive instrument, the WJ IV ACH can be used with confidence in a variety of settings and for multiple purposes. The wide age

≡ Rapid Reference 1.4

Reliabilities for the WJ IV ACH Tests

WJ IV ACH Test	Median Reliability Across Age
Letter-Word Identification	.94
Applied Problems	.92
Spelling	.92
Passage Comprehension	.89
Calculation	.93
Writing Samples	.90
Word Attack	.90
Oral Reading	.96
Sentence Reading Fluency	.94
Math Facts Fluency	.96
Sentence Writing Fluency	.82
Reading Recall	.92
Number Matrices	.92
Editing	.91
Word Reading Fluency	.92
Spelling of Sounds	.88
Reading Vocabulary	.88
Science	.84
Social Studies	.87
Humanities	.87

≡ Rapid Reference 1.5

WJ IV ACH Cluster Reliabilities

WJ IV ACH Cluster	Median Reliability Across Age
Reading	.95
Broad Reading	.97
Basic Reading Skills	.95

WJ IV ACH Cluster	Median Reliability Across Age
Reading Comprehension	.93
Reading Comprehension-Extended	.96
Reading Fluency	.96
Reading Rate	.96
Mathematics	.96
Broad Mathematics	.97
Math Calculation Skills	.97
Math Problem Solving	.95
Written Language	.94
Broad Written Language	.95
Basic Writing Skills	.95
Written Expression	.92
Academic Skills	.97
Academic Fluency	.97
Academic Applications	.96
Phoneme-Grapheme Knowledge	.94
Academic Knowledge	.95
Brief Achievement	.97
Broad Achievement	.99

range and breadth of coverage allow the tests to be used for educational, clinical, or research purposes from preschool to the geriatric level. Uses of the WJ IV ACH include: (a) establishing an individual's present achievement performance levels, (b) determining academic strengths and weaknesses, (c) comparing an individual's performance to age or grade peers, (d) exploring eligibility for special programs, (e) monitoring educational progress across the school years, (f) investigating the effectiveness of curricula, and (g) assisting with rationales for recommendations that propose specific curricular adaptations and modifications.

The fact that the WJ IV ACH was co-normed with the WJ IV COG and the WJ IV OL provides a "best-practice" scenario for identifying an individual's unique strengths and weaknesses, as well as for obtaining information for instructional planning and programming. The combined and co-normed information provided is especially useful for documenting the nature of, and differentiating among, intra-ability variations and ability/achievement comparisons and discrepancies.

Intra-ability (intracognitive, intra-oral language, intra-achievement) variations are useful for understanding an individual's strengths and weaknesses, diagnosing and documenting the existence of specific disabilities, and acquiring the most relevant information for educational and vocational planning. The intra-achievement variation procedure is available when using only the WJ IV ACH, whereas the other two variation procedures require use of the WJ IV COG and WJ IV OL.

Ability/achievement comparisons or discrepancies (intellectual ability/achievement, oral language ability/achievement) are sometimes used as part of the selection criteria for learning disability programs. Within the WJ IV ACH the Academic Knowledge/achievement comparison is available. The oral language ability/achievement discrepancy is available when using the WJ IV OL and the WJ IV ACH, and additional ability/achievement discrepancy procedures are available when using the WJ IV COG. See Chapter 4 and Chapter 5 for further discussion about the use and interpretation of these procedures.

DON'T FORGET
••
Purposes and Uses of the Test

- Describe individual strengths and weaknesses.
- Determine present performance levels.
- Assist with diagnosis of disabilities.
- Determine ability/achievement and intra-achievement variations.
- Assist with program planning and the selection of accommodations.
- Assess growth.
- Evaluate programs.
- Conduct research.

CAUTION
••
Possible Kinds of Test Misuse

- Being unfamiliar with the content and organization of the test
- Not completing proper training or study for test use
- Not understanding the applications and limitations of test scores

RESOURCES FOR THE WJ IV ACH

The *WJ IV Tests of Achievement Examiner's Manual* (Mather & Wendling, 2014a) and the *WJ IV Technical Manual* (McGrew et al., 2014) currently provide the most detailed information about the WJ IV. The Examiner's Manual presents the basic principles of individual clinical assessment, specific information regarding use of the test, and suggested procedures for learning to administer, score, and complete the interpretative portions of the WJ IV ACH. The development, standardization, and technical characteristics of the tests are described in the separate Technical Manual.

🐊 TEST YOURSELF 🐊

1. What are the four major curricular areas included in the WJ IV ACH?
2. For what age range is the WJ IV ACH appropriate?
3. What grade range is available in the WJ IV ACH norms?
4. Which of the following tests is new to the WJ IV ACH?
   (a) Letter-Word Identification
   (b) Sentence Writing Fluency
   (c) Reading Recall
   (d) Applied Problems
5. Which of the following tests is not new to the WJ IV ACH?
   (a) Word Reading Fluency
   (b) Spelling of Sounds
   (c) Oral Reading
   (d) Number Matrices
6. Which of the following clusters is new to the WJ IV ACH?
   (a) Reading Comprehension
   (b) Reading Rate
   (c) Phoneme-Grapheme Knowledge
   (d) Written Expression
7. The WJ IV ACH contains a procedure for calculating an ability/achievement discrepancy.
   True or False?
8. The WJ IV ACH does not share common norms with the WJ IV Tests of Cognitive Abilities and the WJ IV Tests of Oral Language.
   True or False?

9. **There are three forms of the Standard and Extended Batteries.**
   True or False?

10. **It is not necessary to administer all 20 tests in the WJ IV ACH.**
    True or False?

Answer: 1. reading, mathematics, written language, and academic knowledge; 2. 2 to 95+ years; 3. K.0 to 17.9; 4. c; 5. b; 6. b; 7. True; 8. False; 9. False; 10. True

Two

HOW TO ADMINISTER THE WJ IV ACH

Proper WJ IV ACH administration requires training, study, and practice. Although individuals in a wide range of professions can learn the actual procedures for administering the test, a higher degree of skill is required to interpret the results to others or to test individuals who have special problems or specific disabilities. Some examiners can adequately administer a test but may need help interpreting and explaining the results correctly. Only properly trained individuals should interpret the results of standardized tests, especially in high-stakes situations, such as making decisions for special education eligibility.

Standards applicable to testing have been developed through a collaborative effort of three professional organizations: the American Educational Research Association (AERA), the American Psychological Association (APA), and the National Council on Measurement in Education (NCME). These standards are published in a document titled *Standards for Educational and Psychological Testing* (AERA, APA, & NCME, 2014). The standards referenced in this chapter are from that publication.

A selective testing table (see Figure 2.1), included in each Test Book and Manual, illustrates which tests need to be administered to obtain the various cluster scores. Based on the principle of selective testing, it is seldom necessary to administer all of the WJ IV ACH tests or to complete all of the available interpretive options for one person. For example, if an individual was referred for a reading evaluation, you may only want to administer the tests that are related to reading performance. In addition, you may wish to administer several tests from the WJ IV COG and WJ IV OL that are related to reading performance.

CAUTION

Examiner Qualifications

Standard 10.1: Those who use psychological tests should confine their testing and related assessment activities to their areas of competence, as demonstrated through education, training, experience, and appropriate credentials (AERA et al., 2014, p. 164).

Standard 10.3: Professionals should verify that persons under their supervision have appropriate knowledge and skills to administer and score tests (AERA et al., 2014, p. 164).

Standard 12.16: Those responsible for educational testing programs should provide appropriate training, documentation, and oversight so that the individuals who administer and score the test(s) are proficient in the appropriate test administration and scoring procedures and understand the importance of adhering to the directions provided by the test developer purpose (AERA et al., 2014, p. 200).

			Reading						Math				Writing				Cross-Domain Clusters					
			Reading	Broad Reading	Basic Reading Skills	Reading Comprehension	Reading Fluency	Reading Rate	Mathematics	Broad Mathematics	Math Calculation Skills	Math Problem Solving	Written Language	Broad Written Language	Basic Writing Skills	Written Expression	Academic Skills	Academic Fluency	Academic Applications	Academic Knowledge	Phoneme-Grapheme Knowledge	Brief (or Broad) Achievement
Standard Easel	ACH-01	Letter-Word Identification	■	■	■												■					■
	ACH-02	Applied Problems							■	■		■							■			■
	ACH-03	Spelling											■	■	■		■					■
	ACH-04	Passage Comprehension	■	■		■													■			◆
	ACH-05	Calculation							■	■	■						■					◆
	ACH-06	Writing Samples											■	■		■			■			◆
	ACH-07	Word Attack			■																■	
	ACH-08	Oral Reading					■															
	ACH-09	Sentence Reading Fluency		■			■	■										■				◆
	ACH-10	Math Facts Fluency								■	■							■				◆
	ACH-11	Sentence Writing Fluency												■		■		■				◆
Extended Easel	ACH-12	Reading Recall				■																
	ACH-13	Number Matrices										■										
	ACH-14	Editing													■							
	ACH-15	Word Reading Fluency						■														
	ACH-16	Spelling of Sounds																			■	
	ACH-17	Reading Vocabulary				□																
	ACH-18	Science																		■		
	ACH-19	Social Studies																		■		
	ACH-20	Humanities																		■		

■	Tests required to create the cluster listed.
□	Additional test required to create an extended version of the cluster listed.
◆	Additional tests required to create Broad Achievement.

Figure 2.1 WJ IV ACH Selective Testing Table

APPROPRIATE TESTING CONDITIONS

Testing Environment

Prior to testing, select a testing room that is quiet, comfortable, and has adequate ventilation and lighting. Ideally, only you and the examinee should be in the room. Ensure that the room has a table or desk and two chairs, one of which is an appropriate size for the examinee, and that the seating arrangement allows you to view both sides of the easel book, point to all parts on the examinee's test page in the Test Book and in the Response Booklet, and record responses out of view. The easel format of the Test Book provides easy access to all administration directions. When positioned properly, the Test Book provides a screen so that you can record responses on the Test Record out of the examinee's view and shield the correct answers that are printed on the Test Record. The best seating arrangement is one in which you sit diagonally across from the examinee at the corner of a table. Another possible arrangement is to sit directly across the table. With this arrangement, the table must be narrow and low enough so you can see over the upright Test Book to point to the examinee's test page when necessary.

Testing Materials

The basic materials necessary for administering the WJ IV ACH are the Test Books, a Test Record, a Response Booklet (RB), a CD player, headphones or earbuds, the test audio recording, at least two sharpened pencils with erasers, and a stopwatch. The test kit does not include the CD player, headphones, pencils, or stopwatch.

Getting Ready to Test

Prior to beginning the test, fill in the examinee's name and date of birth and check to see whether the individual should be wearing glasses or a hearing aid. Spaces are provided on the Test Record to record the number of years an individual has been retained or has skipped in school. Some examiners prefer to complete this information with the examinee during the rapport building time at the beginning of the session.

When testing a school-age individual, the online scoring program will automatically calculate the exact tenth-of-a-year grade placement for the standard school year once you enter the grade level. If the individual is tested during the summer months, record the grade that has just been completed. For example, the grade placement for a student evaluated in July who had just completed eighth grade would be 8.9. If an examinee is enrolled in some type of nongraded program, the normal grade placement for students of this examinee's age at that time of the school year may provide the most appropriate grade level for test interpretation. An option is also available for recording the exact starting and ending dates of the school year. This option is used for year-round schools, as well as for schools with starting and ending dates that fall more than 2 weeks before or after the default dates of August 16 and June 15. It is recommended that you use this option for all examinees to ensure precision of the grade norms used in generating the scores. After you enter the starting and ending dates, the online scoring program automatically calculates the exact grade placement in tenths of the school year.

If an individual is not attending school (i.e., kindergarten through college), it is not necessary to record a grade placement unless it would be useful to compare the individual's performance with the average performance of students at some specified grade placement. For example, if a 25-year-old woman was just going to begin a 4-year college, it may be helpful to compare her performance to students who are entering grade 13.0.

Establishing and Maintaining Rapport

In most instances, you will have little difficulty establishing a good relationship with the examinee. However, do not begin testing until the person seems relatively at ease. If the examinee does not feel well or does not respond appropriately, do not attempt testing. Often, examiners begin the testing session with a short period of conversation, discussing something of interest to the person, such as what he or she enjoys doing in leisure time or what sports the student plays. You do not need to provide a lengthy explanation of the test. A suggested statement labeled "Introducing the Test" is provided in the introductory section of each Test Book.

Throughout the testing session, tell the examinee that he or she is doing a good job, using such comments as "fine" and "good" and encouraging a response even when items are difficult. It is fine to say, "Would you like to take a guess on that one?" During the test, make sure the examinee feels that the experience is enjoyable. Take care, however, that your comments do not reveal whether answers are correct or incorrect. For example, do not say "good" only after correct responses or pause longer after incorrect responses as if waiting for the examinee to change a response.

CAUTION

....

Appropriate Examiner/Examinee Interactions

- Be careful not to reveal the correct answers to items.
- Do not indicate whether responses are correct or incorrect.
- Provide encouragement throughout the administration, not just when the examinee answers correctly or incorrectly.

TESTING INDIVIDUALS WITH SPECIAL NEEDS

At times you may need to adapt the standard test procedures in order to accommodate an individual who has special limitations. Because accommodations may have a compromising effect on the validity of the test results, determine whether the procedures have been altered to the extent that you must be cautious when interpreting the results. Note and describe all accommodations on the Test Record and in the test report. Three broad classes of individuals often require accommodations in the assessment process: young children or preschoolers, English language learners (ELLs), and individuals with disabilities.

DON'T FORGET

....

An accommodation is a comparable measure that maintains the intended construct.

A modification is a noncomparable measure that changes the intended construct.

The term *accommodation* is used to denote changes with which the comparability of scores is retained, and the term *modification* is used to denote changes that affect the construct measured by the test (AERA et al., 2014, p. 58).

CAUTION

For norm-based score interpretations, any modification that changes the construct will invalidate the norms for score interpretations (AERA et al., 2014, p. 61).

An adaptation for a particular disability is inappropriate when the purpose of a test is to diagnose the presence and degree of that disability. For example, allowing extra time on a timed test to determine distractibility and speed-of-processing difficulties associated with attention deficit disorder would make it impossible to determine the extent to which the extent and processing-speed difficulties actually exist (p. 62).

Regardless of the individual's characteristics that make accommodations necessary, it is important that test accommodations address the specific access issue(s) that otherwise would bias an individual's test results (p. 60).

Preschool Examinees

Some young children are uncomfortable with unfamiliar adults and may perform better if a parent is nearby. If a parent will be present during the testing session, briefly explain the testing process before actual testing begins, including the establishment of test ceilings and the importance of not assisting the child on any item. Initially, some children may be shy and refuse to speak to a stranger. If after several rapport-building activities, such as interacting with a puppet, the child still refuses to speak, discontinue testing and try again at a later date. Some tests are more useful than others with preschool children.

DON'T FORGET

Possible Accommodations When Testing Preschool Children
- Allow a parent to remain in the room but not directly in view of the child.
- Allow the child to sit on a parent's lap if separation is not possible.
- Provide breaks between tests.
- Vary the activity level of tasks (e.g., fine-motor activity, oral activity).
- Provide reinforcements (e.g., stickers, snacks).
- Sit on the floor with the child when administering the test.
- Maintain a fun, interesting, and appropriate pace.

English Language Learners (ELLs)

Before using the WJ IV ACH (or any English test) with a student whose first language is not English, determine the individual's English proficiency and language dominance. One option when evaluating an individual who speaks Spanish and English is to administer the three parallel English and Spanish tests in the WJ IV Tests of Oral Language (WJ IV OL) (Schrank, Mather, et al., 2014b). Comparing an individual's performance on parallel English and Spanish tests and clusters can help determine language dominance and proficiency.

If the individual is English dominant, use the WJ IV ACH. If conducting a bilingual assessment, use the WJ IV ACH as the English achievement measure.

The vocabulary and syntax used in the test instructions may be too complex for some individuals who are just learning English. Although the test instructions are controlled for complexity, in some cases you may need to provide further explanation of the task. Note and explain this modification of the standardized testing procedures in the evaluation report because in some cases you would need to interpret the scores with caution.

DON'T FORGET

Possible Accommodations When Testing English Language Learners
- Use English words that may be more familiar to the individual when presenting directions.
- Provide supplemental practice or review test directions to enhance understanding.
- Do not modify standardized procedures when measuring some aspect of an individual's English language ability (i.e., reading, writing, listening, or speaking skills).
- Do not translate test items into another language. When available, use a test in the individual's primary language. For example, begin an evaluation with the three Spanish tests in the WJ IV OL if Spanish is the primary language.

CAUTION

Standards to Consider When Testing English Language Learners
Standard 3.13: A test should be administered in the language that is most relevant and appropriate to the test purpose (AERA et al., 2014, p. 69).

> *Excerpt from Comments:*
> Test users should take into account the linguistic and cultural characteristics and relative language proficiencies of examinees who are bilingual or use multiple languages. Identifying the most appropriate language(s) for testing also requires close consideration of the context and purpose for testing. Except in cases where the purpose of testing is to determine the test taker's level of proficiency in a particular language, the

test takers should be tested in the language in which they are most proficient. (AERA et al., 2014, p. 69)

Standard 3.14: When testing requires the use of an interpreter, the interpreter should follow standardized procedures and, to the extent feasible, be sufficiently fluent in the language and content of the test and examinee's native language and culture to translate the test and related testing materials and to explain the examinee's test responses, as necessary (AERA et al., 2014, p. 69).

Individuals With Disabilities

In modifying test procedures and interpreting test results for individuals with disabilities, be sensitive to the limitations that different impairments may impose on an individual's abilities and behavior. Some tests cannot be administered to individuals with profound impairments. You will need to determine the most appropriate tests on a case-by-case basis. Table 2.1 presents considerations and possible accommodations for individuals with sensory or physical impairments.

Table 2.1 Considerations and Possible Adaptations When Testing Individuals With Sensory or Physical Impairments

Hearing Impairments	Visual Impairments	Physical Impairments
Be sure hearing aid is worn and functioning.	Place yellow acetate over test pages to reduce glare.	Provide rest periods or breaks during testing session.
Use examinee's mode of communication (e.g., American Sign Language, Signed English, written responses).	Make environmental modifications (e.g., positioning lamp to provide additional light or dimmed illumination).	Modify response mode when necessary (e.g., allow oral responses when individual is unable to write).
Use interpreter if examiner is not proficient in examinee's mode of communication.	Allow examinee to hold test pages closer or alter position of Test Book.	When appropriate, allow use of special equipment (e.g., keyboard for writing responses).
	Enlarge test materials. If available, use the Braille version of the test when necessary.	

Learning disabilities and reading disabilities. Accommodations are usually not provided on standardized achievement tests for students who struggle with learning or reading. Although an accommodation may improve performance, the resulting score will not be an accurate reflection of a person's capabilities. In most instances, the purpose of the assessment is to document the severity of the impairment in learning or reading. Clearly, you would not read the reading tests to an individual with reading difficulties, as the main purpose of the evaluation is to determine the extent and severity of the reading problem, not to measure oral language comprehension. The goal of the evaluation is to determine an individual's unique pattern of strengths and weaknesses and then to use this assessment data to suggest appropriate classroom accommodations and recommend possible teaching strategies and interventions.

For some children with severe perceptual impairments, you may need to use a card or piece of paper to highlight or draw attention to specific items. Individuals with poor fine-motor control may need to use a keyboard for responses rather than writing in the Response Booklet. Individuals who are easily frustrated by tasks that become too difficult may respond better to several short testing sessions, rather than one lengthy session.

Behavioral disorders/attention-deficit/hyperactivity disorder. Clinical expertise is needed to assess children with severe behavior or attention difficulties. You can often use specific behavioral management techniques that will increase the likelihood of compliance. It is a good idea to become familiar with the typical classroom behaviors of individuals who exhibit severe attention or behavior challenges prior to conducting an assessment. You will need to determine whether the test results provide a valid representation of the individual's present performance level. When evaluating individuals with challenging behaviors, attempt to determine the effects of the problem behaviors on the assessment process and how the behaviors affect performance. For example, Robert, a third-grade student with severe behavioral challenges, completed three items on the Writing Samples test. He then refused to write any more sentences, stating that he hated writing and had to do too much in school anyway. The examiner tried to encourage Robert, but he was adamant that he was not doing any more. In this situation, the test results would not be representative of Robert's writing abilities, but they do suggest how his behavior affects his school performance.

CAUTION

Modifying Standardized Procedures
- May invalidate the normative interpretation of test results.
- Note modifications on the Test Record and report.
- Use professional judgment on a case-by-case basis.

DON'T FORGET

Standard 3.9: Test developers and/or test users are responsible for developing and providing accommodations, when appropriate and feasible, to remove construct-irrelevant barriers that otherwise would interfere with examinees' ability to demonstrate their standing on target constructs (AERA et al., 2014, p. 67).

Excerpt from Comments:
An appropriate accommodation is one that responds to specific individual characteristics but does so in a way that does not change the construct the test is measuring or the meaning of the scores. (AERA et al., 2014, p. 67)

CONFIDENTIALITY OF TEST MATERIALS

Test security is the responsibility of test users and has two aspects: careful storing of the materials and protecting test content. Keep tests such as the WJ IV ACH in locked cabinets if they are stored in an area accessible to people with a nonprofessional interest in the tests. Do not leave the test unattended where others may see the materials and look at the test items. During a discussion of the test results, you may describe the types of items included in general but avoid actual review of specific test content. Use examples similar to the test items without revealing the actual test items.

The issue of test confidentiality is also important. Do not share test content or results with curious nonprofessionals or make materials available for public inspection. During testing or after testing has been completed, do not inform examinees of whether answers are correct or incorrect and do not explain the correct answers to any of the questions. For example, after testing is finished, you would not show a student how to solve a computational problem on the Calculation test. Occasionally, individuals will request information. Usually you will be able to recognize whether it is appropriate or inappropriate to supply the requested information. If you should not supply the requested information, respond with a comment such as "I'm not supposed to help you with that."

CAUTION

Responsibility for Test Security
Standard 6.7: Test users have the responsibility of protecting the security of test materials at all times (AERA et al., 2014, p. 117).

Standard 10.18: Professionals and others who have access to test materials and test results should maintain the confidentiality of the test results and testing materials consistent with scientific, professional, legal, and ethical requirements. Tests (including obsolete versions) should not be made available to the public or resold to unqualified test users (AERA et al., 2014, p. 168).

Disclosing specific test content can invalidate future administrations. As noted on the copyright pages, the WJ IV is not to be used in programs that require disclosure of questions or answers.

ADMINISTRATION CONSIDERATIONS

The goal of standardized testing is to see how well a person can respond when given instructions identical to those presented to individuals in the norm sample. If you are learning to administer the WJ IV ACH, study the contents of the Test Book, paying particular attention to the information after the tabbed page, the specific instructions on the test pages, and the boxes with special instructions. In addition, Appendix C of the WJ IV ACH Examiner's Manual (Mather & Wendling, 2014a) includes a reproducible test-by-test checklist designed to help you build competency with administration of the achievement tests. You can use the checklist as a self-study or observation tool. Administer several practice tests, treating them as if they were actual administrations. Strive for administrations that are both exact and brisk.

DON'T FORGET

Exact Administration
- Bold, blue type in the Test Book presents the directions the examiner reads to the examinee.
- Directions to the examiner, such as when to point, are printed in black in the Test Book.
- Special instructions are presented in boxes in the Test Book.

Brisk Administration
- Proceed to the next item as soon as the examinee completes a response.
- Do not stop and "visit" during the testing session.
- Keep testing brisk to enhance rapport and help maintain attention.

Order of Administration

In many cases, you will follow the order of tests as they are presented in the easel Test Books, particularly the core set of tests, Tests 1 through 6. The tests have been ordered so that tasks alternate between different formats and achievement areas (e.g., writing versus math). However, you may administer the tests in any order. As a general rule, you would not administer two timed tests or two tests involving sustained writing (such as the Writing Samples and Sentence Writing Fluency tests) in a row. For example, Tests 9 through 11 in the WJ IV ACH Standard Battery are all timed tests. If you wish to administer these three fluency measures, intersperse them with other types of tasks. Also, consider the likes and dislikes of the person being evaluated. For example, if a student struggles with math, separate administration of the math tests. In addition, you may discontinue testing between the administration of any two tests and resume on another day, if needed.

Suggested Starting Points

Using the Suggested Starting Points with basal and ceiling levels helps to reduce testing time. The Suggested Starting Points are located in the Test Book following the tabbed title page for each test. Select a starting point based on an estimate of the examinee's actual *achievement level* rather than by the current age or grade placement. For example, individuals who are low-functioning will need to begin with a lower item than indicated by their present grade placement, whereas an individual participating in a gifted education program would usually be started at a higher level.

Time Requirements

As a general rule, experienced examiners require about 40 minutes to administer the core set of tests (Tests 1–6). The Writing Samples test requires approximately 15 minutes to administer, whereas the other tests, on average, require about 5 minutes each. The tests in the Extended Battery require an additional 5 to 10 minutes each. The amount of time varies depending on an examinee's particular characteristics, age, and speed of response. When testing, allow a reasonable amount of time for a person to respond and then suggest moving on to the next item. If requested, you may provide more time on a specific item, provided that the test directions allow for additional time. For example, on the Letter-Word Identification test, instructions say to move on if the person has not responded within 5 seconds. If, when asked to try the next one, the person responds that he is still trying to figure out the current word, you would allow more time. Essentially, Letter-Word Identification is not a timed test and the 5-second guideline is provided to keep the pace moving. Rarely would an individual read the word correctly if he did not respond within 5 seconds.

As another example, on Passage Comprehension, an individual may reread the sentences several times. Although you would note this behavior, rereading is perfectly acceptable on an untimed test. This would not, however, be acceptable on a test like Reading Recall, in which the examinee is instructed to read through the passage one time only.

Basal and Ceiling Rules

The purpose of basal and ceiling rules is to limit the number of items administered but still be able to estimate, with high probability, the score that would have been obtained if all items had been administered. Test items span a wide range of difficulty, with the easiest item presented first and the most difficult item last. Consequently, a number of items in the test will be beyond a given individual's operating range (the set of items between the basal and ceiling levels). The basal level is the point below which a person is very likely to respond correctly to all items. The ceiling level is the point above which there is almost no chance the person will respond correctly to any items.

Criteria for basal and ceiling levels are included at the beginning of each test in the Test Book and are stated briefly at the top of each test in the Test Record. Before testing, review the starting and stopping points of each test and choose an appropriate starting point by consulting the Suggested Starting Points table. Many of the achievement tests indicate that the basal level is established after six consecutive correct responses. If an examinee responds correctly to the first six or more consecutive items administered, continue testing until the ceiling criterion is met. If you do not obtain a basal when the first six items are administered, test backward page by page until six consecutive items are correct or until the page with Item 1 has been administered. Then return to the point at which testing was interrupted and continue testing from there until the ceiling criterion of failing the six highest-numbered consecutive items is met, or until you have administered the page with the last test item.

The best practice is to test by complete pages when stimulus material appears on the examinee's side of the easel. Because examinees do not see any of the pages that fall below the basal level or above the ceiling level, they are essentially unaware of the other test questions in the Test Book. If an individual reaches a ceiling in the middle of a test page and there is no material on the examinee's side, you may discontinue testing.

If a basal has not been established, then Item 1 serves as the basal. Some examiners mistakenly think that if a basal cannot be established, then the test cannot be given. This is not the case. If a young child missed the first item, got the next two correct, and then missed the next six items (the ceiling), the number correct would be recorded as two. Similarly, when a ceiling is not reached, the last item on the test serves as the ceiling.

In a case where there appears to be two basals, use the six lowest-numbered consecutive correct responses as the true basal. Conversely, when there appears to be two ceilings, use the six highest-numbered consecutive incorrect responses as the ceiling. The best procedure for estimating a person's true score is to take into account all items passed and all items missed. The basal and ceiling rules are simply guides to minimize testing time and reduce frustration.

DON'T FORGET

Basal/Ceiling Rules

Tests with basal of five consecutive correct and ceiling of five consecutive incorrect:
Applied Problems, Reading Vocabulary

Tests with basal of six consecutive correct and ceiling of six consecutive incorrect:
Letter-Word Identification, Spelling, Passage Comprehension, Calculation, Word Attack, Number Matrices, Editing, Spelling of Sounds, Science, Social Studies, and Humanities

Timed tests:
3-minute limit: Sentence Reading Fluency, Math Facts Fluency, Word Reading Fluency
5-minute limit: Sentence Writing Fluency

Test with blocks or sets of items and continuation instructions:
Writing Samples, Oral Reading, Reading Recall

Figure 2.2 illustrates how a basal and a ceiling were determined on Test 1: Letter-Word Identification for an eighth-grade girl, Crystal, who was referred for reading difficulties.

Step 1. The examiner estimated Crystal's reading level to be at Grade 5 to 6. The Suggested Starting Points table indicates testing should begin with Item 38. Crystal answered Items 38 to 42 correctly, but missed Item 43. Although she missed Item 43, the examiner administered the rest of the page, following the complete page rule. Crystal answered Item 44 correctly but missed Item 45, so no basal was established.

Step 2. The examiner then flipped back one page and presented Items 30 to 37. Although Crystal missed Item 36, a basal level was established. She correctly answered the six consecutive lowest-numbered items (30–35).

Step 3. The examiner returned to the point at which testing was interrupted and resumed testing with Item 46. Crystal missed Items 46 to 51. Although

Crystal had now missed six consecutive items (46–51), the examiner completed the page because there was stimulus material visible on the examinee's side of the Test Book. In the process of completing the page, Crystal missed Item 52 but answered Item 53 correctly. Therefore, a ceiling was not established (six consecutive highest-numbered items administered incorrect) and testing continued.

Step 4. The examiner administered all the items on the next page (54–61) and obtained a ceiling when Crystal mispronounced them all. Although Crystal had missed six items (54–59), the page had to be completed.

Step 5. The examiner stopped testing with Item 61 because the ceiling level had been reached and the page had been completed.

Step 6. The examiner calculated the number correct by totaling the number of items read correctly and included all items below the basal. The number correct was 43.

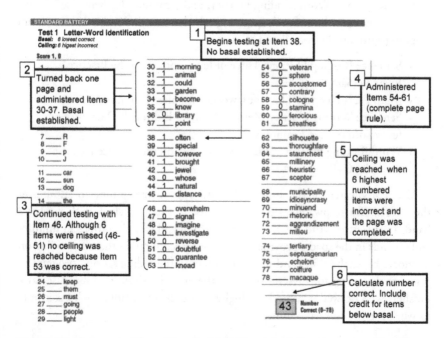

Figure 2.2 Determination of Basal and Ceiling Levels for Crystal, an Eighth Grader, on Test 1: Letter-Word Identification

Tests Requiring the Response Booklet

You will need the WJ IV ACH Response Booklet (RB) when administering any of the following tests: Test 3: Spelling, Test 5: Calculation, Test 6: Writing Samples, Test 9: Sentence Reading Fluency, Test 10: Math Facts Fluency, Test 11: Sentence Writing Fluency, Test 15: Word Reading Fluency, and Test 16: Spelling of Sounds. In addition, the RB also contains a worksheet to use with Test 2: Applied Problems and Test 13: Number Matrices. Give the examinee the RB and a pencil when directed to do so by instructions in the Test Book.

Timed Tests

The following tests are timed: Test 9: Sentence Reading Fluency, Test 10: Math Facts Fluency, Test 11: Sentence Writing Fluency, and Test 15: Word Reading Fluency. The time limit is 3 minutes each for Sentence Reading Fluency, Math Facts Fluency, and Word Reading Fluency, and 5 minutes for Sentence Writing Fluency. The guidelines for determining whether to administer the test or for stopping early on the four timed tests are:

- Sentence Reading Fluency: Three or fewer correct on the Practice Exercise (Samples C–F)
- Math Facts Fluency: Three or fewer correct after 1 minute
- Sentence Writing Fluency: Zero on Samples B through D or three or fewer correct after 2 minutes
- Word Reading Fluency: One or zero correct on the Practice Exercise (Samples C–F)

Use a stopwatch or the stopwatch feature on a smartphone to administer these tests. If a stopwatch is unavailable, use a watch or clock with a second hand. In this case, write down the exact starting and stopping times in minutes and seconds in the spaces provided in the Test Record rather than depending on memory. Enter the times and number correct in the online scoring program to generate the scores for these tests. Enter the exact finishing time because early finishers who do well will receive a higher score than individuals who continue to work for the full time limit.

Audio-Recorded Tests

Test 16: Spelling of Sounds is the only WJ IV ACH test that is presented using an audio recording. When administering this test, use high-quality audio equipment and, if available, headphones or earbuds. Use audio equipment with a good speaker so that a clear reproduction of the test items is produced. If using a computer to administer the audio tests, make sure that the sound quality is clear. Good quality external speakers or good quality headphones are beneficial and help ensure the sound quality.

Use of the test audio recording is expected and headphones are recommended unless the person being tested resists wearing headphones or has difficulty attending to a recorded presentation. Although you may present the test items using live voice, make sure to practice pronouncing the nonsense words accurately.

CAUTION

Common Administration Errors
- Not following standardized administration procedures
- Providing too much assistance to an examinee
- Not testing by complete pages when stimuli are visible on examinee's page
- Not establishing a basal or ceiling
- Not following cutoff or continuation instructions
- Not querying when indicated
- Not following directions in the Error or No Response boxes
- Not adhering to time limits on timed tests
- Being too lenient or stringent on scoring responses
- Administering all tests to all examinees

DON'T FORGET

Keys to Competent Administration
- Know the correct pronunciation of all test items.
- Be fluent in administration.
- Understand the basal/ceiling rules.
- If the examinee gives more than one response to an item, score the last response given.
- Do not penalize for errors due to articulation or for regional or dialectical speech differences.
- Test by complete pages when items are visible on the examinee's test page.

Behavioral and Qualitative Observations and Recording Errors

Because standardized testing occurs in a one-on-one situation, you can gain valuable insights by noting the examinee's reaction to the tests and the response style, as well as how he or she responds to items as they increase in difficulty. The WJ IV ACH includes two types of observation checklists: the Test Session Observations Checklist and Qualitative Observation Checklists for Tests 1 through 11. Information from these checklists can be entered into the scoring program for inclusion in the score report. In addition, you can analyze any errors after testing is completed.

Test Session Observations Checklist. This checklist on the first page of the Test Record is a brief, seven-category behavior rating scale intended to systematize and document a number of general observations. The categories include levels of conversational proficiency, cooperation, level of activity, attention and concentration, self-confidence, care in responding, and response to difficult tasks. Each category has a range of possible responses in order to help identify whether the behavior is typical or atypical for the age or grade of the individual being assessed. Complete this checklist at the end of the testing session.

Qualitative Observation Checklists. Each of the 11 tests in the Standard Batteries (Forms A, B, C) has a Qualitative Observation Checklist in the Test Record. These checklists are designed to document examinee performance on the test through qualitative observations, or in the case of Test 8: Oral Reading, a quantitative observation. Although optional, use of these checklists can provide important insights about how the individual completed the task. For example, on Test 1: Letter-Word Identification, you may observe that the examinee lacked automaticity when reading the words, reading them accurately but slowly. Or, you may observe that the examinee did not apply phoneme–grapheme relationships. Figure 2.3 illustrates the Qualitative Observation Checklist for Test 1: Letter-Word Identification.

Qualitative observation data. During standardization, data were collected on 9 of the 11 tests with Qualitative Observation Checklists. Data are not available for Test 7: Word Attack or Test 8: Oral Reading, which offers a quantitative tally of types of errors made by the examinee. This information, described in Chapter 5 of the WJ IV ACH Examiner's Manual (Mather & Wendling, 2014a), helps determine whether an examinee's response to the task is typical or atypical compared to agemates. For example, on the Letter-Word Identification test, at age 10, 5% of children identified words rapidly and accurately with little effort (Rating 1); 74% had the typical behavior in Rating 2; 11% identified initial items rapidly and accurately but had difficulty applying phoneme–grapheme relationships to latter

Qualitative Observation

On Letter-Word Identification, which of the following best describes the ease with which the individual identified words? (Mark only one response.)

___ 1. Identified words rapidly and accurately with little effort (automatic word identification skills)

___ 2. Identified initial items rapidly and accurately and identified more difficult items through increased application of phoneme-grapheme relationships (typical)

___ 3. Identified the initial items rapidly and accurately but had difficulty applying phoneme-grapheme relationships to latter items

___ 4. Required increased time and greater attention to phoneme-grapheme relationships to determine the correct response (nonautomatic word identification skills)

___ 5. Was not able to apply phoneme-grapheme relationships

___ 6. None of the above, not observed, or does not apply

Figure 2.3 Qualitative Observation Checklist for Test 1: Letter-Word Identification

items (Rating 3); 6% required increased time and greater attention to determine the correct response (Rating 4); 4% were not able to apply phoneme–grapheme relationships (Rating 5), and 1% were not observed or none of the ratings applied (Rating 6). If an examinee receives a rating of 2, his performance is typical for his agemates. However, if an examinee receives a rating of 5, his performance is atypical because only 4% of agemates received a rating that low.

Recording errors. It is often helpful to write down any errors that the examinee makes for later analysis, which can assist in making specific recommendations and planning an instructional program. Attempt to analyze the types of errors across tests rather than just within a single test. For example, a third-grade girl's errors on the Letter-Word Identification and Word Attack tests indicated that she was having trouble with short vowel sounds, whereas a fourth-grade boy's errors on Calculation and Math Facts Fluency indicated that he was experiencing difficulty with multiplication facts.

TEST-BY-TEST RULES OF ADMINISTRATION

Although the WJ IV ACH Examiner's Manual and Test Books provide detailed rules for test-by-test administration, this section presents important reminders

DON'T FORGET

Qualitative Information
- Observe behavior during testing. Note reactions to the various tests, response style, level of effort, attention, persistence, level of cooperation, and conversational proficiency.
- Use the Test Session Observations Checklist included on each WJ IV Test Record to facilitate the collection of observational data.
- Use the Qualitative Observation Checklists in the Test Record for Tests 1 through 11 to document how the examinee performed on each task.
- Use the qualitative observation data (Chapter 5 of the WJ IV ACH Examiner's Manual) to determine how typical or atypical an examinee's performance was compared to agemates.
- Record errors for further analysis. Error analysis often provides important information for developing educational recommendations and planning instruction.

about each test. Whether you are familiar with the WJ III Tests of Achievement or just learning the WJ IV ACH, this section serves as a guide or a good refresher. The information presented applies to all three forms (A, B, and C), as well as to the Extended Battery. While studying the following descriptions of test administration procedures, you may also wish to review the material in the Test Book and Test Record.

HOW TO ADMINISTER THE STANDARD BATTERY, FORMS A, B, AND C

Test 1: Letter-Word Identification

Letter-Word Identification measures the examinee's word identification skills. The task ranges from identification of letters to reading aloud isolated letters and words. The examinee does not need to know the meaning of the words.

Administration. Select an appropriate starting point by consulting the Suggested Starting Points table located on the page after the tab in the Test Book. Establish a basal by testing in complete pages until the six consecutive lowest-numbered items are correct or until Item 1 has been administered. Continue testing by complete pages until the examinee misses the six highest-numbered items administered or until the page with the last item has been administered.

Know the correct pronunciation of each item. Following some of the more difficult items, correct pronunciations are shown in parentheses in the Test Book.

Refer to a standard dictionary for additional assistance. Do not tell or help the examinee with any letters or words during this test or read any items.

If the examinee sounds out the word first and then says the correct word fluently, score it as correct. This is not a test of automatic word recognition. Many examinees need to employ decoding strategies to read unfamiliar words, and they are not penalized for this. For example, if the examinee reads the stimulus word *island* as *is-land* and then says, "Oh, that's island" (pronouncing the word correctly), you would score the item as correct. However, if the examinee reads *island* as *is-land* and does not blend it together to pronounce the word correctly, score the item as incorrect. If the examinee's last response to an item is read phoneme by phoneme or syllable by syllable, score that item 0 and then suggest that the examinee "first read the word silently and then say the whole word smoothly." Give this reminder only once during the test.

To keep administration brisk, use the 5-second guideline shown in the Error or No Response boxes to encourage a response if no response has been given. However, if the examinee is still attempting to read the word or requests more time, you would allow more time. The 5-second guideline is not a time limit.

If unsure of a response to a specific item, do not ask the examinee to repeat that item. Instead, have the person repeat all of the items on that page. Score only the item in question; do not rescore the other items.

Record incorrect responses for later error analysis. This analysis can provide valuable insights into the examinee's knowledge of phoneme–grapheme relationships. Rapid Reference 2.1 lists the key administration points for Letter-Word Identification.

Qualitative observation checklist. Check the one statement that best describes the ease with which the examinee identified and read the words. Although this checklist is optional, it provides important qualitative information that informs instructional planning. If using the data in Chapter 5 of the WJ IV ACH Examiner's Manual, determine whether the examinee's performance was typical or atypical compared to agemates.

Item scoring. Score each correct response 1 and each incorrect response 0. Do not penalize an examinee for mispronunciations resulting from articulation errors, dialects, or regional speech patterns. Record the total number of items answered correctly and all items below the basal in the Number Correct box in the Test Record.

Common examiner errors. Common examiner errors include: (a) having the examinee repeat a specific word, (b) failing to complete a page, (c) accepting responses that are sounded out but not blended back together, (d) treating the 5-second guideline as a time limit, and (e) telling the examinee letters or words on the test.

≡ Rapid Reference 2.1

Key Administration Points for Test 1: Letter-Word Identification
- *Materials needed:* Standard Battery Test Book and Test Record.
- Use Suggested Starting Points.
- Follow basal/ceiling rules: six consecutive correct/six consecutive incorrect.
- Know the exact pronunciation of each word.
- Do not tell the examinee any words or letters.
- Do not ask the examinee to repeat a specific word.
- Only accept correct responses that are pronounced as a complete word.
- Remember to complete the page, even after a ceiling has been reached. If the examinee gives any correct responses in the process of completing the page, continue testing to reach a new ceiling.
- Record errors for analysis.
- Allow more than 5 seconds if the examinee requires more time to respond.
- Do not penalize for articulation errors or regional/dialectical speech differences.

Test 2: Applied Problems

Applied Problems requires the individual to analyze and solve practical math problems. The examiner presents each item orally, so the examinee is not required to read.

Administration. Using the table in the Test Book, select a starting point based on an estimate of the examinee's present level of math skill. When prompted, give the examinee a pencil with an eraser and the RB. Provide these materials prior to the prompt if the examinee requests them or appears to need them. Test by complete pages until the examinee correctly answers the five lowest-numbered items administered, or until the page with Item 1 has been administered. Continue testing by complete pages until the examinee misses the five highest-numbered items administered or you have administered the page with the last item. Upon request by the examinee, you may repeat any item. The optional Qualitative Observation Checklist helps describe the examinee's performance on this test and compares the examinee's performance to that of agemates. Rapid Reference 2.2 lists the key administration points for Applied Problems.

Item scoring. Score each correct response with a 1 and each incorrect response with a 0. Unit labels (e.g., hours, inches, dollars) are not required unless specified in the correct key. If the unit label is required, both the answer and the label must be correct to receive credit. If the unit label is not required and the examinee gives a

≡ Rapid Reference 2.2

Key Administration Points for Test 2: Applied Problems
- *Materials needed:* Standard Battery Test Book, Test Record, RB, and two pencils.
- Use Suggested Starting Points.
- Follow basal/ceiling rules: five consecutive correct/five consecutive incorrect.
- Test by complete pages.
- Provide the RB and pencil when prompted, or earlier if needed.
- Repeat items if requested by the examinee.
- Score the item as incorrect if the wrong unit label is provided, even if the label is not required.

correct answer and provides a correct label, score the item as correct. However, if an incorrect label is given, required or not, score the item as incorrect. Record the total number of items answered correctly and all items below the basal in the Number Correct box in the Test Record.

Common examiner errors. Common examiner errors include: (a) forgetting to test by complete pages, (b) not repeating items upon request, and (c) not scoring items correctly based on the rules governing unit labels.

Test 3: Spelling

Spelling requires the examinee to write words that are presented orally. Initial items measure prewriting skills followed by items that require the examinee to write individual upper- and lowercase letters. All remaining items measure the person's ability to spell words correctly.

Administration. Before administering this test, be sure to know the pronunciation of all test items. Using the table in the Test Book, select a starting point based on an estimate of the examinee's present level of spelling skill. When prompted, give the examinee a sharpened pencil with an eraser and the RB. Printed responses are requested because they are typically more legible than cursive responses, but cursive responses are acceptable. Administer the test following the basal and ceiling rules: either six consecutive lowest-numbered items correct or Item 1, and either six consecutive highest-numbered items failed or the last item. The complete page rule does not apply to this test. Completing the optional Qualitative Observation Checklist helps describe the examinee's automaticity on this task and you can compare performance to that of agemates by consulting

≡ Rapid Reference 2.3

Key Administration Points for Test 3: Spelling
- *Materials needed:* Standard Battery Test Book, Test Record, RB, and two pencils.
- Know the pronunciation of all test items.
- Use Suggested Starting Points.
- Follow basal/ceiling rules: six consecutive correct/six consecutive incorrect.
- Request printed responses but accept cursive writing.
- Do not penalize for poor handwriting or reversals, unless the reversal becomes a new letter.
- Accept upper- or lowercase responses unless case is specified.

Chapter 5 of the WJ IV ACH Examiner's Manual. Rapid Reference 2.3 lists key administration points for the Spelling test.

Item scoring. Score each correct response with a 1 and each incorrect response with a 0. Accept upper- or lowercase letters unless case is specified. Do not penalize for reversed letters as long as the letter does not become a new letter. For example, a reversed lowercase *c* is not penalized, but a reversed lowercase letter *b* would be penalized because it becomes the letter *d*. Record the total number of items answered correctly and all items below the basal in the Number Correct box in the Test Record.

Common examiner errors. Common examiner errors include: (a) mispronouncing words, (b) scoring items incorrectly, or (c) penalizing for reversed letters that do not become new letters.

Test 4: Passage Comprehension

Passage Comprehension requires the examinee to silently read a short passage and then supply a key missing word that makes sense in the context of the passage. Initial items involve symbolic learning (matching a rebus to a picture) followed by items that require pointing to a picture that goes with a printed phrase.

Administration. Using the table in the Test Book, select a starting point based on an estimate of the examinee's present level of reading skill. Test by complete pages until the examinee correctly answers the six lowest-numbered items administered or until Item 1 has been administered. Continue testing by complete pages until the examinee misses the six highest-numbered items administered or until the page with the last item has been administered.

The passages should be read silently. Some individuals, especially younger ones, may read aloud. When this happens, remind the examinee to read silently. If the person continues to read aloud, do not insist on silent reading. Do not help the examinee with any words on this test. The examinee needs only to identify the specific word that goes into the blank. If the examinee reads the sentence aloud with the correct answer, say "Tell me the one word that should go in the blank." If the examinee cannot provide the word, score the response as incorrect. For Items 12 and higher, if the examinee does not respond after 30 seconds, encourage a response. If there is still no response, score the item 0, point to the next item, and say "Try this one." The 30 seconds is a guideline, not a time limit. If the examinee requests more time on an item, you would allow more time. Results on the optional Qualitative Observation Checklist help describe the examinee's performance on this task. Rapid Reference 2.4 lists the key administration points for Passage Comprehension.

Item scoring. Score each correct response 1 and each incorrect response 0. Unless noted in the key, accept only one-word responses. If a person gives a two-word or longer response, ask for a one-word answer. Responses are correct when they differ from the correct response only in verb tense or number (singular/plural). Score the response as incorrect if the examinee substitutes a different part of speech, such as a noun for a verb. Do not penalize for mispronunciations resulting from articulation errors, dialects, or regional speech patterns. Record the total number of items answered correctly and all items below the basal in the Number Correct box in the Test Record.

≡ *Rapid Reference 2.4*

Key Administration Points for Test 4: Passage Comprehension
- *Materials needed:* Standard Battery Test Book and Test Record.
- Use Suggested Starting Points.
- Follow basal/ceiling rules: six consecutive correct/six consecutive incorrect.
- Test by complete pages.
- When necessary, remind the examinee to read silently.
- If the examinee reads a passage aloud, the word that belongs in the blank must be identified separately.
- Do not provide help with any words on this test.
- Do not penalize for responses that differ in tense or number.
- Score responses that substitute a different part of speech as incorrect.
- Do not penalize for articulation errors or regional, dialectical speech differences.

Common examiner errors. Common examiner errors include: (a) providing help with words, (b) not completing queries, (c) not asking for a one-word response when a longer response is given, (d) penalizing for responses that differ only in verb tense or number, and (e) counting responses that are a different part of speech as correct.

Test 5: Calculation

Calculation measures the ability to perform mathematical computations, ranging in difficulty from simple addition facts to complex equations.

Administration. Using the Suggested Starting Points located in the Test Book, select an appropriate starting point based on the examinee's present estimated level of math skills. When prompted, give the examinee a pencil with an eraser and the RB. If the examinee misses one or both sample items, discontinue testing and score the test a 0. Administer the test following the basal and ceiling rules: six consecutive lowest-numbered items correct or until Item 1 has been administered, and six consecutive highest-numbered items incorrect or until the last item has been administered. The complete page rule does not apply to this test. Do not draw the examinee's attention to the operation signs in the problems. The results on the optional Qualitative Observation Checklist can help describe the examinee's rate and automaticity on this task. Rapid Reference 2.5 lists key administration points for Calculation.

Item scoring. Score each correct calculation 1 and each incorrect response 0. Score any items the examinee skipped before the last completed item as 0. Do not

---

≡ Rapid Reference 2.5

Key Administration Points for Test 5: Calculation
- *Materials needed:* Standard Battery Test Book, Test Record, RB, and two pencils.
- Select a starting point based on examinee's present estimated level of math skill.
- Follow basal/ceiling rules: six consecutive correct/six consecutive incorrect.
- Discontinue testing and record a score of 0 if both sample items are missed.
- Complete all appropriate queries.
- Do not provide additional guidance, such as pointing out the signs.
- Score skipped items as 0.
- Do not penalize for poorly formed numbers or reversed numbers.
- Score transposed numbers as 0 (e.g., 12 for 21).

penalize for poorly formed or reversed numbers on this test; however, score a transposition of numbers (e.g., 13 for 31) as incorrect. Record the total number of items answered correctly and all items below the basal in the Number Correct box in the Test Record.

Common examiner errors. Common examiner errors include: (a) failing to complete queries; (b) failing to establish a basal or ceiling; and (c) providing inappropriate guidance, such as alerting the examinee to pay attention to the signs.

Test 6: Writing Samples

Writing Samples measures the examinee's skill in writing sentences in response to a variety of demands that increase in complexity. Responses are evaluated based on quality of expression.

Administration. To begin, select a starting point based on an estimate of the examinee's present level of writing ability. You may administer this test to a small group of two or three individuals at one time if, in your judgment, it will not affect any individual's performance and the examinees are taking the same block of items.

Administer the appropriate block of items as indicated on the table in the Test Book on the page after the Writing Samples tab. When prompted, give the examinee a pencil with an eraser and the RB. If an examinee's response to an item is illegible or difficult to read, ask the person to write as neatly as possible. Do not, however, ask the examinee to read aloud what was written for scoring purposes. Score illegible responses as 0. If requested by the examinee, you may read any words during this test or repeat the instructions. When an examinee asks if spelling is important or how to spell a word, encourage the examinee to just do the best he or she can. The overall quality of the examinee's written sentences can be described by completing the Qualitative Observation Checklist in the Test Record. Rapid Reference 2.6 lists the key administration points for Writing Samples.

Item scoring. Score Writing Samples after the testing is completed. Items 1 through 6 are scored 1 or 0. Items 7 and higher may be scored 2, 1.5, 1, 0.5, or 0 points using a modified holistic procedure that requires examiner judgment. Because scoring of this test is more involved and subjective than the scoring of other WJ IV ACH tests, special rating and scoring procedures are provided in Appendix B of the WJ IV ACH Examiner's Manual that accompanies the test. The Scoring Guide for all three forms of this test is in Appendix B so be sure to consult the pages that correspond to the form administered (Form A, B, or C).

≡ Rapid Reference 2.6

Key Administration Points for Test 6: Writing Samples
- *Materials needed:* Standard Battery Test Book, Test Record, RB, and two pencils.
- Use the examinee's estimated writing ability to select a block of items to administer.
- Score the items after the testing is complete.
- Administer additional items if the examinee's score falls in a shaded area.
- Read words to the examinee as he or she requests.
- Do not spell any words for the examinee.
- Do not ask the examinee to read his or her response for scoring purposes.
- Be sure the raw score is based on only one of the established blocks of items.
- Encourage the examinee to attempt a response to each item in the block.

This section presents a summary of item-scoring procedures, and Chapter 3 presents additional details regarding scoring.

- Items 1 through 6
  - 1 point: Standard response that meets task requirements.
  - 0 points: Inadequate response that does not meet task requirements.
- Items 7 through 28
  - 2 points: A 2-point response is a superior response. Excluding beginning items, it is a complete sentence that satisfies task demands and includes additional descriptive words or embellishments.
  - 1.5 points: A response scored 1.5 points is a borderline response that does not fit the exact pattern of the Scoring Guide. If it is not clear whether a response is superior (2 points) or standard (1 point), credit the response with a score of 1.5 points.
  - 1 point: A 1-point response is a standard response. Excluding beginning items, it is a complete sentence with adequate content.
  - 0.5 points: A response scored 0.5 points is a borderline response that does not fit the exact pattern of the Scoring Guide. If it is not clear whether a response is standard (1 point) or inadequate (0 points), credit the response with a score of 0.5 points.
  - 0 points: A no-credit response is an inadequate response. It may be an incomplete sentence, a sentence with minimal content, an illegible response, or a sentence that does not follow the task demands.

If the individual's raw score falls within one of the seven shaded areas in the Scoring Table, administer the additional items that are noted in the Adjusted Item

Blocks chart in the Test Record. Base the examinee's score on just one block of items, even if more than one block was administered. The block of items that falls more in the middle of the range of scores (unshaded areas) provides the most accurate representation of the examinee's writing ability. If the individual's score for a block of items ends in a .5, for example 15.5, round to the nearest even number. In this case the score would be 16. If in another case the score is 16.5, it also would be 16 since that is the nearest even number.

Common examiner errors. Common examiner errors include: (a) failing to administer the appropriate block of items, (b) scoring the items incorrectly, (c) being either too lenient or too harsh when evaluating responses, (d) failing to administer additional items when necessary, (e) calculating the raw score incorrectly, (f) asking the examinee to read his or her written response for scoring purposes, and (g) rounding a score that ends in .5 up, rather than to the nearest even number.

Test 7: Word Attack

Word Attack requires the examinee to read aloud nonsense or low-frequency words that conform to English spelling patterns. Initial items require the examinee to produce the sound a letter makes. Remaining items require the examinee to apply phonic and structural analysis skills in reading the nonsense words.

Administration. Review the correct pronunciation of all items before administering this test. Pronunciation for the more difficult items is shown in parentheses following the item in the Test Book. Refer to a standard dictionary for additional assistance. If the examinee has any special speech characteristics resulting from articulation errors or dialect, an examiner who is familiar with the examinee's speech pattern should administer this test.

Using the table in the Test Book, select a starting point based on an estimate of the individual's present level of reading skill. Test by complete pages until the examinee has responded correctly to six consecutive items, or until Item 1 has been administered. Continue testing until the examinee has missed six consecutive items, or until the last item has been administered.

If a response to a specific item is unclear, do not ask the examinee to repeat the specific item. Instead, complete the entire page and then ask the examinee to repeat all of the items on that page. Score only the item in question and not the other items.

If the examinee pronounces the word phoneme-by-phoneme or syllable-by-syllable instead of reading it in a natural and fluent way, score the item 0 and suggest that the examinee "first read the word silently and then say the whole word

≡ Rapid Reference 2.7

Key Administration Points for Test 7: Word Attack

- *Materials needed:* Standard Battery Test Book and Test Record.
- Know pronunciation of all items prior to administering this test.
- Use Suggested Starting Points.
- Follow basal/ceiling rules: six consecutive correct/six consecutive incorrect.
- Test by complete pages.
- Do not tell the examinee any letters or words.
- Only accept correct responses that are pronounced as a complete word.
- Do not ask the examinee to repeat a specific word. Instead, have the examinee repeat entire page and rescore only the item in question.
- Record errors for analysis after testing is completed.
- Score the last response given on each item.

smoothly." Give this reminder only once during the administration of this test. However, if the examinee first sounds out the stimulus word and then pronounces it correctly, score the item 1. Score the last response given. Record incorrect responses for error analysis and complete the Qualitative Checklist in the Test Record to describe how the examinee performed the task. Rapid Reference 2.7 lists the key administration points for Word Attack.

Item scoring. Score each correct response 1 and each incorrect response 0. Do not penalize the examinee for mispronunciations resulting from articulation errors, dialects, or regional speech patterns. Record the total number of items answered correctly and all items below the basal in the Number Correct box in the Test Record.

Common examiner errors. Common examiner errors include: (a) failing to know the correct pronunciation of all of the items, (b) accepting responses that are sounded out and not blended back together, and (c) failing to have the examinee repeat an entire page when one response was not heard.

Test 8: Oral Reading

Oral Reading is a measure of word reading accuracy and prosody. The examinee reads aloud sentences that gradually increase in difficulty. Performance is scored for both accuracy and fluency of expression.

Administration. Oral Reading is composed of a set of sentences that gradually increase in difficulty. Although the sentences are not presented in

≡ Rapid Reference 2.8

Key Administration Points for Test 8: Oral Reading

- *Materials needed:* Standard Battery Test Book, Test Record.
- Know the pronunciation of all of the words in the test.
- Start at the suggested starting point based on the person's estimated reading achievement.
- Know the different error types and what is and is not an error.
- Mark all errors in sentences with a slash (/).
- Follow the continuation rules at the bottom of each page to determine which items to administer and when to discontinue testing.
- Enter the number of points into the online scoring program for each group of sentences administered. Enter an X for any group not administered.
- If needed, remind the examinee to read carefully, not as fast as he or she can.

a paragraph, the set is organized around one specific content area theme: bees (Form A), whales (Form B), and trees (Form C). There are two different starting points based on an individual's estimated reading level. This test uses continuation instructions rather than basal and ceiling rules. The continuation instructions are found at the bottom of each examiner page in the Test Book and also on the Test Record. For example, when starting with Item 1, if the examinee has 5 or fewer points on Items 1 through 5, testing is discontinued. If the examinee has 6 or more points on Items 1 through 5, testing continues with Items 6 through 10. Rapid Reference 2.8 lists key administration points for Oral Reading.

Item scoring. As the examinee is reading a sentence, mark all errors with a slash at the point in the sentence where the error occurs. This process is simplified because the sentences are reproduced in the Test Record. The types of errors that are marked include: mispronunciations, omissions, insertions, substitutions, hesitations of 3 seconds, repetitions, transpositions, and ignoring punctuation. For all error types except insertions, place the slash mark on the word or punctuation mark that was incorrect. For insertions, place the slash mark between the two printed words where the insertion occurred. If the examinee self-corrects within 3 seconds, do not count the word as an error. Also, if an examinee repeats a word or words as part of the self-correction, do not count the repetition as an error. As an option, record and total each error type on the Qualitative Observation Tally that is in the Test Record. Analyses of the error types can assist in instructional planning.

For scoring purposes, a sentence with no errors receives a 2, a sentence with one error receives a 1, and a sentence with two or more errors receives a 0. Record the number of points for each group of sentences administered in the corresponding Number of Points boxes on the Test Record. Use those totals for entry in the online scoring program and for obtaining an estimated age or grade equivalent in the Scoring Table in the Test Record. Enter an X for any group of sentences that was not administered.

When first learning to administer and score this test, it may be helpful to complete several practice administrations. During these practice administrations, record the examinee's reading of the sentences to check your scoring accuracy. Some examinees read quickly and it may be difficult to write down and classify the error types until you are more familiar with the process. It is recommended that you only do this during practice administration. If testing someone who reads quickly, you can remind the examinee to read carefully, not as fast as he or she can. In some cases, you may need to ask the examinee to pause after each sentence, giving you time to record the errors.

DON'T FORGET
....
During practice administrations, recording the examinee as he or she reads aloud for Test 8: Oral Reading may improve your accuracy in scoring and recording of types of errors.

Common examiner errors. Common examiner errors include: (a) not knowing the correct pronunciation of a specific word, (b) marking a self-correction that is done within 3 seconds as an error, (c) failing to mark the different types of reading errors accurately, and (d) not following the continuation instructions.

Test 9: Sentence Reading Fluency

Sentence Reading Fluency is a timed test that requires the examinee to silently and quickly read and comprehend simple sentences. The examinee must decide if the statement is true or false and then circle *Yes* or *No* in the Response Booklet.

Administration. All examinees begin this test with the sample items. If the examinee has three or fewer correct answers on Practice Exercises C through F, discontinue testing and record a score of 0 in the Sentence Reading Fluency Number Correct box in the Test Record. You may administer this test to a small group of two or three individuals at one time if, in your judgment, it will not affect any individual's performance.

When you are ready to begin the test, give the examinee a sharpened pencil and the Response Booklet. The 3-minute time limit begins with the administration of

Item 1. Be sure to record the exact starting time in minutes and seconds if a stopwatch is not being used. During the test, if the examinee appears to be answering items without reading the sentences, remind him or her to read each sentence. If the examinee stops at the bottom of a page, remind him or her to continue to the top of the next column or on to the next page. Due to the way this test is scored, examinees need to read the sentences in order, only skipping the ones that cannot be read. If the examinee stops to erase an answer, remind him or her to just quickly cross out the incorrect one, rather than erasing.

Discontinue testing after exactly 3 minutes and collect the pencil and RB. Record the exact finishing time, because early finishers who do well will receive higher scores than individuals who work for the full 3 minutes. Complete the optional Qualitative Checklist in the Test Record to describe how the examinee performed the task. Rapid Reference 2.9 lists the key administration points for Sentence Reading Fluency.

Item scoring. Score each correct response 1 and each incorrect response 0. A scoring guide overlay is provided for convenience and accuracy. Ignore skipped items. Record the total number of correct items and the total number of incorrect items.

≡ Rapid Reference 2.9

Key Administration Points for Test 9: Sentence Reading Fluency

- Materials needed: Standard Battery Test Book, Test Record, RB, two pencils, and stopwatch or watch with second hand.
- Administer sample items to all examinees.
- Do not administer test if the examinee has three or fewer correct on Practice Exercises C through F.
- Begin with Item 1 for all examinees.
- Observe the 3-minute time limit.
- When not using a stopwatch, record exact starting time in minutes and seconds.
- Remind examinees to try to read the sentences if it appears they are simply circling answers randomly.
- Do not help the examinee with any words on this test.
- Remind examinees to continue working if they stop at the bottom of a page.
- Remind examinees to work in numerical order if it appears they are skipping around. It is acceptable to skip items that are not known.
- Remind examinees to quickly cross out (rather than erase) responses they wish to change.

CAUTION

Do not administer Test 9: Sentence Reading Fluency to a person who cannot read. Due to the response requirements, a nonreader could randomly circle yes or no without ever reading a sentence and receive a score. That score would not reflect the person's reading ability.

Common examiner errors. Common examiner errors include: (a) failing to record exact starting or finishing times in minutes and seconds when not using a stopwatch, (b) failing to provide appropriate guidance during the test, (c) providing help on reading words or sentences, (d) counting skipped items as errors, and (e) failing to record two totals: number correct and number incorrect.

Test 10: Math Facts Fluency

Math Facts Fluency is a timed test that requires rapid calculation of simple, single-digit addition, subtraction, and multiplication facts.

Administration. All examinees begin this test with Item 1. When prompted, give the examinee a sharpened pencil and the Response Booklet. If the examinee has three or less correct after 1 minute, discontinue testing and record a time of 1 minute in the Test Record as well as the number correct (0 to 3). For all others, discontinue testing after exactly 3 minutes and then collect the pencil and RB. Once testing has started, do not point to the signs or remind the examinee to pay attention to the signs.

If the examinee finishes in less than 3 minutes, record the exact finishing time in minutes and seconds on the Test Record. Exact finishing times are important because early finishers who do well will receive higher scores than individuals who continue to work for the full 3 minutes. Complete the optional Qualitative Checklist in the Test Record to describe how the examinee performed the task. Rapid Reference 2.10 lists the key administration points for Math Facts Fluency.

Item scoring. Score each correct response 1 and each incorrect response 0. A scoring guide overlay is provided to facilitate scoring. Do not penalize for poorly formed or reversed numerals. Transposed numbers (e.g., 41 for 14) are incorrect.

Common examiner errors. A common examiner error is providing inappropriate guidance during the test, such as pointing out the signs or reminding a student that he or she knows how to solve that type of problem.

≡ Rapid Reference 2.10

Key Administration Points for Test 10: Math Facts Fluency

- Materials needed: Standard Battery Test Book, Test Record, RB, two pencils, and stopwatch or watch with second hand.
- When not using a stopwatch, record the exact starting time in minutes and seconds.
- Begin with Item 1 for all examinees.
- Observe the 3-minute time limit.
- Discontinue testing if the examinee has three or less correct after 1 minute. Record 1 minute and the number correct (0 to 3).
- Do not point out the signs.
- Base the score on the total number of items completed correctly.

Test 11: Sentence Writing Fluency

Sentence Writing Fluency is a timed test that requires formulating and writing simple sentences quickly. Each sentence must relate to a given stimulus picture and incorporate a given set of three words.

Administration. Complete the sample items and then begin with Item 1 for all examinees. If the examinee receives a zero on Samples B through D after error correction, discontinue testing and record a score of 0 for the test. If the examinee has three or fewer correct within the first 2 minutes, you may discontinue testing. Record a time of 2 minutes and enter the number correct (0 to 3). For all other examinees, discontinue testing after exactly 5 minutes and collect the pencil and RB. If the examinee finishes before the 5-minute time period has elapsed, record the actual finishing time in minutes and seconds on the Test Record. Exact finishing times are important because early finishers who do well will receive higher scores than individuals who continue to work for the full 5 minutes. In this test, you may read the stimulus words to the examinee if requested. You may administer this test to a small group of two or three individuals at one time if, in your judgment, this procedure will not affect any examinee's performance. Complete the optional Qualitative Checklist in the Test Record to describe how the examinee performed the task. Rapid Reference 2.11 lists key administration points for the Sentence Writing Fluency test.

Item scoring. Score each correct response with a 1 and each incorrect response with a 0. Score any items skipped prior to the last item the examinee completed as incorrect. Do not penalize for errors in spelling, punctuation, or capitalization or for poor handwriting, unless the writing on an item is illegible. Sometimes it may not be immediately apparent whether to score an item as correct or incorrect. To receive credit for an item the examinee must: (a) use the three stimulus words in a complete sentence, (b) not change the stimulus words in any way, and (c) provide a response that is a reasonable sentence. Stimulus words that are miscopied or misspelled can still receive credit if the word has not changed tense, number, part of speech, or become a different word, and the examinee wrote a reasonable, complete sentence. For example, if a person wrote "The foot is litle," the misspelling of *little* would not be penalized. Awkward sentences (if the meaning is clear) and sentences with the understood subject "you" are scored as correct. Sentences that use alternate characters such as an ampersand (&) or a plus sign (+) for the word *and* or an abbreviation like "w/" instead of the full word *with* are scored as correct if the response meets all other criteria. If the examinee omits a word that is critical to the sentence meaning, score the response as incorrect. Do not penalize for an accidental omission of a less meaningful word (e.g., *a, the, an*) in a sentence, unless it is one of the stimulus words.

If, after reviewing these guidelines, it is still unclear how to score one or more items, balance the scores given to these responses. For example, if two items are unclear, score one item with a 1 and the other with a 0.

⟹ *Rapid Reference 2.11*

Key Administration Points for Test 11: Sentence Writing Fluency
- *Materials needed:* Standard Battery Test Book, Test Record, RB, two pencils, and stopwatch or watch with second hand.
- Test may be administered to a small group of two to three individuals.
- Complete sample items with all examinees.
- Discontinue testing if examinee has a 0 on Samples B through D after error correction.
- Begin test with Item 1 for all examinees.
- Observe the 5-minute time limit.
- Testing may be discontinued if the examinee has three or fewer correct in the first 2 minutes.
- Read any word requested by the examinee.
- To receive credit, the examinee must use three stimulus words and may not change them.
- Do not penalize for poor writing or errors in capitalization, punctuation, or spelling, as long as the response is legible.
- Score all skipped items as 0.

Common examiner errors. Examiner errors include: (a) being too lenient or too stringent on scoring the sentences, (b) failing to note that the examinee has changed or not included one of the three stimulus words, and (c) counting a miscopied stimulus word as an error in every case.

ADMINISTRATION OF THE EXTENDED BATTERY

Test 12: Reading Recall

Reading Recall requires the examinee to silently read a short story one time and then retell as much of the story as he or she can recall.

Administration. Use the examinee's present level of reading ability as an estimate of where to begin testing. Consult the table in the Test Book to choose the appropriate starting point. The examinee is asked to read a story once silently. If necessary, remind the examinee of this rule. Turn the page after the examinee has completed reading the story once. Prompt the examinee as directed to retell the story. Do not tell the examinee any words on this test. This test uses continuation instructions rather than basal and ceiling rules. The continuation instructions are presented after each set of two stories, and they provide direction regarding whether additional stories should be administered or testing should be discontinued. The administration of this test is very similar to the Story Recall test in the WJ IV COG. Rapid Reference 2.12 lists the key administration points for Reading Recall.

Item scoring. On the Test Record, slashes (/) separate the story elements. When scoring the test, place a check mark over each element recalled correctly. Each element is scored based on a key word or words shown in bold type. The examinee must recall the bold word or words exactly, or a synonym that preserves meaning, to receive credit for the element. If the examinee gives a derivation of a proper name, allow credit for the element (e.g., Annie for Ann). If the examinee gives a response that differs from the correct response only in verb tense or number (singular/plural) or uses possessive case (e.g., Joe's instead of Joe), give credit for the element. The examinee may recall the elements in any order.

In addition, do not penalize for mispronunciations resulting from articulation errors, dialects, or regional speech patterns (e.g., *browing* for *blowing*).

Record the number of correctly recalled elements for each story and then the cumulative total for each set of two stories administered in the appropriate Number of Points boxes on the Test Record. The number of points for the last two sets of stories administered is used to obtain an estimated age and grade equivalent from the Scoring Table in the Test Record. Record the numbers for

≡ Rapid Reference 2.12

Key Administration Points for Test 12: Reading Recall

- *Materials needed:* Extended Battery Test Book, Test Record.
- Use the examinee's current level of reading achievement to estimate a starting point.
- Select the appropriate starting point from the table in the Test Book.
- The examinee reads the story through silently one time.
- The examinee must recall elements in bold type exactly (except for examples previously noted) to receive credit.
- In the Test Record, place a check mark over each element the examinee correctly recalled.
- The elements may be recalled in any order.
- Follow the continuation instructions to determine when to administer additional stories or when to discontinue testing.
- Enter the number of points in the Score Entry section of the Test Record and into the online scoring program for each set of two stories administered. Enter an X for any set not administered.

each set of stories in the Score Entry table in the Test Record, and enter X for sets of stories that were not administered. Follow this same procedure when entering scores into the scoring program.

Common examiner errors. Common examiner errors include: (a) not scoring the elements correctly and (b) not following the continuation instructions.

Test 13: Number Matrices

Number Matrices is a measure of quantitative reasoning. The examinee must identify the missing number in a matrix.

Administration. Number Matrices has two sample items. Sample A is for people with estimated math ability from kindergarten to grade 8, and Sample B is the starting point for grade 9 to adult. After administering Sample B, there are two suggested starting points. When beginning the test, provide the examinee with a pencil and the worksheet found in the Response Booklet. Some examinees may be confused by more than one matrix on a page. In these cases, it is permissible to show one matrix at a time by covering one with a paper or hand. Administer the test by complete pages following the basal and ceiling rules: six consecutive lowest-numbered items correct or until Item 1 has been administered, and six consecutive highest-numbered items incorrect or the last

≡ Rapid Reference 2.13

Key Administration Points for Test 13: Number Matrices

- *Materials needed:* Extended Battery Test Book, Test Record, and RB.
- Administer Sample A to examinees with estimated mathematical abilities of kindergarten to grade 8 and Sample B to grade 9 to adult.
- If the examinee is confused by more than one matrix per page, use a paper to uncover one matrix at a time.
- Follow basal/ceiling rules: six consecutive correct/six consecutive incorrect.
- Test by complete pages.
- Encourage a response after 30 seconds on Items I through I I or I minute on Items 12 through 30 if the examinee does not seem to be working on the problem.
- Place the worksheet in the RB in front of the examinee with a pencil with an eraser, and tell him or her to use the worksheet if needed.

item has been administered. On Items 1 through 11, encourage a response after 30 seconds; on Items 12 through 30, encourage a response after 1 minute. These times are guidelines rather than time limits, so if an examinee is actively engaged in trying to solve a problem, allow for more time. Also, if the examinee provides a response that is not a whole number, request that he or she use whole numbers only to solve the problems. Rapid Reference 2.13 lists the key administration points of Number Matrices.

Item scoring. Score each item with a 1 for a correct response and with a 0 for an incorrect response. To be correct, the answer must solve the problem both horizontally and vertically. Record the total number of items answered correctly and all items below the basal in the Number Correct box in the Test Record.

Common examiner errors. Common examiner errors include: (a) not following the instructions in the Error or No Response box, (b) not providing the examinee with a pencil and the worksheet in the RB, and (c) not prompting the examinee to move on after 30 seconds (Items 1–11) or 1 minute (Items 12–30) if he or she is not actively engaged in solving the matrix.

Test 14: Editing

Editing requires identifying and correcting errors in written passages. The error in the passage may be incorrect punctuation or capitalization, inappropriate word usage, or a misspelled word.

≡ Rapid Reference 2.14

Key Administration Points for Test 14: Editing
- Materials needed: Extended Battery Test Book and Test Record.
- Administer Samples A through D to all individuals.
- Select a starting point based on the individual's estimated writing ability.
- Follow basal/ceiling rules: six consecutive correct/six consecutive incorrect.
- Test by complete pages.
- Discontinue testing if an individual has a 0 on Samples A through D or on Items 1 through 4.
- Do not read any words or test items to the examinee.
- Be sure to query when necessary.
- Do not give credit unless the examinee both identifies and corrects the error.

Administration. Administer Sample Items A through D to all individuals, then select a starting point based on an estimate of the examinee's present level of writing ability. If the examinee has a score of 0 correct on the four sample items, discontinue the test and record a score of 0 without administering any test items. Test by complete pages until the examinee correctly answers the six lowest-numbered items administered or until the page with Item 1 has been administered. Test by complete pages until the examinee misses the six highest-numbered items administered or until you have administered the page with the last item. If the examinee has a score of 0 correct on Items 1 through 4, discontinue testing and record a score of 0.

Do not tell the examinee any words on this test. If an examinee reads the sentence aloud and inadvertently corrects the error in context, say "Tell me how to correct the error." If the examinee indicates the error without explaining how to correct it, say "How would you correct that mistake?" Unless the examinee can both identify and correct the error in the passage, score the item as incorrect. Rapid Reference 2.14 lists the key administration points for Editing.

CAUTION

Do not administer Test 14: Editing to a person who cannot read. Because the examinee must read each item to take this test, a nonreader's performance would reflect the inability to read rather than proofreading skills.

Item scoring. Score each correct response as 1 and each incorrect response as 0. For a response to be correct, the examinee must indicate both where the error is located and how the mistake should be corrected. Record the total number of items answered correctly and all items below the basal in the Number Correct box in the Test Record.

Common examiner errors. Common examiner errors include: (a) reading any words in the test items to the examinee, (b) failing to have the examinee both identify and correct the error, and (c) failing to query when necessary.

Test 15: Word Reading Fluency

Word Reading Fluency is a timed test that requires vocabulary knowledge and semantic fluency. The examinee must quickly mark two words that share a semantic relationship in a row of four words.

Administration. Place the Response Booklet in front of the examinee and administer the Sample Items and Practice Exercise. Follow all directions for error correction or no response during the administration of the Sample Items and Practice Exercise to ensure the examinee understands the task. If the examinee has one or no items correct on the Practice Exercise, record a score of 0 for the test and do not administer the test. Once the Practice Exercise has been completed, the person is given 3 minutes to work on the test items. Remind the examinee to continue to the next page or the next column if he or she stops at the bottom of a page. Do not tell the examinee any of the words on this test. If the examinee finishes before the 3-minute time period has elapsed, record the actual finishing time in minutes and seconds on the Test Record. Recording exact finishing times is important because early finishers who do well will receive higher scores than individuals who continue to work for the full 3 minutes. Rapid Reference 2.15 lists the main administration points for Word Reading Fluency.

≣ Rapid Reference 2.15

Key Administration Points for Test 15: Word Reading Fluency
- Materials needed: Extended Battery Test Book, Test Record, RB, stopwatch, and two pencils.
- Administer Samples A and B and the Practice Exercises C through F to all examinees.
- Discontinue testing if the examinee has 1 or no items correct on the Practice Exercise.
- Follow all error correction and no response directions carefully for Sample Items and the Practice Exercise.
- Give the examinee the RB and pencil and then begin timing for 3 minutes.
- Score all items 1 or 0.
- Do not read any items to the examinee during this test.
- Use the scoring guide overlay to facilitate scoring.

Item scoring. Score each correct response 1 and each incorrect response 0. A scoring guide overlay is provided for convenience and accuracy.

Common examiner errors. Examiner errors include: (a) not reminding the examinee to keep going if he or she stops on an item or at the bottom of the page, (b) failing to stop the test at exactly 3 minutes, and (c) reading any of the words to the examinee.

> ## CAUTION
> ....
> Do not administer Test 15: Word Reading Fluency to a person who cannot read. Due to the response requirements, a nonreader could randomly mark two words in each line without ever reading a word and receive a score. That score would not reflect reading ability and could be quite misleading.

Test 16: Spelling of Sounds

Spelling of Sounds requires the examinee to use both phonological and orthographic coding skills to spell nonwords that conform to English spelling patterns. Initial items require the examinee to write single letters that represent one speech sound.

Administration. Present Sample Items A through D and Items 1 through 5 orally. When a letter is printed within slashes, such as /m/, say the most common sound (phoneme) of the letter, not the letter name. Present the remaining items using the audio recording. Before beginning the test, locate Item 6 on the audio recording and adjust the volume to a comfortably loud level. When prompted, give the examinee a sharpened pencil with an eraser and the Response Booklet.

Select a starting point based on an estimate of the examinee's present spelling level. Test until the examinee correctly answers the six lowest-numbered items administered or until Item 1 has been administered. Continue testing until the examinee misses the six highest-numbered items administered or until the last test item has been administered. Because the examinee does not see the test item stimulus, the complete page rule does not apply to this test.

Although the audio recording provides adequate time for most individuals to write responses, pause or stop the audio recording if the examinee needs more time. You may replay items whenever the examinee requests. In rare cases when an examinee experiences difficulty with the audio recording, you may present the items orally.

The examinee is asked to repeat the sound or nonsense word before writing a response. The oral repetition is not used for scoring but does provide qualitative information. If the examinee mispronounces the item, do not repeat the item or ask the examinee to try again. Note the mispronunciation in the Test Record and then compare it to the written response to obtain instructional insights. For example, Martha, a high school student, repeated the nonsense word *foy* as *voy* and then proceeded to spell the word as *voy*. This type of error suggests difficulty discriminating between the /f/ and /v/ sounds, rather than problems with spelling. Rapid Reference 2.16 lists key administration points for Spelling of Sounds.

Item scoring. Score correct written responses as 1 and incorrect written responses as 0. Record the total number of correct responses and all items below the basal in the Number Correct box in the Test Record.

Do not penalize for reversed letters as long as the letter does not become a new letter. For example, a reversed lowercase *c* would not be penalized, but a reversed lowercase letter *b* would be penalized because it becomes a new letter, *d*.

The answers shown in the Test Book represent the most commonly occurring orthographic patterns (visual sequences of letters) in the English language and are the only correct responses. Although some responses may appear to be correct sound spellings, if they do not represent the most common and frequent orthographic pattern, the response is scored as incorrect. Use only the correct answers shown in the Test Book. For example, Todd, a sixth-grade student, spelled the nonsense word *scritch* as *skrich*. Although *skrich* is a correct sound spelling and indicates that he can put sounds in order, the /skr/ sound is nearly always spelled using the letters *scr* in

≡ Rapid Reference 2.16

Key Administration Points for Test 16: Spelling of Sounds

- *Materials needed:* Extended Battery Test Book, Test Record, RB, audio recording, audio equipment, and two pencils.
- Know pronunciation of samples and Items 1 through 5 before administering the test.
- Select starting point based on the examinee's current spelling achievement level.
- Administer Samples A through D and Items 1 through 5 orally.
- Use the audio recording beginning with Item 6.
- Give the examinee the RB and pencil when prompted.
- Follow the basal/ceiling rules: six consecutive correct/six consecutive incorrect.
- Score all items 1 or 0.
- Use only the answers listed in the Test Book as correct responses.
- Repeat items if the examinee requests.
- Do not penalize examinee if he or she mispronounces the test item before writing it. Score only the written response.

English, and the letters *tch* are the most common spelling pattern of that sound in a one syllable word with a short vowel sound. Error analyses can help determine if the examinee is able to sequence sounds correctly but has difficulty recalling common orthographic patterns.

> **DON'T FORGET**
> ....
> Use the test audio recording when administering Spelling of Sounds.

Common examiner errors. Examiner errors include: (a) incorrectly scoring items, (b) giving credit for an answer that is not listed in the Test Book as a correct response, and (c) failing to replay items if the examinee asks for the item to be repeated.

Test 17: Reading Vocabulary

Reading Vocabulary presents two tasks: Synonyms and Antonyms. The examinee reads a stimulus word and then provides an appropriate synonym or antonym.

Administration. Review the correct pronunciation of all items while learning to administer the test. You must administer both subtests (Synonyms and Antonyms) to obtain a score for this test. For each subtest, administer the sample items to all examinees and then select a starting point based on an estimate of current reading ability. Test by complete pages until the examinee correctly answers the five lowest-numbered items administered or until you have administered the page with Item 1. For each subtest, test by complete pages until the examinee misses the five highest-numbered items administered or until the page with the last item has been administered. After administering the sample items, do not read any other items or tell the examinee any other words. Examinees are asked to read the stimulus words out loud, but do not use this for scoring purposes. The score is based only on the synonym or antonym the examinee provides. It may be helpful to make note of oral reading errors for error analysis and instructional planning. For example, Renee, a fifth-grade student, responded that the opposite of *cellar* was *buyer*. This response may be more indicative of spelling difficulties than poor vocabulary knowledge. The administration of the test is similar to Test 1: Oral Vocabulary in the WJ IV COG. Comparing results from the parallel tasks of Oral Vocabulary and Reading Vocabulary can help pinpoint whether the examinee has difficulty with word knowledge or decoding or both areas. Rapid Reference 2.17 lists the key administration points for Reading Vocabulary.

Item scoring. Score each correct response 1 and each incorrect response 0. Unless noted, accept only one-word responses. If a person gives a two-word or longer response, ask for a one-word answer. Responses are correct when they differ

≡ Rapid Reference 2.17

Key Administration Points for Test 17: Reading Vocabulary
- *Materials needed:* Extended Battery Test Book and Test Record.
- Know the pronunciation of each item.
- Administer both subtests.
- Administer sample items for each subtest to all examinees.
- Select an appropriate starting point for each subtest based on the examinee's current reading ability.
- Follow the basal/ceiling rules for both subtests: five consecutive correct/five consecutive incorrect.
- Test by complete pages.
- Do not tell the examinee any words on the test items.
- Unless noted, accept only one-word responses.
- Record errors for further analysis.
- Do not penalize the examinee if he or she misreads the stimulus word. Score only the synonym or antonym response.

from the correct response only in verb tense or number (singular/plural). A response is incorrect if the examinee substitutes a different part of speech, such as a noun for a verb. If an examinee responds to an antonym item by giving the stimulus word preceded by *non-* or *un-,* ask for another answer unless otherwise indicated by the scoring key. Do not penalize for mispronunciations resulting from articulation errors, dialects, or regional speech patterns. For each subtest, record the total number of correct responses and all items below the basal in the Number Correct box in the Test Record.

Common examiner errors. Examiner errors include: (a) reading items to examinees, (b) failing to administer both subtests, (c) failing to apply the basal/ceiling rules to each subtest, and (d) miscalculating the total score.

Tests 18 Through 20: Science, Social Studies, and Humanities

Science, Social Studies, and Humanities measure the examinee's knowledge in the corresponding area. These three tests compose the Academic Knowledge cluster. Science includes items related to anatomy, biology, chemistry, geology, medicine, and physics. Social Studies measures knowledge of history, economics, geography, government, and psychology. Humanities includes items related to art, music, and literature.

≡ Rapid Reference 2.18

Key Administration Points for Tests 18: Science, 19: Social Studies, and 20: Humanities

- *Materials needed:* Extended Battery Test Book and Test Record.
- Know the pronunciation of all items.
- Select a starting point for each test based on an estimate of the examinee's present achievement level.
- Follow basal/ceiling rules for each test: six consecutive correct/six consecutive incorrect.
- Test by complete pages.
- Repeat any item upon request of examinee.
- Complete all queries as needed.
- Do not penalize for articulation errors or regional or dialectical speech differences.

Administration. Review the exact pronunciation for all the words while learning to administer these three tests. The pronunciations for more difficult items follow in parentheses. For other items, consult a standard dictionary. Select a starting point for each test based on an estimate of the individual's present achievement level. For each test, test by complete pages until the examinee correctly answers the six lowest-numbered items administered or the page with Item 1 has been administered. For each test, test by complete pages until the examinee misses the six highest-numbered items administered or you have administered the page with the last item. You may repeat items if the examinee requests. Rapid Reference 2.18 lists the key administration points for the Science, Social Studies, and Humanities tests.

Item scoring. Score each correct response 1 and each incorrect response 0. Do not penalize for mispronunciations resulting from articulation errors, dialects, or regional speech patterns. Record the total number correct including all items below the basal in the Number Correct box for each test.

Common examiner errors. Examiner errors include: (a) mispronouncing items, (b) failing to ask any queries, and (c) failing to apply basal/ceiling rules.

🐟 TEST YOURSELF 🐟

....

1. **You must administer all of the tests in the Standard Battery before using the Extended Battery.**
   True or False?

2. **Which test has two subtests that must be administered to get the score?**

3. **Which test requires the use of an audio recording?**

4. **List the timed tests.**

5. **All of the reading tests have the same basal/ceiling rules.**
   True or False?

6. **Which test does not require the use of the Response Booklet?**
   (a) Applied Problems
   (b) Editing
   (c) Number Matrices
   (d) Sentence Reading Fluency

7. **The WJ IV ACH may not be used if the individual has physical or sensory impairments.**
   True or False?

8. **What materials that are not included with the test kit may be needed to administer some of the tests?**

9. **On Letter-Word Identification, an examiner began the test with Item 30. The examinee got Items 30 to 35 correct, but missed Item 36. What should the examiner do?**
   (a) Continue testing until the examinee misses six in a row.
   (b) Discontinue testing and give the examinee a 0.
   (c) Go back to Item 1 and administer Items 1 to 6.
   (d) Complete the page (Item 37) and then turn back one page and administer all items on that page beginning with the first item (Items 22–29).

10. **How would you score the following items (using a 1 or a 0 for each item)?**
    (a) On Calculation—correct answer is 14, examinee wrote 41.
    (b) On Calculation—correct answer is 3, examinee wrote a backward 3.

11. **How would you score the following items?**
    (a) On Passage Comprehension—correct answer is *cars*, examinee said *car*.
    (b) On Passage Comprehension—correct answer is *lie*, examinee said *liar*.

12. **How would you score the following items?**
    (a) On Letter-Word Identification—correct answer is *island*, examinee said *i . . . i . . . land* and did not pronounce the word as a whole.
    (b) On Spelling of Sounds—correct answer is *gat*, examinee wrote *gate*.
    (c) On Spelling—correct answer is *table*, examinee wrote *tadle*.

13. **When a letter is shown between slashes as /m/, you would say the most common sound for that letter, not the letter name.**
    True or False?

14. Which two tests use continuation instructions instead of basal/ceiling rules?

15. If a sentence were read perfectly on Test 8: Oral Reading, it would be scored with a 0 indicating no errors.
True or False?

Answer: 1. False; 2. Test 17: Reading Vocabulary; 3. Test 16: Spelling of Sounds; 4. Test 9: Sentence Reading Fluency, Test 10: Math Facts Fluency, Test 11: Sentence Writing Fluency, Test 15: Word Reading Fluency; 5. False; 6. b; 7. False; 8. stopwatch, audio player, headphones or earbuds, pencils; 9. d; 10. a. 0, b. 1; 11. a. 1, b. 0; 12. a. 0, b. 0, c. 0; 13. True; 14. Test 8: Oral Reading and Test 12: Reading Recall; 15. False.

Three

HOW TO SCORE THE WJ IV ACH

The WJ IV Tests of Achievement provide a wide array of scores: raw scores, age equivalents, grade equivalents, standard scores, percentile ranks, relative proficiency indexes (RPIs), and instructional zones. A unique aspect of the WJ IV ACH is that it provides both age and grade norms. The age norms are presented in 1-month intervals from ages 2-0 through 18-11 and then by 1-year intervals from ages 19-0 through 95+ years. The grade norms are available by tenths of a year from K.0 through 17.9.

Due to the precision and variety of scores available on the WJ IV, it is scored using a scoring program. The only scores that you need to calculate manually are the raw scores. If desired, estimates of the age and grade equivalents for each test may be obtained manually by using the Scoring Tables in the Test Record. All other test scores and all cluster scores are generated using the Woodcock-Johnson online scoring and reporting program (Schrank & Dailey, 2014).

ITEM SCORING

Because the individual's pattern of correct and incorrect responses is needed to determine basal and ceiling levels or appropriate blocks of items, item scoring is done during test administration (with the exception of the Writing Samples test). The number correct, or *raw score,* is usually calculated after testing is completed. On most of the tests, each item administered is scored by writing 1 or 0 in the appropriate space in the Test Record (1 = correct, 0 = incorrect). There are two exceptions: Writing Samples and Oral Reading. Both of these tests use a multiple-point scoring system. Leave spaces blank that correspond to items not administered. After completing a test, the only spaces that will be blank are items below the basal, above the ceiling, or not in the assigned block of items. Rapid Reference 3.1 lists notations that may be helpful when recording items.

≡ Rapid Reference 3.1

Notations for Recording Responses
1: correct response
0: incorrect, or no response
Q: indicates a query
DK: indicates the response of "Don't Know"
NR: indicates "No Response"
SC: indicates a self-correction

CAUTION

Do not use an alternate scoring system such as using check marks or plus signs for correct responses when scoring the test. Use a 1 for a correct response and a 0 for an incorrect response.

CORRECT AND INCORRECT KEYS

The Test Books include correct and incorrect keys that serve as guides for scoring certain responses. The keys show the most frequently given correct or incorrect answers. On occasion, an examinee's response will not be listed in the key. In these cases, you will need to use judgment in determining whether the response is correct or incorrect. Sometimes more information is needed before a response can be scored as correct or incorrect. For some responses, a query is designed to elicit another answer from the examinee. If the prompted response still does not fall clearly into the correct or incorrect category, record the response and score it after testing has been completed. Use professional judgment in querying responses that are not listed in the query key.

Occasionally a response does not require a query but, at the moment, it is hard to decide how to score the item. In this case, record the actual response in the Test Record and score it later. Do not use that item to determine a basal or ceiling and continue testing until the basal or ceiling criterion is met. After testing has been completed, return to the item or items in question and score the responses. If, after further consideration, it is still not clear how to score two responses, balance the scores by scoring one item a 1 and the other a 0.

SCORING MULTIPLE RESPONSES

When an examinee provides more than one response to an item, the general principle to follow is to *score the last answer given*. The new response, whether correct or incorrect, is used as the final basis for scoring. Follow this procedure even if the examinee changes a response given much earlier in the testing session. In cases in which the examinee provides two answers simultaneously, query the response by asking something like "Which one?" or "Give me just one answer." For example, on the Word Attack test, Katy, a second-grade student, responded "That's either wags or wugs." The examiner then replied, "Which is it?"

> ### DON'T FORGET
> ....
> **Error Analysis**
> Whenever possible, record incorrect responses in the Test Record. Analyze these responses later for clinical inferences and instructional implications. Look for patterns of errors across all tests administered as well as within the individual tests.

TESTS REQUIRING SPECIAL SCORING PROCEDURES

Of the 20 tests in the WJ IV ACH, 5 tests have special scoring procedures: Writing Samples, Oral Reading, Sentence Reading Fluency, Reading Recall, and Reading Vocabulary. On the Writing Samples test, the raw score is based only on one "block" of items, even if more than one block is administered. The raw score for the Oral Reading test is based on the number of points earned on a group of administered sentences. The Sentence Reading Fluency test requires counting both the number correct and the number incorrect. The raw score for the Reading Recall test is based on the number of correctly recalled elements on a group of administered stories. The Reading Vocabulary test requires adding together the scores on the two subtests: Synonyms and Antonyms. The following section summarizes the details for scoring Writing Samples, Oral Reading, Sentence Reading Fluency, and Reading Recall. It is recommended that you have a copy of the WJ IV ACH Test Record in hand while reading the following section. For further information, consult the WJ IV ACH Examiner's Manual.

TEST 6: WRITING SAMPLES

Score Writing Samples after administering a block of items. Use the Scoring Guide in Appendix B of the WJ IV ACH Examiner Manual to score responses. Make sure to use the section of Appendix B that applies to the form of the WJ IV ACH administered (Form A, B, or C). The guide includes several examples of different point-value responses that occurred frequently in the standardization. Chapter 2 of this book summarizes item scoring guidelines.

Two raters. When first learning this test, the most desirable procedure is to have two different examiners score it. Ideally, one of the examiners is experienced with scoring the Writing Samples test. After independent scoring, the two individuals should attempt to resolve any score differences of more than one point. Average the two raw scores to obtain the final raw score.

Administering additional items. On occasion, a better estimate of an examinee's writing skill may be obtained by administering additional items that are easier or more difficult. If it is apparent that the examinee is experiencing undue ease or difficulty with the assigned block of items, it would be appropriate to administer the additional items immediately. Because Writing Samples is usually scored after testing is completed, it may be necessary to administer the additional items at a convenient time within the next few days. The Writing Samples Scoring Table in the Test Record allows you to determine if the most appropriate block of items has been administered. If the individual's raw score falls within one of the seven shaded areas on the Scoring Table, administer the additional items that are noted in the Adjusted Item Block chart on page 7 in the Test Record. This chart also indicates the block of items to use for calculating the raw score. Figure 3.1 illustrates the Scoring Table and the Adjusted Item Block chart for Writing Samples.

CAUTION
••
Scoring Writing Samples

Examiners frequently score items too liberally on this test. Adhere to the samples and criteria in Appendix B of the Examiner's Manual. In addition, if the score for the selected block falls in a shaded area of the Scoring Table, administer the additional items as directed. Base the score on the adjusted block indicated in the Test Record.

When you cannot decide how to score an item (e.g., you can't decide if it is a 1 or a 0.5), assign the lower score. On the next item in question, assign the higher score. If you always assign the higher score, the resulting score will be too high and overestimate the person's writing ability.

Calculating the number of points. Record the number of points for each item in the administered block in the Number of Points box on the Test Record. The raw score (number of points) is based only on the items in the assigned block. Do not give credit for items below or above this block. Raw scores that result in fractions of one-half are rounded to the nearest even number. For example, a score of 17.5 rounds to 18, and a score of 18.5 also rounds to 18. On the Test Record in the Score Entry section, enter the number of points for the most appropriate block

Adjusted Item Block

Note	Administer Additional Items	Base Number of Points on Items
①	7 to 12	1 to 12
②	13 to 18	7 to 18
③	1 to 6	1 to 12
④	19 to 24	13 to 24
⑤	7 to 12	7 to 18
⑥	25 to 28	19 to 28
⑦	13 to 18	13 to 24

When a score falls in a shaded area on the scoring table, use the Adjusted Item Block table above to determine what additional items to administer.

Test 6   Writing Samples
Scoring Table

Encircle row the Number of Points.

Items 1–6	Items 1–12	Items 7–18	Items 13–24	Items 19–28	AE (Est)*	GE (Est)*
0	0				<5-0	<K.0
1	1				5-0	<K.0
2	2				5-10	K.4
3	3				6-3	K.8
—	4				6-5	1.0
4	5	③			6-8	1.2
—	6	2			6-11	1.5
5	7	—			7-0	1.6
①	8	3			7-2	1.7
—	—	4			—	—
	9	5			7-6	2.0
	10	6	⑤		7-7	2.0
	11	7	2		7-11	2.5
	12	8	—		8-2	2.8
	—	9	3		8-5	3.0
	13	10	—		8-8	3.3
	—	—	4		—	—
	—	11	—		9-1	3.7
	14	12	5		9-6	4.0
	—	13	—	⑦	9-11	4.5
		—	6	2	10-2	4.6
	15	14	—	—	10-5	5.0
		—	7	—	10-8	5.2
		15	—	—	10-0	5.6
		—	8	3	11-2	5.8
		16	9	—	11-8	6.2
	16	—	—	—	—	—
	②	17	10	4	12-3	6.8
		—	11	—	12-11	7.5
	18	—	5		13-2	7.7
		12	—		13-7	8.1
	19	—	6		14-0	8.6
		13	—		14-2	8.8
		14	—		15-0	9.6
	20	—	7		15-4	9.9
		15	—		16-8	11.3
		—	8		18-6	>12.9
		16			28	>12.9
	21–22	—	—	—	—	—
	④	17–19	>8	>30	>12.9
	20–22	—	—	—
	⑥			

*AE and GE are estimates of the precise values provided by the scoring program.

Figure 3.1   Writing Samples Scoring Table and Adjusted Item Block Chart

of items administered. The score is based on a single block, even if more than one block has been administered.

TEST 8: ORAL READING

The Oral Reading test uses Continuation Instructions instead of basal and ceiling rules. It also uses multipoint scoring (2, 1, or 0). When a sentence is read with no errors it is scored 2, with one error it is scored 1, and with two or more errors it is scored 0. Follow the Continuation Instructions to determine when to administer additional sentences or when to discontinue testing. Once a criterion for discontinuing has been met, total the number of points earned on the sentences administered. The score for this test is based on the administered sentences only. Enter the number of points earned in the Number of Points box at each continuation instruction point reached. Then enter the cumulative total number of points in the Number of Points box at the end of the test.

TEST 9: SENTENCE READING FLUENCY

The score for the Sentence Reading Fluency test is based on both the number of correct responses and the number of incorrect responses. Skipped items and items that fall outside of the range of attempted items are not counted as errors. For example, if the examinee only completed Items 1 to 77, Items 78 to 110 would not be factored into the score. When using the online scoring program, enter both the number correct and the number incorrect. When obtaining estimated age or grade equivalents, subtract the number of errors from the number correct. If the result is a negative number, enter a score of 0. This would usually only happen when an individual is just circling *Yes* or *No* without reading or without comprehending the sentence.

TEST 12: READING RECALL

The Reading Recall test uses Continuation Instructions instead of basal and ceiling rules. Follow the Continuation Instructions to determine when to administer additional stories or when to discontinue testing. The test is administered in two-story sets and Continuation Instructions follow each set. Within each story, a point is given for each correctly recalled element. After each story, the number of elements correctly recalled is entered in the Number of Points box for that one story. After each set of two stories, the cumulative total for the two stories is entered into the Number of Points box. Use the total for each set of two stories when consulting the Continuation Instructions.

STEP-BY-STEP: HOW TO SCORE THE WJ IV ACH

Step 1: Compute the Raw Scores

With the exception of the five tests previously described (Writing Samples, Oral Reading, Sentence Reading Fluency, Reading Recall, and Reading Vocabulary), the procedure for computing the raw scores is the same. The raw score is the number of correct responses plus a score of 1 for every item in the test that falls below the basal. Be careful not to include scores for sample items in the calculation of raw scores. Although responses to the sample items are recorded in the Test Record, they appear in tinted panels and thus are clearly distinct from the actual test items.

After adding up the raw score, record this score in the Number Correct tinted box in each test section in the Test Record. The scoring for each test is usually completed after the testing session is over or as the examinee is working on a test like Sentence Writing Fluency.

DON'T FORGET

●●●

- For Writing Samples, the raw score is based on the most appropriate block of items.
- For Oral Reading, the raw score is based on the number of points earned on a group of administered sentences.
- For Sentence Reading Fluency, the score is based on both the number correct and the number incorrect.
- For Reading Recall, the score is based on the number of correctly recalled elements in a group of administered stories.
- For Reading Vocabulary, the score is based on adding together the scores from the two subtests, Synonyms and Antonyms.

CAUTION

●●●

Common Errors in Calculating Raw Scores
- Forgetting to include credit for all items not administered below the basal
- Including the sample items in the raw score
- Making simple addition errors
- Incorrectly transferring the number correct to the scoring program or Scoring Table

- Neglecting to enter the raw scores for each subtest within a test (Reading Vocabulary)
- Miscalculating scores for tests that have multiple point options (Writing Samples, Oral Reading)
- Including points on more than the specified block or set of items (Writing Samples)
- Miscalculating scores for tests that use Continuation Instructions (Oral Reading, Reading Recall)
- Neglecting to count both the number correct and number incorrect on Sentence Reading Fluency

Step 2: Obtain Estimated Age and Grade Equivalent Scores

This optional procedure is available if you wish to obtain immediate feedback on an examinee's performance. In the Test Record, each test has scoring tables that provide the estimated age (AEs) and grade equivalents (GEs). The estimated scores for certain tests may differ slightly (less than one standard error of measurement) from the actual AE and GE scores that are reported by the scoring program, which is more accurate. For all reporting purposes, use the AE and GE scores generated by the scoring program.

Once the raw score has been calculated, locate that number in the first column of the test's Scoring Table in the Test Record and circle the entire row. The circled row includes the number correct, the estimated AE, and the estimated GE. For tests that have raw scores based on a block or group of items (i.e., Writing Samples, Oral Reading, Reading Recall), locate the number correct in the column that corresponds to the block or group of items administered. Computing the number correct and checking the AE or GE scores provide immediate feedback regarding the individual's level of performance during the testing session. These results may refine the selection of starting points in later tests or suggest the need for further testing in specific areas. Figure 3.2 illustrates the completion of this step for Rhia, an eighth-grade girl, who obtained a raw score of 46 on Test 1: Letter-Word Identification.

Step 3: Use the Woodcock-Johnson Online Scoring and Reporting Program

Complete the remainder of the scoring procedure using the online scoring program. Each Test Record includes access to a basic scoring report. Future releases of the scoring program will include additional fee-based features, such as

Test 1   Letter-Word Identification
Scoring Table

Encircle row the Number of Correct.

Number Correct	AE (Est)*	GE (Est)*	Number Correct	AE (Est)*	GE (Est)*
0	<2-4	<K.0	40	7-2	1.8
1	2-4	<K.0	41	7-3	1.9
2	3-0	<K.0	42	7-4	1.9
3	3-4	<K.0	43	7-6	2.0
4	3-7	<K.0	44	7-7	2.2
5	3-10	<K.0	45	7-8	2.3
6	4-0	<K.0	46	7-10	2.4
7	4-2	<K.0	47	7-11	2.5
8	4-4	<K.0	48	8-1	2.7
9	4-6	<K.0	49	8-3	2.8
10	4-8	<K.0	50	8-5	3.0
11	4-10	<K.0	51	8-7	3.1
12	5-0	<K.0	52	8-9	3.3
13	5-1	<K.0	53	8-11	3.5
14	5-3	<K.0	54	9-2	3.7
15	5-5	K.0	55	9-5	4.0
16	5-6	K.1	56	9-8	4.2
17	5-7	K.2	57	9-11	4.5
18	5-8	K.3	58	10-3	4.8
19	5-9	K.4	59	10-7	5.2
20	5-10	K.4	60	11-0	5.5
21	5-11	K.5	61	11-5	6.0
22	6-0	K.6	62	11-10	6.5
23	6-1	K.6	63	12-5	7.0
24	6-1	K.7	64	13-0	7.6

Figure 3.2 Obtaining the Estimated Age Equivalent and Grade Equivalent for a Number Correct of 46 on Test 1: Letter-Word Identification

interventions and narrative reports. The initial release of this program includes the following features:

- Scores for all tests and clusters administered
- Options to select age or grade norms, levels of discrepancies and variations, and types of scores
- Test Session Observations information from Test Record (optional)
- Qualitative Checklist information from Test Record for Tests 1 through 11 (optional)
- Age/Grade Profiles
- Standard Score/Percentile Rank Profiles

> **CAUTION**
> ....
> Any report produced by an online scoring program or a computer-generated report is not intended to serve as a final, comprehensive report. The examiner is responsible for interpreting the results.

In addition to saving time, the scoring program virtually eliminates the possibility of clerical errors. To obtain derived scores, enter the examinee identification information, the number correct for each test administered (Sentence Reading Fluency requires entering both the number correct and the number incorrect), and the information from the Test Session Observations Checklist and the Qualitative Checklists, if completed. You may score any single test or a combination of WJ IV tests may be scored. Chapter 8 contains an example of a score report for the WJ IV ACH and WJ IV OL produced by this program.

SPECIFIC SCORING REMINDERS FOR EACH TEST

Test 1: Letter-Word Identification

Range: A core test appropriate for preschool through adult
  Scoring reminders:

- Score correct responses with a 1, incorrect responses with a 0.
- Score 1 if the response differs from the correct answer in verb tense or number.
- Score 0 if response is a different part of speech from the correct answer.
- Enter the number of items answered correctly plus one point for each item below the basal in the Number Correct box.

Test 2: Applied Problems

Range: A core test appropriate for preschool through adult
  Scoring reminders:

- Score correct responses with a 1, incorrect responses with a 0.
  - If a label is required, both the numeric response and the label must be correct to receive a 1.
  - If an incorrect label is given, whether it is required or not, the item is scored 0.
- Enter the number of items answered correctly plus one point for each item below the basal in the Number Correct box.

Test 3: Spelling

Range: A core test appropriate for preschool through adult
Scoring reminders:

- Score correct responses with a 1, incorrect responses with a 0.
- Score correctly spelled responses that contain a reversed letter with a 1 unless the reversed letter makes a different letter (e.g., a reversed *b* becomes a *d*).
- Enter the number of items answered correctly plus one point for all items below the basal in the Number Correct box.

Test 4: Passage Comprehension

Range: A core test appropriate for preschool through adult
Scoring reminders:

- Score correct responses with a 1, incorrect responses with a 0.
- Score the item 1 if the response differs from the correct answer in verb tense or number.
- Score the item 0 if the response is a different part of speech from the correct answer.
- Unless noted otherwise, score two-word or longer responses with a 0.
- Enter the total number of items answered correctly plus one point for each item below the basal in the Number Correct box.

Test 5: Calculation

Range: A core test appropriate for preschool through adult
Scoring reminders:

- Score correct responses with a 1, incorrect responses and skipped items with a 0.
- Score correct responses that have poorly formed or reversed numerals with a 1.
- Score transposed numerals (e.g., 17 and 71) with a 0.
- Enter number of items answered correctly plus one point for each item below the basal in the Number Correct box.

Test 6: Writing Samples

Range: A core test appropriate for preschool through adult
Scoring reminders:

- Score responses using the multiple-point rating guide (2, 1.5, 1, 0.5, or 0).
  - Items 1 through 6 are scored 1 or 0 (0.5 is an option).
  - Items 7 and higher are scored 2, 1, or 0 (1.5 and 0.5 are options).
- Score 2 if the response is superior and meets all criteria.
- Score 1.5 if the response falls between average and superior.
- Score 1 if the response is average and meets criteria.
- Score 0.5 if the response falls between unacceptable and average.
- Score 0 if the response does not meet criteria or is illegible.
- Add points for items within the selected block to obtain the total number of points.
- If the number of points falls in a shaded area on the scoring table, administer the additional items as directed.
- Base the final score on the most appropriate block of items regardless of how many blocks were administered. The most appropriate block is the one with number of points closest to the middle of the column in the range of possible scores.
- Enter the number of points and the letter corresponding to that block of items when using the scoring program.
- If obtaining estimated AE/GE, circle the row for the number of points in the column corresponding to the block of items administered.

Test 7: Word Attack

Range: A supplemental test appropriate for preschool through adult
Scoring reminders:

- Score correct responses with a 1, incorrect responses with a 0.
- Enter the number of items answered correctly plus one point for each item below the basal in the Number Correct box.

Test 8: Oral Reading

Range: A supplemental test appropriate for grade 1 through adult
Scoring reminders:

- Mark each error with a slash (/) as the person is reading.
- Score the sentence with a 2 if there are no errors, with a 1 if there is one error, and with a 0 if the examinee reads the sentence with two or more errors.

- Score self-corrections within 3 seconds as correct. Do not count a repetition during a self-correction as an error.
- Count a hyphenated word as one word.
- Score a repetition of two or more consecutive words as one error.
- Base the number correct on points earned on a group of administered sentences.

Test 9: Sentence Reading Fluency

Range: A supplemental test appropriate for grade 1 through adult
Scoring reminders:

- Score correct responses with a 1, incorrect responses with a 0.
- Enter total number of items answered correctly within the time limit in the Number Correct box on the Test Record.
- Enter total number of items answered incorrectly within the time limit in the Number Incorrect box on the Test Record. Do not include skipped items or items that fall beyond the last item the examinee attempted during the time limit as incorrect.
- If obtaining estimated AE/GE, subtract the number incorrect from the number correct to calculate total points. If a negative number results, use 0.
- When using the scoring program, enter both the number correct and the number incorrect.

Test 10: Math Facts Fluency

Range: A supplemental test appropriate for kindergarten through adult
Scoring reminders:

- Score correct responses with a 1, incorrect responses with a 0.
- Score skipped items as 0.
- Score correct responses that have poorly formed or reversed numerals with a 1.
- Enter the number of items answered correctly within the 3-minute time limit in the Number Correct box.

Test 11: Sentence Writing Fluency

Range: A supplemental test appropriate for grade 1 through adult
Scoring reminders:

- Score correct responses with a 1, incorrect responses with a 0.
- Score skipped items as a 0.

- Score correct responses that have errors in spelling, punctuation, capitalization, or poor handwriting with a 1 as long as the responses are legible, complete sentences that use all three words.
- Score the item with a 0 if one of the three stimulus words is not included in the sentence.
- Score the item with a 0 if one of the three stimulus words is changed in any way, for example, is a different part of speech, changes tense, or changes number. Miscopying a stimulus word does not automatically result in a 0 score unless the word was changed as noted.
- Score the item with a 0 if a word critical to sentence meaning is omitted.
- Score the item with a 1 if the sentence is awkward but the meaning is clear.
- Score the item with a 1 if the subject of the sentence is an understood "you" and the response meets all other criteria (e.g., Dress the pretty doll).
- Score the item with a 1 if the response is correct but leaves out less significant words, such as *a* or *the*.
- Enter the total number of items written correctly within the 5-minute time limit in the Number Correct box.
- If three or fewer are correct within the first 2 minutes, discontinue the test and record the time of 2 minutes and the number correct (0–3) in the Number Correct box.

Test 12: Reading Recall

Range: A supplemental test appropriate for grade 1 through adult
    Scoring reminders:

- Place a check mark over each element recalled correctly during retelling.
- Each correctly recalled element counts as 1 point.
- Do not penalize for mispronunciations due to articulation errors or regional/dialectical speech differences.
- Do not count as correct a response that differs from a bold element in any way, with three exceptions: Accept derivations of words (e.g., Bob or Bobby), accept synonyms that are very close in meaning to the words in bold type (e.g., father for dad), and accept words that differ only in possessive case (e.g., Amy, Amy's), verb tense (drive, drove), or number (singular/plural—thief, thieves).
- Count the number of points earned in each story administered and record it in the appropriate box.

- Enter the cumulative scores for each set of two stories administered in the appropriate box.
- Record an X for each set of stories that was not administered.
- If obtaining estimated AE/GE and more than four stories were administered, combine the points for the last four stories and use the column corresponding to that set of stories.

Test 13: Number Matrices

Range: A supplemental test appropriate for kindergarten through adult
Scoring reminders:

- Score correct responses with a 1, incorrect responses with a 0.
- Enter the number of items answered correctly plus one point for each item below the basal in the Number Correct box.

Test 14: Editing

Range: A supplemental test appropriate for grade 2 through adult
Scoring reminders:

- Score correct responses with a 1, incorrect responses with a 0.
- Score the item 0 if the examinee does not identify *and* correct the error.
- Enter the number of items answered correctly plus one point for each item below the basal into the Number Correct box.

Test 15: Word Reading Fluency

Range: A supplemental test appropriate for grade 1 through adult
Scoring reminders:

- Score correct responses with a 1, incorrect responses with a 0.
- Enter the total number of items answered correctly within the 3-minute time limit in the Number Correct box.

Test 16: Spelling of Sounds

Range: A supplemental test appropriate for preschool through adult
Scoring reminders:

- Score correct responses with a 1, incorrect responses with a 0.
- The only correct responses are shown in the Test Book.

- Score as correct spelled responses that contain a reversed letter, unless the reversed letter becomes another letter (e.g., a reversed *b* becomes a *d*).
- Score only the written response, not the oral repetition of the stimulus word.
- Enter the total number of all items answered correctly plus one point for each item below the basal in the Number Correct box on the Test Record.

Test 17: Reading Vocabulary

Range: A supplemental test appropriate for grade 1 through adult
Scoring reminders:

- Score correct responses with a 1, incorrect responses with a 0.
- Score the item with a 1 if the response differs from the correct answer in verb tense or number.
- Score the item with a 0 if the response is a different part of speech from the correct answer.
- Score only the response, not the oral reading of the stimulus words.
- Unless noted otherwise, score two-word or longer responses with a 0.
- For both subtests, record the number of items answered correctly plus one point for each item below the basal in the Number Correct box.
- Enter the number correct for both subtests when using the scoring program.
- If obtaining estimated AE/GE, add the scores for both subtests together (A + B).

Test 18: Science, Test 19: Social Studies, Test 20: Humanities

Ranges: Supplemental tests appropriate for preschool through adult
Scoring reminders:

- Score correct responses 1, incorrect responses 0.
- For each test, record the number of items answered correctly plus one point for each item below the basal in the Number Correct box.
- Enter the number correct for each test when using the scoring program.

DON'T FORGET

Computer Generated Scores

Use the online scoring program to generate all derived scores. You can only obtain estimated AEs and GEs for the individual tests manually. In addition, cluster scores, based on the tests administered, are only available using the scoring program.

EVALUATING TEST BEHAVIOR

It is important to determine whether the test results accurately reflect the individual's abilities. During the testing process, be alert for signs in the examinee's behavior that indicate the test results may be of questionable validity. The following question on the front page of each Test Record assists examiners in documenting the issue: "Do these test results provide a fair representation of the subject's present functioning?" If there is some reason for questioning the test results, mark the no box and provide an explanation in the space provided. Possible reasons for questioning validity include: (a) an examinee's problems with hearing or vision, (b) behavioral or attention issues that interfere with the examinee's ability to concentrate, and (c) certain background factors (e.g., limited English proficiency). Note any unusual test behaviors or answers encountered during the session because this type of qualitative information can take on unexpected significance when analyzing the test results. As described in Chapter 2, a Test Session Observations Checklist and Qualitative Observation Checklists for Tests 1 through 11 are provided in the Test Record to assist in recording observations systematically throughout the testing session.

 TEST YOURSELF

1. **All derived scores may be calculated manually or by using the online scoring program.**
   True or False?

2. **Indicate incorrect responses with an X.**
   True or False?

3. **For which test(s) are items not administered below the basal included in the raw score?**
   (a) Calculation
   (b) Writing Samples
   (c) Word Attack
   (d) Sentence Reading Fluency

4. **Do not include sample items in the raw score.**
   True or False?

5. **Which test has subtests that must be added together to obtain estimated age and grade equivalents?**
   (a) Science
   (b) Spelling of Sounds
   (c) Applied Problems

(d) Reading Vocabulary

(e) Oral Reading

6. **On Writing Samples, how would you record a score of 20.5?**

7. **On the Oral Reading test, ignoring punctuation is counted as an error.**
    True or False?

8. **You can read any words the examinee requests on Word Reading Fluency.**
    True or False?

9. **You can only obtain cluster scores using the scoring program.**
    True or False?

10. **Which test requires entry of both the number correct and the number incorrect to obtain the derived scores?**

Answer: 1. False; 2. False; 3. a and c; 4. True; 5. d; 6. 20 (round to nearest even value); 7. True; 8. False; 9. True; 10. Sentence Reading Fluency.

Four

HOW TO INTERPRET THE WJ IV ACH

The WJ IV ACH provides a rich variety of interpretive options and scores. You must know what scores are available, when to use the various scores, and how to interpret these scores. The purpose of the assessment dictates what scores are most appropriate to use. In addition, you need to know what each test and cluster measure, what skills and abilities are required to perform the tasks, and what implications may be derived. Interpreting the WJ IV ACH requires a higher level of skill than administering the test. Prior to scoring, you must first decide whether to use grade- or age-based norms.

GRADE- OR AGE-BASED NORMS

The WJ IV ACH provides the option for using either grade- or age-based norms. When making school-based decisions regarding achievement levels, grade-based norms are generally preferable. Age-based norms are more applicable in clinical settings or with adults, and should be used in cases in which the results will be compared to scores from another test that only provides age norms (e.g., comparing the WISC-V to the WJ IV ACH). Selection of grade or age norms does not affect the obtained age equivalents (AEs) or grade equivalents (GEs), but differences will be noted in the standard scores, percentile ranks, and relative proficiency index scores. The Woodcock-Johnson online scoring and reporting program (Schrank & Dailey, 2014) provides the option to make grade or age comparisons. The grade norms are available for grades K.0 to 17.9. Although it is usually clear which grade norm group to select in the scoring program, there may be some confusion if you wish to compare an examinee's performance to individuals in the first year of graduate school (17.0 to 17.9). There is not a separate entry for graduate school. You must select the 4-year college norms, which include the first year of graduate school. Be sure to clearly indicate in reports which norm group was used for scoring.

TYPES OF SCORES

When reporting results to parents, teachers, and examinees, select the scores that are most meaningful and easily explained. Some metrics are easier to interpret than others. Age and grade equivalents or percentile ranks can be useful for discussions with parents and teachers who may more easily understand these types of scores than standard scores. As an examiner, you need to understand the purpose and interpretation of each type of score and be able to describe and discuss each type of score accurately.

The next section presents a detailed description of the WJ IV ACH scores. This overview includes AEs, GEs, relative proficiency indexes, instructional zones, Cognitive Academic Language Proficiency (CALP) levels, percentile ranks, and standard scores. It also presents additional optional standard score scales (i.e., z scores, t scores, normal curve equivalents, and stanines). The scoring program generates all of the derived scores for all tests and clusters.

DON'T FORGET

Assessment Creates Opportunity

Examiners have an opportunity to observe how an individual approaches tasks during an assessment. The purpose of testing should not be limited to determining eligibility for services or diagnosing a disability. Through qualitative observations, you can analyze many facets of academic performance, as well as note the types of strategies an individual uses.

CAUTION

USE THE SAME TYPE OF NORM GROUP

When comparing results from two different tests, such as the WISC-V and the WJ IV ACH or the KeyMath3 and the WJ IV ACH, be sure to use the same type of norm reference group for scoring each (i.e., age to age or grade to grade).

Raw Score/Number Correct

For most tests, the raw score is the number of correct responses plus the number of items below the basal that were not administered, each receiving one point. Two tests (Test 6: Writing Samples, Test 8: Oral Reading) use multiple-point scoring so the raw score is based on the total number of points earned; Test 9: Sentence Reading Fluency uses both the number correct and the number incorrect on the range of items attempted in obtaining the scores; and Test 12: Reading Recall uses the points earned on administered stories. As shown in Figure 4.1, the number correct is listed in the first column on the left in the Scoring Table that appears for each test in the Test Record. This information is followed by the corresponding AEs and GEs. Chapter 3 presents procedures for calculating the number correct.

Zero Scores

In cases in which an individual receives a zero on any test, you must decide whether that score represents a true assessment of ability or reflects an inability to perform the task. If the individual has not been exposed to the type of task in question, it may be more appropriate not to score the test rather than interpreting a zero raw score. For example, Jamie, a kindergarten student, obtained a zero on the Word Attack test. This score may indicate that she has not yet been exposed to letters and sounds and, therefore, this score should not be interpreted. Max, a fifth-grade student, also had a score of zero on the Word Attack test. In this case, that score may be an accurate reflection of his very limited reading ability and, therefore, should be interpreted. Even when a zero score is considered an accurate reflection of ability and is entered into the scoring program, it produces only age and grade equivalents. Because of the problems associated with interpretation, no other derived scores are available for zero scores at the individual test level. All of the derived scores, however, are reported for clusters that include a test with a zero raw score. If all tests within a cluster have a raw score of zero, then no derived scores are reported.

W Score

The W score (Woodcock, 1978; Woodcock & Dahl, 1971) is a special transformation of the Rasch ability scale (Rasch, 1960; Wright & Stone, 1979). The W scale for each test is centered on a value of 500, which is set to approximate the average performance at age 10-0 and grade 5.0. Cluster scores are the average (arithmetic mean) W score of the tests included in that cluster. For example, the cluster score for Broad Written Language is the average W score of Test 3: Spelling, Test 6: Writing Samples, and Test 11: Sentence Writing Fluency. In the WJ IV, the W score is not shown

CAUTION

Some examiners make the mistake of assuming that the clusters are based on the average of the standard scores for the tests included in each cluster. Remember that the WJ IV ACH clusters are based on the average of the W scores for the tests within a cluster, not the standard scores.

Test 1   Letter-Word Identification
Scoring Table

Encircle row for the Number Correct.

Number Correct	AE (Est)*	GE (Est)*	Number Correct	AE (Est)*	GE (Est)*
0	<2-4	<K.0	40	7-2	1.8
1	2-4	<K.0	41	7-3	1.9
2	3-0	<K.0	42	7-4	1.9
3	3-4	<K.0	43	7-6	2.0
4	3-7	<K.0	44	7-7	2.2
5	3-10	<K.0	45	7-8	2.3
6	4-0	<K.0	46	7-10	2.4
7	4-2	<K.0	47	7-11	2.5
8	4-4	<K.0	48	8-1	2.7
9	4-6	<K.0	49	8-3	2.8
10	4-8	<K.0	50	8-5	3.0
11	4-10	<K.0	51	8-7	3.1
12	5-0	<K.0	52	8-9	3.3
13	5-1	<K.0	53	8-11	3.5
14	5-3	<K.0	54	9-2	3.7
15	5-5	K.0	55	9-5	4.0
16	5-6	K.1	56	9-8	4.2
17	5-7	K.2	57	9-11	4.5
18	5-8	K.3	58	10-3	4.8
19	5-9	K.4	59	10-7	5.2
20	5-10	K.4	60	11-0	5.5
21	5-11	K.5	61	11-5	6.0
22	6-0	K.6	62	11-10	6.5
23	6-1	K.6	63	12-5	7.0
24	6-1	K.7	64	13-0	7.6
25	6-2	K.8	65	13-7	8.2
26	6-3	K.8	66	14-3	8.8
27	6-4	K.9	67	15-0	9.6
28	6-4	K.9	68	16-0	106
29	6-5	1.0	69	17-7	12.1
30	6-6	1.1	70	21	>12.9
31	6-6	1.1	71	25	>12.9
32	6-7	1.2	>71	>30	>12.9
33	6-8	1.2			
34	6-9	1.3			
35	6-9	1.4			
36	6-10	1.4			
37	6-11	1.5			
38	7-0	1.6			
39	7-1	1.7			

*AE and GE are estimates of the precise values provided by the scoring program.

Figure 4.1 Scoring Table for Test 1: Letter-Word Identification From the Test Record

in the Test Record but appears in the score report generated by the online scoring program. Each raw score has a corresponding W score. The scoring program converts raw scores into W scores. Because W scores are equal-interval scores, they are the preferred metric for use in statistical procedures.

Age and Grade Equivalents

An age equivalent (AE), or age score, reflects performance in terms of the age level in the norm sample at which the median raw score and corresponding W score are the same as the examinee's score. For example, if the median raw score or number correct for 10-year-olds in the norm sample is 43 on a particular test, then any examinee who obtains a raw score of 43 on that test receives an AE of 10-0. AEs may be more useful in some applications than grade equivalents, especially as they relate to the abilities of young children or adults not attending school. The AE is useful when attempting to determine an approximate level of development.

A grade equivalent (GE), or grade score, reflects the examinee's performance in terms of the grade level in the norm sample at which the median raw score and corresponding W score are the same as the examinee's score. In other words, if the median W score (or corresponding raw score) on a test for students in the sixth month of the second grade is 488, then an individual who earns a W score of 488 would receive 2.6 as a grade score. The GEs on tests like the WJ IV ACH represent the midpoint of the individual's instructional zone and can be used for instructional planning. Because the test includes items distributed over a wide range of difficulty levels (rather than a limited range typically found on group-administered tests), the age and grade scores reflect the actual level of task difficulty an individual can perform. The GE is useful when attempting to determine an appropriate, approximate level for instructional materials.

At the lower ends of the age and grade scales, less-than signs (<) are used for levels of performance that fall below the median score of the lowest age or grade group reported. Greater-than signs (>) are used for levels above the median for the age or grade of peak performance. For example, if the age of peak performance is 34 years, an examinee who scored above the median for that age group receives an age score of >34.

You can obtain an estimate (Est.) of age and grade equivalents by using the scoring tables for each test in the Test Record (as shown in Figure 4.1). Precise age or grade equivalents for tests are obtained from the Woodcock-Johnson online scoring and reporting program (Schrank & Dailey, 2014). Both age equivalents and grade equivalents can be displayed in the same score report by selecting the additional score option. For example, if you are using grade norms, the score report automatically displays grade equivalents. To add in age equivalents, you would select a new score selection template and choose to include age equivalents. Age and grade equivalent scores for clusters are available only when using the scoring program. Examples of the types of statements that are used for grade and age equivalent scores are:

- Jacob's grade equivalent score (GE) on basic reading skills indicates that he is reading at approximately a beginning third-grade level (GE = 3.1).
- Marco, a 10th-grade student, scored similarly to the average student in early seventh grade (GE = 7.2) on the Applied Problems Test.
- Diana's science knowledge as measured by Test 18: Science is comparable to average 8-year-olds.
- The number of items Tom, a seventh grader, answered correctly on the math calculation task is comparable to the average student in early fourth grade.

W Difference Score

The W difference scores are based on the difference between an examinee's test or cluster W score and the median test or cluster W score (REF W) for the reference group in the norm sample (same age or same grade) with which the comparison is being made. W difference scores are used when deriving other scores such as the relative proficiency index and the standard score.

Relative Proficiency Index

The relative proficiency index (RPI) was originally called the *relative mastery index* (RMI) in the WJ-R (Woodcock & Johnson, 1989). The RPI allows statements to be made about an examinee's proficiency on the task and the predicted quality of performance on tasks similar to the ones tested. The RPI is expressed as a fraction. The denominator is a constant of 90. The numerator ranges from 0 to 100 and reflects the examinee's proficiency on the task and the predicted level of performance on similar tasks.

RPIs are based on the distance along the W scale that an individual's score falls above or below the median score for the reference group (Reference W or REF W). This is the W difference (W Diff) and reflects the individual's absolute distance from the average performance for age or grademates on the task. You would interpret an RPI of 45/90 on the Spelling test for Natalie, a sixth-grade girl, to mean that she is only half as proficient on the task as her average age or grademates. When others at her age or grade show 90% success, Natalie is predicted to show only 45% success on similar tasks. On the other hand, if her RPI were 99/90, you

≡ Rapid Reference 4.1

●●●

Verbal Labels for RPI Scores

RPI	W Diff	Proficiency Label	Developmental Label	Functional Level
100/90	+31 and above	Very advanced	Very advanced	Very advanced
98/90 to 100/90	+14 to +30	Advanced	Advanced	Advanced
95/90 to 98/90	+7 to +13	Average to advanced	Age-appropriate to advanced	Within normal limits to advanced
82/90 to 95/90	−6 to +6	Average	Age-appropriate	Within normal limits
67/90 to 82/90	−13 to −7	Limited to average	Mildly delayed to age-appropriate	Mildly impaired to within normal limits
24/90 to 67/90	−30 to −14	Limited	Mildly delayed	Mildly impaired
3/90 to 24/90	−50 to −31	Very limited	Moderately delayed	Moderately impaired
0/90 to 3/90	−51 and below	Extremely limited	Severely delayed	Severely impaired

would predict that she would perform spelling tasks with 99% success that average age or grademates perform with 90% success. Rapid Reference 4.1 provides verbal labels for describing performance when using the RPI. Technically, the verbal labels are driven by the *W* Diff score rather than the RPI itself. This means that on occasion the same RPI may yield two different verbal labels. Note that there is overlap between the RPI ranges in Rapid Reference 4.1, but there is no overlap in the *W* Diff ranges. For example, the RPI of 100/90 appears in both the "advanced" and "very advanced" categories. Looking at the *W* Diff ranges, we can see that if one person has a +30 *W* Diff and another person has a +31 *W* Diff, they will get the same RPI of 100/90 but have different labels.

Depending on the purpose of the evaluation, one type of label may be more appropriate than another. For example, a developmental label may be more appropriate when testing a younger child, whereas a proficiency label may be more appropriate for describing the performance of a school-age student. Examples of the types of sentences used to describe RPIs are:

- Akeisha's RPI of 30/90 on the Phoneme/Grapheme cluster indicates that when average sixth-grade students have 90% proficiency, Akeisha has only 30% proficiency. Her knowledge of sound–symbol relationships is limited.
- Marla's RPI of 99/90 in Broad Mathematics indicates advanced proficiency in basic math skills and mathematical concepts. When average age peers have 90% success on similar tasks, Marla is predicted to have 99% success. Grade-level tasks in mathematics will be easy for Marla.
- Bennett's RPI of 92/90 on the Academic Knowledge cluster indicates average proficiency compared to peers.
- Although Judith's standard scores on both Broad Reading and Broad Writing are in the low range (standard scores of 70 and 72), her proficiency in reading (RPI = 4/90) is lower than her proficiency in mathematics (RPI = 35/90).

CALP Levels

Cognitive Academic Language Proficiency (CALP) levels, another application of the RPI, are helpful in determining an individual's language proficiency. CALP is defined as language proficiency in academic situations and includes those aspects of language that emerge with formal schooling. Aspects of language that are acquired naturally, without formal schooling, are referred to as *Basic Interpersonal Communication Skills* (BICS). Cummins (1984) formalized the distinction between these two types of language proficiency (BICS and CALP). When evaluating English language learners, it can be helpful to consider an individual's CALP levels in determining language proficiency, language dominance, or for planning an appropriate educational program. CALP levels are also helpful when considering the instructional needs of native English speakers with delayed or limited language. In addition, the WJ IV OL provides three parallel English and Spanish tests that can be helpful in evaluating language dominance and proficiency (see Chapter 5 for more information). CALP levels are available for certain WJ IV ACH clusters (see Table 4.1).

To display CALP levels for any of these clusters, select the option to include CALP when using the online scoring program. Rapid Reference 4.2 illustrates the six CALP levels available plus two regions that fall between two levels, the relationship to the RPI, and the instructional implications of each.

Table 4.1 Clusters for Which CALP Levels Are Available

Reading Clusters	Written Language Clusters	Other ACH Clusters
Reading	Written Language	Academic Skills
Basic Reading Skills	Basic Writing Skills	Academic Applications
Reading Comprehension	Written Expression	Academic Knowledge
Reading Comprehension–Extended		Brief Achievement

≡ Rapid Reference 4.2

Relationship Between RPI and CALP Levels

	CALP Level	W Diff	RPI	Instructional Implications
6	Very Advanced	+31 and above	100/90	Extremely easy
5	Advanced	+14 to +30	98/90 to 100/90	Very easy
4–5 (4.5)	Fluent to Advanced	+7 to +13	95/90 to 98/90	Easy
4	Fluent	−6 to +6	82/90 to 95/90	Manageable
3–4 (3.5)	Limited to Fluent	−13 to −7	67/90 to 82/90	Difficult
3	Limited	−30 to −14	24/90 to 67/90	Very difficult
2	Very Limited	−50 to −31	3/90 to 24/90	Extremely difficult
1	Extremely Limited	−51 and below	0/90 to 3/90	Nearly impossible

DON'T FORGET

Determine an Individual's Level of English Language Proficiency

Use the CALP levels to consider the individual's language proficiency before interpreting test results or making instructional recommendations. In addition, you can use CALP levels to help determine eligibility for ESL or bilingual programs. Use the achievement clusters as well as clusters from the WJ IV OL when making entrance or exit decisions.

Examples of the types of sentences used to describe CALP levels are:

- Kai met the criteria for fluency on all of the WJ IV Oral Language clusters (CALP 4–4.5).
- Raul's performance on the Basic Reading Skills cluster suggests extremely limited functioning in reading English (CALP = 1). It will be nearly impossible for him to read grade-level English books.
- Daniel's CALP level of 2 on the Written Expression cluster suggests that he will find 12th-grade-level writing tasks to be extremely difficult.

Percentile Rank

A percentile rank uses a scale from 1 to 99 to describe performance relative to a specific age- or grade-level segment in the norm sample. The examinee's percentile rank indicates the percentage of people in the selected segment of the norm sample who had scores the same as or lower than the examinee's score. Percentile ranks are particularly useful for describing a person's relative standing in the population. For example, Ivan's percentile rank of 6 on the Reading Cluster indicates that his performance was the same as or better than only 6% of the population, whereas Susie's percentile rank of 94 indicates that her score was the same as or better than 94% of the population. In other words, only 6% of her age peers would have a higher score.

Extended percentile ranks (Woodcock, 1987) provide scores that extend down to a percentile rank of one tenth (0.1) and up to a percentile rank of 99 and nine tenths (99.9). If an individual's percentile rank is 0.2, this indicates that only two persons out of 1,000 (0.2%) would have a score as low or lower. If an individual's percentile rank is 99.8, this indicates that the person's performance was as good as or better than that of 998 persons out of 1,000 (99.8%) in the reference group, or that two persons out of 1,000 would have a score as high or higher. Extending the percentile rank scale adds discriminating measurement to the range of a traditional percentile rank scale—about three fourths of a standard deviation at the top and three fourths of a standard deviation at the bottom.

DON'T FORGET

....

Remember when you see a decimal in the percentile rank, the comparison group is 1,000 people, not 100.

Examples of statements describing percentile ranks include:

- Martha's percentile rank of 99.5 on the Basic Math Skills cluster indicates that only five out of 1,000 students would have a score as high or higher (or her score was as high or higher than 995 out of 1,000 people).
- Angela's percentile rank of 1 on the Basic Writing Skills cluster indicates that only one out of 100 third-grade students would obtain a score as low or lower (or only 1% of grademates scored as low or lower than Angela).
- On the Broad Mathematics Cluster, Dominick's percentile rank of 0.5 indicates that only five out of 1,000 people would have a score as low or lower.

Standard Score

The standard score scale used in the WJ IV is based on a mean of 100 and a standard deviation of 15. This scale is the same as most deviation-IQ scales and may be used to relate standard scores from the WJ IV to other test scores based on the same mean and standard deviation. The WJ IV standard score range (0 to 200+) provides more discrimination at the ends of the scale. Because standard scores are more difficult for parents and other nonprofessionals to understand, many examiners use the more meaningful and equivalent percentile rank to interpret the standard score.

In writing reports or communicating test results to parents and others, you may prefer to use verbal labels rather than numbers to describe test performance. Rapid Reference 4.3 provides suggested verbal labels to use when describing test results. Exercise care when using descriptors of a disability. Use person-first language when describing an individual with a disability (e.g., "an individual with an intellectual disability" rather than "an intellectually disabled individual"). Use caution and professional judgment in the selection and application of verbal labels to describe a range of scores. Although labels may assist in communicating test results, the terminology is at times ambiguous or the meaning of the labels can be misunderstood.

⚋ Rapid Reference 4.3

Verbal Labels for Standard Score and Percentile Rank Ranges

Standard Score	Percentile Rank	Verbal Label
151 and above	Above 99.9	Exceptionally superior
131 to 150	98 to 99.9	Very superior, very high

Standard Score	Percentile Rank	Verbal Label
121 to 130	92 to 97	Superior, high
111 to 120	76 to 91	High average, above average
90 to 110	25 to 75	Average
80 to 89	9 to 24	Low average, below average
70 to 79	3 to 8	Low, well below average
50 to 69	0.1 to 2	Very low
49 and below	Below 0.1	Exceptionally low

Examples of statements using standard scores would be:

- Arnold's low to low average performance on the Math Problem Solving cluster reflects his current difficulty with mathematical concepts and reasoning.
- When Mr. Begley's performance is compared to students entering graduate school, his Academic Knowledge cluster is competitive (Standard Score = 120).
- Rhia's standard score of 125 (+/− 1 SEM: 120–130) indicates that her performance on the WJ IV Broad Written Language cluster is in the superior range.

Four other types of standard scores—z-scores, T-scores, stanines, and normal curve equivalents (NCEs)—are available when using the online scoring program. To display any of these scores, add a new score selection template that includes the additional score or scores you wish to report. The additional standard score selected appears for all tests and clusters. Rapid Reference 4.4 shows the means and standard deviations for each type of standard score available. Appendix C of this book presents a table for converting z-scores to percentile ranks or standard scores.

≡ Rapid Reference 4.4

....

Means and Standard Deviations for Common Standard Scores

Score	Mean	Standard Deviation
z	0	1
T	50	10

Score	Mean	Standard Deviation
Stanine	5	2
NCE	50	21.06
SS	100	15

Standard Error of Measurement

Every test score, from any test, has error associated with it. To improve accuracy when describing an individual's scores, the standard error of measurement (SEM) is used to determine the range of scores around the obtained score. This provides an indication of the degree of confidence professionals can have in an obtained score. Rather than using an average SEM, every possible score in the WJ IV has a unique SEM reported. These SEMs are primarily used to build confidence bands for standard scores and percentile ranks that are presented on the score report.

LEVELS OF INTERPRETIVE INFORMATION

The WJ IV provides four hierarchical levels of information in an interpretive framework. Information from one level cannot be used interchangeably with information from another. Each level provides unique information about a person's test performance and builds on information from the previous level. Consider information from all four levels when describing a person's performance. Rapid Reference 4.5 provides a brief summary of the four levels of information.

≡ Rapid Reference 4.5
....

Four Hierarchical Levels of Information

Level	Score or Source of Information	Application
1	Qualitative, error analysis	Aids instructional planning
	Test Session Observations Checklist	Aids behavioral observations
2	Age equivalents	Help to determine level of development
	Grade equivalents	Help to determine level of instruction

Level	Score or Source of Information	Application
3	RPIs, CALP levels	Help to determine level of proficiency
	Instructional zone	Provides a range (easy to difficult)
4	Standard scores, percentile ranks	Show relative standing compared to peers

Level 1 information is useful in interpreting results and planning the appropriate instructional program. Informal and qualitative in nature, this information is obtained through behavioral observations during testing and through error analysis of responses to individual items. Each test in the Standard Battery (Tests 1–11) has a Qualitative Checklist that can be used to help document the examinee's performance on the task. In addition, a framework for recording behavioral observations, the Test Session Observations Checklist, is located on the first page of the WJ IV ACH Test Record. Level 1 information can include comments that the examinee makes (e.g., "I really don't like math"), as well as behavioral observations (e.g., the student was inattentive during timed tests). It also can help with forming hypotheses about the nature of a problem. For example, Phillip, a fourth-grade student, missed several items on both the Letter-Word Identification and Word Attack tests that involved short vowel sounds. One instructional recommendation was that Phillip should be retaught short vowels and practice reading consonant-vowel-consonant words with these sounds.

Watching how the individual performs the task can also provide insights into instructional recommendations. Two ninth-grade students, John and Rebekkah, solved this problem in different ways, although they both arrived at the correct solution:

Form A, Item 31, Applied Problems: The Roberts have four people in their family. For breakfast they each eat three muffins. If the muffins come in packages of six, how many packages do they need each morning?

John multiplied 4 by 3 and then divided 12 by 6 to get the answer of two packages. Rebekkah drew four people and then put three muffins under each of the people. She then drew a package around two groups of six. Although both students have a conceptual understanding of the problem, Rebekkah's approach is more concrete and reveals that she does not understand how to use multiplication and division to solve such a word problem.

Level 2 information indicates an individual's stage of development and is expressed as age or grade equivalents. You can use these scores to help estimate an appropriate developmental or instructional level.

Level 3 information indicates the quality of a person's performance on criterion tasks of a given difficulty level and can be helpful in determining an appropriate instructional level. The RPI compares the examinee's proficiency on a task to the proficiency of average age- or grademates. The RPI can be used to help determine an appropriate instructional level. The instructional zone, based on the RPI, defines the range of tasks that a person would perceive as quite easy (96% successful) to a level that a person would perceive as quite difficult (75% successful). As noted, this is similar to the independent and frustration levels typically found on informal reading inventories. CALP levels, also determined by the RPI, can be helpful in describing an individual's language proficiency.

Level 4 information provides a basis for making peer comparisons. In educational and clinical settings, percentile ranks and standard scores are the most common metrics used to describe an individual's relative group standing as compared to age or grade peers. These scores are often the scores used in making placement decisions, such as a need for special education.

> **DON'T FORGET**
> ....
> ### Include Qualitative Information in the Report
> Complete the Qualitative Checklists for Tests 1 through 11
> Use the Test Session Observation Checklist to describe the following for each examinee:
> - Level of attention/concentration
> - Relevant behaviors
> - Attitude toward the testing
> - Motivation
> - Level of engagement
> - Persistence/effort
> - Response style
>
> Record and analyze errors:
> - Look for patterns
> - Identify strengths and weaknesses

INTERPRETING TESTS

The interpretation of test results is a complex process. Simply reporting the derived scores or printing out a computer report is not an interpretation. An analysis of the individual's performance on a test must consider the stimulus material, task demands, task complexity, language requirements needed to complete the task, developmental nature of the task, and any factors that may have affected performance. Furthermore, understanding the Cattell-Horn-Carroll Theory of Cognitive Abilities (CHC theory) (Carroll, 1993; Cattell, 1963; Horn, 1988, 1991; Horn &

≡ Rapid Reference 4.6

Definitions of CHC Factors

Reading/Writing Ability (*Grw*)—Depth of lexical knowledge, including spelling, vocabulary, language comprehension, and English language usage.

Quantitative Knowledge (*Gq*)—Store of acquired mathematical declarative and procedural knowledge.

Comprehension-Knowledge (*Gc*)—Breadth and depth of a person's acquired knowledge of a culture and the effective application of this knowledge (i.e., crystallized intelligence).

Fluid Reasoning (*Gf*)—Mental operations an individual uses when faced with a novel task that cannot be performed automatically. Inductive and deductive reasoning are indicators of *Gf*. Typically requires deliberate and flexible control of attention to solve "on the spot" problems.

Long-Term Retrieval (*Glr*)—Storage and consolidation of information in long-term memory and fluent retrieval of it later through association. This is not the store of knowledge (*Gc* or *Gq*), but rather the process of storing and retrieving that information.

Short-Term Working Memory (*Gwm*)—Apprehension, manipulation, and retention of information in immediate awareness and then use of it within a few seconds.

Cognitive Processing Speed (*Gs*)—Fluent performance of cognitive tasks automatically, especially when under pressure to maintain focused attention and concentration.

Auditory Processing (*Ga*)—Perception, analysis, and synthesis of auditory stimuli (includes phonological awareness abilities).

Visual Processing (*Gv*)—Perception, analysis, synthesis, and manipulation of visual stimuli (includes thinking with visual patterns).

Cattell, 1966; McGrew, 2005, 2009; Schneider & McGrew, 2012; Woodcock, 1990, 1998) can provide guidance in interpreting test results. Rapid Reference 4.6 provides definitions of the various factors in CHC theory.

INTERPRETING THE READING TESTS

Many children find learning to read a formidable task. For about 20% of children, learning to read is the most difficult challenge they face in school (Lyon, 1998; Shaywitz, 2003). Because reading is a major foundational skill for all school-based learning, it is critical that examiners evaluate reading performance and plan appropriate instructional programs. Rapid Reference 4.7 provides a list of some of the common characteristics of individuals with low reading performance.

To interpret the reading tests, you must be aware of the skills involved in each task, know what abilities underlie each test, and recognize any additional

≡ Rapid Reference 4.7

Characteristics of Individuals With Low Reading Performance

An individual with low basic reading skills:

- Has poor phonological awareness
- Has poor orthographic awareness (knowledge of spelling patterns)
- Has trouble learning sight words
- Has difficulty sounding out words
- Has trouble applying strategies for word analysis
- Overrelies on context clues when reading
- Reads slowly
- Hesitates and repeats words and phrases
- Loses place when asked to read aloud
- Misreads words
- Avoids reading

An individual with low reading comprehension skills:

- Has difficulty recalling what is read
- Has trouble using syntactic and semantic cues
- Has trouble understanding what is read
- Has a limited vocabulary
- Becomes easily frustrated with tasks requiring reading
- May read well orally but does not comprehend
- Has weaknesses in oral language comprehension
- Has difficulty with all academic tasks involving reading

factors that may facilitate or inhibit performance, such as attention. You will also want to consider the impact of poor oral language skills when evaluating reading performance as well as the relationships between reading and written language performance.

The skills measured in the eight reading tests range from lower-level (less complex) abilities, such as recognizing letters and sounds in isolation, to the higher-level (more complex) abilities, such as comprehending and recalling connected discourse. Figure 4.2 displays an interpretive model of the skills measured by the WJ IV reading tests. Using the framework of CHC theory to interpret the reading tests shows that the tests are primarily measures of reading ability, an aspect of reading/writing ability (*Grw*).

Other aspects of processing, particularly auditory processing (*Ga*), long-term retrieval (*Glr*), comprehension-knowledge (*Gc*), cognitive processing speed (*Gs*), and short-term working memory (*Gwm*), are also measured by the WJ IV reading

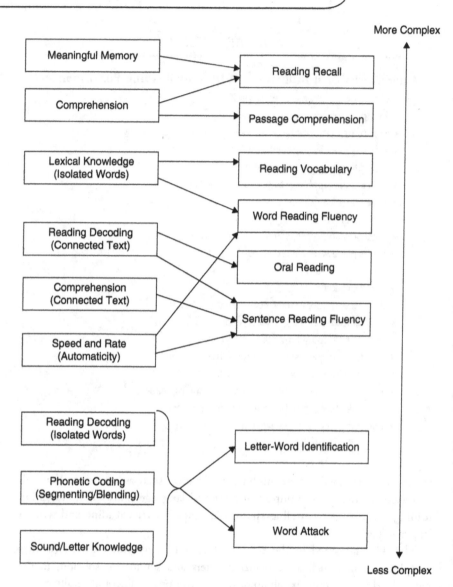

Figure 4.2 Skills Measured by the WJ IV ACH Reading Tests

tests. McGrew and Wendling (2010) report that *Gc, Ga, Gs,* and *Gwm* have a consistent, significant relationship with reading achievement. *Gc* is strongly related to basic reading skills and reading comprehension across all ages. Phonetic coding, an aspect of auditory processing (*Ga*), is important to basic reading skills in particular.

Short-term working memory (*Gwm*) appears to contribute to reading achievement. This seems to be particularly true as it relates to working memory (*Gwm*-WM), which is significant at all ages for both basic reading skills and reading comprehension. Memory span (*Gwm*-MS) is related to reading comprehension for individuals at the high school level. In addition, naming facility and associative memory, aspects of long-term retrieval (*Glr*), appear to be important predictors of early reading failure. Fluid reasoning (*Gf*) is important to comprehension (Nation, Clarke, & Snowling, 2002), but research has not linked *Gf* to decoding. Perceptual speed, a narrow (*Gs*) ability, adds significantly to the explanation of reading performance. Some developmental differences are noted. For example, the significance of comprehension-knowledge (*Gc*) and working memory (*Gwm*-WM) to reading achievement increases with age, whereas the significance of long-term retrieval (*Glr*) and processing speed (*Gs*) declines with age. Visual processing abilities (*Gv*) have little significance in explaining or predicting reading achievement. However, some visual abilities, such as orthographic coding (the ability to recall letters and letter strings) (Berninger, 1990; Hale & Fiorello, 2004), are important to reading success.

> **DON'T FORGET**
> ....
> **The Difference Between Phonological and Orthographic Awareness**
> Phonological awareness involves the ability to manipulate language sounds (phonemes). Orthographic awareness involves the ability to recall written letters and letter strings (graphemes).

Test I: Letter-Word Identification

This test requires the individual to read isolated letters and words orally. It is a measure of reading decoding (sight recognition), including reading readiness skills. The items are presented in a list rather than in context. The reader does not need to know the meaning of the words. Individuals with good sight-word recognition skills recognize the letters and words rapidly and with little effort. Automatic and fluent sight-word identification facilitates reading performance.

Individuals with inefficient or limited strategies for word identification typically have low performance on this test. These individuals may identify several words accurately but require increased time and greater attention to phonic analysis to determine the correct response. Word identification skills are not automatic. Individuals with poor word recognition skills tend to read slowly and make numerous errors. They may be unwilling to try, are easily frustrated, or are afraid to risk making an error. In many cases, you will want to evaluate the types of errors that the individual makes during testing. Table 4.2 indicates the task demands and categories of the

Table 4.2 Categories of Phonic Elements for Items in Letter-Word Identification, Forms A, B, and C

Phonic Element/ SyllableType	Item	Form A	Item	Form B	Item	Form C
Letter Recognition (pointing response)	1	L	1	T	1	D
	2	A	2	S	2	E
	3	S	3	B	3	S
	4	W	4	C	4	G
	5	k	5	i	5	d
	6	y	6	r	6	a
Letter Identification (oral response)	7	R	7	X	7	A
	8	F	8	s	8	c
	9	p	9	z	9	e
	10	J	10	T	10	D
Word Recognition (pointing response)	11	car	11	cat	11	dog
	12	sun	12	rug	12	mat
	13	dog	13	tree	13	see
Word Identification (oral response)						
Irregular and high frequency	14	the	17	will	15	to
	22	have	22	was	17	one
	23	into	29	only	22	two
	38	often			30	does
					31	been
					38	piece
Short vowel closed syllable (CVC or VC)	15	at	14	in	14	is
	16	and	15	dog	16	can
	18	man	16	it	18	if
	20	cup	18	but	20	hot
	21	fish	20	big	29	rabbit

Table 4.2 (Continued)

Phonic Element/ SyllableType	Item	Form A	Item	Form B	Item	Form C
	25	them	25	then	35	quick
	26	must	27	family	40	million
	31	animal	32	children	41	studying
	54	veteran	34	different		
	59	stamina	48	toxic		
	70	minuend	71	nuptial		
Open syllable (ends on vowel with long vowel sound)	17	no	19	play	32	because
	19	she	31	grow	44	decide
	27	going	43	diamond		
	34	become	62	diatom		
	36	library				
Long vowel –*igh*	29	light				
Long vowel	61	breathes	57	leagues	19	like
					25	time
					26	cake
					43	island
Consonant -*le* syllable	28	people	76	inveigle	60	whittles
					67	chortle
Vowel team (digraph or diphthong)	24	keep	28	new	24	soon
	32	could	33	great	27	each
	37	point	37	own	28	about
	40	however	41	through	34	town
	41	brought	45	sausage	39	build
	42	jewel	49	statue	55	seized
	53	knead	72	poignant		
	66	heuristic				

(*continued*)

Table 4.2 (Continued)

Phonic Element/ SyllableType	Item	Form A	Item	Form B	Item	Form C
R-controlled syllable	30	morning	26	more	50	fierce
	33	garden	44	liberty	51	whirled
	44	natural	54	portrait		
	52	guarantee				
Soft c or soft g	39	special	40	sentence	37	change
	45	distance	42	pledge	61	porcelain
	48	imagine	47	social	65	gist
			56	ancient	74	taciturn
			63	prestige		
			67	deficiencies		
Hard c or hard g	47	signal	39	guess	58	domesticated
					77	casuistry
Consonant blend	55	sphere	21	from	57	scowled
			24	just	59	justifiable
			30	hand		
Consonant digraph	35	knew	23	when	21	that
	43	whose	46	bachelor	23	they
	63	thoroughfare	50	nephew	36	father
			69	blithe	48	character
					49	phrase
					66	labyrinth
Affixes	46	overwhelm	35	faster	33	really
	49	investigate	36	beautiful	42	famous
	50	reverse	38	building	45	lacked
	51	doubtful	51	curious	47	announcer
	56	accustomed	52	hesitate	56	courageous

Table 4.2 (Continued)

Phonic Element/ SyllableType	Item	Form A	Item	Form B	Item	Form C
	57	contrary	53	tremendous	62	controversial
	60	ferocious	55	evidence	63	ravenous
	64	staunchest	59	particularly	64	nutritive
	65	millinery	61	infectious	69	subsidiary
	68	municipality	64	trajectory	71	denotative
	72	aggrandizement	68	unscrupulous	73	quadruped
	74	tertiary	73	impetuosity	75	ubiquitous
	75	septuagenarian			76	perspicacity
French origin	58	cologne	66	opaque	52	moustache
	62	silhouette	74	pique	78	frisson
	73	milieu	78	bourgeois		
	76	echelon				
	77	coiffure				
	78	macaque				
Greek origin	69	idiosyncrasy	60	psychology	53	thermostat
	71	rhetoric	70	pterodactyl	68	aesthetic
			75	rhetorician	70	euphemism
			77	chimerical	72	psoriasis
Qu: /kw/			58	quarreled	54	quite

phonic elements or syllable types for items in Forms A, B, and C. Although many of the words could be placed in multiple categories, each word was assigned to only one category. For example, the word *must* could be placed in both the short vowel and consonant blend categories. The examples in each category are designed to help you identify other phonic elements or syllable types that may appear in each word. Rapid Reference 4.8 defines the various categories and phonics terminology used in Table 4.2. These terms also apply to categories in Table 4.3 for Word Attack and Table 4.6 for Spelling. Analyzing the types of errors an individual makes on a test or across tests can provide valuable information that helps guide instruction.

≡ *Rapid Reference 4.8*

Phonics and Word Identification Terminology

Phoneme: a single speech sound (e.g., /s/, /m/) that combines with others to form words

Short (or lax) vowels: vowel sounds produced with little tension in the vocal cords (e.g., *man, tub*)

Long (or tense) vowels: vowel sounds produced with more tension in the vocal cords (e.g., *tame, hose*)

Grapheme: a letter or letter combination that spells a single phoneme (e.g., *igh*)

Irregular or exception words: words that contain a part that does not follow common English spelling rules or patterns (e.g., the *ai* in *said*)

Consonant blend: adjacent consonants before or after a vowel in a syllable that maintain their identity when pronounced (e.g., *st* in *stop*)

Consonant digraph: two consonant letters that make one new speech sound (e.g., *ph* = /f/)

Vowel digraph: two vowel letters that make a single speech sound (e.g., *ea* = /E/)

Vowel diphthong: vowel sounds that have a glide when pronounced (e.g., *ou, ow, oi, oy*)

Syllable Types

  Closed: a syllable that includes a short vowel sound ending in one or more consonants (e.g., *tap, bump*)

  Open: a syllable that ends in a long vowel sound with a single vowel letter (e.g., *no, return*)

  Vowel consonant silent e (VCe): a syllable with a single vowel, a consonant, and then a silent e (e.g., *ace, mice*)

  R-controlled: a syllable with a single vowel that is followed by the letter *r*, which often affects the vowel sound (e.g., *car, motor*)

  Vowel team: a syllable that uses a vowel combination (a digraph or diphthong) for spelling (e.g., *team, coin*)

  Consonant -le: a final syllable that contains a consonant, plus *le* (e.g., *candle, turtle*)

Affixes: a morpheme (the smallest meaning unit) added to the beginning (prefix) or ending (suffix) of a word to change its meaning

Multisyllabic: having more than one syllable

You may wish to compare the results of this test with Passage Comprehension, Oral Reading, Sentence Reading Fluency, Reading Recall, Word Reading Fluency, and Reading Vocabulary to develop insights into the individual's level of reading skills with and without the context of meaning. Although all of the tests require word identification, these other tests also require knowledge of word meanings, sentence structure, and comprehension. You may also wish to compare the results of Letter-Word Identification and Word Attack to determine whether differences exist between the reader's word identification and his or her ability to apply phonic skills.

Test 4: Passage Comprehension

This test requires the individual to read a short passage silently, comprehend the information, and provide a missing word. It is a measure of reading comprehension and lexical knowledge. This modified cloze task requires the ability to use both syntactic and semantic clues in comprehending text.

Low performance on Passage Comprehension may be a function of limited basic reading skills, comprehension difficulties, or both. Analysis of the types of errors made will help in determining the most appropriate instructional plan. You may consider three different types of errors: (1) syntactically correct but semantically incorrect, (2) semantically correct but syntactically incorrect, or (3) both incorrect.

To help clarify whether the problem is with reading alone or reflects limited language comprehension, you can compare the results from the Passage Comprehension test to Test 2: Oral Comprehension in the WJ IV OL, a similar task that does not require reading (see Chapter 5 for more information). If the individual does well on the oral test, then language comprehension is not likely to be the reason for poor performance on the reading test. If the individual does poorly on Oral Comprehension, however, then limited language comprehension must also be considered as a contributing factor to poor reading performance.

Test 7: Word Attack

This test requires the individual to orally read phonically regular nonsense words. Word Attack measures aspects of both phonological (using speech sounds to read words) and orthographic (using common letter patterns or strings to read nonsense words) coding. Phoneme–grapheme knowledge is necessary to perform well on this test.

Low performance on Word Attack may result from poor phonological processing, limited phoneme–grapheme knowledge, poor decoding skills and strategies, or a lack of fluency. Impaired decoding is frequently thought to be the basis of reading problems. You may wish to evaluate the types of errors the individual makes on this test in order to make the most appropriate instructional recommendations. Table 4.3 shows the tasks and phonic elements for the items

Table 4.3 Categories of Phonic Elements for Items in Word Attack, Forms A, B, and C

Phonic Element	Item	Form A	Item	Form B	Item	Form C
Sound Recognition (point to picture that starts with sound specified)	1	/k/	1	/k/	1	/k/
	2	/f/	2	/f/	2	/f/
Letter/Sound Recognition (point to letter or letters that make the sound specified)	3	/p/	3	/r/	3	/f/
	5	/sh/	5	/gr/	5	/sh/
Sound Identification (says sound of letter or letters)	4	/k/	4	/m/	4	/k/
	6	/t/	6	/n/	6	/z/
	7	/sp/	7	/gl/	7	/k/
	8	/kl/	8	/tw/		
Nonsense Word Identification (reads nonsense word aloud)						
Short vowel	9	tiff	9	hap	9	lat
	11	ven	10	mell	11	bix
	12	wugs	11	fim	12	lish
	13	mip	12	rox	14	jop
	16	jox	13	gugs	15	zent
	23	centizen	15	tisp		
	27	hudned	28	depnonlel		
Long vowel	17	bine	18	cade	22	rotion
	19	blighten	19	sluke	25	ligtite
	26	cythe	23	frime		

Table 4.3 (Continued)

Phonic Element	Item	Form A	Item	Form B	Item	Form C
Vowel digraph or diphthong	10	zoop	21	comfrain	8	/oi/
	14	foy	26	mafreatsun	17	pawk
	21	baunted			18	loast
	25	saist				
R-controlled	18	artible	24	cirdon	16	snirk
					20	yerdle
Consonant blend	29	fleighted	14	floxy	19	thrept
			16	gusp	21	trond
			17	splist		
Consonant digraph	15	leck	20	shomble	10	fash
	20	wreet	27	phigh	13	vack
	24	phintober			27	paraphonity
Multisyllabic	28	intestationing	29	mivocative	28	subdirement
	31	sylibemeter	30	apertuate	29	botrationary
	32	armophodelictedness	31	psypenoptimeter	30	redigitation
			32	pretrationistic	31	sophomibistry
Qu: /kw/	22	quade	22	quantric	23	quog
Silent g			25	gnib	24	gnobe
Silent k					26	knoink
Soft g	30	coge			32	mefgest

on Word Attack, Forms A, B, and C. Each item appears in just one category in Table 4.3, although many items could be assigned to more than one category. For example, *gusp* appears in the Consonant Blend category but could also be assigned to the Short Vowel category. Review of the examples in Table 4.3 will help you determine additional phonic elements that may apply to each item. This information, along with error analysis, can be helpful in planning instruction.

If an individual has a low score on Word Attack, you will want to evaluate the individual's phonological awareness. You may administer Test 3: Segmentation, Test 7: Sound Blending, and Test 9: Sound Awareness from the WJ IV OL, as well as Test 5: Phonological Processing from the WJ IV COG. An individual who has strong auditory processing (*Ga*) but does poorly on Word Attack has an excellent prognosis for improvement. The underlying abilities to analyze and synthesize sounds are intact, so systematic instruction in phoneme–grapheme relationships should help improve reading skills.

> **DON'T FORGET**
> ....
> An analysis of errors can help you determine appropriate instructional recommendations.

An individual who has poor auditory processing (*Ga*) in addition to poor performance on Word Attack would benefit from an instructional program that focuses on both developing phonological awareness and phonic skills. Individuals need a prerequisite amount of phonological awareness to develop decoding skills. Specific training in sound blending and phonemic segmentation, in particular, improves decoding skills (Ehri, 2006; National Reading Panel, 2000). Focused instruction can help an individual increase his or her understanding of the relationship between the sounds (phonemes) and the written symbols (graphemes).

Test 8: Oral Reading

This test requires oral reading of a set of sentences that gradually increases in complexity. The test measures decoding skill, automaticity with reading, and prosody (reading with expression). Within the Test Record, you can use the Qualitative Observation Tally to code the type of errors an individual makes while reading the sentences; this may lead to specific instructional implications. For example, a fourth-grade student, Roberto, made numerous hesitations and repetitions while reading the passages. This suggests that Roberto has a problem with fluency and automaticity, so a method to address these issues would be appropriate.

Test 9: Sentence Reading Fluency

This test requires the individual to read simple sentences quickly and indicate whether the statement is true or false by circling *Yes* or *No*. It is a measure of reading speed and automaticity. Low performance on Sentence Reading Fluency may be a result of difficulty sustaining attention, limited basic reading skills, slow processing speed, or comprehension difficulties. An individual's processing speed (*Gs*) (see Cognitive Processing Speed Cluster from WJ IV COG) may facilitate or inhibit performance on this test. The speed and fluency with which an individual performs basic skills can influence performance on higher-level skills. You may wish to compare Sentence Reading Fluency with Test 15: Word Reading Fluency to see if performance is similar on both timed tests. If Sentence Reading Fluency is higher than Word Reading Fluency, this suggests that increased context improves word recognition skill.

Test 12: Reading Recall

This test requires the individual to read a story and then recall the elements of that story. Both reading and expressive language skills are required to perform this story-retelling task. Reading Recall measures reading comprehension, meaningful memory, and language development. Poor attention, poor memory, poor decoding, limited vocabulary, low expressive language, or limited comprehension may negatively impact performance on this test. You may compare performance on the Reading Recall test to Test 6: Story Recall on the WJ IV COG. If performance is higher on Story Recall than Reading Recall, this suggests that the problem is not with memory or attention, but rather with reading skills. Conversely, if Reading Recall is higher than Story Recall, this suggests that reading comprehension is stronger than listening comprehension.

Test 15: Word Reading Fluency

This test is a timed test that requires the examinee to silently and quickly read four words and mark the two that share a semantic relationship. Low performance on this test may result from poor basic reading skills, limited vocabulary, or slow processing speed. An individual's processing speed (*Gs*) (see Cognitive Processing Speed Cluster from the WJ IV COG) may facilitate or inhibit performance on this test.

As noted previously, you may wish to compare performance on this test to Test 9: Sentence Reading Fluency since both are timed reading tests. If performance is higher on Test 15: Word Reading Fluency, this suggests that the increased context of language in Sentence Reading Fluency does not help the individual. You also may wish to compare the results of Word Reading Fluency to tests that require vocabulary knowledge such as Test 17: Reading Vocabulary, or Test 1: Picture Vocabulary from the WJ IV OL, or Test 1: Oral Vocabulary from the WJ IV COG, all of which are untimed tests. This comparison may help determine whether speed or vocabulary knowledge is influencing performance.

Test 17: Reading Vocabulary

This test has two parts: 17A: Synonyms and 17B: Antonyms. The individual is required to read words and to orally supply synonyms in 17A and antonyms in 17B. Low performance on this test may result from poor basic reading skills, limited vocabulary, or both. If the individual reads the stimulus words correctly but provides an incorrect response, he or she may be better at decoding than comprehending. If the individual misreads the stimulus words but provides the correct response, he or she may be better at comprehending than decoding. For example, a ninth-grade student read the word *receive* as *recover* and then said that *retrieve* was a synonym. Although this response would be scored as incorrect, the examiner noted that it was a decoding, not a vocabulary or comprehension, error.

You may wish to compare Reading Vocabulary directly to the individual's performance on Test 1: Oral Vocabulary in the WJ IV COG, a similar task that does not require reading. If the individual's performance is higher on the oral task than on the reading task, then the focus of instruction should be on developing basic reading skills. If the individual's performance is low on both the oral task and the reading task, then the focus of instruction should be on developing oral vocabulary, as well as basic reading skills.

READING CLUSTERS

The WJ IV ACH has seven reading clusters: Reading, Broad Reading, Basic Reading Skills, Reading Comprehension, Reading Comprehension-Extended, Reading Fluency, and Reading Rate. You can use each of these clusters when calculating intra-achievement variations or ability/achievement comparisons. Rapid Reference 4.9 illustrates typical instructional implications for individuals with reading difficulties.

≡ Rapid Reference 4.9

Instructional Implications for Individuals With Low Reading Achievement

- Match the level of instructional materials to the individual's reading level.
- Provide support so that the individual can succeed while skills are being developed.
- Match the type of instruction to the specific needs of the individual.
- Provide explicit instruction in phonological awareness and phoneme–grapheme relationships.
- Provide direct instruction to develop basic reading skills (both sight words and phonic skills).
- Use a procedure such as repeated reading to increase reading rate.
- Have the student engage in oral reading 10–15 minutes daily, receiving immediate corrective feedback for errors.
- Develop oral language abilities.
- Teach and provide practice with comprehension strategies.
- Teach self-monitoring techniques.

Reading Cluster

The Reading cluster consists of two tests: Letter-Word Identification, a measure of word recognition skill, and Passage Comprehension, a measure of reading comprehension. Because it includes a measure of basic skills and comprehension, this cluster may be used when you want an estimate of a person's general reading ability. The cluster does not include a timed test, so it provides a measure of reading accuracy rather than reading speed.

Broad Reading Cluster

Composed of three tests, Letter-Word Identification, Passage Comprehension, and Sentence Reading Fluency, this cluster provides a broad overview of the individual's overall reading level. Because it is a mix of three different aspects of reading (basic skills, comprehension, and fluency), interpretation of this cluster is most meaningful when performance is similar on all three tests.

Basic Reading Skills Cluster

For this cluster, Letter-Word Identification and Word Attack provide a broad view of the individual's basic word reading skills, including sight-word recognition and phonic skills. Comparing the results of the two tests will help you determine if word recognition skills, phonic skills, or both are limited and require remediation. Analysis of errors made on both tests can help you target specific instructional elements.

If an individual has trouble decoding words, few resources are left for comprehension. Slow, labored reading with many errors will have a negative impact on comprehension. Analyzing an individual's performance on the basic reading skill tests is important to the interpretation of the reading comprehension tests. Be sure to consider the effect of decoding problems before identifying a problem in reading comprehension.

Reading Comprehension Cluster

The Reading Comprehension cluster is composed of Passage Comprehension and Reading Recall. This cluster provides a broad view of the individual's reading comprehension skill. Both tests measure comprehension in the context of connected discourse. Reading Recall also has a meaningful memory component that requires reconstruction of the passage that was read. Because of the retelling aspect of Reading Recall, expressive language demands are increased and must be considered when interpreting results.

The Reading Comprehension-Extended cluster also includes Passage Comprehension and Reading Recall, but adds a third test, Reading Vocabulary. Reading Vocabulary measures comprehension in a decontextualized format, that is, the knowledge of word meanings in isolation. Comparing the results of the three tests in this cluster will help determine whether a meaningful context helps or interferes with an individual's comprehension.

You may want to compare the results of the Reading Comprehension cluster to the Basic Reading Skills cluster, the Academic Knowledge cluster, and the Listening Comprehension cluster available in the WJ IV OL. Low performance on reading comprehension tasks may result from low basic reading skills or limited oral language or background knowledge. Considering the impact of these various factors will help you determine the most appropriate instructional program for the individual.

Reading Fluency

The Reading Fluency cluster contains two tests: Oral Reading and Sentence Reading Fluency. This cluster includes a measure of untimed oral reading and a measure of silent reading that is timed. Although the Oral Reading test is not timed, you can evaluate a person's ease of reading, accuracy, and expression (prosody) as he or she reads the set of sentences aloud. In addition, you can document the number and type of errors the person makes while reading. You can record this information in the Qualitative Observation Tally located in the Test Record and then use the results to help inform instructional planning. Sentence Reading Fluency is a timed silent reading task that requires comprehending simple sentences quickly. When comparing the individual's performance on the two tests in this cluster, consider how the differences in task and response demands may have influenced performance.

Reading Rate

The Reading Rate cluster consists of Sentence Reading Fluency and Word Reading Fluency. Both of these tests are timed and read silently. Sentence Reading Fluency requires comprehension of simple sentences, whereas Word Reading Fluency involves the understanding of vocabulary and the semantic relationships among pairs of words. Results on this cluster can be compared to Basic Reading Skills and Reading Comprehension. In addition, you may want to investigate how the person performs on other timed measures (e.g., Math Facts Fluency and Sentence Writing Fluency), as well as on measures of processing and perceptual speed on the WJ IV COG. In some cases, the results of this cluster, when substantiated with additional information, can be used to help document a need for extended time on tests.

Sheila was applying for graduate school. Although she had been diagnosed with dyslexia in third grade, she had never received special education services at school. She was concerned that she would need certain accommodations on tests, such as extended time, if she was going to be successful. In the past, she remembered never being able to complete exams even though she could have answered more questions if she had been provided with more time. The WJ IV ACH assessment results indicated superior Academic Knowledge, but very low scores on Word Attack, Spelling, Sentence Reading Fluency, and Word Reading Fluency. Additional scores on the WJ IV COG and OL helped establish the rationale for Sheila's need for more time (e.g., slow perceptual speed but above average oral language and reasoning abilities).

INTERPRETING THE MATHEMATICS TESTS

Interpretation of the mathematics tests requires that you are aware of the skills involved in each task, know what abilities underlie each test, and recognize

≡ Rapid Reference 4.10

Characteristics of Individuals With Low Math Achievement

An individual with low basic math skills:
- Appears anxious or resistant to solving math problems
- Lacks confidence when presented with math problems
- Uses finger counting long after it is developmentally appropriate
- Reverses and transposes numbers (e.g., 12 for 21)
- Does not attend to signs
- Has trouble understanding the number line
- Has trouble determining differences in the magnitude of numbers
- Has difficulty aligning numbers when performing calculations
- Has difficulty remembering steps in computing or solving problems

An individual with low math reasoning skills:
- Has limited math vocabulary
- Lacks age-appropriate quantitative concepts
- Has trouble with estimation
- Has limited strategies for solving math problems
- Does not recognize or self-correct errors
- Has difficulty recognizing relevant information in word problems
- Has difficulty eliminating extraneous information from word problems

additional factors that may influence performance. Rapid Reference 4.10 indicates common characteristics of individuals with low math achievement. The four mathematics tests measure skills that range from lower-level abilities, such as writing numbers, to higher-level abilities, such as analyzing and solving problems. Figure 4.3 provides an interpretive model of the various skills measured by the WJ IV mathematics tests.

Using the CHC theory as the interpretive framework, the mathematics tests primarily measure quantitative knowledge (*Gq*). The WJ IV math tests also measure aspects of fluid reasoning (*Gf*), comprehension-knowledge (*Gc*), cognitive processing speed (*Gs*), short-term working memory (*Gwm*), auditory processing (*Ga*), and visual processing (*Gv*). McGrew and Wendling (2010) found that *Gf*, *Gc*, and *Gs* abilities, as well as some narrow abilities, were correlated consistently and significantly with basic math skills and math reasoning. Some

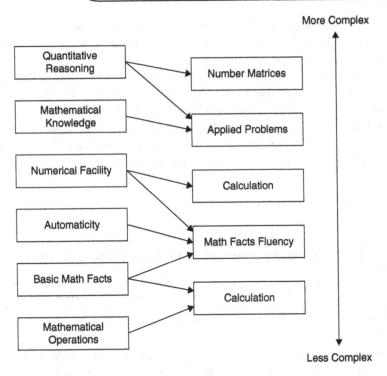

Figure 4.3 Various Skills Measured by the WJ IV ACH Mathematics Tests

developmental differences were also noted. For example, the *Gc* relationship to math reasoning increases with age, whereas *Gf* was related consistently and significantly across all ages. The narrow abilities of perceptual speed (*Gs*-P) and working memory (*Gwm*-WM) were also significantly related to both basic skills and math reasoning across all ages. The narrow *Ga* ability of phonetic coding (*Ga*-PC) correlated with mathematics, especially at the younger ages. *Gv* appears to be related to math tasks that require higher-level skills and thinking, but is not related to basic math skills (Flanagan, Ortiz, & Alfonso, 2013).

Test 2: Applied Problems

This test requires the individual to analyze and solve practical math problems. It is a measure of quantitative reasoning, math achievement, and math knowledge. Because no reading is required, low performance will most likely be related to limits in mathematical knowledge (*Gq*). Low performance may result from poor attention, limited fluid reasoning (*Gf*), limited math skills, or oral language comprehension difficulties (*Gc*).

Compare results on this test to reading and writing clusters to determine whether the individual does better when no reading is required. Oral language comprehension, limited vocabulary (*Gc*), working memory (*Gwm*-WM), perceptual speed (*Gs*-P), and fluid reasoning (*Gf*) can impact performance on Applied Problems. Analyzing the individual's errors may help provide ideas for instructional planning. Table 4.4 indicates the categories for the problems in Forms A, B, and C.

Table 4.4 Categories of Problems on Test 2: Applied Problems, Forms A, B, and C

Category	Form A Items	Form B Items	Form C Items
Number Concepts	1–10	1–8, 10	1–12
Subtraction	11–14, 21–23, 26, 29–30	9, 11, 13, 15–17, 26, 30, 37	13–14, 16, 20, 22, 24–25, 29
Addition	15, 17–18, 33	12, 14, 19	15, 17, 19, 21
Money	22–23, 28	20, 23, 28, 32	27–28
Division	24, 31, 35	24, 31, 33, 40, 42	23, 31
Multiplication	25, 32	27, 29, 34	26, 32, 34, 38
Fractions	27, 42	35, 38, 41	21
Time	34, 37	18, 25, 36, 39, 44	30, 35–37
Probability	36, 39, 46–47	51, 56	55
Algebra	38, 43–44, 49–50	48, 50, 54–55	33, 43, 48–49, 53–54, 56
Percentages	40–41	49	40, 42, 46
Interest	45	46	44, 52
Geometry	48, 52–56	43, 45, 52–53	41, 47, 50–51
Measurement		33, 42	
Averaging		47	39, 45

Test 5: Calculation

This test requires the individual to perform a variety of calculations ranging from simple addition and subtraction to complex calculus. Tasks progress from: (a) basic addition, subtraction, multiplication, and division; (b) advanced calculations of each operation with regrouping; (c) advanced calculation of each operation with negative numbers (except division); (d) fractions; (e) percentages; (f) algebra; (g) trigonometry; (h) logarithms; and (i) calculus. Calculation measures the ability to perform mathematical computations that are fundamental to more complex math reasoning and problem solving. Fluency with basic math skills is fundamental to more complex math. Low performance may result from limited basic math skill, weaknesses in short-term working memory (Gwm-WM), limited fluency or automaticity with math facts (Gs-P), poor or limited instruction, or difficulty with attention.

Be sure to observe the examinee's behaviors; categorize errors that are made; note which concepts are known and unknown; and interview the examinee, if needed. For example, Anna, a sixth-grade girl, made numerous errors in Calculation. To try to understand the reasons for her errors, the examiner presented Anna with a set of similar problems and asked her to talk through what she was doing as she performed the calculations. This helped the examiner pinpoint Anna's confusions regarding math algorithms. Bart, an eighth-grade student, made errors on all problems involving fractions. For example, in adding fractions, he would combine the numerators and denominators (e.g., $\frac{1}{2} + \frac{1}{4} = \frac{2}{6}$). Observations of these types of errors lead to specific instructional recommendations. Bart needs explicit instruction in how to add, subtract, multiply, and divide with numbers that have fractions. Table 4.5 indicates the number of items in each category for Forms A, B, and C.

Test 10: Math Facts Fluency

This test requires the individual to quickly solve simple addition, subtraction, and multiplication facts. Low performance on this test may result from poor attention, limited basic math skills, lack of automaticity, or slow processing speed (Gs-P). Some individuals work slowly and make no errors, whereas other individuals work very quickly and make several errors. If numerous errors are made, attempt to determine the reasons for the mistakes. As examples, a student may be confused or not pay careful attention to the signs, may not know multiplication facts, or may be confused about the properties of zero (e.g., $6 + 0 = 0$).

Table 4.5 Categories of Problems on Test 5: Calculation, Forms A, B, and C

Category	Form A (Number of items)	Form B (Number of items)	Form C (Number of items)
Basic addition	12	10	10
Basic subtraction	6	8	8
Basic multiplication	4	4	4
Basic division	2	3	2
Advanced addition	3	3	4
Advanced subtraction	1	1	2
Advanced multiplication	3	3	4
Advanced division	2	2	2
Algebra	5	4	4
Derivatives	2	2	2
Factorials	1	1	1
Fractions	4	4	4
Geometry	1	1	1
Integrals	2	3	3
Logarithms	1	1	1
Matrices and determinants	1	1	1
Percentages	2	1	1
Powers and roots	2	2	1
Trigonometry	2	2	1

Test 13: Number Matrices

The task in Number Matrices requires the individual to look at a matrix of numbers, figure out the pattern, and then provide the missing number. It is a measure of quantitative reasoning (RQ), an aspect of fluid reasoning (*Gf*), and also requires working memory (*Gwm*-WM) and perceptual speed (*Gs*-P).

Low performance on this test will most likely result from limited fluid reasoning (*Gf*), especially the narrow ability of quantitative reasoning (RQ). In addition, limited attention, working memory, and perceptual speed may impact performance.

Math Clusters

The WJ IV ACH has four math clusters: Mathematics, Broad Mathematics, Math Calculation Skills, and Math Problem Solving. Each of these clusters may be used in the intra-achievement variation procedure or the ability/achievement comparisons. Rapid Reference 4.11 lists possible instructional implications for individuals with low math achievement.

Mathematics

The Mathematics cluster consists of two tests: Applied Problems and Calculation. Because it includes a measure of basic math skills and a measure of math reasoning,

≡ Rapid Reference 4.11

Instructional Implications for Individuals With Low Math Achievement
- Match materials to individual's instructional level.
- Provide a high-interest, success-oriented math curriculum.
- Use manipulatives to help teach concepts.
- Reduce the number of problems.
- Provide additional time for completion of assignments.
- Teach the use of a calculator.
- Use graph paper to aid alignment and organization of calculation problems.
- Provide systematic and extended practice to reinforce learning.
- Be sure the individual understands the task by closely monitoring performance.
- Use fact charts.
- Teach meaningful applications of mathematics.
- Use an evidence-based math program that teaches skills and concepts sequentially.
- Develop math vocabulary.
- Teach functional mathematics.

this cluster may be used to estimate a person's general mathematics ability. The cluster does not include a timed test, so it provides a measure of math knowledge, rather than automaticity with math facts.

Broad Mathematics

This cluster is composed of three tests: Applied Problems, Calculation, and Math Facts Fluency. It provides a broad, comprehensive view of the individual's math achievement level. The Broad Mathematics cluster measures computational skill, automaticity with math facts, and problem solving and reasoning. Because this cluster measures three different aspects of math ability, interpretation of the cluster is most accurate when performance is similar on all three of the tests.

Math Calculation Skills

This cluster is composed of two tests: Calculation and Math Facts Fluency. It provides a measure of basic math skills including computational skills and automaticity with basic math facts. Relative ease with computations is an important factor in predicting math performance. You may wish to compare the results of the two tests in this cluster to help determine whether processing speed (*Gs*) or mastery of basic math facts is impacting performance.

Math Problem Solving

This cluster is composed of two tests: Applied Problems and Number Matrices. It provides a measure of mathematical knowledge and reasoning. You can compare results of this cluster to the Math Calculation Skills cluster to help determine whether basic math skills are impacting performance. In addition, you can compare results of this cluster to oral language if using the WJ IV OL and to comprehension-knowledge (*Gc*) and fluid reasoning (*Gf*) clusters if using the WJ IV COG. Individuals with low oral language may have difficulty with quantitative terminology or math vocabulary. Individuals with low comprehension-knowledge may lack prerequisite knowledge for acquiring and identifying mathematical concepts. Individuals with low fluid reasoning may have difficulty identifying and thinking through the various steps of a mathematical problem.

INTERPRETING THE WRITTEN LANGUAGE TESTS

Interpretation of the written language tests requires awareness of the skills involved in each task, what abilities underlie each test, and the additional factors that may be affecting writing performance. Rapid Reference 4.12 lists common characteristics of individuals with low written language performance.

The skills measured in the four written language tests range from lower-level abilities, such as copying shapes, to the higher-level abilities, such as expressing ideas in writing. The WJ IV ACH measures several aspects of writing skill: spelling, usage and proofreading, writing fluency, and the quality of written expression. Figure 4.4 provides an interpretive model of the various skills measured by the WJ IV written language tests.

≡ Rapid Reference 4.12

**Characteristics of Individuals With Low
Written Language Achievement**

An individual with low basic writing skills:

- Has poor phonological awareness
- Has poor orthographic awareness
- Usually has poor basic reading skills
- Has poor handwriting
- Reverses or transposes letters
- Has poor spelling
- Fails to self-monitor errors
- Uses simple vocabulary to avoid misspelling words
- Does poorly under time constraints
- Has limited editing skills

An individual with low written expression:

- Has a poor attitude toward writing
- Has poor basic skills that affect his or her ability to express ideas
- Has limited background knowledge, limited experiences, and low vocabulary
- Has low oral language abilities
- Has poor organizational skills
- Has low reasoning abilities

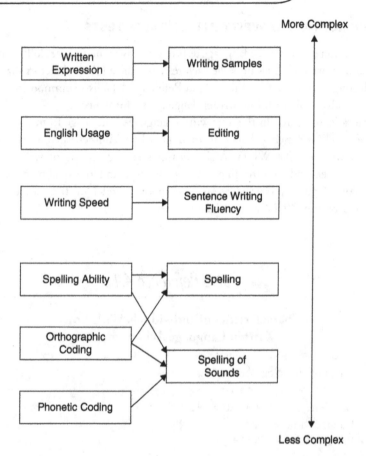

Figure 4.4 Various Skills Measured by the WJ IV ACH Written Language Tests

Using CHC theory as the interpretive framework, the written language tests primarily measure writing ability, an aspect of reading/writing ability (*Grw*). The WJ IV written language tests also measure aspects of comprehension-knowledge (*Gc*), cognitive processing speed (*Gs*), short-term working memory (*Gwm*), fluid reasoning (*Gf*), long-term retrieval (*Glr*), and auditory processing (*Ga*) (Flanagan et al., 2013; Floyd, McGrew, & Evans, 2008).

Test 3: Spelling

This test requires the individual to produce, in writing, single letters or words in response to oral prompts. Several factors that may influence performance include: fine-motor skill, handwriting, phonological coding, and orthographic coding. This test measures prewriting skills and spelling. A careful analysis of errors can often result in specific instructional recommendations. For example, an examiner noted that Caleb, a third-grade student, was having trouble spelling medial short vowel sounds and was also reversing certain letters (e.g., *b* and *d*). The examiner provided specific recommendations for spelling instruction in consonant-vowel-consonant words, as well as a strategy to use to help eliminate *b–d* reversals.

Table 4.6 indicates phonic elements in the items for Forms A, B, and C. Many words could appear in more than one category. For example, the word *comb* could appear in the long vowel and silent *b* categories. However, each word was assigned to only one category. Review of the examples in Table 4.6 will help you determine additional phonic elements that may be in each word. This information, along with error analysis, can help you make recommendations for planning instruction. (See Rapid Reference 4.8 for the definitions of the categories and phonics terminology in Table 4.6.)

Table 4.6 Categories of Phonic Elements for Items in Spelling, Forms A, B, and C

Skill	Item	Form A	Item	Form B	Item	Form C
Prewriting (copy after demonstration)	1	horizontal line	1	box	1	horizontal line
	2	triangle	2	vertical line	2	circle
(copy from model)	3	H	3	E	3	S
Print letters	4	A or a	4	M or m	4	O or o
	5	T or t	5	B or b	5	C or c
	6	P or p	6	X or x	6	U or u
	7	W or w	7	R or r	7	E or e
	8	L	8	F	8	B
	9	i	9	e	9	i

(*continued*)

Table 4.6 (Continued)

Skill	Item	Form A	Item	Form B	Item	Form C
Spelling (write dictated words)						
Short vowel	10	is	10	hat	13	had
	11	fun	16	under	14	ten
	12	got	27	gallon	19	funny
	13	am			28	second
	14	with				
	22	dinner				
Consonant blend	15	from	14	jump		
	16	camp	36	crystal		
Consonant digraph	26	laugh	21	who	17	mother
			31	elephant	23	shoe
			38	whisper	31	laughing
			59	pharaoh	50	zephyr
Vowel digraph or diphthong	17	saw	11	book	15	bee
	25	because	19	yellow	18	house
	27	already	24	friend	25	early
	28	juice	25	young	32	mountain
	36	calorie	29	unfair	40	tomorrow
	44	leisure	46	crouton	42	coax
	52	nuisance	52	maneuver		
Long vowels	19	nice	12	she	10	he
	23	fight	13	green	12	my
	34	clothes	18	cake	21	place
	42	cocoa	30	remember	26	before
					38	concrete

Table 4.6 (Continued)

Skill	Item	Form A	Item	Form B	Item	Form C
R-controlled vowels	31	important	26	tore	22	first
	43	calendar	49	separate	44	squirrel
					46	mortgage
					55	questionnaire
Irregular	18	water	15	are	11	the
	21	once	17	they	16	was
			23	any	20	said
			42	yacht	24	were
					37	beautiful
Affixes	20	cooked	35	reliable	34	international
	24	walked	39	actually	41	advertisement
	30	vacation	41	profession	45	necessary
	32	manager	43	carriage	47	arrogance
	33	electric	47	sufficient	49	anonymous
	37	subscription	51	repetitious	52	acquaintance
	39	skiing	56	vacillate	53	exacerbate
	41	enthusiastic			54	conscientious
	51	treacherous				
Silent *b*	29	comb			36	doubt
Silent *w*	35	sword				
Silent *g*			34	design		
			45	foreign	58	impugn
Qu: /kw/			57	soliloquy	29	question
					48	exquisite

(continued)

Table 4.6 (*Continued*)

Skill	Item	Form A	Item	Form B	Item	Form C
French origin	48	bouquet	48	bureau	56	camouflage
	50	lacquer	54	rendezvous		
	57	crevasse	55	parquet		
	59	bouillon	58	liaison		
Greek origin	40	gymnasium	60	hemorrhage	51	dilemma
	55	chimerical				
Words ending in consonant -*le*	47	tenta<u>cle</u>	20	tab<u>le</u>	27	han<u>dle</u>
			22	peo<u>ple</u>	39	bicy<u>cle</u>
Soft *c* or *g*	45	<u>c</u>yst	53	ven<u>ge</u>ance	35	<u>g</u>eneral
	49	exa<u>gg</u>erate			43	con<u>g</u>enial
Hard *c* or *g*	38	lea<u>gu</u>e	44	dialo<u>gu</u>e	33	<u>g</u>arage
	46	ne<u>g</u>otiate				
-*ough* pattern			28	bou<u>gh</u>t		
			33	cou<u>gh</u>		
-*eigh* pattern			37	nei<u>gh</u>bor		
-*sc* pattern			40	<u>sc</u>enery	57	iride<u>sc</u>ent
					59	<u>sc</u>intillant
Multisyllabic	53	vituperative	32	adventure	30	popular
	54	omniscient	50	anthropomorphic	60	lachrymose
	56	sergeant				
	58	lackadaisical				
	60	camaraderie				

Test 6: Writing Samples

This test requires the individual to produce meaningful written sentences in response to a variety of tasks. Low performance may result from limits in: (a) oral language, (b) vocabulary, (c) organizational ability, (d) knowledge, or (e) spelling skill. The individual's attitude toward writing may also influence performance. Although errors in spelling and usage are not penalized on this test (unless the response is illegible), you can gain additional qualitative information through a careful analysis of the individual's responses. For example, you may note that the individual does not: (a) start sentences with capital letters, (b) use ending punctuation, (c) spell words accurately, or (d) write using complete sentences. Or you may observe that the individual makes errors in spelling and usage, but writes descriptive, interesting sentences that address the task demands. You may also wish to compare Writing Samples to measures of oral language to see if writing ability is commensurate with receptive and expressive language.

Test 11: Sentence Writing Fluency

This test requires the individual to produce, in writing, legible, simple sentences with acceptable English syntax. Low performance on this test may result from poor attention, poor motor control and handwriting, limited spelling or reading skills, slow cognitive processing speed (*Gs*), or a response style that interferes with performance (slow and accurate, fast and inaccurate, slow and inaccurate, etc.). You may wish to compare the results on this test to other timed measures to see whether the person generally works slowly or has a particular difficulty with writing speed.

Test 14: Editing

This test requires the ability to identify and correct errors in punctuation, capitalization, spelling, and usage in short written passages read by the examinee. Low performance may result from limited instruction, lack of knowledge of writing conventions, failure to self-monitor or self-correct errors, or poor reading skill.

Test 16: Spelling of Sounds

This test requires the individual to spell nonsense words that conform to conventional phonics and spelling rules. Both phonological coding (*Ga*) and orthographic coding are measured by this test. Low performance may result from poor attention, poor phonological processing, poor orthographic awareness, or low phoneme–grapheme knowledge. You can compare results from this test to the Word Attack test or to tests from the WJ IV OL (Segmentation, Sound Blending, and Sound Awareness) to help determine whether difficulties result from phonological problems or limited knowledge of phoneme–grapheme relationships.

An analysis of errors can be particularly valuable on this test. Brady, a sixth-grade student, spelled the nonsense words exactly like they sound (e.g., *quib* as *kwib* and *scritch* as *skrich*). Although this indicates good skill with phonemic segmentation, it indicates a lack of sensitivity to common English spelling patterns. Brady does not need practice sequencing sounds, but rather needs to be taught common English spelling patterns, such as -*tch*.

Written Language Clusters

The WJ IV ACH has four written language clusters: Written Language, Broad Written Language, Basic Writing Skills, and Written Expression. All of these clusters may be used when calculating intra-achievement variations and ability/achievement discrepancies. Rapid Reference 4.13 lists several possible instructional recommendations for individuals with low written language performance.

≡ Rapid Reference 4.13

Instructional Implications for Individuals With Low Written Language Achievement

- Match instruction to developmental level.
- Teach the use of a computer, including the spell-check feature.
- Provide alternatives to writing (e.g., oral responses).
- Provide preferential seating for copying tasks, or limit or omit copying tasks.
- Simplify or shorten spelling lists or other written assignments.
- Teach the spellings of high-frequency words.
- Teach a word-study strategy that will enhance spelling skill.
- Teach editing skills.
- Provide extended time for completing written tasks.
- Teach different types of sentence structures.
- Use sentence-combining exercises.
- Help the individual increase vocabulary and other oral language abilities.
- Use story frames or other graphic organizers.
- Teach the student how to write various types of text structures (e.g., descriptive, compare–contrast, persuasive).

Written Language

This cluster contains two tests: Spelling and Writing Samples. Because it includes a measure of basic writing skills and a measure of written expression, this cluster may be used to estimate a person's general writing ability. This cluster does not include a timed test, so it provides a measure of written language rather than automaticity and ease of writing.

Broad Written Language

This cluster includes three tests: Spelling, Writing Samples, and Sentence Writing Fluency. It provides a broad, comprehensive view of the individual's written language achievement. Task demands include spelling single-word responses, expressing ideas to various tasks, and writing simple sentences quickly. You may want to compare the results from this cluster to the results on the Broad Reading cluster and to the Oral Language cluster from the WJ IV OL to help determine the impact of oral language and/or reading skills on written language performance.

Basic Writing Skills

This cluster comprises two tests: Spelling and Editing. It provides a measure of basic writing skills in isolated and context-based formats. Task demands include writing letters, spelling single words, and identifying and correcting errors in spelling, usage, capitalization, and punctuation. Because Editing requires the examinee to read the items and then identify and correct the errors, you will want to consider the impact of the examinee's reading ability on performance. You may also wish to compare the results of this cluster with the Written Expression cluster to determine whether basic writing skills are affecting performance. Mastery of basic skills is a fundamental part of complex meaningful written expression. Error analysis of the two tests in this cluster may help identify the individual's developmental level in spelling.

Written Expression

This cluster includes two tests: Writing Samples and Sentence Writing Fluency. It provides a measure of meaningful written expression and automaticity with writing. You may compare the results of this cluster to the results on the Reading

Comprehension and Basic Writing Skills clusters, or the Oral Expression cluster from the WJ IV OL. Low performance may result from low oral language or limited basic writing skills.

INTERPRETING THE CROSS-DOMAIN CLUSTERS

Cross-domain clusters represent a mix of reading, writing, and math tasks grouped in the areas of academic skills, academic fluency, or academic applications. Additional clusters include Brief Achievement, Broad Achievement, Academic Knowledge, and Phoneme–Grapheme Knowledge.

Academic Skills Cluster

This cross-academic cluster is composed of the three basic skill tests: Letter-Word Identification, Calculation, and Spelling. It provides a general, basic skills achievement level and can help determine whether the individual's level of basic skills is similar or variable across the three academic areas. Consider whether basic skills facilitate or inhibit the individual's performance. Low performance may suggest particular curricular adaptations, such as use of books on CD during reading time or a calculator during math activities. Students with low performance in one or more areas often require direct, explicit instruction to improve the accuracy of skills.

Academic Fluency Cluster

This cross-domain cluster is composed of the three fluency tests: Sentence Reading Fluency, Math Facts Fluency, and Sentence Writing Fluency. It provides a general academic fluency level. This cluster can help determine whether the individual's level of automaticity with basic skills is facilitating or inhibiting academic performance. Note whether the individual's speed of performance is similar or variable across the three academic areas. For example, a person may work slowly on reading and writing tasks, but at an average rate on measures of mathematics. In many cases, low performance on this cluster when contrasted with measures of (Gc), such as the Academic Knowledge cluster, may suggest a need for extended time or shortened assignments. Additional information can be obtained by comparing the Academic Fluency cluster to the Perceptual Speed (Gs-P) and the Cognitive Processing Speed (Gs) clusters in the WJ IV COG. This may help determine whether speed is generally slow or performance on one or more academic tasks is slowed because of low basic skills.

Academic Applications Cluster

This cross-domain cluster is composed of the three application tests: Passage Comprehension, Applied Problems, and Writing Samples. It provides a general measure of an individual's ability to reason and apply academic knowledge. As with the other cross-domain clusters, note whether the individual's performance on the tests in this cluster is similar or variable. Also, consider the impact of basic skills, fluency, and oral language proficiency when interpreting this cluster. Low performance may suggest a need for adjusting the difficulty level of the instructional materials. Students with low Academic Applications often need adjustment in the difficulty levels of instructional tasks.

Academic Knowledge

Academic Knowledge contains three tests: Science, Social Studies, and Humanities. These tests require the individual to respond orally to questions. Early items require the examinee only to point to a response. This test measures acquired curricular knowledge, an aspect of comprehension-knowledge (Gc). A broad sample of the individual's range of scientific knowledge, general knowledge, cultural knowledge, and geographic knowledge is measured by the Academic Knowledge cluster. Some individuals will have high scores in one area, but not another. Todd, a ninth-grade student, knew a lot about science, but little about humanities. Nicole, a college sophomore and English major, knew a lot about humanities, but recalled little about science.

Low performance may result from limited vocabulary, limited exposure to curricular areas, or both. This cluster can provide valuable insights into the interests of the individual as well as the level of crystallized intelligence. No reading is required. Therefore, the results can help determine whether the individual's knowledge base is impacting performance in the other academic areas. If the WJ IV COG has been administered, results from this test can be compared to the comprehension-knowledge (Gc) cluster. If the WJ IV OL has been administered, results can be compared to the Oral Language and Listening Comprehension clusters. In addition, within the WJ IV ACH, this cluster can be used as the ability score in an ability/achievement comparison procedure to help determine whether reading, writing, and/or mathematics are in line with the person's content knowledge.

Phoneme–Grapheme Knowledge

This cluster is a combination of two tests: Word Attack and Spelling of Sounds. It may be used to evaluate the individual's proficiency using phonics for reading and spelling. The tasks require the individual to decode (read) and encode (spell) pseudo words or nonsense words. Although they have no meaning, these words all use possible English spelling patterns (orthography). Low performance may result from poor phonological skills or limited orthographic skills, or both. A low score may also be attributable to poor or limited instruction. To help understand the reasons for an individual's low performance, compare this cluster to the auditory processing (*Ga*) cluster in the WJ IV COG or the Phonetic Coding cluster in the WJ IV OL. The Phoneme–Grapheme cluster can be especially useful in documenting specific reading disabilities (dyslexia).

Brief Achievement Cluster

The Brief Achievement cluster is a combination of three tests: Letter-Word Identification, Applied Problems, and Spelling. This cluster provides a quick screening of the person's levels of performance in reading, writing, and math.

Broad Achievement Cluster

This cluster is composed of nine tests in the Standard Battery. These nine tests are used to create the Broad Reading, Broad Mathematics, and Broad Written Language clusters. The purpose of the Broad Achievement cluster is to provide a general level of academic proficiency. The cluster can be used to identify students with very limited or advanced performance levels across curricular areas. It is also helpful when you need a global view of the individual's overall performance across the various achievement domains. The tests required for obtaining the Broad Achievement cluster also yield the four additional cross-

> ### CAUTION
> ....
> #### Interpretation of Global Scores
>
> Use care when interpreting global scores that are composed of tests measuring many different skills or abilities, such as the Broad Achievement score. Although this score provides an estimate of general academic performance, it reveals little about the underlying scores upon which it is based. Examine how the person did on the clusters and tests to obtain information about the examinee's unique achievement patterns.

domain clusters (Skills, Fluency, Applications, and Brief Achievement) previously described.

INTERPRETING INSTRUCTIONAL ZONES

The instructional zone, a special application of the RPI, identifies an individual's present level of functioning from easy (the independent level) to difficult (the frustration level). The instructional zone extends from an RPI of 96/90 to an RPI of 75/90. An individual will perceive tasks that fall at an RPI of 96/90 as "easy" (EASY), whereas tasks that fall at an RPI of 75/90 will be "difficult" (DIFF). When using the online scoring program, select the Age/Grade Profile report to get a graphic representation of the examinee's instructional or developmental zone, ranging from the independent level to the frustration level. The grade equivalent (GE) printed below the left end of the shaded band represents the easy or independent level. The GE printed below the right end of the shaded band represents the difficult or frustration level. The obtained GE represents the midpoint of the zone and provides an estimate of instructional level. If you choose age norms, the developmental zone is represented with age equivalents (AEs). The concept of the RPI is similar to that found in informal reading inventories, in which instructional reading levels are identified that range from the independent (easy) level to the frustration (difficult) level.

> **DON'T FORGET**
> ....
>
> Independent level = RPIs of 96/90 or higher (easy)
>
> Instructional level = RPIs of 76/90 to 95/90
>
> Frustration level = RPIs of 75/90 or lower (difficult)

Vygotsky's (1978) zone of proximal development is a similar concept to the instructional zone. This learning zone represents the distance between an individual's actual developmental level and the level of potential development when assisted by a more knowledgeable other. The concept of developmental ranges is helpful in planning instruction to support growth. Ideally, within a school setting, both homework and seatwork would be at the independent level, whereas work that is supported by others (teachers, peers, parents) would be at the instructional level.

Examples of the types of statements used to describe the instructional zone include:

- Arnold's instructional zone on the Basic Writing Skills cluster indicates that spelling and editing tasks will be easy at the beginning second-grade level but difficult at the beginning third-grade level.
- Appropriate instructional materials for June in basic math skills would range from beginning fifth-grade level (easy) to end of sixth-grade level (difficult).
- Jared's instructional zone on the Math Problem Solving cluster indicates that he will find math reasoning tasks at the 9th-grade level to be easy, whereas tasks at the 11th-grade level will be very difficult.

The instructional zone also depicts the rate of growth in a particular ability at a particular point in time. A narrow range means that growth is rapid during the stage of development, whereas a wide range means that growth is slow. For example, the range on the Word Attack test for a ninth-grade student is wide because the student's ability to pronounce pseudo words (phonically regular nonsense words) is not changing much during this time period. In contrast, the range on a test such as Letter-Word Identification is narrow because the ability to decode increases at a steady rate across the school years.

Table 4.7 illustrates the instructional zones for several achievement clusters for Toby, a student near the end of fifth grade (5.8). First, note the grade equivalents in the column labeled GE. These are the obtained grade equivalents on the task and represent the midpoint of the instructional zone. Next, note the EASY to DIFF columns, which represent the instructional zone ranging from the independent to frustration levels for Toby. A review of this information helps us understand Toby's instructional needs. We can see that reading is problematic whereas math is not. Every instructional zone for a reading cluster is below Toby's grade placement of grade 5.8. His frustration level on the reading clusters is in the third- to fourth-grade range with the exception of reading fluency, which is at the second-grade level. The

Table 4.7 Instructional Zones for Several Achievement Clusters

Cluster/Test	W	GE	EASY to DIFF	
Reading	485	3.3	2.6	4.3
Broad Reading	466	2.4	2.0	3.0
Basic Reading Skills	483	3.0	2.3	4.0
Reading Fluency	450	1.8	1.4	2.1
Broad Mathematics	539	13.4	10.5	>17.9
Math Calc Skills	540	13.0	9.1	>17.9

extreme limits in reading fluency explain why the instructional zone for Broad Reading, which includes fluency, is lower than the instructional zone for Reading, which does not include fluency. Clearly, Toby will have little success on grade-level reading tasks. To ensure success and classroom participation, the level of instruction will need to be adapted for Toby, or he will need the textbooks to be recorded.

INTERPRETING STANDARD SCORE OR PERCENTILE RANK RANGES

Viewing a range of scores is often preferred to interpreting a single score because every score includes some error. To account for this error, confidence bands are used. For example, at the 68% level of confidence, the standard score or percentile rank range portrays the ±1 SEM confidence band. This band, extending from a point 1 SEM below the individual's obtained score to a point 1 SEM above the individual's obtained score, is the area in which the true score falls two out of three times. If a higher degree of confidence is desired, the online scoring program provides an option to select a 90% or 95% level of confidence. A 95% confidence band (±2 SEM) represents the region in which an individual's true ability would fall 19 times out of 20.

Table 4.8 illustrates the standard score confidence bands at the 68% level of confidence for several achievement clusters. Although most of the ranges for the clusters shown are three to four standard scores above and below the obtained score, Reading Fluency has a larger range of scores, meaning there is more error associated with the score. Reporting the range of scores increases confidence that the individual's true score is represented. Select the Standard Score/Percentile

Table 4.8 Standard Score Confidence Bands (68% level) for Several Achievement Clusters

Cluster/Test	SS (68% Band)
Reading	83 (80–86)
Broad Reading	70 (66–73)
Basic Reading Skills	82 (79–85)
Reading Fluency	64 (58–69)
Broad Mathematics	133 (129–137)
Math Calc Skills	128 (124–132)

Rank Profile report when using the online scoring program to obtain a graphic representation of this information.

You can use the SS confidence bands to evaluate differences in an individual's performance on administered tests. Use caution, however, when interpreting these differences because some degree of variability in performance is to be expected. The significance of observed differences decreases as the number of comparisons increases. In addition, you must determine whether a statistically significant difference has any practical or educational implications. A statistically significant discrepancy may exist between measures but have little educational relevance.

For example, Ralph's standard score of 100 on Broad Mathematics was significantly lower than his advanced performance in other areas of achievement. He is unlikely to need intervention, however, because this ability falls within the average range. As a general rule, do not use single scores on individual tests to attempt precise descriptions of specific academic skills; rather, use scores to generate hypotheses about academic performance. You can derive more reliable estimates of achievement from cluster scores than from individual test scores.

One way to approach test or cluster analysis is to evaluate the scores in reference to the norm group. For the SS ranges, the reference point is a mean of 100 (coupled with a standard deviation of 15). For analysis purposes, (a) standard scores above 115 always indicate a strength (one or more standard deviations above the mean), (b) standard scores of 85 to 115 usually indicate average ability (within one standard deviation from the mean), and (c) standard scores below 85 usually indicate a weakness (one or more standard deviations below the mean).

Sometimes, clinicians discuss "relative" strengths and weaknesses. This concept becomes particularly relevant when analyzing the performance of very low-functioning or high-functioning students. For example, a person may obtain a standard score of 80 in Broad Reading and 60 in Broad Mathematics. Although both scores are below average, reading could be described as a "relative" strength for this individual. A "twice exceptional" student (e.g., a gifted student who also has a reading disability) may have superior scores in Broad Mathematics (e.g., a standard score of 130), but only average scores in Reading (e.g., a standard score of 95). Reading would be viewed as a relative weakness.

Because all of the WJ IV ACH clusters and tests have a mean of 100 and a standard deviation of 15, you can statistically evaluate performance across the clusters and the test scores. To say that one score is meaningfully (i.e., statistically significantly) higher than another score, you first need to determine that the difference between the two scores does not represent chance variation. It is not possible to simply look at two scores and say that one is statistically higher or lower than the other score. A statistically significant difference indicates a high probability that the academic skills measured by the two scores differ. In other words, the difference is greater than that which is expected to occur simply by chance.

The main questions to ask are:

- Do the individual's scores on the clusters differ significantly from each other?
- Do the individual's test scores differ significantly from one another?

The following list provides three guidelines for determining the likelihood that a true difference in abilities is represented by the difference between the scores on any two tests or any two clusters.

1. If the 68% confidence bands for any two tests or clusters overlap at all, assume no difference exists between the person's two abilities.
2. If a separation exists between the ends of the two test confidence bands that is less than the width of the wider of the two confidence bands, assume that a possible difference exists between the individual's two abilities. A difference of this size would occur on average about eight times in 100 if a single comparison is made. A common practice with batteries such as the WJ IV ACH is to compare more than one pair of tests at a time or to look only at the most extreme examples. Under these conditions, the probability increases that at least one difference will be observed even though the two abilities do not differ. For example, if 10 comparisons are being made, a difference of this size would occur by chance about 57 times in 100.
3. If the separation between the two confidence bands is greater than the width of the wider band, assume that a real difference exists between the individual's two abilities. A difference this size would occur on average about two times in 1,000 if a single comparison is being made. (The actual probability ranges from 0 to five times in 1,000 depending on the amount of separation.) If 10 comparisons were being made, a difference of this size would occur by chance about 20 times in 1,000.

You need to determine the significance of both high and low scores. For example, in testing an adult, Ms. Garrigus, you observed that she had a significant weakness in spelling. Her job as an engineer, however, does not require that her reports and memos have accurate spelling. Thus, in this situation, there are currently no vocational implications because the spelling weakness does not cause

CAUTION

Do Not Overinterpret Differences in Scores

A certain amount of variability is expected in the general population. The significance of observed differences decreases as the number of comparisons increases. You must determine whether observed differences have any practical applications or educational implications.

any problems. If, however, Ms. Garrigus decides to become an English teacher, her lower spelling abilities may become an issue.

The goal of profile analysis is to generate hypotheses about a person's achievement. The hypotheses generated need to be compared with other information gathered about the examinee, including relevant background knowledge, additional testing, and interviews with teachers and parents. When the hypotheses are reasonable, you can use them to: (a) clarify the specific nature of an individual's academic performance, (b) clarify the severity of any problems in academic development, (c) develop intervention recommendations, (d) select appropriate educational programs, or (e) consider an appropriate academic or vocational placement.

To determine the factors that might account for a certain pattern of scores, consider both the extrinsic (or external) factors, as well as the intrinsic (or internal) factors. Extrinsic factors include the person's socioeconomic status, education, past services and interventions, special training, social and physical environment, family background, and so forth. In some cases, differences among scores may be factors associated with examiner characteristics or factors associated with the assessment situation. Internal factors include the examinee's attention, health, temperament, physical and mental status, and motivation and interest.

INTERPRETING VARIATIONS AND COMPARISONS

Two types of procedures are available on the WJ IV: intra-ability variations (variations among abilities) and ability/achievement comparisons (discrepancies between a predictor score and measured academic performance). The primary purpose of the intra-ability variation procedures is diagnosis, whereas the primary function of the ability/achievement comparison procedures is prediction. The following section describes these options in more detail. Table 4.9 indicates the variations or comparisons that are available when using the WJ IV ACH alone or with the WJ IV OL or the WJ IV COG.

Because all norms for the WJ IV ACH, the WJ IV OL, and the WJ IV COG are based on data from the same sample, actual discrepancy norms are available. This eliminates the need to estimate the discrepancy by using a regression equation

Table 4.9 Variation and Comparison Calculations Available in the WJ IV

Intra-Ability Variation	Ability/Achievement Comparisons
Intra-achievement (ACH only)	Academic knowledge/achievement (ACH only)
Academic skills/Academic fluency/Academic Applications (ACH only)	Oral language/achievement (OL and ACH)
Intra-oral language (OL only)	GIA/achievement (COG and ACH)
Intra-cognitive (COG only)	Scholastic aptitude/achievement (COG and ACH)
	Gf-Gc/other ability (COG and ACH and OL)

or a table based on the equation. The co-norming of the WJ IV also provides an accurate means for evaluating the significance of a variation or a discrepancy. These advantages are available to the examiner when using any of the variation or comparison procedures shown in Table 4.9.

Interpreting the Significance of a Variation or Discrepancy

Understanding the "significance" of a variation or discrepancy is based on interpretation of either of two scores: the discrepancy percentile rank (Discrepancy PR) or the discrepancy standard deviation (Discrepancy SD). These scores help

DON'T FORGET
....

The Purpose of WJ IV Variation and Comparison Procedures

Intra-ability variations are designed for diagnosis.
- Used to identify strengths and weaknesses
- Used to help with early identification of problems
- Used to help document a specific learning disability

Ability/achievement comparisons are designed for prediction.
- Used to estimate expected performance in the near term based on a selected ability
- Used to illustrate performance relative to peers
- Used to help document the concept of "unexpected" underachievement

interpret the presence and severity of the variations and discrepancies. The Discrepancy PR reflects the percent of the population that possesses a discrepancy (difference score) of that magnitude, such as 1% or 95%. The Discrepancy PR score differs from other percentile ranks in that it compares the person to age or grade mates of the same ability or other score, not to the entire age or grade norm group. The Discrepancy SD is a standardized z-score that changes the obtained percentile rank into standard deviation units, related to a criterion such as −1.5 standard deviations.

When describing certain variations or discrepancies, refer to differences as being *relative* (compared to the person's other abilities) strengths or weaknesses. For example, on the intra-achievement variation procedure, a student had standard scores in the low 60s on Broad Reading, Broad Mathematics, and Broad Written Language. In contrast, the student's standard score on Academic Knowledge was 80. The score report identifies Academic Knowledge as a significant strength. In the report or description of performance, you would describe this as a relative strength because none of the scores fell within the average range.

Intra-Ability Variation Procedures

The intra-ability variation procedures are based on the practice of examining test performance to determine patterns of strengths and weaknesses. As noted in Table 4.10, four types of intra-ability variations are available on the WJ IV. With these variations, equal interest exists in either strengths or weaknesses in one area relative to the average of all other areas being considered. Only two intra-ability variation procedures are available when using just the WJ IV ACH: Intra-achievement and Academic Skills/Academic Fluency/Academic Applications. The others require using the WJ IV COG or WJ IV OL.

Table 4.10 Four Types of Intra-Ability Variations in the WJ IV

WJ IV ACH	WJ IV COG	WJ IV OL
Intra-achievement (Requires a minimum of ACH Tests 1–6)	Intra-cognitive (Requires a minimum of COG Tests 1–7)	Intra-oral language (Requires a minimum of OL Tests 1–4)
Academic Skills/Academic Fluency/ Academic Applications (Requires a minimum of ACH Tests 1–6 and Tests 9–11)		

Intra-Achievement Variation Procedure

The intra-achievement variation allows examiners to analyze an individual's academic test and cluster scores and to explore strengths and weaknesses. For example, a person may have a strength in reading, but a weakness in mathematics. These variations within achievement can help determine a person's present educational needs.

Examiners can calculate intra-achievement variations for three curricular areas (reading, mathematics, and writing) if Tests 1 through 6 have been administered. Additional tests and clusters can be added into this variation procedure (see Table 4.11). Individuals who have specific achievement strengths or weaknesses,

Table 4.11 WJ IV Intra-Achievement Variation Procedure

Intra-Achievement Variations	
Required from WJ IV ACH (Tests 1-6)	Optional from WJ IV ACH
Test 1: Letter-Word Identification	Uses same predictor as Letter-Word Identification Test 7: Word Attack Test 8: Oral Reading Basic Reading Skills Reading Fluency (also requires Test 9: Sentence Reading Fluency)
Test 2: Applied Problems	Uses same predictor as Applied Problems Test 13: Number Matrices Math Problem Solving
Test 3: Spelling	Uses same predictor as Spelling Test 14: Editing Test 16: Spelling of Sounds Basic Writing Skills
Test 4: Passage Comprehension	Uses same predictor as Passage Comprehension Test 9: Sentence Reading Fluency Test 12: Reading Recall Test 15: Word Reading Fluency Test 17: Reading Vocabulary Reading Comprehension Reading Comprehension-Extended Reading Rate
Test 5: Calculation	Uses same predictor as Calculation Test 10: Math Facts Fluency Math Calculation Skills
Test 6: Writing Samples	Uses same predictor as Writing Samples Test 11: Sentence Writing Fluency Written Expression

Table 4.12 Results from the Intra-Achievement Variation Procedure

Variations	Standard Scores			Discrepancy		Interpretation
Intra-achievement (Extended)	Actual	Predicted	Difference	PR	SD	+/−1.50 (SEE)
Basic Reading Skills	82	110	−28	0.1	−2.97	Weakness
Reading Comprehension	81	108	−27	0.3	−2.76	Weakness
Reading Fluency	64	109	−45	<0.1	−4.26	Weakness
Reading Rate	71	107	−36	<0.1	−3.12	Weakness
Math Calculation Skills	128	97	31	99.9	+2.98	Strength
Math Problem Solving	141	100	41	>99.9	+3.62	Strength
Basic Writing Skills	98	108	−10	13	−1.11	—
Written Expression	99	106	−7	27	−0.62	—

such as superior math skills relative to the average of all other achievement areas, exhibit an intra-achievement variation. Table 4.12 illustrates results from an intra-achievement variation for Rebecca, a fifth-grade student. Because this variation includes more than Tests 1 through 6, it is labeled (Extended).

Interpreting the intra-achievement variation procedure. The Actual Standard Score (SS) column in Table 4.12 shows the standard score the individual actually obtained on the test. The Predicted SS column shows the individual's predicted or expected SS. The Difference column shows the difference between the actual SS and the predicted SS. A negative difference indicates the actual score was lower than predicted. A positive difference indicates the actual score was higher than predicted. The PR column shows the discrepancy percentile rank (Discrepancy PR). This score indicates the percentage of the individual's peer group (same age or grade and same predictor score) that achieved variations or differences of the same size as the individual achieved. The Discrepancy SD column shows the difference, in units of the standard error of estimate, between the individual's actual and predicted scores. A negative value in the Discrepancy SD column indicates the individual's actual achievement was lower than predicted. A positive value indicates the individual's actual achievement was higher than predicted. This statement of significance (Discrepancy SD) can be used instead of the percentile rank in programs with selection criteria based on a difference equal to or greater than, for example, one and one-half times the standard deviation. Any individual who had a Discrepancy SD of −1.5 or lower would meet this selection criterion. The final column indicates whether the variation is a significant strength or weakness. If performance is at or above +1.5 SD, a relative strength is documented. If performance is at or below −1.5 SD, a relative weakness is documented. Dashes in the final column indicate the variation was not significantly different than expected.

Using Basic Reading Skills as an example (see Table 4.12), the actual SS is 82 and the predicted score is 110. Because the actual SS (82) is lower than predicted (110), there is a negative difference (−28). The discrepancy PR of 0.1 indicates that only one out of 1,000 grademates with the same predictor score had a negative difference as large or larger between his or her actual and predicted scores on Basic Reading Skills. In other words, less than 1% of peers (same age or grade and same predictor) scored this low or lower on Basic Reading Skills. The actual score is nearly three standard deviations (−2.97) below prediction, indicating a significant weakness for this individual. The weakness in Basic Reading Skills is relative to performance on the other areas, but it is also a normative weakness (SS < 85).

Other results shown in Table 4.12 indicate that this individual had significant weaknesses in Reading Comprehension, Reading Fluency, and Reading Rate. In addition, this person had significant strengths in Math Calculation Skills and Math Problem Solving, but did not have significant variations in Basic Writing Skills or Written Expression. The following list presents a few examples of how to discuss these scores in a report.

- In Math Calculation Skills, only one out of 1,000 grade peers with the same predicted achievement score as Rebecca would obtain a standard score of 128 or higher (or her score exceeded 999 out of 1,000 grade peers with the same predicted score) (Discrepancy PR = 99.9).
- On the intra-achievement variations, less than one in 1,000 grademates with the same predicted score would obtain a score as high or higher on the Math Problem Solving cluster (Discrepancy PR = >99.9).
- Math Problem Solving and Math Calculation skills are significant strengths relative to performance in the other achievement areas and are also normative strengths (SS > 115).
- Rebecca has significant weaknesses in reading and significant strengths in math, suggesting the presence of a specific reading disability.

Although professionals must evaluate the examinee's entire performance, clinical history, and background information to arrive at the most reasonable hypothesis that accounts for significant differences among abilities, significant intra-achievement variations may indicate one or more of the following:

- Varied interests
- Strengths or weaknesses in processing information
- Strengths or weaknesses in academic performance
- Strengths or weaknesses in speed of processing (e.g., as demonstrated on the timed tests versus the skills and/or application tests)
- Strengths or weaknesses in the curricula
- Sensory impairments
- Specific learning disabilities
- Limited educational opportunities

Academic Skills/Academic Fluency/Academic Applications Variation Procedure

Nine achievement tests are required for this variation procedure: three in reading (Letter-Word Identification, Passage Comprehension, Sentence Reading Fluency), three in written language (Spelling, Writing Samples, Sentence Writing Fluency), and three in mathematics (Applied Problems, Calculation, Math Facts Fluency). The person's performance in skills, fluency, and applications is compared across the academic areas of reading, written language, and mathematics.

Three additional clusters can be added to this variation procedure: Reading Rate from the WJ IV ACH and Cognitive Processing Speed and Perceptual Speed from the WJ IV COG. Table 4.13 illustrates an example of the Academic Skills/ Academic Fluency/Academic Applications variation procedure.

Other Intra-Ability Variation Procedures

The two remaining procedures, intra-cognitive and intra-oral language, require use of the WJ IV COG and the WJ IV OL. When using the WJ IV COG, the intra-cognitive variation procedure helps document specific cognitive strengths

Table 4.13 Example of Academic Skills/Academic Fluency/Academic Applications Variation Procedure

Variations Academic Skills/Academic Fluency/Academic Applications	Standard Scores			Discrepancy		Interpretation ±1.50 (SEE)
	Actual	Predicted	Difference	PR	SD	
Academic Skills	103	95	8	85	+1.05	—
Academic Fluency	84	95	−11	14	−1.10	—
Academic Applications	106	103	3	59	+0.22	—

and weaknesses often required in determining the presence of a specific learning disability. The intra-oral language procedure requires the WJ IV OL and allows examiners to analyze an individual's strengths and weaknesses across several domains of oral language. See Chapter 5 for more information about the intra-oral language variation procedure.

Ability/Achievement Comparisons

Ability/achievement models use certain abilities to predict academic performance. The five ability/achievement comparison procedures available in the WJ IV provide a means for comparing an individual's current academic performance with the average academic performance for all others in the population with similar ability. Only one ability/achievement comparison option (academic knowledge/achievement) is available when using the WJ IV ACH. The other four procedures require the use of the WJ IV COG or the WJ IV OL in conjunction with the WJ IV ACH.

Academic Knowledge/Achievement Comparison Procedure

Since Academic Knowledge is a strong measure of acquired knowledge, or Gc, and does not require reading, writing, or math, it serves as a good predictor of academic ability. This procedure allows the examiner to determine if current achievement levels are commensurate with the individual's store of acquired content knowledge.

The Academic Knowledge cluster comprises Test 18: Science, Test 19: Social Studies, and Test 20: Humanities. The standard score for this cluster is used as the predictor of expected achievement. The individual's expected achievement is then compared to his or her actual achievement. Examinees with expected scores significantly higher than their actual achievement scores exhibit a relative strength in academic knowledge with weaknesses in one or more areas of achievement. If expected scores are significantly lower than actual achievement, the individual exhibits a relative weakness in academic knowledge with strengths in one or more areas of achievement. In addition, you can include two clusters from the WJ IV OL in this comparison procedure. Table 4.14 lists the various clusters than can be included in this ability/achievement comparison procedure. Table 4.15 illustrates an example of the Academic Knowledge/Achievement comparison for Heather, a high school sophomore. The Academic Knowledge cluster score in this example is a standard score of 127. It is used as the ability score, or predictor, to predict achievement.

Table 4.14 Academic Knowledge/Achievement Comparisons

Predictor	Achievement Clusters That May Be Compared	Oral Language Clusters That May Be Compared
Academic Knowledge	Brief Achievement	Phonetic Coding
	Broad Achievement	Speed of Lexical Access
	Reading	
	Broad Reading	
	Basic Reading Skills	
	Reading Comprehension	
	Reading Comprehension–Extended	
	Reading Fluency	
	Reading Rate	
	Mathematics	
	Broad Mathematics	
	Math Calculation Skills	
	Math Problem Solving	
	Written Language	
	Broad Written Language	
	Basic Writing Skills	
	Written Expression	
	Academic Skills	
	Academic Fluency	
	Academic Applications	

The correlations between Academic Knowledge (the ability score) and each achievement area are used to create the predicted score shown in the predicted score column. The final column indicates whether the achievement area was significantly higher (Yes +) or lower (Yes −) than predicted based on the Academic Knowledge cluster score. In the example shown in Table 4.15, achievement was significantly lower than predicted in Broad Achievement and all the reading clusters reported. Achievement was significantly higher than predicted in Broad Mathematics and Math Problem Solving.

Table 4.15 Example of Academic Knowledge/Achievement Comparisons

Comparisons Academic Knowledge/ Achievement	Standard Scores			Discrepancy		Significant at ±1.5 SD (SEE)
	Actual	Predicted	Difference	PR	SD	
Broad Achievement	95	114	−19	7	−1.51	Yes (−)
Broad Reading	70	112	−42	<0.1	−3.27	Yes (−)
Basic Reading Skills	82	113	−31	1	−2.39	Yes (−)
Reading Comprehension	81	111	−30	1	−2.18	Yes (−)
Broad Mathematics	133	113	20	94	+1.55	Yes (+)
Math Calculation Skills	128	111	17	90	+1.26	No
Math Problem Solving	141	116	25	98	+2.08	Yes (+)
Broad Written Language	93	113	−20	8	−1.42	No
Basic Writing Skills	98	114	−16	10	−1.27	No
Written Expression	99	110	−11	23	−0.73	No

Examples of statements that may be used to describe the results of this procedure would be:

- Using Heather's Academic Knowledge score (SS = 127) to predict her achievement, less than one out of 1,000 of her peers (same grade, same predictor) would obtain a Broad Reading score as low or lower (Discrepancy PR = <0.1).
- In Reading Comprehension, only one out of 100 grademates with the same predictor would have a negative difference of this magnitude or greater between their actual and predicted scores (Discrepancy PR = 1). Heather's actual Reading Comprehension score (SS = 81) is significantly lower than predicted (SS = 111).
- Heather's Math Problem Solving score (SS = 141) is significantly higher than predicted. Only two out of 100 peers (same grade, same predictor) would have a score as high or higher on this cluster (or her score exceeded 98 out of 100 grade peers with the same predicted score) (Discrepancy PR = 98).
- Although Heather's Math Calculation Skills score (SS = 128) falls in the superior range and is a normative strength, it is not significantly higher than predicted based on her Academic Knowledge score (SS = 127).
- There is not a significant difference between Heather's actual Written Expression score (SS = 99) and her predicted score (SS = 110).

Other Ability/Achievement Comparison and Discrepancy Procedures

The oral language/achievement comparison procedure is available when using the WJ IV OL in conjunction with the WJ IV ACH. This procedure is particularly helpful in exploring the role oral language plays in the individual's academic performance. See Chapter 5 for more information about the oral language/ achievement comparison procedure.

The remaining procedures require the use of the WJ IV COG. Examiners may use the General Intellectual Ability (GIA) cluster, the Scholastic Aptitudes, or the *Gf-Gc* Composite as the ability score. The general intellectual ability/ achievement procedure can be used to determine the presence and severity of a discrepancy between general intellectual ability (*g*) and any particular area of achievement. When the *Gf-Gc* composite is the predictor, it can be used to determine the presence and severity of a discrepancy between the high *g*, complex cognitive abilities, and any area of achievement, as well as oral language and other cognitive abilities. In each academic area, the scholastic aptitude/ achievement comparison procedure can be used to determine whether an examinee is achieving commensurate with his or her current levels of associated cognitive abilities. More information about these procedures can be found in the WJ IV COG Examiner's Manual (Mather & Wendling, 2014b).

STEP-BY-STEP INTERPRETATION OF THE WJ IV ACH

A standardized test, such as the WJ IV ACH, is designed to be a tool used during the evaluation process, and is not meant to be the only source of information about an examinee. A test does not interpret or diagnose—that is the role of the examiner. The emphasis on standard scores and determining eligibility has led some examiners to ignore important qualitative information about the examinee's instructional needs. The following provides a step-by-step plan for analyzing performance on the WJ IV ACH and goes beyond consideration of standard scores alone.

Step 1. Interpret the Clusters

Cluster scores are the most valid and reliable scores to interpret. They indicate a more representative array of abilities as well as a larger number of items than are found in individual tests. Twenty-two clusters are available.

Reading: Reading, Broad Reading, Basic Reading Skills, Reading Comprehension, Reading Comprehension-Extended, Reading Fluency, Reading Rate

Mathematics: Mathematics, Broad Mathematics, Math Calculation Skills, Math Problem Solving

Written Language: Written Language, Broad Written Language, Basic Writing Skills, Written Expression

Cross-Domain: Academic Skills, Academic Fluency, Academic Applications, Academic Knowledge, Phoneme/Grapheme Knowledge, and Brief and Broad Achievement

- Compare results of clusters across academic areas. For example, compare reading clusters to written language, academic knowledge, or mathematics clusters. Examine the Broad Achievement clusters to determine which achievement areas are intact and which are of concern. For example, is achievement low in all academic areas or primarily in one area?
- Use the Brief or Broad Achievement score as an estimate of academic abilities if a general indicator of overall academic performance is needed.
- Compare results of clusters within an academic area. For example, when looking at a particular academic area such as reading, compare the scores from Basic Reading Skills to Reading Comprehension. Is performance low on all clusters (generalized) in that area? Is performance lower on Basic Reading Skills than on Reading Comprehension or lower on the Reading Comprehension cluster than on the Basic Reading Skills cluster?
- Use the cross-domain clusters to determine if the individual has a generalized problem in basic skills (accuracy), fluency (speed), or application of the skills (reasoning).

Step 2. Interpret the Variations and Discrepancies

- Determine whether significant intra-ability variations exist by using the intra-achievement or Academic Skills/Academic Fluency/Academic Applications variation procedures.
- Determine whether significant ability/achievement discrepancies exist by using the academic knowledge/achievement comparison procedure.
- Consider the implications of any significant variations or discrepancies.

Step 3. Interpret Instructional Ranges

- Examine the grade ranges (EASY/DIFF) to determine instructional zones. For each cluster or test, you can identify an independent (easy), instructional, and frustration (difficult) level.

Step 4. Interpret SS or PR Confidence Bands

- Examine the SS or PR ranges to determine relative standing of the individual in comparison to the peer group. Interpretation of the confidence bands can help you identify statistically significant discrepancies in the individual's performance. Determine whether the discrepancy has both practical and instructional implications.
- Analyze the differences among cluster scores to develop hypotheses about strengths and weaknesses.
- Determine whether significant differences exist among cluster scores.
- Determine whether significant differences exist among the tests that constitute a specific cluster.
- Determine whether significant differences exist among the individual test scores.

Step 5. Interpret Individual Tests (20 possible tests)

- Consider the results of each test in each cluster obtained. Are the results similar or different? It is often informative to analyze performance among the tests measuring a broad achievement area. For example, make comparisons among the three tests of the Broad Reading Cluster: Letter-Word Identification, Passage Comprehension, and Sentence Reading Fluency. Although these comparisons are open to the errors associated with multiple comparisons, they are valuable for generating hypotheses about the examinee's reading abilities. Evaluating results at the individual test level can help determine instructional plans.
- Analyze the differences among all of the test scores to see the patterns that go across different domains. For example, you may note that a person responds slowly on all timed tests or has difficulty on all tasks involving basic skills, but not on tasks involving reasoning and problem solving.

Step 6. Complete an Error Analysis

- Analyze the pattern of errors within each test. Evaluating the quality of responses will help determine the individual's level of understanding. Some responses are very close to being correct, whereas others reveal minimal understanding or limited knowledge.

Within a test, the items are arranged in order of difficulty, which will help you to evaluate the responses. For example, an examinee may complete addition problems correctly but make errors on subtraction problems involving regrouping.

- Examine a person's correct and incorrect responses to individual items to help identify error patterns and determine instructional objectives. For example, you may find that on the reading and spelling tests the individual has not learned specific phoneme–grapheme correspondences. This type of observation can lead to specific recommendations and additional assessments to investigate certain findings in more depth.

Step 7. Review and Summarize Behavioral Observations

- Review the information compiled when completing the Test Session Observations Checklist in the Test Record.
- Use the Qualitative Observation Checklists that are available for Tests 1 through 11 to help document the individual's performance on the various tasks. Consider the individual's reaction to different tasks as well as his or her response to increased difficulty of tasks. How does the individual handle increasingly difficult tasks? Does the individual respond carefully or impulsively, quickly or slowly, accurately or inaccurately? Is there a noticeable difference in attitude or behavior between academic areas?
- Consider the strategies used by the individual. Are they appropriate for the task? Is the individual flexible or rigid in applying strategies?
- Note whether the individual used self-monitoring or made self-corrections on certain tasks.
- Note any comments that were made by the examinee during the testing session. For example, Sheila, a second-grade student, told the examiner, "I like to read, but I hate math and so does my mother."

DON'T FORGET
....

Standard 10.15: The interpretation of test or test battery results for diagnostic purposes should be based on multiple sources of test and collateral information and on an understanding of the normative, empirical, and theoretical foundations, as well as the limitations, of such tests and data (AERA et al., 2014, p. 167).

Step 8. Integrate Information

- Integrate the information obtained from the current evaluation with information from other sources (e.g., classroom work, observations, interviews, other testing data, RTI data, and school records).

🐟 TEST YOURSELF 🐟

1. What is the primary purpose of the intra-ability variation procedure on the WJ IV ACH?
2. What is the primary purpose of the ability/achievement comparison procedure?
3. What cluster is used as the predictor score when calculating an ability/achievement comparison from just the WJ IV Tests of Achievement?
4. What does the EASY/DIFF grade range illustrate?
5. What does the SS confidence band illustrate?
6. Which two tests are needed for the Phoneme–Grapheme Knowledge cluster?
7. What does it mean if two tests have overlapping confidence bands?
8. Write a statement describing an intra-achievement variation PR of 0.1 on Broad Reading for an individual in eighth grade.
9. On which written language test would a weakness in oral language comprehension have the greatest impact?
   a. Writing Fluency
   b. Spelling of Sounds
   c. Writing Samples
   d. Editing
10. Which WJ IV OL test would you want to compare to the results from Passage Comprehension?
    a. Picture Vocabulary
    b. Oral Comprehension
    c. Sentence Repetition
    d. Understanding Directions

Answer: 1. Diagnosis, determination of strengths and weaknesses; 2. Prediction of achievement based upon Academic Knowledge; 3. Academic Knowledge; 4. Indicates the independent to frustration instructional levels; 5. Presents an estimate of the error around an obtained score; 6. Word Attack and Spelling of Sounds; 7. There is no statistically significant difference between the two test scores; 8. Compared to grade peers with the same predicted score, only one in 1,000 individuals would have a score as low or lower on Broad Reading; 9. c; 10. b.

Five

USE AND INTERPRETATION OF THE WJ IV TESTS OF ORAL LANGUAGE

The WJ IV Tests of Oral Language (WJ IV OL) (Schrank, Mather, et al., 2014b) are a set of tests that may be administered in conjunction with the WJ IV COG or the WJ IV ACH. The fact that the WJ IV OL is co-normed with the WJ IV COG and WJ IV ACH provides a "best-practice" scenario for identifying an individual's unique strengths and weaknesses as well as for obtaining information for instructional planning and programming. The combined and co-normed information provided by the WJ IV OL, the WJ IV COG, and the WJ IV ACH is especially appropriate for examining ability/achievement compari-sons and intra-ability variations. Ability/achievement (scholastic aptitude/achieve-ment, *Gf-Gc*/other ability, intellectual ability/achievement, academic knowledge/achievement, or oral language ability/achievement) comparisons and intra-ability variations are often used as one part of the selection criteria for learning disability programs. The oral language ability/achievement comparison is available when using the WJ IV OL and the WJ IV ACH, which is described later in the chapter. The purpose of this chapter is to explain the tests, clusters, and interpretive features of the WJ IV OL, as well as how it can be used with the WJ IV ACH.

ORGANIZATION OF THE WJ IV OL

The WJ IV OL has nine English tests and three Spanish counterparts to measure varied aspects of oral language. The three Spanish tests are adaptations of Test 1: Picture Vocabulary, Test 2: Oral Comprehension, and Test 6: Understanding Directions. These tests are all contained within one easel test book. Figure 5.1 depicts the Selective Testing Table of the WJ IV OL. Although many of these tests were included in the WJ III COG or the WJ III ACH, the extensive renorming and addition of new tests and interpretive procedures improve and increase the diagnostic capabilities. The WJ IV OL includes measures of both expressive and receptive language. Table 5.1 provides an overview of the content and task

			Oral Language Clusters									OL + COG	
			Oral Language	Broad Oral Language	Oral Expression	Listening Comprehension	Phonetic Coding	Speed of Lexical Access	Lenguaje oral	Amplio lenguaje oral	Comprensión auditiva	Vocabulary (VL/LD)	Auditory Memory Span (MS)
Oral Language Battery	OL-01	Picture Vocabulary	■	■	■							■	
	OL-02	Oral Comprehension	■	■		■							
	OL-03	Segmentation					■						
	OL-04	Rapid Picture Naming						■					
	OL-05	Sentence Repetition			■								■
	OL-06	Understanding Directions		■		■							
	OL-07	Sound Blending					■						
	OL-08	Retrieval Fluency						■					
	OL-09	Sound Awareness											
	OL-10	Vocabulario sobre sibujos							■	■			
	OL-11	Comprensión oral							■	■	■		
	OL-12	Comprensión de indicaciones								■	■		
Other Tests	COG-01	Oral Vocabulary										■	
	COG-18	Memory for Words											■

■ Tests required to create the cluster listed.

Figure 5.1 WJ IV OL Selective Testing Table

Table 5.1 Content and Task Demands of WJ IV OL Tests

Test Name	Description	Task Demands
Test 1: Picture Vocabulary Test 10: Vocabulario sobre dibujos	Measures aspects of word knowledge, a comprehension-knowledge (*Gc*) ability.	Requires naming familiar to less familiar objects in English (or Spanish).
Test 2: Oral Comprehension Test 11: Comprensión oral	Measures oral comprehension of contextual information, an aspect of comprehension-knowledge (*Gc*).	Requires listening to a short passage in English (or Spanish) and supplying a key missing word.
Test 3: Segmentation	Measures phonetic coding, a narrow auditory processing (*Ga*) ability.	Requires listening to a word and breaking it into its parts (compound words, syllables, phonemes).

Table 5.1 *(Continued)*

Test Name	Description	Task Demands
Test 4: Rapid Picture Naming	Measures speed of word retrieval, an aspect of cognitive processing speed (*Gs*).	Requires naming simple pictures quickly.
Test 5: Sentence Repetition	Measures memory span, a narrow ability of short-term working memory (*Gwm*).	Requires listening to a word, phrase, or sentence and repeating it verbatim.
Test 6: Understanding Directions Test 12: Comprensión de indicaciones	Measures working memory for language, an aspect of short-term working memory (*Gwm*).	Requires listening to a sequence of directions in English (or Spanish), and then following those directions by pointing to objects in a picture.
Test 7: Sound Blending	Measures phonetic coding, a narrow auditory processing (*Ga*) ability.	Requires listening to a series of syllables or phonemes and then blending the sounds into a word.
Test 8: Retrieval Fluency	Measures speed of lexical access, an aspect of long-term retrieval (*Glr*).	Requires naming as many items as possible in a given category within a 1-minute time limit.
Test 9: Sound Awareness	Measures phonetic coding, a narrow ability of auditory processing (*Ga*).	Requires providing a rhyming word in 9A and deleting a word part or sound to form a new word in 9B.

demands for each of the oral language tests. Figure 5.2 illustrates the types of items that are included in each of the tests. The items shown are only illustrations, not actual test items.

DON'T FORGET

....

Reminders to Examiners
- Many of the WJ III oral language tests are now included in the WJ IV OL.
- Oral language may be used as an ability to predict achievement.
- Important additional diagnostic information can be obtained by using the co-normed WJ IV COG and WJ IV ACH.
- It is not necessary to administer all of the tests in the WJ IV OL.
- The Spanish tests can provide English–Spanish comparisons in a bilingual evaluation.

HOW TO ADMINISTER THE WJ IV OL TESTS

As with the WJ IV ACH, proper administration of the WJ IV OL requires training. Although individuals in a wide range of professions can learn the actual administration procedures, a higher degree of skill is required to interpret the tests or integrate the results with the WJ IV COG and WJ IV ACH.

Test 1: Picture Vocabulary
The task requires naming common to less familiar pictured objects.
    What is this person holding? (Correct: gavel)

Test 2: Oral Comprehension (audio)
The task requires listening to short passages and then supplying the missing final word.
    Without a doubt, his novels are more complex than the novels of many other contemporary _____
(Correct: writers, novelists, authors)

Test 3: Segmentation
This task requires breaking a word into its parts, progressing from compound words, to syllables, to individual phonemes.

    Baseball. If we took the word apart, it would be . . . (Correct: base-ball)
    Say the word *puppet* and then say the two parts. (Correct: pup-pet)
    Say each sound in the word *dog*. (Correct: d-o-g /d//o//g/)

Test 4: Rapid Picture Naming (timed)
This task requires naming common pictured objects presented in rows as quickly as possible.

Figure 5.2 Item Types for the WJ IV OL Tests

Test 5: Sentence Repetition (audio)
This task requires listening to and then repeating sentences that increase in length and syntactic complexity.

Joanna went to the zoo.

Arnold decided that he wanted to go scuba diving next year on his spring break.

Test 6: Understanding Directions (audio)
The task requires pointing to objects in a picture after listening to instructions that increase in linguistic complexity.

Point to the man on the bike. Go.

Point to the car in the intersection after you point to one of the flying birds. Go.

Before you point to the tallest building, point to the tree closest to a corner. Go.

Test 7: Sound Blending (audio)
This test requires synthesizing words and word parts, progressing from two parts and syllables to individual phonemes.

Tell me what each word is: pur-ple, /b//a//t/

Test 8: Retrieval Fluency (timed)
This test requires the examinee to name as many examples as possible in a given category within a 1-minute period. The task consists of three different categories.

I want you to name different articles of clothing that you can wear. You will have 1 minute to name as many as you can.

Test 9: Sound Awareness (audio)
The task includes two measures of phonological awareness (rhyming and deletion).

Tell me a word that rhymes with goat. (rhyming)

Say the word *cat* without the /k/ sound. (deletion)

Figure 5.2 (Continued)

Refer to Chapter 2 for additional information about general principles of administration; most procedures apply to both the WJ IV OL and WJ IV ACH.

Testing Materials

The WJ IV OL requires the Test Book, the Test Record, audio equipment and the audio recording, at least two sharpened pencils with erasers, and a stopwatch.

Language Exposure and Use Questionnaire

When evaluating an English language learner or when using the Spanish tests in the WJ IV OL, you may wish to complete the Language Exposure and Use Questionnaire on the last page of the Test Record, which includes a number of questions about the history of the examinee's language use.

ADMINISTRATION CONSIDERATIONS

Prior to administering the WJ IV OL, read the Examiner's Manual, study the contents of the Test Book, review the information on the tabbed page, and review the specific instructions and boxes on the test pages. Administer several practice tests before an actual administration.

Order of Administration

You may administer the WJ IV OL tests in any order and you do not have to administer all of the tests. However, it is generally recommended that you administer the core tests, Tests 1 through 4, first.

Time Requirements

As a general rule, experienced examiners require about 40 minutes to administer the first eight tests. This will vary, of course, depending on the age and ability level of the examinee. Test 9: Sound Awareness is a screening measure for younger students or those who have poor phonological awareness, so you do not administer it in most cases. If the Spanish tests will be administered, allow for an extra 15 to 20 minutes.

Timed Tests

The WJ IV OL contains two timed tests: Rapid Picture Naming and Retrieval Fluency. The time limits are noted on the test page, as well as on the Test

Record. Be sure to administer these tests using a stopwatch or a watch with a second hand.

Tests Using the Audio Recording

Use the standardized audio recording to present Oral Comprehension, Sentence Repetition, Understanding Directions, Sound Blending, and Sound Awareness (Deletion). As described with the WJ IV ACH, when administering these tests, use good-quality audio equipment and headphones. The audio equipment must have a good speaker, be in good working order, and produce a faithful, clear reproduction of the test items.

Although the WJ IV OL Examiner's Manual and Test Book provide detailed rules for test-by-test administration, this section presents important reminders about each test. Whether the reader is familiar with the WJ III oral language tests or just learning these tests, this section will serve as a guide or a good refresher. While studying the following descriptions of test administration procedures, you may also want to follow along with the material in the Test Book and Test Record. Appendix A.2 provides an overview of the finer points of administration of the WJ IV OL tests.

DON'T FORGET
....
If you are administering the Spanish tests (Tests 10–12) or testing an English language learner, you may wish to complete the Language Exposure and Use Questionnaire on the last page of the Test Record.

TEST 1: PICTURE VOCABULARY AND TEST 10: VOCABULARIO SOBRE DIBUJOS

Administration

Be sure to know the correct pronunciation of the items. Pronunciation for more difficult items follows in parentheses. Refer to a standard dictionary for additional help with pronunciation. Select a starting point based on an estimate of the individual's present level of oral language skill. When administering each item, point to the appropriate picture or the specific part of the picture as directed in the instructions for each item in the Test Book. Be sure to complete any queries listed in the Test Book. Testing is conducted in complete page units because the examinee sees stimuli in the Test Book. The basal is established when the examinee correctly answers the six lowest-numbered items administered or until you have administered the page with Item 1. The ceiling is reached when the examinee misses the six

≡ Rapid Reference 5.1

Key Administration Points for Test 1: Picture Vocabulary and Test 10: Vocabulario sobre dibujos

- Materials needed: WJ IV OL Test Book and Test Record.
- Know the pronunciation of all test items.
- Use the Suggested Starting Points.
- Follow basal/ceiling rules: six consecutive lowest-numbered items correct/six consecutive highest-numbered items incorrect.
- Test by complete pages.
- Complete all queries as indicated in the Test Book.
- Be sure to point to the picture or picture part as directed.
- Record errors for further analysis.

highest-numbered items administered or until you have administered the page with the last item. Rapid Reference 5.1 lists the key administration points for Picture Vocabulary. All administration instructions and scoring procedures also apply to the parallel Spanish test, Test 10: Vocabulario sobre dibujos.

Item Scoring

Score each correct response with a 1 and each incorrect response with a 0. Do not penalize an examinee for mispronunciations resulting from articulation errors, dialects, or regional speech patterns.

Common Examiner Errors

Examiner errors include: (a) failing to point to the picture or specific picture part as directed, (b) failing to complete queries, and (c) failing to test by complete pages.

TEST 2: ORAL COMPREHENSION AND TEST 11: COMPRENSIÓN ORAL

Administration

Administer Sample Items A and B to all examinees and then select a starting point based on an estimate of the examinee's present oral language skill. Present Sample Items A and B orally. Present Sample Items C and D and all test items using the audio recording. In rare cases, you may present the items orally. Attempt to say the sentence in exactly the same manner that it is presented on the audio recording. The basal is established when the examinee correctly answers the six lowest-numbered items administered or until you have administered Item 1. Continue testing until the examinee misses the six highest-numbered items administered or until you have administered the last item. Rapid Reference 5.2 lists the key administration points for Oral Comprehension. All administration instructions and scoring procedures also apply to the parallel Spanish test, Test 11: Comprensión oral.

Item Scoring

Score each correct response 1 and each incorrect response 0. Unless noted, only one-word responses are acceptable. If a person gives a two-word or longer response, ask for a one-word answer. Responses are correct when they differ from the correct response only in verb tense or number (singular/plural). A response is incorrect if the examinee substitutes a different part of speech, such as a noun for a verb. Do not penalize for mispronunciations resulting from articulation errors, dialects, or regional speech patterns.

Common Examiner Errors

Examiner errors include: (a) failing to use the audio recording, (b) failing to ask for one-word responses when a longer response is given, and (c) failing to imitate the recording if administering the test orally.

≡ Rapid Reference 5.2

Key Administration Points for Test 2: Oral Comprehension and Test 11: Comprensión oral

- *Materials needed:* WJ IV OL Test Book, Test Record, audio recording, and audio equipment.
- Use the Suggested Starting Points.
- Orally administer Samples A and B to all examinees.
- Use audio recording for Samples C and D and all test items.
- Follow basal/ceiling rules: six consecutive lowest-numbered items correct/six consecutive highest-numbered items incorrect.
- Accept only one-word responses unless otherwise noted.
- Request one-word responses if examinee gives longer responses.
- Do not penalize for articulation errors or regional/dialectical speech differences.
- Do not penalize for responses that differ in tense or number.
- Score as incorrect answers that are a different part of speech.

TEST 3: SEGMENTATION

Administration

Present Introduction 1 to examinees with estimated ability of preschool to grade 1, and Introduction 2 to grade 2 through adults. The basal is established when the examinee correctly answers the five lowest-numbered items correctly or when you have administered Item 1. The ceiling is reached when the examinee misses the five highest-numbered items administered or until you have administered the last item. If necessary, you may repeat any item during the test. Score the examinee's last response for each item. You may wish to record incorrect responses for later error analysis. Rapid Reference 5.3 lists the key administration points for Segmentation.

Item Scoring

Score correct responses 1 and incorrect responses 0.

Common Examiner Errors

Examiner errors include: (a) saying the letter name rather than the sound when a letter is presented within slashes (e.g., /s/); (b) on Items 11 through 20,

---

≡ Rapid Reference 5.3

Key Administration Points for Test 3: Segmentation
- *Materials needed:* WJ IV OL Test Book, Test Record.
- Use the Suggested Starting Points.
- Follow the basal/ceiling rules: five consecutive lowest-numbered items correct/five consecutive highest-numbered items incorrect.
- If starting with Introduction 2 and the examinee does not get the first five items correct, continue testing until a ceiling is reached. Then return to Introduction 1 and administer Items 1 through 10.
- For Items 11 through 20, even if the sounds are not pronounced perfectly, score the response as correct if the person has broken the word into the correct number of segments or parts.
- For Items 21 through 37, listen carefully for each sound. All sounds must be pronounced to receive credit.

scoring a response as incorrect if it's not pronounced perfectly even though it had the correct number of segments; and (c) scoring a response as correct on Items 21 to 37 when all of the sounds are not provided.

CAUTION

Some examiners may not be able to hear word parts or phonemes. In these cases, the examiner should enlist the help of a speech-language therapist or reading specialist to administer and score this test.

TEST 4: RAPID PICTURE NAMING

Administration

All examinees begin with the sample items to ensure that the task is understood. For each error made on the sample items, provide immediate corrective feedback as indicated in the Test Book. The examinee must name all 10 samples correctly before beginning the test. This test has a 2-minute time limit and requires the use of a stopwatch or a watch with a second hand. Turn the page immediately after the examinee has named the last item on the page. The Test Record is designed to help you keep your place. It has extra space after each group of five items that constitutes a row on the test page, and it has a solid line below the last item on each test page. As you approach each solid line, make sure you are ready to turn the Test Book page. If the examinee pauses for more than 2 seconds, say "Try the next one." If needed, point to the next picture. If the examinee finishes before the end of 2 minutes, record the exact finishing time in minutes and seconds on the Test Record. It is important to record the exact finishing time because early finishers who do well on the task will receive higher scores than others that work for the full time limit. Rapid Reference 5.4 lists the key administration points for Rapid Picture Naming.

Item Scoring

Score correct responses 1 and incorrect responses 0. If the examinee uses a synonym, such as *kitty* or *kitten* for *cat,* or a word that is similar in meaning, such as *plant* for *flower,* score the item as correct. It may not be feasible to write separate 1s for each correct response if the examinee is naming quickly. If you have trouble keeping up with the examinee, you may use a continuous line for all correct responses or you may write in just the 0s. After testing, go back and add the 1s.

≡ Rapid Reference 5.4

Key Administration Points for Test 4: Rapid Picture Naming
- *Materials needed*: Test Book, Test Record, stopwatch.
- Administer all sample items to all examinees.
- Follow the error correction procedure on sample items until examinee gets all 10 correct.
- Testing begins with Item 1 for all examinees.
- Adhere to the 2-minute time limit and record exact finishing time in minutes and seconds.
- Accept synonyms and words similar in meaning as correct.
- Turn the page immediately after the examinee responds to the last item on a page.

Common Examiner Errors

Common examiner errors include: (a) not following the error correction procedure correctly on all sample items, (b) not pointing to the next picture if the examinee pauses for more than 2 seconds, (c) not accepting as correct common synonyms for the pictures, (d) not turning the page immediately after the examinee gets to the bottom, and (e) exceeding the time limit of 2 minutes.

TEST 5: SENTENCE REPETITION

Administration

Locate the appropriate starting point for each examinee by consulting the Suggested Starting Points table in the Test Book. Sample A and Items 1 through 8 are presented orally. Present Sample B and all remaining items from the audio recording. You may pause the recording if the examinee requires more time to respond, but do not replay any items except as noted in the Test Book. Samples A and B and Items 1 and 2 may be repeated. Key administration points for Sentence Repetition are listed in Rapid Reference 5.5.

Item Scoring

Score each verbatim response 1 and each incorrect response 0.

Common Examiner Errors

Common examiner errors include: (a) replaying items, (b) not using the audio recording, and (c) scoring an item correct when it is not repeated verbatim.

≡ Rapid Reference 5.5

Key Administration Points for Sentence Repetition
- *Materials needed*: Test Book, Test Record, audio recording, and audio equipment.
- Use examinee's current level of oral language ability to estimate a starting point.
- Follow the basal/ceiling rules: four consecutive lowest-numbered items correct/ four consecutive highest-numbered items incorrect.
- Do not repeat any test items except as allowed on Items 1 and 2.
- Pause the recording if the examinee needs more response time.

TEST 6: UNDERSTANDING DIRECTIONS AND TEST 12: COMPRENSIÓN DE INDICACIONES

Administration

Select a starting point based on an estimate of the examinee's present level of listening comprehension. Consult the Suggested Starting Points table located in the Test Book to determine which picture or set of pictures to administer first. The three Suggested Starting Points are Picture 1 (preschool), Pictures 2 and 3 (kindergarten through grade 4), or Pictures 4 and 5 (grade 5 through adult). Administer all items for each picture in the suggested set. Follow the Continuation Instructions shown at the end of each set of pictures to determine when to discontinue testing or what additional pictures to administer. Continue testing until you reach the discontinue criterion for a particular set of pictures.

Before administering each picture, allow the examinee to review the picture for about 10 seconds. Do not repeat or replay an item. In rare cases, you may present the items orally. Attempt to say the item in the same manner that it is presented on the audio recording. Rapid Reference 5.6 lists key administration points for Understanding Directions. All administration instructions and scoring procedures also apply to the parallel Spanish test, Test 12: Comprensión de indicaciones.

Item Scoring

Score each correct response 1 and each incorrect response 0. For the item to be scored as correct, the examinee must complete all of the steps of the direction. Many of the items require the examinee to point to certain objects before pointing to other objects. If the direction does not specify the sequence, the examinee may point in any order.

≡ Rapid Reference 5.6

Key Administration Points for Test 6: Understanding Directions and Test 12: Comprensión de indicaciones

- *Materials needed:* Test Book, Test Record, audio recording, and audio equipment.
- Use examinee's current level of listening comprehension to estimate starting point.
- Use the audio recording to administer this test.
- Allow examinee to review the picture for 10 seconds before administering items for that picture.
- Do not allow the examinee to begin pointing until the word "go" is stated for each item.
- Complete all items for each picture administered.
- The examinee must complete all steps to receive credit on an item.
- The examinee must recall steps in order unless order is not specified.
- Follow the continuation instructions shown after each set of pictures to determine when to discontinue or what additional pictures to administer.
- Do not repeat any items.
- Become familiar with the pictures and items in order to facilitate scoring the examinee's pointing responses.

Common Examiner Errors

Common examiner errors include: (a) not using the audio recording, (b) not scoring the items correctly, (c) not allowing the examinee to review the picture for 10 seconds before administering the items, and (d) not reading the directions as presented on the audio recording if administering the test orally.

TEST 7: SOUND BLENDING

Administration

Before beginning the test, locate the track for Sample B on the audio recording and adjust the volume to a comfortable level. Present Sample Item A orally. If the examinee does not understand the task, demonstrate further with the additional items provided in the Error or No Response box on the page in the Test Book. Present Sample Item B and all test items from the audio recording. Although the audio recording provides adequate time for most examinees to respond, you may pause or stop the recording if the examinee needs more response time. Because it is difficult to replicate the items orally, present this test using the audio recording;

however, in rare cases, you may present Items 1 through 16 orally. Attempt to say each item in the same manner that it is presented on the audio recording. Do not repeat any item during the test.

If the examinee only pronounces the word phoneme-by-phoneme or syllable-by-syllable (like it is presented on the recording) instead of saying it fluently (sounds blended into a whole word), tell the examinee to "Say the word smoothly." Give this reminder only once during the test. Score the examinee's last response for each item. You may wish to record incorrect responses for later error analysis. Rapid Reference 5.7 lists the key administration points for Sound Blending.

> **DON'T FORGET**
> ....
> After the first reminder, words that are pronounced in parts and not blended into a whole word are scored as incorrect.

Item Scoring

Score correct responses 1 and incorrect responses 0.

Common Examiner Errors

Common examiner errors include: (a) not using the audio recording, (b) scoring responses correct that are not blended together into a whole word, (c) failing to remind the examinee to say the word smoothly the first time the response is not blended, and (d) not scoring the examinee's last response as correct or incorrect for each item.

≡ Rapid Reference 5.7
....

Key Administration Points for Test 7: Sound Blending
- *Materials needed*: Test Book, Test Record, audio recording, and audio equipment.
- Administer sample items to all examinees.
- Follow the basal/ceiling rules: six consecutive correct/six consecutive incorrect.
- Words must be pronounced as a blended whole to receive credit.
- Only give the reminder to say the whole word smoothly one time during the entire test.
- Pause the audio if more response time is needed.
- Do not replay any items.

TEST 8: RETRIEVAL FLUENCY

Administration

Retrieval Fluency requires a stopwatch or a watch or clock with a second hand. Administer all three items to all examinees. Each item has a 1-minute time limit. Do not count duplicate answers; for example, if the examinee says "giraffe" three times, mark only one correct response. If you cannot remember whether the examinee has duplicated a word, do not stop the examinee or ask if the response was already named. Instead, give the response credit and balance the scores if you are unsure of another response. If the examinee pauses for 10 seconds, say "Go ahead. Say the words as fast as you can." Key administration points for Retrieval Fluency are listed in Rapid Reference 5.8.

Item Scoring

Use tally marks on the lines provided in the Test Record to record the number of correct responses for each item. Group the tally marks by fives for easier totaling (i.e., ⦀⦀). For Item 1, you may accept brand names of foods or drinks as correct (e.g., Coke®, Spaghetti-Os®). You may also accept different variations of the same type of food or drink (e.g., Swiss cheese, cheddar cheese, American cheese). For Item 2, accept variations of the same name as correct (e.g., Bob, Bobby, Robert). For Item 3, accept variations of the same type of animal (e.g., bear, grizzly bear, black bear, polar bear).

Common Examiner Errors

Common examiner errors include: (a) failing to give credit for variations of correct responses, (b) not stopping each item after one minute, and (c) counting exact duplicate responses as correct.

⇒ Rapid Reference 5.8

Key Administration Points for Retrieval Fluency
- *Materials needed*: Test Book, Test Record, stopwatch.
- Administer all three items to all examinees.
- Allow 1 minute for each item.
- Use tally marks to record correct responses.
- Do not count duplicate responses.
- Do not ask examinee to repeat a response.
- Accept variations as correct.

TEST 9: SOUND AWARENESS

Administration

Administer both subtests (Rhyming and Deletion) to obtain a raw score for this test. For 9A Rhyming, consult the Suggested Starting Points table to determine an appropriate starting point. The basal is established when the examinee has correctly answered six consecutive lowest-numbered items administered or when you have administered Item 1. For 9B Deletion, all examinees begin with sample items and then Item 1. For both subtests, a ceiling is reached when the examinee misses the six highest-numbered items administered or when you have administered the last item. Administer subtest 9A: Rhyming orally. You may repeat items upon request. For subtest 9B: Deletion, administer Sample Item A orally and Sample B and all test items from the audio recording. Letters printed within slashes, such as /s/, indicate that you should say the most common sound of the letter (the phoneme), not the letter name. Consider recording errors for later error analysis. Rapid Reference 5.9 lists the key administration points for Sound Awareness.

Item Scoring

Score each correct response 1 and each incorrect response 0. For 9A Rhyming, responses must be real words to receive credit, so score rhyming nonsense words as 0. Do not penalize for mispronunciations resulting from articulation errors, dialects, or regional speech patterns.

≡ Rapid Reference 5.9

Key Administration Points for Sound Awareness
- *Materials needed:* Test Book, Test Record, audio recording, and audio equipment.
- Administer both subtests to obtain a raw score.
- Know the pronunciation of samples and items that are presented orally.
- Administer the sample items to all individuals for each subtest.
- Choose an appropriate starting point for 9A Rhyming.
- Begin with Item 1 on 9B Deletion for all examinees.
- Follow the ceiling rules for both subtests (9A and 9B): six consecutive incorrect.
- For 9A Rhyming, responses must be real words to receive credit.
- Record errors for further analysis.
- Use the audio recording as directed on 9B Deletion.

DON'T FORGET

Sound Awareness is a screening measure intended for use with younger children (K–3). It can be used with older individuals who may have limits in phonological processing.

Common Examiner Errors

Common examiner errors include: (a) mispronouncing the samples and items that are presented orally, (b) failing to administer both subtests to obtain a score, and (c) not using the audio recording for 9B: Deletion.

HOW TO SCORE THE WJ IV OL

Tests Requiring a Special Scoring Procedure

Only two of the tests in the WJ IV OL have a special scoring procedure: Understanding Directions and Retrieval Fluency. The score on Understanding Directions is based on the number of correct responses the examinee has on the set of pictures administered. Each correct response is scored 1 and each incorrect response is scored 0. On the Test Record, write the number of points earned for each picture in the space provided. When indicated on the Test Record, record the cumulative total for the two pictures specified. In the Score Entry section on the Test Record, enter the number of points for each picture or set of pictures administered and enter an X if the set was not administered. To obtain estimated age and grade equivalents, locate the number of points in the appropriate column corresponding to the group of pictures administered. If you have administered more than one group of pictures, use the last group administered following the continuation instructions to estimate age and grade equivalents.

On Retrieval Fluency, the raw score is based on the total number of tally marks recorded for each of the three items. Record a tally mark for each correct response, grouping them by fives. For each item, count the correct responses and record the total in the Number Correct box. The maximum number that can be entered for each item is 99. To obtain estimated age and grade equivalents, add the three item totals together and locate that sum in the Scoring Table.

Scoring Reminders for Each Test

Test 1: Picture Vocabulary and Test 10: Vocabulario sobre dibujos
Scoring Reminders:
- Score correct responses 1 and incorrect responses 0.
- Enter the number of items answered correctly plus one point for each item below the basal in the Number Correct box on the Test Record.

Test 2: Oral Comprehension and Test 11: Comprensión oral
Scoring Reminders:
- Score correct responses 1 and incorrect responses 0.
- Score 1 if the response differs from the correct answer in verb tense or number.
- Score 0 if the response is a different part of speech from the correct answer.
- Unless noted otherwise, score two-word or longer responses 0.
- Enter the number of items answered correctly plus one point for each item below the basal in the Number Correct box on the Test Record.

Test 3: Segmentation
Scoring Reminders:
- Score correct responses 1 and incorrect responses 0. Examinee must provide all parts of the word, or all sounds in the word, for the item to be correct.
- Do not penalize for dialect variations or articulation errors.
- For Items 11 through 20, do not penalize the examinee if he or she does not say the letter sounds perfectly as long as the word has been broken into the correct number of parts.
- Enter the number of items answered correctly plus one point for each item below the basal in the Number Correct box on the Test Record.

Test 4: Rapid Picture Naming
Scoring Reminders:
- Score correct responses 1 and incorrect responses 0.
- If the examinee provides a synonym (e.g., *puppy* for *dog*) or a word similar in meaning (e.g., *plant* for *flower*), score the response as correct.
- Do not penalize mispronunciations resulting from articulation errors, dialect variations, or regional speech patterns.
- Record the total completion time, in minutes and seconds, in the Time boxes of the Test Record. There is a 2-minute time limit for this test.
- Record the total number of correct responses in the Number Correct box on the Test Record.

Test 5: Sentence Repetition
Scoring Reminders:
- Score correct responses 1 and incorrect responses 0.
- Do not penalize mispronunciations resulting from articulation errors, dialect variations, or regional speech patterns.

- Enter the number of items answered correctly plus one point for each item below the basal in the Number Correct box on the Test Record.

Test 6: Understanding Directions and Test 12: Comprensión de indicaciones
Scoring Reminders:
- Score correct responses 1 and incorrect responses 0.
- The examinee must complete all steps in the direction to receive credit.
- Except where order is noted, the examinee may respond to the directions in any order to receive a 1.
- Enter the number of points for each picture administered in the appropriate box.
- Enter the cumulative number of points for the sets of pictures (as directed in the Test Record).
- In the Score Entry section, enter the number of points for each group of pictures administered or an X if not administered.
- If obtaining estimated AE/GE, combine the points for the highest set of pictures administered and find the total in the corresponding column.

Test 7: Sound Blending
Scoring Reminders:
- Score correct responses 1 and incorrect responses 0.
- Items that are pronounced in parts (as they are on the audio recording) are considered as errors and scored 0.
- Score the last response given, including self-corrections.
- Add the number of points for all items answered correctly plus one point for each item below the basal and record the total in the Number Correct box on the Test Record.

Test 8: Retrieval Fluency
Scoring Reminders:
- Use tally marks to record each correct response on the Test Record.
- Duplicate responses do not receive credit.
- Variations of a response do receive credit (e.g., Bob, Bobby, Robert).
- Record the total number of correct responses in the Number Correct box after each item on the Test Record.
- If the total score for an item exceeds 99, enter 99 as the number correct.
- Enter the number correct for each of the three items when using the online scoring program.

Test 9: Sound Awareness
Scoring Reminders:
- Score correct responses 1 and incorrect responses 0.
- For 9A, record the number of items answered correctly plus one point for each item below the basal in the Number Correct box on the Test Record.
- For 9B, record the number of items answered correctly in the Number Correct box on the Test Record.
- Enter the number correct for both subtests when using the online scoring program.
- If obtaining estimated AE/GE, add together the scores for the two subtests (A + B).

HOW TO INTERPRET THE WJ IV OL TESTS

The tests on the WJ IV OL measure several different linguistic abilities, including phonological awareness, speed of lexical access, memory, vocabulary, and listening comprehension. Figure 5.3 illustrates the various skills measured by the WJ IV OL and their relationship to CHC theory.

> **DON'T FORGET**
> ....
> See Chapter 4 of this book for information on all of the scores available in any of the WJ IV batteries: WJ IV ACH, WJ IV OL, or WJ IV COG.

Test 1: Picture Vocabulary and Test 10: Vocabulario sobre dibujos

This test requires the individual to name pictured objects, ranging from familiar objects to less familiar objects. Early items only require a pointing response (receptive vocabulary). All other items require an oral response (expressive vocabulary). This test measures vocabulary, verbal ability, and cultural knowledge, all of which are aspects of comprehension-knowledge (*Gc*). Picture Vocabulary is primarily a single-word expressive vocabulary task.

Low performance may result from limited vocabulary, limited exposure to English (or Spanish if Test 10: Vocabulario sobre dibujos is administered), or word retrieval problems. Observation, as well as an analysis of errors, will help you determine whether poor performance is a result of limited vocabulary or retrieval problems. Errors that are related to the correct response (e.g., describe an attribute or function) may indicate a retrieval problem. Errors that are not directly associated with the correct response may indicate a weakness in vocabulary

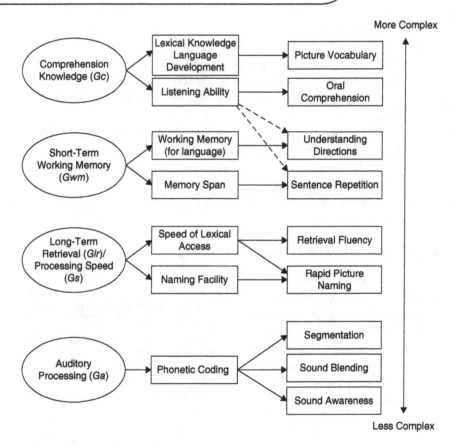

Figure 5.3 Various Skills Measured by the WJ IV OL Tests and Their Relationship to CHC Theory

knowledge. In contrast, errors that are associated with the word meaning indicate a strength in vocabulary knowledge, even though the response is scored as incorrect. Sometimes a student may know the function of an object, but not be able to come up with the exact name. For example, Eric, a fourth-grade student, described *hinges* as the things that let the door swing back and forth. Dan, a student at a community college, noted that the caduceus was a medical symbol, but he didn't know exactly what it was called.

Vocabulary knowledge is highly related to reading comprehension. The importance of this knowledge increases as reading skill develops. Thus, instruction that is designed to increase vocabulary should help improve reading comprehension. An individual could have low scores on this test for several

≡ Rapid Reference 5.10

Interpretation of Test 1: Picture Vocabulary and Test 10: Vocabulario sobre dibujos
Primary Broad CHC Factor: Comprehension-Knowledge (Gc)
Narrow CHC Abilities: Lexical knowledge (VL), Language development (LD)
Stimuli: Visual (pictures)
Task Requirements: Orally identifying pictures of objects
Cognitive Processes Used: Object recognition, lexical access and retrieval
Response Modality: Oral (words)
Related Educational Interventions or Accommodations: Building vocabulary and knowledge, text talks, semantic maps, reading aloud to the individual

reasons: English as a second language, limited experiences and opportunities, cultural differences, or limited knowledge of word meanings. Rapid Reference 5.10 summarizes interpretive information for Picture Vocabulary and Vocabulario sobre dibujos.

Test 2: Oral Comprehension and Test 11: Comprensión oral

This test requires the individual to listen to a short passage and then provide the final word to complete it. This task measures listening ability and language development, both of which are aspects of comprehension-knowledge (*Gc*). The individual must use previously acquired knowledge, syntax, and context clues to identify the missing word. Oral Comprehension is primarily a receptive language task.

Low performance may result from limited semantic or syntactic knowledge, limited exposure to English, or poor attention. This oral test is similar in format to the WJ IV ACH Passage Comprehension test but the examinee listens to a passage instead of reading a passage. Comparing the results of these two tests will help you determine whether limited oral language or decoding skill is impacting reading comprehension performance. Both reading and listening comprehension involve several of the same abilities, such as vocabulary, reasoning, and background knowledge. Students with oral language impairments and intellectual disabilities may obtain similar scores on both measures of listening and reading comprehension. Oftentimes, students with learning disabilities will score higher on measures of listening comprehension than on measures of reading comprehension. Some students, however, have higher scores on Passage Comprehension than on Oral Comprehension. This suggests that comprehension improves when reading rather than when listening. For example, students with language impairments may score higher on Passage Comprehension because the printed words remain in front of them. The text facilitates comprehension and reduces the effects of memory on comprehension. Thus, consideration of the discrepancies between listening and reading comprehension can provide you with useful information.

As noted, some students may have difficulty on this task because they have trouble retaining information in memory. Analysis of other tests involving memory, such as Sentence Repetition and Understanding Directions, can help clarify and pinpoint memory difficulties. An individual could have low scores on this for several reasons: poor attention, weak memory, low oral language, or limited background knowledge. A summary of interpretive information is presented in Rapid Reference 5.11.

DON'T FORGET

Consideration of the discrepancies between listening comprehension and reading comprehension is useful information for learning disability evaluations.

Test 3: Segmentation

This test requires the person to break apart words, progressing from compound words, to syllables, to individual phonemes. Segmentation, the ability to break apart the sounds within a word, is a critical phonological awareness ability that

≡ Rapid Reference 5.11

Interpretation of Test 2: Oral Comprehension and Test 11: Comprensión oral

Primary Broad CHC Factor: Comprehension-Knowledge (Gc)

Narrow CHC Abilities: Listening ability (LS)

Stimuli: Auditory (oral sentences)

Task Requirements: Listening to short passages that increase in linguistic complexity and providing the final word

Cognitive Processes Used: Construction of propositional representations through syntactic and semantic integration of orally presented passages in real time

Response Modality: Oral (words)

Related Educational Interventions or Accommodations: Providing shortened directions, increasing knowledge of English (or Spanish) syntax, building vocabulary and knowledge underlies aspects of spelling. If a student does poorly on Segmentation, it is likely that he or she will have difficulty putting sounds in the correct order when spelling words. Segmentation is the opposite of blending, which requires pushing the sounds together to form a word. Both of these abilities are critical for reading and spelling words. An individual could have low scores on this test for several reasons: poor phonological awareness, English as a second language, articulation difficulties, weak memory, or inadequate instruction. Fortunately, most students can learn how to segment speech sounds. Rapid Reference 5.12 provides an instructional sequence for teaching segmentation skills and Rapid Reference 5.13 summarizes interpretive information.

> **DON'T FORGET**
> ....
> It is easiest to segment compound words, then syllables, and then phonemes.

Test 4: Rapid Picture Naming

Rapid Picture Naming (Rapid Reference 5.14) measures the narrow abilities of naming facility and speed of lexical access (i.e., the speed of producing names for objects). This test measures the speed or fluency of recognition, retrieval, and oral production of the names of common pictured objects. A considerable body of research suggests that speed of lexical access or how quickly individuals can name highly familiar visual stimuli is a strong predictor of reading performance and a cognitive marker of developmental dyslexia (Georgiou & Parrila, 2013). This type of task appears most related to reading fluency. An individual could have low scores on this test for several reasons: poor attention, slow articulation speed, or slow processing speed.

≡ Rapid Reference 5.12
....

Instructional Sequence for Segmentation
- Progress from compound words, to syllables, to phonemes.
- Begin with words with two sounds, then three, and then four.
- Use chips or tiles to represent the sounds or word parts.
- Have the person say the whole word.
- Say a word and have the person represent the sounds with blocks.
- Say a word and have the person represent the sounds with letter tiles.

≡ *Rapid Reference 5.13*

Interpretation of Test 3: Segmentation

Primary Broad CHC Factor: Auditory Processing (*Ga*)

Narrow CHC Abilities: Phonetic coding (PC)

Stimuli: Auditory (oral words)

Task Requirements: Listening to a word and breaking it into parts and phonemes

Cognitive Processes Used: Analysis of phonological elements in immediate awareness

Response Modality: Oral (word parts, phonemes)

Related Educational Interventions or Accommodations: Provide direct instruction in segmentation with letter tiles, provide practice segmenting words for spelling

≡ *Rapid Reference 5.14*

Interpretation of Test 4: Rapid Picture Naming

Primary Broad CHC Factors: Long-term Retrieval (*Glr*), Processing Speed (*Gs*)

Narrow CHC Abilities: Naming facility (NA), Speed of lexical access (LA)

Stimuli: Visual (pictures)

Task Requirements: Recognizing objects then retrieving and saying their names rapidly

Cognitive Processes Used: Speed/fluency of retrieval and oral production of recognized objects; speeded serial naming, rapid object recognition

Response Modality: Oral (words)

Related Educational Interventions or Accommodations: Increase reading fluency through speed drills, record and monitor progress

Test 5: Sentence Repetition

Sentence Repetition (Rapid Reference 5.15) measures auditory memory span (i.e., attention to temporally ordered, verbalized acoustic stimuli; registration of the stimuli sequence in immediate memory; and repetition of the sequence). Unlike repeating a string of unrelated words, such as on the WJ IV COG Memory for Words test, performance on this task can be aided by meaning and use of the sentence context. When Sentence Repetition is combined with the WJ IV COG Memory for Words test, the two tests form the narrow ability cluster Auditory Memory Span. Auditory memory span can be considered a

≡ Rapid Reference 5.15

Interpretation of Test 5: Sentence Repetition

Primary Broad CHC Factor: Short-term Working Memory (*Gwm*), Comprehension-Knowledge (*Gc*)

Narrow CHC Abilities: Auditory memory span (*Gwm*-MS), Listening ability (*Gc*-LS)

Stimuli: Auditory (words, sentences)

Task Requirements: Listening to and repeating phrases or sentences in correct sequence

Cognitive Processes Used: Formation of echoic memories aided by a semantic, meaning-based code

Response Modality: Oral (words and sentences)

Related Educational Interventions or Accommodations: Rehearsal, provide visual cues, associate new information with prior knowledge, shorten instructions

---

narrow ability within the broader construct of working memory because the tasks require controlled, focused attention to retain a string of orally presented information, often the first part of a working memory task. Because no transformation or manipulation of information is involved in tasks such as Sentence Repetition and Memory for Words, they measure short-term memory span. These tests require the individual to recall a string of words that increases in length or sentences that increase in both length and complexity. An individual could obtain low scores on this test for several reasons, such as limited attention, poor memory, or limited oral language.

Test 6: Understanding Directions and Test 12: Comprensión de indicaciones

This test requires the individual to listen to a sequence of oral instructions and then follow the directions by pointing to various objects in a colored picture. The directions gradually increase in linguistic complexity. This test measures listening ability and language development, both of which are aspects of comprehension-knowledge (*Gc*). Understanding Directions also measures memory span and working memory, two aspects of short-term working memory (*Gwm*). Some of the items are simple measures of memory span (e.g., Point to the tree); others measure working memory because they involve rearranging or reordering the sequence (e.g., Before you point to the tree, point to the flower and then the butterfly). An individual may have low scores on this test for several reasons: poor

≡ Rapid Reference 5.16

Interpretation of Test 6: Understanding Directions and Test 12: Comprensión de indicaciones

Primary Broad CHC Factor: Short-term Working Memory (Gwm), Comprehension-Knowledge (Gc)

Narrow CHC Abilities: Memory span and working memory (Gwm-MS, WM), Listening ability (Gc-LS)

Stimuli: Visual (pictures) and auditory (oral sentences)

Task Requirements: Studying a picture then listening to a sequence of directions and then following the directions by pointing to items in the picture

Cognitive Processes Used: Creation of a mental schema or plan of action in immediate awareness

Response Modality: Motoric (pointing)

Related Educational Interventions or Accommodations: Simplify language used and reduce the amount of material to decrease the memory load; provide visual cues; repeat important information, as needed.

attention, limited receptive vocabulary knowledge, or weaknesses in listening comprehension, attention, or memory. Rapid Reference 5.16 presents a summary of interpretive information for Understanding Directions.

Test 7: Sound Blending

Sound Blending is a key ability of phonemic processing. Sound blending and segmentation are the most essential skills for accurate reading and spelling and are good predictors of reading and spelling achievement. The Sound Blending test involves the ability to push together or synthesize sounds to form words. As with the Segmentation test, an individual could have low scores on this test for several reasons: poor phonological awareness, English as a second language, articulation difficulties, weak memory, or inadequate instruction. An individual who has a low score on Sound Blending is also likely to have a low score on the WJ IV ACH Word Attack test. In order to read phonically regular nonsense words, one has to push together the sounds to form the word. Conversely, a

DON'T FORGET

Blending and segmentation are the most important phonemic awareness tasks for word reading and spelling. They measure the synthesis and analysis processes involved in decoding and encoding.

≡ Rapid Reference 5.17

Sequence for Teaching Sound Blending

- Begin the instruction with continuous sounds that can be prolonged (e.g., /s/, /f/, /m/); you can sustain the sound as long as you have air.
- Progress from compound words to syllables to phonemes.
- Present words with two sounds, three, and then four (e.g., /m//e/; /sh//oe/; /c//a//t/; /s//a//n//d/).
- Gradually increase the interval between sounds from one-quarter second to a 1-second break.
- Using moveable letters, practice blending and segmenting (breaking apart the sounds) in words.

student with a high score on Sound Blending is likely to have good phonics skills, unless this type of instruction has been limited. Fortunately, most students can be taught how to blend sounds together to form words. Rapid Reference 5.17 illustrates a recommended sequence for teaching sound blending. Rapid Reference 5.18 presents a summary of interpretive information for Sound Blending.

Test 8: Retrieval Fluency

The Retrieval Fluency test requires fluent retrieval and oral production of examples of words for a category. This task does not include the encoding and storage

≡ Rapid Reference 5.18

Interpretation of Test 7: Sound Blending

Primary Broad CHC Factor: Auditory Processing (Ga)

Narrow CHC Abilities: Phonetic coding (PC)

Stimuli: Auditory (phonemes)

Task Requirements: Synthesizing language sounds (phonemes) into real words

Cognitive Processes Used: Synthesis of phonological elements in immediate awareness, matching the sequence of sounds to known words

Response Modality: Oral (words)

Related Educational Interventions or Accommodations: Early exposure to language sounds, promoting phonological awareness, direct instruction in sound blending and segmentation, practice blending sounds into words and breaking them apart using letter tiles

processes, but rather measures the rate or automaticity of word retrieval. In CHC theory, the cognitive abilities measured by Retrieval Fluency are ideational fluency and speed of lexical access. Martin (2009) described this type of retrieval task as *associative* or *encyclopedic knowledge* having three principle characteristics:

1. Retrieval is explicit (specific names).
2. There is no intrinsic limit on the amount of information that can be retrieved.
3. This type of knowledge is idiosyncratic—some people will produce many responses; others will not.

An individual may have a low score on this test for several reasons: poor attention, limited vocabulary, weaknesses in word retrieval, or limited use of categorical strategies. For example, when thinking of foods to eat, one may picture the aisle of a grocery store; when thinking of names, one may picture the students in a classroom; and when thinking of animals, one may begin with animals at the zoo. Rapid Reference 5.19 summarizes interpretive information for Retrieval Fluency.

Test 9: Sound Awareness

This test requires the individual to analyze and manipulate phonemes by performing rhyming and deletion tasks. No reading is required. Because this test measures two specific aspects of phonological awareness, it is particularly useful in evaluating both beginning readers and older individuals who are experiencing reading difficulty. Additional information regarding phonological

---

≡ Rapid Reference 5.19

Interpretation of Test 8: Retrieval Fluency

Primary Broad CHC Factor: Long-term Retrieval (*Glr*)

Narrow CHC Abilities: Ideational fluency (FI), Speed of lexical access (LA)

Stimuli: Auditory (directions only)

Task Requirements: Naming as many examples as possible from a given category (food, first names, and animals)

Cognitive Processes Used: Recognition, fluent retrieval, and oral production of examples of semantic category; activation of semantic network

Response Modality: Oral (words)

Related Educational Interventions or Accommodations: Oral elaboration, use of cues, allowing more time, building vocabulary and knowledge

awareness can be obtained by administering Test 7: Sound Blending and, from the WJ IV COG, Test 5: Phonological Processing, which includes three subtests: Word Access, Word

Fluency, and Substitution. You may also want to compare the results of these tests to the WJ IV ACH Word Attack test to determine if problems are with phonological awareness, phoneme–grapheme knowledge, or both. Interventions will often focus on increasing the ability to rhyme words. Rapid Reference 5.20 provides a sequence of rhyming skills from the easiest to the most difficult, and

Rapid Reference 5.21 provides an overview of skill development in phonological awareness. Rapid Reference 5.22 provides a summary of interpretive information for Sound Awareness.

≣ Rapid Reference 5.20

Sequence of Rhyming Development
- Recognition: Do these two words rhyme?
- Oddity: Tell me the word that does not rhyme.
- Completion: Finish what I say with a rhyming word.
- Production: What word rhymes with . . . ?

≣ Rapid Reference 5.21

Sequence of Skill Development for Phonological Awareness
- Discriminating rhymes
- Producing rhymes
- Isolating initial and final sounds
- Blending sounds (compound words, syllables, phonemes)
- Segmenting sounds (compound words, syllables, phonemes)
- Manipulating sounds (e.g., deleting, substituting, transposing)

≡ Rapid Reference 5.22

Interpretation of Test 9: Sound Awareness

Primary Broad CHC Factor: Auditory Processing (*Ga*)

Narrow CHC Abilities: Phonetic coding (PC)

Stimuli: Auditory (questions, words)

Task Requirements: Providing rhyming words, deleting word parts and phonemes from whole words to create a new word

Cognitive Processes Used: Access, retrieval, and application of English phonology

Response Modality: Oral (words)

Related Educational Interventions or Accommodations: Explicit instruction in rhyming and sound manipulation, orally (rhyming) and with letter tiles (deletion)

Oral Language Clusters

The WJ IV OL has nine oral language clusters: Oral Language, Broad Oral Language, Oral Expression, Listening Comprehension, Phonetic Coding, Speed of Lexical Access, and three Spanish clusters: Lenguaje oral, Amplio lenguaje oral, and Comprensión auditiva. Two additional clusters are available when using tests from the WJ IV COG: Vocabulary and Auditory Memory Span.

You will want to consider an individual's performance on the oral language clusters in relation to his or her performance on the reading, math, and written language tests. Rapid Reference 5.23 lists possible instructional implications for individuals with limited oral language ability.

Oral Language and Broad Oral Language

Two broad oral language clusters exist: Oral Language and Broad Oral Language. The first cluster is composed of two tests: Picture Vocabulary and Oral Comprehension. The Broad Oral Language cluster is composed of three tests: the two in Oral Language plus Understanding Directions. These clusters provide estimates of the individual's verbal ability. The two parallel Spanish clusters are Lenguaje oral and Amplio lenguaje oral. Broad Oral Language or Amplio lenguaje oral can be used as the predictor in the oral language/achievement comparison procedure.

Oral Expression

This cluster is composed of two tests: Picture Vocabulary and Sentence Repetition. It measures vocabulary knowledge and memory span. A significant

Rapid Reference 5.23

Possible Instructional Implications for Individuals With Limited Oral Language

- Consider the impact on reading, math, and written language performance.
- Refer the individual to a speech/language specialist for a comprehensive language evaluation.
- Develop oral vocabulary and oral language comprehension prior to or simultaneously when providing instruction in other academic areas.
- Use visual displays and concrete examples to support and enhance language comprehension, such as outlines, pictures, graphs, and story frames.
- Prior to assigning a task, demonstrate or model what is expected of the individual.
- Limit the length of oral directions and instructions.
- Provide rich language experiences (e.g., read aloud or have conversations with the individual).
- When asking a question, provide additional time for the individual to respond or speak.
- Prior to beginning a unit or new topic, preteach the important vocabulary words related to the content.
- Pair the individual with a peer who will encourage and facilitate verbal communication.
- Provide opportunities for the individual to use modalities other than language to communicate understanding (e.g., making a model rather than an oral book report).
- Exempt the student from foreign language requirements or choose a language that is more visual in nature (e.g., American Sign Language).
- Provide positive reinforcement regarding the person's unique nonlinguistic strengths (e.g., artistic ability, athletic ability, mathematical ability).

difference between the two tests of this cluster may indicate a specific strength or weakness in vocabulary or memory.

Listening Comprehension

This cluster is composed of two tests: Oral Comprehension and Understanding Directions, which are measures of listening ability and verbal comprehension. Both of these tasks involve receptive language as well as memory span and working memory. The parallel Spanish cluster is Comprensión auditiva.

Phonetic Coding

This cluster has two tests: Segmentation and Sound Blending, both of which are aspects of phonetic coding and auditory processing. Segmentation involves the ability to break apart the sounds in words, which is a fundamental skill underlying spelling. Sound Blending involves pushing together sounds to form words, which underlies the application of phonics.

Speed of Lexical Access

This cluster consists of Rapid Picture Naming and Retrieval Fluency, both of which are timed measures of word retrieval. A difference between these two tests may occur because of the type of task. Rapid Picture Naming is a confrontational naming task in which the person must label specific pictures, whereas Retrieval Fluency is a measure of ideational fluency and the person must produce words that belong to a specific category.

Vocabulary and Auditory Memory Span

You can obtain two additional cluster scores by administering two tests from the WJ IV COG: Test 1: Oral Vocabulary and Test 18: Memory for Words. The Vocabulary cluster includes two expressive vocabulary measures. In some cases, a difference may exist between Picture Vocabulary and Oral Vocabulary, as the latter involves more reasoning. The Auditory Memory Span cluster includes two measures of memory. A difference may exist in a person's performance on these two tests as well. Sentence Repetition has more linguistic context than Memory for Words, which just requires repeating a string of unrelated words.

Intra-Oral Language Variation Procedure

The intra-oral language variation procedure is a norm-based method for evaluating the presence of significant strengths or weaknesses among an individual's linguistic abilities. To calculate this variation procedure, you must administer a minimum of four tests (Tests 1 through 4). The individual's performance on one test is then compared to his or her predicted performance based on the average performance on the other three tests. For example, when evaluating a person's performance on Test 1: Picture Vocabulary, the average of the other three tests (Test 2: Oral Comprehension, Test 3: Segmentation, and Test 4: Rapid Picture Naming) is used to obtain the predicted score. The actual score is then compared to the predicted score. If the actual score is higher than predicted, a positive difference is obtained. If the actual score is lower than predicted, a negative difference is obtained. Depending on the magnitude of the positive (or negative) difference, the person may have a significant strength (or weakness) in a specific area. If, for

> **CAUTION**
> ....
> Intra-ability variations show patterns of strengths and weaknesses among an individual's abilities, so these are relative strengths and weaknesses. Even though a variation may show statistical significance, the evaluator must determine practical significance.

example, Picture Vocabulary is significantly higher than predicted, the person exhibits a relative strength in vocabulary knowledge. If the person's actual Picture Vocabulary score is significantly lower than predicted, he or she exhibits a relative weakness in vocabulary knowledge. This type of information is valuable when documenting a pattern of strengths and weaknesses or determining a specific area of weakness rather than generalized low performance. In addition, Tests 5 through 8 can be included in the variation procedure along with any cluster that results from the tests that are administered. As an option, three tests from the WJ IV COG (Test 1: Oral Vocabulary, Test 5: Phonological Processing, and Test 12: Nonword Repetition) and the Vocabulary and Auditory Processing clusters also can be entered into the oral-language variation procedure. Whenever additional tests or clusters are included in the variation procedure, it is called the "Extended" variation. Table 5.2 illustrates the results of an intra-oral language (Extended) variation for Josh, a third grader. When Josh's oral language abilities are evaluated for strengths and weaknesses, he demonstrates a significant strength in Vocabulary and the two tests that constitute that cluster: Picture Vocabulary and Oral Vocabulary. However, these strengths are relative to his other oral language abilities rather than normative strengths because the cluster and the tests have standard scores falling in the average range. In addition, he has a significant weakness in Understanding Directions and Retrieval Fluency. While these weaknesses are significant relative to his other oral language abilities, they are also normative weaknesses with standard scores of 73 and 74, respectively, which are in the low range.

Oral Language Ability/Achievement Comparisons

The WJ IV OL provides an option to use oral language as a predictor score in the ability/achievement comparison calculation. The Broad Oral Language cluster may be used to predict levels of achievement based upon the individual's level of oral language development.

Table 5.2 Josh's Intra-Oral Language (Extended) Variation

Variations Intra-Oral Language (Extended)	Standard Scores			Discrepancy		Interpretation at
	Actual	Predicted	Difference	PR	SD	± 1.50 SD (SEE)
Oral Expression	98	88	10	81	+0.86	—
Listening Comprehension	81	93	−12	14	−1.08	—
Phonetic Coding	90	97	−7	32	−0.46	—
Speed of Lexical Access	78	97	−19	7	−1.48	—
Vocabulary[+]	110	88	22	97	+1.94	Strength
Auditory Processing[*]	79	97	−18	9	−1.35	—
Picture Vocabulary[^]	109	89	20	95	+1.87	Strength
Oral Comprehension[^]	92	93	−1	43	−0.17	—
Segmentation[^]	86	98	−12	20	−0.84	—
Rapid Picture Naming[^]	84	98	−14	16	−1.01	—
Sentence Repetition	92	90	2	55	+0.12	—
Oral Vocabulary[*]	109	88	21	96	+1.76	Strength
Understanding Directions	73	94	−21	5	−1.63	Weakness
Sound Blending	100	97	3	57	+0.17	—
Retrieval Fluency	74	97	−23	4	−1.77	Weakness
Phonological Processing[*]	84	97	−13	16	−0.98	—
Nonword Repetition[*]	81	97	−16	12	−1.15	—

[+] Cluster obtained, in part, from WJ IV Tests of Cognitive Abilities
[*] Cluster or test obtained from the WJ IV Tests of Cognitive Abilities
[^] Core test for calculation of intra-oral language variations

DON'T FORGET

....

The Amplio lenguaje oral cluster (composed of three Spanish oral language tests) may be used to predict English achievement.

If testing is completed in Spanish, the Amplio lenguaje oral cluster may be used as the predictor. This allows the individual's Spanish oral language ability to predict his or her ability to perform academically in English.

Table 5.3 Rebecca's Oral Language/Achievement Comparisons

Comparison Oral Language/ Achievement	Standard Scores			Discrepancy		Significant at ± 1.50 SD (SEE)
	Actual	Predicted	Difference	PR	SD	
Reading	83	121	−38	<0.1	−3.18	Yes (−)
Broad Reading	70	119	−49	<0.1	−4.03	Yes (−)
Basic Reading Skills	82	120	−38	0.1	−3.00	Yes (−)
Reading Fluency	64	116	−52	<0.1	−3.88	Yes (−)
Mathematics	146	115	31	99	+2.47	Yes (+)
Broad Mathematics	133	114	19	93	+1.46	No
Math Calculation Skills	128	112	16	88	+1.18	No
Written Language	89	117	−28	2	−2.07	Yes (−)
Broad Written Language	93	117	−24	5	−1.68	Yes (−)
Written Expression	99	113	−14	17	−0.94	No
Academic Skills	103	119	−16	11	−1.24	No
Academic Fluency	84	112	−28	2	−2.12	Yes (−)
Academic Applications	106	119	−13	14	−1.09	No

Note: This procedure compares the WJ IV Broad Oral Language cluster score to selected achievement clusters.

Within this comparison procedure, the standard score from the Broad Oral Language cluster, composed of three tests, may be used to predict achievement on any of the achievement clusters. Individuals with a significant negative discrepancy (≥ −1.50) between oral language ability and achievement exhibit relative strengths in oral language with weaknesses in one or more achievement areas. A discrepancy of this size will occur about six out of 100 times. Table 5.3 illustrates an example of the oral language ability/achievement comparison calculations based on the achievement clusters in the Standard Battery for Rebecca, a fifth-grade girl. Rebecca obtained a standard score of 133 on the Broad Oral Language cluster, so many of her achievement scores, especially in the reading and writing areas, are significantly lower than her oral language ability. The results in Table 5.3 indicate that Rebecca scored significantly lower than predicted by her oral language ability in Reading, Broad Reading, Basic Reading Skills, Reading Fluency, Written Language, Broad Written Language, and Academic Fluency. As noted previously, an individual with poor reading and writing abilities but adequate oral language may have a reading disability. Furthermore, her score on Mathematics (SS = 146) is significantly higher than predicted, which indicates she does not have a flat profile that would be associated with generalized low academic performance.

As noted by Stanovich (1991a, 1991b), use of an oral language measure to predict reading and writing is often preferable to use of a general intelligence score because it is more in line with the concept of "potential" and "unexpected" failure. He further explains that using oral language ability as the aptitude measure moves us closer to a more principled definition of reading disability because it provides a more accurate estimate of what the person could achieve if the reading problem were entirely resolved. Essentially, what distinguishes the individual with a reading disability from other poor readers is that listening comprehension ability is higher than ability to decode words (Rack, Snowling, & Olson, 1992), and thus the difficulty is "unpredicted." An individual with a learning disability may or may not exhibit an oral language ability/achievement discrepancy. For example, an older student with reading difficulties may have depressed performance in oral language because of his or her limited experiences with text. This lack of exposure to print contributes to reduced knowledge and vocabulary.

In some cases, the discrepancy between oral and written language abilities is obvious. Figure 5.4 presents a sentence written by Mark, a fourth-grade student, which illustrates a discrepancy between his oral language and written language abilities. His sentence was written in response to Item 7 on Form B of the WJ IV ACH Writing Samples test. The instructions read: "This woman is a queen. Write a sentence that tells what this man is." If you were to just read the sentence, you would think that Mark did not understand the task or was very limited intellectually. However, this is what he said as he was trying to come up with a sentence: "The man is a king. Uh-oh. Hard words. I don't know how to

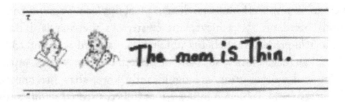

Figure 5.4 Sentence by Mark, a Fourth Grader, Illustrating a Discrepancy Between Oral Language and Writing Ability

spell those words. The man is rich. Another hard word. I don't know how to spell rich. What do I know how to spell? I can spell mom and dad. The mom is a queen. Oh I don't know how to spell queen. What do I know how to spell? Thin, oh I can spell thin." After that, he wrote: "The mom is thin."

Clearly, this illustrates a large discrepancy between Mark's oral language and reasoning abilities and his ability to record his thoughts on paper.

In the field of reading disabilities, one commonly proposed discrepancy model is to compare oral language abilities to specific domains of academic performance. Often individuals with "specific" reading and writing impairments, such as Mark, are described as having a discrepancy between oral and reading and written language abilities. The disability is called "specific" because it primarily affects the development of literacy. The person may struggle with reading, but have no trouble understanding oral discourse or mathematical concepts. The oral language ability/achievement comparison procedure has particular relevance for helping distinguish between individuals who have adequate oral language capabilities but poor reading and writing abilities (i.e., specific reading disabilities) and individuals whose oral language abilities are commensurate with their reading and writing performance. In the first case, intervention would focus on reading and writing development; in the second case, intervention would be directed toward all aspects of language development.

Comparative Language Index (CLI)

The Comparative Language Index (CLI) is a unique comparison procedure available when any of the three parallel English and Spanish clusters have been administered. The CLI is presented as a ratio of the individual's RPI numerators on the two clusters being compared, one in Spanish and one in English. The CLI is helpful in determining language dominance and proficiency. For example, when an individual is administered Tests 1, 2, and 6 in English and Tests 10 through 12 in Spanish, the Broad Oral Language and Amplio lenguaje oral clusters are obtained. Angela, a ninth-grade student, had an RPI for Broad Oral Language of 40/90 and an RPI for Amplio lenguaje oral of 92/90. The CLI is expressed with the Spanish numerator first and the English numerator second resulting in a CLI of 92/40. This CLI indicates that Angela has 92% proficiency on the Spanish cluster and

DON'T FORGET

Information about the Relative Proficiency Index (RPI) can be found in Chapter 4.

40% proficiency on the parallel English cluster. The CLI is available when comparing the following clusters: Oral Language to Lenguaje oral, Broad Oral Language to Amplio lenguaje oral, and Listening Comprehension to Comprensión auditiva.

Cognitive Academic Language Proficiency (CALP)

Another application of the Relative Proficiency Index is the Cognitive-Academic Language Proficiency (CALP) levels that may be reported. (See Chapter 4 for more information about CALP.) If selected in the scoring program, all administered clusters that yield a CALP score are reported in a separate section of the score report. For the WJ IV OL, CALP levels can be reported for the following clusters: Oral Language, Broad Oral Language, Oral Expression, Listening Comprehension, and the three Spanish language clusters: Lenguaje oral, Amplio lenguaje oral, and Comprensión auditiva. Labels attached to the CALP levels describe the individual's proficiency. For example, a person's proficiency on a task may be described as advanced, fluent, or limited. In all, six levels of CALP are available plus two regions that fall between the levels.

STRENGTHS AND WEAKNESSES OF THE WJ IV OL

CAUTION

When a person obtains a low score on a test, consider the reason or reasons for that low score. For example, on Understanding Directions, in one case a low score may be caused by weak memory, whereas in another case, the low score may be caused by inattention.

Because the WJ IV OL was only recently published when this book went to press, no published reviews or critiques existed. During the standardization, we reviewed the instrument carefully and from our initial use we have identified what appear to be its major strengths and limitations. Rapid References 5.24 and 5.25 describe the apparent strengths and weaknesses of the WJ IV OL.

CLINICAL APPLICATIONS OF THE WJ IV OL

Oral language abilities are not only the foundation for success in most academic areas but also the primary avenue through which learning occurs. For this reason, consideration of an individual's oral language abilities is an essential component of a comprehensive evaluation. The WJ IV OL helps explore the

≡ Rapid Reference 5.24

Strengths of the WJ IV OL

- Clusters and tests have high reliability.
- It is normed for use on a wide range of ages and grades.
- It is co-normed with the WJ IV COG and WJ IV ACH, providing more information about the interrelationships among an array of cognitive, linguistic, and academic abilities.
- Use of the Cattell-Hom-Carroll (CHC) theory of cognitive abilities creates a common framework for interpreting results across all three WJ IV batteries.
- It measures several important aspects of oral language that are critical for school and vocational success.
- Broad Oral Language (or Amplio lenguage oral) may be used in an ability/ achievement comparison procedure.
- It includes three parallel Spanish tests that can be used in bilingual evaluations.
- It provides enhanced interpretive options including an intra-oral language variation procedure and an oral language/achievement comparison procedure.
- It is scored by the same online scoring program as the WJ IV ACH and the WJ IV COG.

role of oral language in an individual's achievement performance by providing measures of both receptive and expressive oral language abilities.

Receptive language refers to an individual's ability to understand or comprehend language, including words and gestures. Listening ability is the major skill needed for success in the area of receptive language. Listening requires individuals to receive and correctly interpret the message that is being conveyed. Individuals with

≡ Rapid Reference 5.25

Weaknesses of the WJ IV OL

- Many of the WJ IV OL tests only require single word responses, thus not providing a rich, in-depth measure of expressive language abilities.
- Several of the oral language tests are factorially complex. For example, the Understanding Directions test measures both *Gc* and *Gwm*. Although this makes the test clinically more useful, interpretation of the results may be more difficult.
- Performance on the timed tests may be influenced by cultural differences.
- Several WJ IV OL tests require the use of an audio recording and headphones, increasing the amount of equipment needed for testing.

poor receptive language have difficulty understanding what has been said and difficulty following directions. They become confused listening to lectures and have difficulty understanding what they read. Although they may decode and spell words accurately, they may have limited knowledge of word meanings and limited experiential knowledge. When children are in school, teachers expect them to be able to follow verbal instructions, lectures, and guidelines. For students who have difficulties in listening, the ability to follow through on a given verbal task can be a challenge. Poor receptive language can result in lower grades, gaps in a knowledge base, and difficulty working effectively with others. It can also affect social interactions due to difficulties listening to and understanding language. As children reach adulthood and become employed, poor receptive language abilities can hinder job performance. If the problem is severe enough, the individual may be classified as having a receptive language impairment.

Some students have adequate receptive language but poor expressive language. They understand what is said to them but have difficulty responding orally. Expressive oral language relates to our abilities to retrieve ideas and vocabulary and express these thoughts in an appropriate manner through speaking. Speaking requires developing an intention to speak and formulating thoughts into words and sentences. Deficiencies in the use of expressive language in preschool children have been found to predict subsequent academic difficulties. Individuals with weaknesses in expressive language have difficulty organizing their thoughts, choosing the right words, and expressing their ideas in a clear and fluent manner. They may understand what they hear but not be able to express what they know. These individuals may have trouble expressing their ideas in speaking as well as in writing. Deficits in rapid automatized naming have been associated with individuals with speech and language and reading disorders (Georgiou & Parrila, 2013; Windsor & Kohnert, 2008), so the Rapid Picture Naming test may provide valuable insights. If the problem is severe enough, the student may be classified as having an expressive language impairment.

Weaknesses in oral language affect performance in many areas, in particular reading comprehension, written expression, and math problem solving. A student with weaknesses in oral language may perform adequately on basic skill tests, such as pronouncing and spelling words, but have difficulty on tasks involving the comprehension and use of language. Tasks such as Sentence Repetition require language and memory, both of which are frequently problematic for individuals with language impairments. In addition, these individuals demonstrate difficulty on Understanding Directions and Oral Comprehension. A developmental trend exists on these tasks: Difficulties increase with age. This may be due in large part to the increased language and memory demands as students progress through school.

≡ Rapid Reference 5.26

Factors That Can Affect Oral Language Performance

Possible Reasons for Low Performance in Receptive Language

- Auditory processing deficits
- Attention problems
- Lack of experience and opportunity
- Limited listening skills
- Reduced vocabulary
- Poor understanding of sentence structure
- Difficulty with oral comprehension
- Limits in memory (e.g., working memory capacity, associative memory)

Possible Reasons for Low Performance in Expressive Language

- Poor receptive language
- Difficulty with articulation
- Cultural differences
- Poor word retrieval (inability to recall known words with ease)
- Difficulty with formulation of ideas or organization of thoughts
- Limits in memory (e.g., working memory capacity, associative memory)

An individual who has low performance on oral language tests may require a more comprehensive evaluation from a speech/language therapist. This evaluation will help uncover the intrinsic and extrinsic factors affecting language development. In addition, the speech/language therapist will develop a treatment plan. Rapid Reference 5.26 indicates some possible reasons for low performance on receptive or expressive language tasks.

TEST YOURSELF

1. **Which test includes only the administered items in the raw score?**
    (a) Picture Vocabulary
    (b) Understanding Directions
    (c) Segmentation
    (d) Sound Blending

2. **For which test do the subtests have to be added together to obtain estimated age and grade equivalents?**
   (a) Sound Awareness
   (b) Oral Comprehension
   (c) Picture Vocabulary
   (d) Rapid Picture Naming

3. **On the Rapid Picture Naming test, if the examinee called a picture of a car an *auto* you would score it as correct.**
   True or False?

4. **The oral language ability/achievement comparison procedure requires administration of the WJ IV COG.**
   True or False?

5. **The oral language ability/achievement comparison procedure compares one area of achievement to the average of the person's other areas of achievement.**
   True or false?

6. **About how often will an SD discrepancy of − 1.50 occur?**
   (a) Two out of 1,000 times
   (b) Two out of 100 times
   (c) Six out of 100 times
   (d) Five out of 1,000 times

7. **Which of the following tests does not have a parallel Spanish version?**
   (a) Picture Vocabulary
   (b) Oral Comprehension
   (c) Sentence Repetition
   (d) Understanding Directions

8. **What is the minimum number of tests needed to calculate an intra-oral language variation procedure?**
   (a) Three
   (b) Four
   (c) Five
   (d) Six

9. **The primary purpose of the oral-language variation procedure is:**
   (a) To determine if there is a discrepancy between ability and achievement
   (b) To determine the individual's overall oral language ability
   (c) To determine if the individual requires further evaluation
   (d) To determine the individual's pattern of strengths and weaknesses among oral language abilities

10. **Which of the following is not indicative of difficulty with receptive language?**

(a) Choosing the right words

(b) Comprehending language

(c) Following directions

(d) Understanding a lecture

Answers: 1. b; 2. a; 3. True; 4. False; 5. False; 6. c; 7. c; 8. b; 9. d; 10. a

Six

STRENGTHS AND WEAKNESSES OF THE WJ IV ACH

John O. Willis

Rivier University

Ron Dumont

Fairleigh Dickinson University

We still have our worn, dog-eared copies of the Goldman-Fristoe-Woodcock Auditory Skills Test Battery (GFW) (Goldman, Fristoe, & Woodcock, 1974) and the four previous editions of the Woodcock-Johnson (Woodcock & Johnson, 1977, 1989; Woodcock, McGrew, & Mather, 2001, 2007), but we have also used many other tests of academic achievement and oral language over the past 45 years, so this assessment of strengths and weaknesses is based on reasonably broad and deep experience with the Woodcock-Johnson and other measures. Because the WJ IV had just been released when this book went to press, no published reviews or critiques existed and examiners had not accumulated much testing experience.

This review identified far more strengths than weaknesses in the WJ IV Tests of Achievement. The assets that made the WJ III (Woodcock, McGrew, & Mather, 2001, 2007) a valuable and popular test battery appear to remain intact in the new WJ IV, and the changes appear to be improvements. The WJ IV ACH appears to be technically sound, with tests meeting or exceeding current psychometric standards and offering both usual and customary features and ones that are unique to the WJ IV. We anticipate using and teaching the WJ IV ACH.

TEST DEVELOPMENT AND STRUCTURE

Tests from the WJ III COG and ACH batteries have been reshuffled and tests have been added to create revised Cognitive and Achievement batteries, and a new Oral Language battery, creating three co-normed batteries: COG, ACH, and OL. As with the WJ III (Woodcock, McGrew, & Mather, 2001, 2007), examiners must purchase three batteries to make full use of the WJ IV.

We have often referred to the entire Woodcock-Johnson as the "Swiss Army knife of assessment." With 20 tests of Achievement (four new), 12 tests of Oral Language (one new and three in Spanish), and 18 Cognitive tests (four new), several of which could be included in an assessment of academic achievement, the WJ IV offers the broadest coverage of discrete skills and abilities of any test we have seen. This breadth of cognitive, oral language, and achievement tests, all normed on the same sample of examinees, is a tremendous asset. Like MacGyver's knife, the WJ IV offers a tool for almost every purpose.

Such a broad array of tests necessitates some brevity of individual tests. With 50 tests in the complete WJ IV, no single test can have a huge number of items, and preference needs to be given in most instances to short-response test items. Examiners seeking a large number of test responses for a detailed item analysis, a long story or essay to evaluate, or a test of comprehension of extended reading passages must supplement the WJ IV, just as MacGyver would need a full-sized wrench to loosen a tight bolt.

The WJ IV ACH also offers some tests and clusters that are rare or unique, such as the Spelling of Sounds test and the cross-domain Academic Skills, Academic Fluency, and Academic Applications clusters cutting across reading, writing, and math. Similarly, an astonishing number of possible comparisons are available among the cognitive, oral language, and achievement tests and clusters, including specific measures of predicted achievement in several domains. The availability of three forms of the WJ IV ACH facilitates periodic reassessment by the same examiner or assessment by another examiner.

As with all test instruments and test scores, the WJ IV ACH results need to be integrated with other data about the examinee, including consideration of test behaviors, data from other previous and concurrent assessments, results of informal procedures, information obtained from parents and teachers, and classroom observations. The Woodcock Interpretation and Instructional Interventions[TM] Package—Online Scoring and Reporting, planned for release in early 2015, is intended to provide access to nine Woodcock-Johnson checklists, which should facilitate the integration process.

Assessment of reading and reading-related skills has been enhanced by the addition of several new tests and clusters. The WJ IV ACH now offers: Broad Reading (Letter-Word Identification, Passage Comprehension, and Sentence Reading Fluency tests), Reading (Letter-Word Identification, Passage Comprehension), Basic Reading Skills (Letter-Word Identification, Word Attack), Reading Comprehension (Passage Comprehension, Reading Recall), Reading Comprehension-Extended (Passage Comprehension, Reading Recall, Reading Vocabulary), Reading Fluency (Oral Reading, Sentence Reading Fluency), Reading Rate (Sentence Reading Fluency, Word Reading Fluency), and Phoneme–Grapheme Knowledge (Word Attack, Spelling of Sounds). This is the widest array of discrete reading measures and composite scores that we have seen in a single achievement test battery. Addition of tests from the Cognitive and Oral Language batteries can provide additional, important reading-related clusters.

A deliberate effort has been made to add easier items to many of the WJ IV ACH tests to provide a sufficient "bottom" for younger and lower-scoring examinees. This is a welcome improvement because scores are much more interpretable when the examinee achieves a genuine basal (rather than simply reaching the first item) and when the raw score is greater than zero. However, for those younger and lower-scoring individuals, it is sometimes necessary to test an exhaustive inventory of all items in a particular skill (such as the names of all upper- and lowercase letters or all addition and subtraction facts to 10), not merely test a sufficient sample for a normative score (see, e.g., Dumont & Willis, 2014). When such an inventory is needed for instructional purposes, the examiner must go beyond the scope of normed, individually administered achievement tests.

For examiners new to the WJ or new to testing achievement in general, the *Tests of Achievement Examiner's Manual* (Mather & Wendling, 2014a) is especially valuable. Each test is described with special consideration given to the fine points of administration and scoring. One of these reviewers (RPD) was totally confused by the scoring criteria presented in the easel for the Spelling of Sounds test. Given the test's name, one might expect that the test was just that: a measure of correctly spelling the sounds being presented. This was not the case, which is very clearly explained in the Examiner's Manual. We cannot stress enough the old mantra of "read the manual!"

Spelling of Sounds, and some COG and OL tests, must be presented with the CD and good-quality audio equipment. The Examiner's Manual (pp. 32–33) is more blunt than was the WJ III in requiring this administration unless the examinee actually has difficulty with or resists using the recording, or has difficulty attending to the recording. Sadly, some WJ III examiners routinely administered audio-recorded tests orally, using the excuse that the examinee would probably dislike the audio-recorded presentation. The recorded presentation is a significant strength of the WJ IV. Examiners vary considerably in their oral reading skills and only a few examiners are able to pronounce isolated speech sounds, such as /b/ (not "buh") correctly. Presentation with good-quality audio equipment ensures accurate administration in conformity with the standardization. Another strength of Spelling of Sounds is the return to the original Goldman-Fristoe-Woodcock administration, in which the examinee repeats the nonsense word before attempting to spell it. Comparison of the spoken response (which is not scored) with the written one can provide valuable diagnostic information.

The WJ IV ACH is conveniently designed so that trained examiners can administer the tests with the Test Books (easels), Test Records, and Response Booklets, but the Examiner's Manual provides essential additional information, including clear, detailed instructions for administration; guidance in testing accommodations for special needs; information on scoring; explanations of the various statistics used; and methods for interpreting the tests, clusters, and variation and comparison scores. Also included are Writing Samples Scoring Guides, an Examiner Training Checklist, and a General Test Observations Checklist. Careful study of the Examiner's Manual is not only helpful but also essential for proper administration, and the manual is necessary for correct scoring of Writing Samples. Rapid Reference 6.1 presents additional information about the test development and structure.

TEST INTERPRETATION

The test development process included a serious effort to enhance and significantly expand the interpretive options for the WJ IV ACH. The new test structure reflects many of the recent changes that have been made in Cattell-Horn-Carroll (CHC) theory (Flanagan et al., 2013), making the WJ IV a good choice as the core battery for a cross-battery assessment as well as a source of tests to supplement other instruments.

The 20 achievement tests yield 22 clusters (eight new). The additional clusters considerably expand the interpretive possibilities for evaluators, but they also require some self-restraint and thoughtful planning. Examiners must resist the temptation to throw everything at the wall (or at parents and teachers) and see what sticks. Clusters, their component tests, and comparisons must be chosen carefully to answer referral questions, help illuminate referral concerns, and provide information that will be useful for instructional planning.

Many possible comparison and discrepancy procedures are offered (some using the COG and OL batteries), including discrepancies between the Academic

≡ Rapid Reference 6.1

Primary Strengths and Weaknesses of the WJ IV ACH: Test Development and Structure

Primary Strengths	Primary Weaknesses
• Addition of a separate Oral Language Battery provides three co-normed batteries: COG, ACH, and OL.	• Examiners must purchase three batteries to make full use of the WJ IV.
• The ACH battery has 20 tests (and examiners can select additional COG and OL tests) covering a very broad array of information.	• The extraordinary breadth of the WJ IV batteries requires that each test be relatively brief.
• For the Standard Battery, parallel, alternate forms (A and B) are provided for repeated testing and a third from (C) is available for later comprehensive assessment by another evaluator.	• Although extremely valuable, the additional forms increase the cost of the WJ IV. (Use of a single form for the Extended Battery does limit the additional cost.)
• Easier items have been added to many tests to provide more "bottom" for younger and lower-scoring examinees.	• As with any normed achievement test, examiners may need to analyze certain skills in more depth.
• Using the ACH and OL batteries together provides important measures of phonetic coding and speed of lexical access.	
• Several new reading and reading-related clusters have been added.	
• A Qualitative Checklist is provided for each Standard Battery test.	
• Science, Social Studies, and Humanities tests have been updated as full-length tests and the composite can be compared to academic achievement.	
• New Oral Reading, Word Reading Fluency, Reading Recall, and Number Matrices tests have been added.	
• Spelling of Sounds has been retained and has been enhanced by including oral repetition of the word before writing it.	
• Administration of Spelling of Sounds by CD reduces examiner error and interexaminer variability.	• Examiners must be persuaded to use good-quality audio equipment for all tests that use a CD. (Some WJ III examiners did not use the CDs at all.)

Primary Strengths	Primary Weaknesses
• Co-normed batteries ensure that all cluster and test comparisons and comparisons of achievement with predicted achievement are based on scores of a single norming sample. • The WJ IV ACH can be administered with only the test books and record forms, but there is also a helpful Examiner's Manual that is needed for scoring of Writing Samples.	

Knowledge cluster and two oral language clusters and other achievement clusters; comparisons among the Academic Skills, Academic Fluency, and Academic Applications clusters; discrepancies between cognitive abilities from the WJ IV COG and achievement scores; discrepancies between oral language ability and levels of achievement; and discrepancies between achievement scores and predicted achievement based on selected groups of cognitive tests.

A variation procedure to explore individual strengths and weaknesses efficiently compares achievement scores to predicted scores based on administration of only the six core achievement tests. Each of the six tests can be compared to a predictor based on the scores of the other five core tests. If additional tests are given, they and their clusters can also be compared to the appropriate five-test predictor score. For example, Oral Reading and the Reading Fluency cluster would each be compared to the same predictor used for Letter-Word Identification.

The same caveat about resisting the temptation to see if one can compulsively sift through all of the possible data and find some significant comparison somewhere must apply here. If, for example, an examiner administered just the 17 achievement tests (excluding Science, Social Studies, and Humanities) and computed the intra-achievement (Extended) variations, a total of 26 discrepancy scores would be produced. Given the vast number of tests and clusters available for comparison when using all three WJ IV batteries, there is a real chance that an examiner would find something that appears significant just by chance.

Eleven of the WJ IV ACH clusters provide levels of cognitive academic language proficiency (CALP) (Cummins, 2003). The distinction between CALP and basic interpersonal communication skills (BICS) is an important one, especially with students who are English language learners or, for other reasons, lack age-appropriate academic oral language skills. The WJ IV CALP scores can be used to alert teachers to potential concerns.

≡ Rapid Reference 6.2

Primary Strengths and Weaknesses of the WJ IV ACH: Test Interpretation

Primary Strengths	Primary Weaknesses
• Application of the most recent reformulations of CHC theory to COG, ACH, and OL batteries provides a common interpretive framework within the WJ IV and with other tests using CHC theory.	• In its current state of development, CHC theory is better defined for cognitive abilities than for achievement measures.
• New clusters have been added, including Reading Fluency and Reading Rate as well as two-test Reading, Mathematics, and Written Language clusters that omit tests of fluency.	• Examiners need to select and report the clusters that provide useful information about the examinee.
• Many new cluster and test comparisons and improved comparison procedures have been added.	• Examiners need to refrain from mindlessly running and reporting all possible comparisons.
• A new variation procedure permits comparison among the Academic Skills, Fluency, and Application clusters.	
• Administration of the six core tests permits calculation of predicted achievement for each test based on the other five scores. Other tests and clusters can also be compared to the appropriate predicted achievement score.	
• Achievement and two oral language clusters can be compared to the Academic Knowledge cluster.	
• CALP scores are provided for 11 WJ IV ACH clusters.	

Rapid Reference 6.2 summarizes the primary strengths and weaknesses related to interpretation of the WJ IV ACH.

TEST SCORING

Scoring for most of the tests is very straightforward. As previously noted, the Examiner's Manual provides detailed guidance for scoring tests that have extensive scoring guidelines. One of the greatest strengths of the WJ IV ACH is the power of the online scoring, which saves time; permits scoring by 1-month rather than 3-, 6-, or 12-month intervals of age or grade; allows a multiplicity of different clusters for various purposes; and precludes errors in looking up, calculating, and recording scores (but not clerical errors in entering raw scores). A few examiners fear that this capability is also a weakness: There is no way to score the test without a computer or computerized device, and examiners must have faith in the reliability and security of the online data storage. Offline scoring by a mobile app is supposed to be available in late 2014. As with any new technology, examiners must take the time to learn the new system. Just as with the WJ III Compuscore program, the new online scoring provides many options the end user will find extremely valuable. These include, to name just a few: the ability to customize scoring templates based upon an individual user's preferences; the choice of a vast array of scores to report (e.g., SS, NCE, stanines, PR, PR ranges); and a new "Roster" report that collects all the scores from various examinees into one report.

As anyone who hand-scored the WJ-R (Woodcock & Johnson, 1989) knows, there simply would be no possible way to provide printed tables of norms at 1-month age and grade intervals for the 20 tests and 22 achievement clusters, for the many scores, for differences between them, and for myriad comparisons between tests and clusters when using all three WJ IV batteries. Having scores based on single months of age or grade rather than spans of several months or even years prevents the sometimes dramatic overnight changes in derived scores on other tests as a student switches, for example, from fall to spring norms (Willis & Dumont, 2002, pp. 115–116). In our opinion, that virtue and the wide variety of clusters and interpretive reports that will become available justify the necessary exclusive reliance on computerized scoring. In addition, the use of computer algorithms to accurately pinpoint a person's abilities (whether cognitive, oral language, or academic achievement) makes the WJ IV one of the most technically sophisticated tests available. Those who use optional computer scoring for other tests will be especially happy. Most of us who generally tend to eschew computer scoring will probably be nervous, but pleased with the results.

The Examiner's Manual warns examiners that "not all possible correct and incorrect answers are listed. Judgment is required when scoring some responses" (p. 36) and it elaborates on this important issue. When given responses that are not listed and are not clearly correct or incorrect, examiners may need to consult dictionaries, thesauruses, and other references to ensure correct scoring.

The Examiner's Manual (p. 27) admonishes us not to administer all three fluency tests in a row, but to intersperse them with other tests. This warning is not repeated in the Administration Overviews for those tests in the test books. (See Rapid Reference 6.3 for further information about scoring.)

≡ Rapid Reference 6.3

Primary Strengths and Weaknesses of the WJ IV ACH: Test Scoring

Primary Strengths	Primary Weaknesses
• Computer scoring permits calculation of many scores and comparisons that would be impossible with hand scoring.	• Scoring exclusively by computer precludes checking by hand scoring and delays preliminary scoring until a computer is available.
• Computer scoring eliminates errors in arithmetic and in looking up scores in printed tables.	• Computer scoring does not prevent typographic errors in entering scores and may make it more difficult to catch those errors.
• Offline score entry through mobile apps is available.	• Initially, only online scoring will be available, which may be difficult for itinerant evaluators.
• Summary and Score Reports in English, Parent Reports in English or Spanish, Longitudinal Reports of all WJ evaluations of a child, and age/grade and SS/PR profiles are available.	• Some examiners will be tempted to enter the scores, print the Score Report and Parent Report, and just sign and distribute the printouts.
• Computer scoring permits norms to be based on 1-month intervals of age or grade, preventing large overnight changes in scores between, for example, fall and spring norms or norms for age 9-0 through 9-6 and 9-7 through 9-11.	• Given the tremendous technical precision of, and broad choices available from, the online scoring, examiners must understand any and all scores chosen for interpretation. Simply letting the software produce scores, or identify differences between scores, could lead to misinterpretations of the results.
• Roster Reports (customizable group reports) are available.	
• Score Reports (scores and calculations of variations and comparisons) are available.	
• The WJ IV Interpretation and Instructional Interventions™ Program (WIIIP) (comprehensive report and optional interventions) is available.	
• Scoring of most tests is straightforward. The Examiner's Manual provides detailed guidance for scoring the other tests.	

STANDARDIZATION, RELIABILITY, AND VALIDITY

The WJ IV ACH was normed on an extremely large, carefully selected sample including 664 preschoolers, 3,891 students in grades K through 12, 775 college and graduate students, and 2,086 other adults drawn from 46 states and the District of Columbia. There were six to eight sampling variables for various age levels, all of which closely matched the 2010 U.S. Census projections, and partial subject weighting was used to make the matches even more accurate. Not all examinees took all tests, but a sophisticated planned incomplete data collection, multiple matrix sampling design was employed, which may actually yield more accurate norms. This procedure is thoroughly explained in the WJ IV Technical Manual, which also provides extensive cluster summary and reliability statistics for all tests and clusters in Appendices B and C. Special Group Studies are reported for nine clinical groups, although not for persons with hearing impairments. However, the WJ IV ACH Examiner's Manual (pp. 44–47) provides valuable information about testing persons with hearing impairments.

Item Response Theory statistics provide specific test reliabilities at each age or grade, not just for entire tests. Those reliabilities for nonspeeded measures (those without time limits) are generally very strong: .70 to .98 (median .91) for ACH tests and .90 to .99 (median .96) for clusters. Test-retest stability coefficients are reported for speeded tests and clusters (.76 to .97; median .91), but not for nonspeeded tests and clusters.

The Technical Manual includes a great deal of information on the latest developments in CHC theory and extensive factor analytic data supporting the internal structure of the WJ IV. Concurrent validity studies show moderate to strong correlations between WJ IV ACH and the Kaufman Test of Educational Achievement (KTEA-II) (Kaufman & Kaufman, 2004), the Wechsler Individual Achievement Test (WIAT-III) (Wechsler, 2009), and the Oral and Written Language Scales: Written Expression (OWLS) (Carrow-Woolfolk, 1996). Correlations between WJ IV ACH tests and clusters and scores for other achievement tests are consistently higher for related measures (e.g., reading comprehension) than for less closely related constructs (e.g., reading decoding and reading comprehension or reading and math). Rapid Reference 6.4 provides additional information about the standardization, reliability, and validity of the WJ IV ACH.

≡ Rapid Reference 6.4

Primary Strengths and Weaknesses of the WJ IV ACH: Standardization, Reliability, and Validity

Primary Strengths	Primary Weaknesses
• Extremely large norming samples (664 preschoolers, 3,891 students in grades K through 12, 775 college and graduate students, and 2,086 adults.	• Not all examinees took all tests, but a sophisticated planned incomplete data collection, multiple matrix sampling design was employed, which may actually yield more accurate norms.
• Examinees were drawn from 46 states and the District of Columbia.	
• There were six sampling variables for preschool, seven for school, five for college, and eight for adults.	
• The norming sample closely matched the 2010 U.S. Census projections on these variables, and partial subject weighting was used to refine the matches.	
• Cluster summary and reliability statistics for all tests and clusters can be found in Appendices B and C of the Technical Manual.	
• Special Group Studies are reported for nine clinical groups.	• Persons with hearing impairments were not included in the clinical groups.
• Item Response Theory statistics provide specific test reliabilities at each age or grade.	
• Reliabilities are generally very strong.	
• Reliabilities of nonspeeded ACH tests are .70 to .98 (median .905). Reliabilities of nonspeeded clusters are .90 to .99 (median .96).	
• Test-retest stability coefficients are reported for speeded tests.	• The Technical Manual does not include test-retest stability coefficients for other tests.
• The Technical Manual includes a great deal of information on the latest developments in CHC theory and extensive factor analytic data supporting the internal structure.	

Primary Strengths	Primary Weaknesses
• Concurrent validity studies show moderate to strong correlations between the WJ IV ACH and the KTEA-II and the WIAT-III. • Related WJ IV tests and other tests and subtests show higher correlations than do less closely related measures.	

TEST YOURSELF

1. **Achievement test and cluster scores can be compared to scores from**
   (a) Only the Achievement Battery
   (b) Only the Oral Language Battery
   (c) Only the Cognitive Battery
   (d) All three batteries

2. **The Cattell-Horn-Carroll theory of cognitive abilities provides a framework for interpretation of the cognitive tests but not the achievement tests.**
   True or False?

3. **The WJ IV ACH has the same reading tests and clusters as the WJ III ACH.**
   True or False?

4. **A strength of the WJ IV ACH is that it can be used alone without the other batteries.**
   True or False?

5. **A strength of the WJ IV ACH is that**
   (a) Although there are only a few tests, each test has a great many items.
   (b) There are many tests in the battery.
   (c) The number of math tests has been reduced.
   (d) The reading and written language tests focus on very long passages.

6. **A strength of the WJ IV ACH is that**
   (a) A Language of Math test has been added.
   (b) A different norming sample exists for the Achievement Battery.
   (c) It tests a very broad array of academic skills.
   (d) It uses only a small number of tightly focused tests.

7. **A strength of the WJ IV ACH is that**
   (a) Qualitative Checklists have been added to all Standard Battery tests.
   (b) Qualitative Checklists have been added to all Standard and Extended Battery tests.

(c) Quantitative Checklists have been added to all mathematics tests.

(d) Qualitative Checklists have been added to Extended Battery tests.

8. The WJ IV ACH

(a) Can be scored by hand on the Special Record Form

(b) Can now be scored online and, in the future, scores will be able to be entered offline

(c) Can be scored offline with the CD and will later be able to be scored online

(d) Can be scored with WJ III software with a downloadable upgrade

9. A weakness of the WJ IV Technical Manual is that

(a) There are extensive reliability data, but no validity data reported.

(b) Test-retest stability data are reported only for speeded tests.

(c) Little information is given about the norming sample.

(d) There are norms for kindergarten, but none for preschool children.

10. A strength of the WJ IV ACH is that

(a) New tests have been added, but there are no new clusters.

(b) New clusters have been added, but there are no new tests.

(c) New tests and clusters have been added.

(d) The familiar WJ III tests and clusters have not been changed.

11. A strength of the WJ IV ACH is that the variation procedure for considering achievement strengths and weaknesses

(a) Requires administration of 17 tests and can be applied to any of them

(b) Requires administration of only six tests but can be applied to 17 tests and nine clusters

(c) Requires administration of only six tests and can be applied only to those tests

(d) Is an informal procedure depending on the examiner's judgment

12. A weakness of normed achievement tests for young children, including the WJ IV ACH, is that examiners may need to completely inventory some basic skills.
True or False?

13. The WJ IV ACH Examiner's Manual is a strength because it is clear and comprehensive, and it

(a) Is needed during administration of some tests

(b) Is needed during scoring of one test

(c) Includes only technical information

(d) Need not be studied until after the examiner has gained experience with the tests

Answers: 1. d; 2. False; 3. False; 4. True; 5. b; 6. c; 7. a; 8. b; 9. b; 10. c; 11. b; 12. True; 13. b.

Seven

CLINICAL APPLICATIONS OF THE WJ IV ACH

Diagnosis must take second place to instruction, and must be made a tool of instruction, not an end in itself.

(Cruickshank, 1977, p. 193)

The purposes of an educational evaluation are to identify an individual's strengths and weaknesses and then design an educational program to meet this person's needs. This plan may include specific accommodations, such as oral testing and extended time on tests, or it may include specific instructional strategies and materials. Although lists of instructional materials and recommendations are beyond the scope of this book, Chapter 4 does provide instructional implications for each academic area. Also, Mather and Jaffe (in press) provide lists of recommendations and summaries of instructional methods that can be appended to reports.

The focus of this chapter is on clinical applications of the WJ IV ACH. The most common clinical use of the WJ IV ACH is for the diagnosis of specific learning disabilities (SLD), particularly for the diagnosis of reading, mathematics, and writing disabilities. The WJ IV ACH is also used to help identify individuals who have exceptionally high or low academic performance. In addition, an analysis of variations in performance can help the evaluator determine specific strengths and weaknesses within academic performance and whether academic knowledge is commensurate with the person's other areas of academic performance.

SPECIFIC LEARNING DISABILITIES

The WJ IV ACH can provide helpful information for documenting a specific learning disability (SLD). A *learning disability* is defined in the Individuals with Disabilities Education Improvement Act (IDEA, 2004) as "a disorder in one or more of the basic psychological processes." In order to be identified as having a learning disability, one of

≡ Rapid Reference 7.1

Six SLD Areas (IDEA, 2004) Measured by the WJ IV ACH
1. Basic reading skills
2. Reading fluency
3. Reading comprehension
4. Math calculation
5. Math reasoning
6. Written expression

Two Additional SLD Areas Measured by the WJ IV OL
1. Oral expression
2. Listening comprehension

eight achievement areas must be significantly affected by the disorder. These eight areas of achievement include: oral expression, listening comprehension, basic reading skill, reading fluency, reading comprehension, written expression, mathematics calculation, and mathematics reasoning. The WJ IV ACH provides cluster scores for six of the required SLD areas, as listed in Rapid Reference 7.1. The WJ IV OL measures the two additional areas: oral expression and listening comprehension.

DON'T FORGET

Even though basic writing skills and academic knowledge are not included under the IDEA categories for SLDs, you will still want to consider these abilities in an evaluation. Many students with SLDs have adequate oral language abilities, and relative strengths are found in academic knowledge with relative weaknesses in basic writing skills, particularly spelling.

An SLD is often characterized as "unexpected" or "unexplained" poor performance based on observations of the person's other capabilities and not predicted by general intellectual competence. In an attempt to operationalize the construct of unexpected underachievement, prior to IDEA 2004, the primary criterion used for identifying an SLD was a discrepancy between intelligence or aptitude (used to predict potential for school success) and achievement (the present levels of academic performance). With the reauthorization, however, an ability–achievement discrepancy is no longer required. School districts may use a discrepancy procedure if they wish, but they cannot be required to do so.

Over the past several decades, considerable controversy has existed regarding the use and implementation of this criterion for SLD identification. Historically, many have objected to the sole use of this criterion for SLD identification. For example, Stanovich (1994) stated: "None of the critics of discrepancy definitions are denying the existence of severe reading disability per se or the importance of remedial help. Instead, they are questioning the rationale of differential treatment and resources being allocated on the basis of IQ-achievement discrepancy" (p. 355). Similarly, Fletcher, Lyon, Fuchs, and Barnes (2007) described evaluating domain-specific achievement skills, the intra-individual differences within these achievement domains, and the abilities related to these skills as a more appropriate approach to the identification of an SLD than use of an IQ-achievement discrepancy model.

If an ability/achievement discrepancy is part of the evaluation process, the WJ IV offers a best practice approach for documenting discrepancies. Because the WJ IV ACH is co-normed with the WJ IV COG and the WJ IV OL, the same norm group is used for all comparisons, eliminating the inherent error introduced when comparing results from tests with different norm groups. In addition, both age and grade norms are provided for all three batteries, allowing you to choose the most relevant norm comparison. Finally, the WJ IV provides actual discrepancy or difference score norms that reflect developmental differences, correlations, and regression.

In addition to the WJ IV COG, results from the WJ IV ACH may also be compared to other intelligence tests. However, when using another test to make comparisons for an ability–achievement discrepancy, you will most likely need to use age norms because most other intelligence tests only offer age norms and then apply a correction for statistical regression.

CAUTION

If comparing the WJ IV ACH to another intelligence test besides the WJ IV COG, score the test with age norms because most intelligence tests only provide age norms. You must also correct for the effects of statistical regression.

DON'T FORGET

Use of the WJ IV ACH in Ability–Achievement Discrepancies

Although IDEA 2004 does not require the existence of an ability–achievement discrepancy for SLD identification, districts may use this criterion as part of the process. The WJ IV ACH and the WJ IV OL can be used in conjunction with the WJ IV COG or with any other intelligence test to determine whether a discrepancy exists between overall ability and any of the eight IDEA achievement areas.

Statistical regression is a phenomenon that occurs when comparing two variables (a predictor and a criterion) that are not perfectly correlated, such as when using a global score from an intelligence test to predict achievement. If performance on the first variable (e.g., IQ) is above average (or below average), then performance on the second variable (e.g., achievement) is likely to move, or regress, toward normal or the mean. This phenomenon must be accounted for or incorrect conclusions may be reached. For example, if an individual obtains a global IQ score of 70 and then receives an achievement score of 80, some examiners may conclude that the individual is overachieving. If the correlation between the intelligence test and the achievement test is .60, then based on an IQ of 70 the predicted achievement score would be 82. On the other hand, if the intelligence score is 130, then some examiners may expect the achievement score to be that high as well. If the individual obtains an achievement score of 120, some may conclude this individual is underachieving. Using the same correlation of .60, the predicted achievement score in this case is 118, again moving toward the mean. When the two variables have higher correlations, the effect of regression is reduced. For example, if the correlation is .70, then an IQ of 70 would yield an expected achievement score of 79. If the two variables were perfectly correlated (1.0), there would be no expected difference in scores. In addition, when the predictor is at or very close to the mean (e.g., an IQ of 100), the effect of regression is minimal.

In an ability–achievement discrepancy calculation, the predicted achievement score (e.g., 79) rather than the obtained intelligence score (70) is compared to the actual achievement score. So if a person obtained a Broad Reading standard score of 60, the difference would be −19 points (79–60). If the IQ score were used, the difference would be −10 points (70–60). If one does not correct for the effects of statistical regression, high performing individuals are overidentified as having a discrepancy, and low performing individuals are underidentified.

The best practice is to use co-normed tests that provide actual difference score norms, like the WJ IV batteries. If the tests being used are not co-normed, then the relationship between the predictor and the criterion must be estimated using a regression equation or a table based on the equation.

There is no one specific test or one specific score that will accurately diagnose an SLD. In addition to test scores, you have to consider family history, educational history, parent and teacher reports, behavioral observations, informal work samples, and the results of other tests to make an accurate diagnosis. For example, in reference to dyslexia, Pennington (2009) stated:

If a child has dyslexia, then certain things ought to be true and not true across heterogeneous domains of data, including presenting symptoms, the early developmental history, the school history, the behavior during testing (including kinds of errors), and the test results. A particular diagnosis is supported by a converging pattern of results across these different domains of data and by a diverging pattern of results for competing diagnoses. (p. 32)

Before diagnosing a student as having an SLD, some states require the identification of a processing disorder. Determining the presence of a processing disorder generally involves using cognitive and linguistic tests (e.g., tests of memory, language, phonological processing, rapid automatized naming, or processing speed) that measure the abilities believed to underlie and affect academic learning. When the WJ IV ACH is used in conjunction with the co-normed WJ IV COG and WJ IV OL, you can obtain comprehensive information about cognitive and linguistic processing, academic performance, and discrepancies and variations using actual discrepancy norms. Fletcher et al. (2007) note: "Generally, the more information that is brought to bear on any eligibility or diagnostic decision, the more reliable the decision" (p. 53). The WJ IV intra-ability variation procedures (see Chapter 4) are designed to help document the individual's strengths and weaknesses within achievement areas, or cognitive abilities or oral language abilities.

Reading

The WJ IV ACH has eight reading tests: Letter-Word Identification, Passage Comprehension, Word Attack, Oral Reading, Sentence Reading Fluency, Reading Recall, Word Reading Fluency, and Reading Vocabulary. These tests provide important measures of various aspects of reading achievement. The Letter-Word Identification and Word Attack tests form a Basic Reading Skills cluster. Both measures of word identification (Letter-Word Identification) and nonsense (pseudo word) reading (Word Attack) are needed in a comprehensive evaluation of reading. The Passage Comprehension and Reading Recall tests create the Reading Comprehension cluster. Oral Reading and Sentence Reading Fluency create the Reading Fluency cluster and provide important information about expression (prosody) and reading fluency. Sentence Reading Fluency and Word Reading Fluency form the Reading Rate cluster and provide information about automaticity and speed of reading. Rapid Reference 7.2 reviews the abilities measured by the WJ IV ACH reading tests as well as which SLD areas are assessed. Rapid Reference 7.3 lists possible reasons for low performance in basic reading skills, reading rate and fluency, and reading comprehension.

≡ Rapid Reference 7.2

Abilities Measured by the WJ IV ACH Reading Tests

Test	Ability	Required LD Area
Letter-Word Identification	Letter and word identification	Basic reading skills
Passage Comprehension	Syntactic and semantic cues	Reading comprehension
Word Attack	Nonsense word reading	Basic reading skills
Oral Reading	Word reading accuracy and prosody	Reading fluency
Sentence Reading Fluency	Automaticity and rate	Reading fluency
Reading Recall	Meaningful memory	Reading comprehension
Word Reading Fluency	Reading rate	Reading fluency
Reading Vocabulary	Lexical knowledge	Reading comprehension

≡ Rapid Reference 7.3

Factors That Can Affect Reading Performance

Possible Reasons for Low Performance in Basic Reading Skills

- Poor phonological awareness
- Poor orthographic awareness
- Slow processing speed
- Limited alphabetic knowledge
- Trouble pronouncing multisyllabic words
- Limited instruction

Possible Reasons for Low Performance in Reading Rate and Fluency

- Poor attention
- Slow rapid automatized naming (RAN)
- Slow processing speed
- Poor basic reading skills
- Limited instruction
- Limited time spent reading

Possible Reasons for Low Performance in Reading Comprehension
- Poor basic reading skills
- Limited oral language
- Low vocabulary
- Low reasoning ability
- Limited use of strategies
- Lack of experiences and exposure
- Low motivation and interest
- Limited instruction

Early Identification of Children at Risk for Reading Failure

Considerable research on the early identification of reading difficulties has focused on identifying measures to predict future reading achievement in preschool or kindergarten children. Three abilities appear to be good predictors of risk for reading failure: letter/sound knowledge (Perfetti, 2007; Shaywitz, Morris, & Shaywitz, 2008), phonological awareness (sensitivity to the sounds in spoken words) (Berninger et al., 2006; Cooper, 2006; Shaywitz et al., 2008; Torgesen, 2002), and rapid naming (the capacity to name arrays of letters, digits, colors, or pictured objects rapidly) (Berninger, Abbott, Thomson, & Raskind, 2001; Georgiou & Parrila, 2013; Kintsch & Rawson, 2005; Wagner & Torgesen, 1987; Wolf, Bowers, & Biddle, 2000).

The WJ IV ACH has several measures of letter–sound knowledge (Letter-Word Identification, Word Attack, and Spelling of Sounds) and two measures of phonological coding (Word Attack and Spelling of Sounds). The WJ IV OL has an adapted measure of rapid naming, the Rapid Picture Naming test, which is designed to measure speed of lexical retrieval.

DON'T FORGET

Best Predictors of Beginning Reading Achievement

- Phonological awareness and phonological coding
  WJ IV ACH tests: Word Attack, Spelling of Sounds
  WJ OL tests: Sound Blending, Segmentation, Sound Awareness
- Letter–sound identification
  WJ IV ACH tests: Letter-Word Identification, Word Attack, Spelling of Sounds
- Rapid naming
  WJ IV OL test: Rapid Picture Naming

≡ *Rapid Reference 7.4*

Symptoms of Dyslexia

- Poor phonological awareness
- Poor orthographic awareness (knowledge and recall of English spelling patterns)
- Slow processing speed and/or rapid automatized naming (RAN)
- Letter reversals and transpositions (e.g., *was* for *saw*) that persist past the age of 7
- Spelling words the way they sound rather than how they look
- Trouble pronouncing multisyllabic words
- Trouble retrieving specific words
- Trouble sequencing sounds in spelling
- Trouble with rapid word recognition
- Slow reading and writing speed

Dyslexia

The most common type of SLD is dyslexia. Students with dyslexia have trouble blending and segmenting phonemes, learning letter–sound correspondences, memorizing letter sequences for sight word reading and spelling, and recognizing words rapidly. One core deficit of dyslexia affects the use of phonological processes in reading (Morris et al., 1998; Rack, Snowling, & Olson, 1992; Stanovich, 1988; Stanovich & Siegel, 1994). These phonological coding skills are the strongest predictor of reading disabilities and are uniquely deficient in most readers with dyslexia; in addition, the deficit is highly heritable (Pennington, 2009; Wise & Olson, 1991). Rapid Reference 7.4 reviews some of the most common symptoms of dyslexia.

DON'T FORGET

Blending ability is critical for acquiring phonics skills and segmentation is needed for spelling.

Decoding (pronouncing words) and encoding (spelling words) involve similar processes, including knowledge of phoneme–grapheme relationships as well as the ability to recall letter strings and words. To pronounce a word, an individual needs to know how to break apart the sounds and then how to blend the sounds back together to make a word; to spell a word, an individual needs to be able to break pronunciations into the component sounds (segmentation).

Another core deficit in dyslexia appears to affect automaticity or rapid symbol processing, often referred to as rapid automatized naming (RAN) (Wolf, 1991).

This type of problem seems to be more related to accuracy in pronouncing words and the rapid processing of words or reading fluency, rather than to phonological abilities and phonics skills. Students with slow symbol processing speeds do not recognize words easily and rapidly. Their lack of automaticity then affects their comprehension (Kintsch & Rawson, 2005; Nation, Marshall, & Snowling, 2001). This ability to recognize words rapidly by sight is the most important variable in predicting reading comprehension for individuals with an SLD (Meltzer, 1994).

When identifying individuals with dyslexia, consider the following to be the most relevant information from the WJ IV ACH: (a) word identification (e.g., out-of-context word decoding of both real words and pseudo words); (b) measures of spelling (e.g., real word and nonsense word spelling); and (c) measures of speed (e.g., reading rate and academic fluency). Students with dyslexia who have not had systematic instruction will have low phoneme–grapheme knowledge and are likely to perform slowly on tasks involving rapid processing (e.g., measures of reading rate and fluency).

When analyzing the reading tests, an individual with dyslexia is likely to have higher scores on tests involving context and language comprehension (e.g., oral vocabulary and knowledge) and mathematics and lower scores on measures of phoneme–grapheme knowledge and reading rate. For example, the person's performance will likely be higher on Passage Comprehension and Reading Recall than on Letter-Word Identification, Word Attack, Sentence Reading Fluency, and Word Reading Fluency. In contrast, an individual with poor reading comprehension will likely have higher scores on measures of basic reading skills and rate. When decoding skills and fluency are intact, most problems in reading comprehension arise from weaknesses in a range of oral language abilities, including poor vocabulary, background knowledge, grammar, and listening comprehension, rather than reading skills per se (Snowling & Hulme, 2012; Spencer, Quinn, & Wagner, 2014). Spencer et al. (2014) indicate that individuals with problems in reading comprehension that do not stem from poor decoding have weaknesses that are general to language comprehension, rather than being specific to reading.

> **DON'T FORGET**
> ....
> Most problems in reading comprehension arise from weaknesses in oral language abilities.

Individuals with dyslexia suffer from a specific impairment that affects reading and spelling development. They require explicit instruction and practice in reading and spelling single words. They often require more repetition, more practice, and more review to acquire basic reading skills. Instruction needs to be more systematic and more carefully designed, aimed at improving the overall level of skill as well as the efficiency of the learner. Effective strategies focus on phonemic awareness instruction coupled with direct reading instruction and a structured phonics approach followed by fluency training (Pennington, Peterson, & McGrath, 2009). Components of effective strategies include: (a) drills and probes, (b) provision of immediate feedback, (c) rapid pacing of instruction, and (d) carefully sequenced instruction (Swanson & Hoskyn, 1998). In addition, teachers need to adapt instruction to the level of reading development and provide appropriate accommodations, such as the use of a spell checker and extended time on tests.

CAUTION

Consider the Effects of Intervention on Test Performance

Many children with reading disabilities, particularly if they have had effective intervention, can obtain average scores on some reading tests, such as untimed measures of single-word reading (Pennington et al., 2009). This does not mean that they no longer have dyslexia, but that the interventions have improved word reading skill. Their performance usually declines, however, when they are asked to read text rapidly and fluently because their speed of word perception and reading rate are still compromised.

CAUTION

Not Everyone With Reading Difficulties Has Dyslexia

To identify dyslexia, look for specific impairments in basic reading skills, reading rate, and spelling. In addition, the individual should show some areas of relative strength (e.g., oral language, academic knowledge, or math).

DON'T FORGET

When doing an evaluation, you will want to document the specific strengths of an individual with dyslexia. These findings can often provide helpful information for accommodations and instruction, as well as ideas for vocational and career planning.

Individuals with dyslexia often have strengths in other areas, including oral language, mathematics, or academic knowledge. Because the impairment does not affect all domains of functioning, individuals may have variations within and among abilities (i.e., intra-ability variations). Thus, you will also want to document specific areas of strength in addition to the areas of weakness.

≡ *Rapid Reference 7.5*

Abilities Measured by WJ IV ACH Written Language Tests

Test	Ability Measured	Required LD Area
Spelling	Spelling of real words	Written expression
Writing Samples	Expression of ideas in writing	Written expression
Sentence Writing Fluency	Automaticity with writing	Written expression
Editing	Identification and correction of errors in written work	Written expression
Spelling of Sounds	Spelling of phonically regular nonsense words	Written expression

Written Language

The WJ IV ACH contains five writing tests that measure different aspects of writing ability. Rapid Reference 7.5 reviews the abilities measured by the WJ IV ACH writing tests. Under IDEA 2004, all of these measures fall under the broad category of written expression. Only two tests, Writing Samples and Sentence Writing Fluency, are required to obtain the Written Expression cluster. The other writing tests, however, can be useful in documenting a specific problem in writing, such as poor basic writing skills. In fact, difficulty with basic skills is often the reason for limited written expression. It is important to consider how these basic or secretarial skills are affecting an individual's written expression.

Individuals who struggle with basic reading skills typically also struggle with spelling. Similarly, individuals who have poor reading comprehension are likely to struggle with written expression. A few individuals, however, have adequate or even advanced reading skills but they struggle with one or more aspects of written language development. Some individuals have adequate written expression but struggle primarily with basic writing skills; other individuals write with ease but have trouble coming up with ideas.

Dysgraphia (difficulty writing) is a disorder resulting from poor visual-motor integration. Individuals with dysgraphia have difficulty writing or copying letters, words, or numbers. These individuals can speak, read, and may even be able to spell orally, but have trouble with the motor movements necessary for writing. Figure 7.1 illustrates the writing of Evan, a high school junior with

19.

(1) Whenever you buy a present, you should consider the interests of the receiver. (2) *If you*

Are selecting a gift for a significant other, you might consider flowers (handwritten)

(3) If, on the other hand, you are selecting a gift for your little cousin, you might choose a caboose for his new electric train set.

20.

Despite his (effort) (crossed out)
Jim was lost at sea, never to be (handwritten)

despite his effort

seen or heard from again. (handwritten)

Transcription of responses to Items 19 and 20:

19. If you are selecting a gift for a significant other, you might consider flowers.
20. Despite his effort, Jim was lost at sea, never to be seen or heard from again.

25.

(1) Two mountain chains traverse the country roughly from east to west forming between them a number of verdant valleys and plateaus. (2) *The town somehow withstood the ferosity of the intimidating and fierce obstacles that nature had provided.* (handwritten) _____ (3) The walls of the town, which is built on a hill, are high, the streets and lanes tortuous and broken, the roads winding and narrow.

Transcription of response to Item 25:

25. The town somehow withstood the ferocity of the intimidating and fierce obstacles that nature had provided.

27.

The world of touch is an amazing and intricate one; the materials that surround us in our day to day life all have a unique signature in the way they feel. (handwritten)

Metal, wood, glass, stone, plant fiber, animal hide, plastic (natural or synthetic)—there just aren't that many raw materials from which the things of the world are made. Because there are so few substances, when we touch an object, tactile clues can be quickly assessed: Does it feel warm or cold, hard or soft, dry or moist? How quickly does the surface warm to the touch? Does it push back? For example, plastic can be made to look convincingly like either wood or leather, but we learn to discriminate between these substances by feel. The things of the world are composed of only a few material substances, and our sense of touch guides us to accurate judgment.

Transcription of Response to Item 27:

27. The world of touch is an amazing and intricate one; the materials that surround us in our day to day life, all have a unique signature in the way they feel.

Figure 7.1 Evan's Writing Samples

28.

Artistic expressions of the world we inhabit go back much farther in time than the well-known art of the ancient Egyptians and Greeks. Carefully realized, well-rendered images of animals and people, created thirty thousand years ago, have been found in ancient caverns in France and elsewhere. Cave paintings, with a variety of colored pigments, depict subjects running or standing still, and cleverly placed shading creates the believable illusion of three dimensions on flat or mildly contoured sections of cave walls. These paintings were made more than twenty-seven millennia before the sculptures decorating the Parthenon in Athens. *The sculptures measured hold a significant place in art history as well as our own; standing tall, bold, and beautiful as a reminder not only of man's accomplishments but also his creativity*

Transcription of response to Item 28:

28. The sculptures themselves hold a significant place in art history as well as our own; standing tall, bold, and beautiful as a reminder not only of man's accomplishments but also his creativity.

Figure 7.1 (Continued)

dysgraphia, on several items of the Writing Samples test. Even though his handwriting is difficult to read, notice how sophisticated his responses are. Fortunately, Evan has developed keyboarding skill and can compose with relative ease on his laptop.

Difficulty in copying text is a key to differentiating between dysgraphia and other types of writing problems. For example, some individuals with writing difficulties may be able to copy, but they have trouble reproducing words from memory. They recognize words when they see them and can copy and read them, but they have trouble writing spontaneously or from dictation. Others have difficulties formulating their thoughts or expressing their ideas in writing. They can communicate orally, copy, and spell correctly, but they have trouble expressing their ideas, and they make errors in writing that they do not make when speaking.

Often, you will want to compare a person's performance on the Basic Writing Skills and Written Expression clusters to determine which aspects of writing are the most difficult. Careful analysis of performance on the various written language tests can help pinpoint the examinee's specific writing difficulties. For example, the Spelling test affords an opportunity to look at copying and spelling, and the Spelling of Sounds test looks at the ability to use phonological and orthographic information to spell nonsense words. The Sentence Writing Fluency test measures the ability to compose sentences quickly, whereas the Writing Samples test looks at sentence construction and ideation. The Editing test looks at the person's

≡ Rapid Reference 7.6

Factors That Can Affect Written Language Performance

Possible Reasons for Low Performance in Basic Writing Skills
- Poor phonological awareness
- Poor orthographic awareness
- Weak fine-motor skills
- Limited phoneme–grapheme knowledge
- Limited instruction

Possible Reasons for Low Performance in Written Expression
- Weak fine-motor skills
- Limited basic writing skills
- Limited oral language
- Lack of experiences and exposure
- Low motivation and interest
- Low reasoning ability
- Limited instruction

ability to proofread, or to detect and correct errors in spelling, punctuation, capitalization, and usage. Rapid Reference 7.6 suggests possible reasons for low performance in basic writing skills and written expression.

Mathematics

Although math problems have not been studied as extensively as reading problems, attempts have also been made to identify specific disorders of mathematics. Most studies have focused on basic numeracy skills. In a large birth cohort, the prevalence of math disability ranged from 6% to 13% depending on the definition that was used (regression-based IQ–achievement discrepancy, unadjusted discrepancy of IQ and math achievement, and low math achievement) (Barbaresi, Katusic, Colligan, Weaver, & Jacobsen, 2005). Although other areas of mathematics need to be studied, we do know that acquisition of mathematical concepts, more than any other content area, is tied closely to the teacher's knowledge of mathematics and the manner in which these concepts are taught (Lyon, 1996). Teachers who do not understand mathematical principles or know how to teach them may create additional learning difficulties for their students.

The complexity of mathematics increases the difficulty of documenting specific disorders. Some students seem to have trouble primarily with the mastery of computational skills such as adding, subtracting, multiplying, and dividing. These individuals have deficits in fundamental arithmetic operations, even though they have adequate reasoning, language, and visual-spatial skills (Novick & Arnold, 1988). Other students have adequate computational skills but trouble with the conceptual component, such as the abilities involved in learning mathematical concepts and solving story problems. Thus, educators need to consider that computational skill and problem-solving skill are two separate aspects of mathematics when diagnosing and planning instruction for students (Fuchs et al., 2008; Fuchs, Fuchs, Schumacher, & Seethaler, 2013).

Dyscalculia, a neurologically based learning disability, is rare (Steeves, 1983), so the term tends to be misused. Novick and Arnold (1988) defined dyscalculia as a "developmental arithmetic disorder, which refers to the failure to develop arithmetic competence" (p. 132). The most universal behavioral characteristics of dyscalculia are: (a) poor learning and retrieval of arithmetic facts from memory, (b) immature counting and problem-solving strategies, (c) slow number naming and calculation fluency, and (d) difficulty comparing the magnitudes of numbers (Price & Ansari, 2013). Just as with dyslexia, from an instructional point of view, it is not enough to label someone as having dyscalculia. It is more appropriate to describe the specific areas of math that are problematic for that individual and then design a specific intervention plan.

On the WJ IV ACH, you can compare a person's performance in math calculation skills and math problem solving. This can help determine if the problem lies in knowledge of how to perform calculations, automaticity with basic math facts, or application of math concepts and knowledge to tasks involving reasoning and problem solving. Rapid Reference 7.7 reviews the abilities measured by the WJ IV ACH math tests, as well as which LD areas are assessed.

≡ Rapid Reference 7.7

Abilities Measured by WJ IV ACH Math Tests

Test	Ability Measured	Required LD Area
Applied Problems	Problem solving and reasoning	Math reasoning
Calculation	Math computation	Math calculation
Math Facts Fluency	Automaticity with math facts	Math calculation
Number Matrices	Quantitative reasoning	Math reasoning

Careful observation during the administration of the math tests may also reveal characteristics typical of individuals with math disabilities. One of the most common characteristics is the use of immature problem-solving procedures even when solving simple arithmetic problems. For example, Randy, a fifth-grade student, still counts on his fingers when performing basic calculations. Another common characteristic is difficulty memorizing and recalling math facts. Many individuals with learning disabilities have persistent trouble memorizing basic number facts in all four operations, despite great effort and adequate understanding of the concepts (Fleischner, Garnett, & Shepherd, 1982; Geary, Hamson, & Hoard, 2000). The most documented research finding regarding students with learning disabilities in math is that they have persistent difficulties memorizing and then retrieving basic arithmetic facts once they have been committed to memory (Geary, 2013).

DON'T FORGET

Students with learning disabilities in math have difficulty memorizing and retrieving math facts.

As with reading comprehension and written expression, multiple factors can affect an individual's ability to effectively solve math problems. Oral language abilities play a key role, as does the ability to shift back and forth between verbal and visual representations. Difficulty with the language aspects of math may result in confusion about terminology, difficulty following verbal explanations, and weak verbal skills for monitoring the steps of complex calculations. Disturbances in visual-spatial organization may contribute to weak understanding of concepts, poor number sense, difficulty with pictorial representations, confused arrangements of numbers and signs on the page, and poor handwriting. Individuals with memory problems may have difficulty learning math facts. Similar to success in reading comprehension and written language, success in mathematics depends largely upon background knowledge, automaticity with math facts, and the use of strategic behaviors. Rapid Reference 7.8 lists several factors that can affect math performance. Rapid Reference 7.9 lists specific behaviors across the grades that were associated with basic math skills and problem-solving abilities (Bryant, Smith, & Bryant, 2008).

≡ Rapid Reference 7.8

Factors That Can Affect Math Performance

Possible Reasons for Low Basic Math Skills
- Limited attention
- Slow processing speed

- Poor working memory
- Inadequate number sense
- Weak fine-motor skills
- Poor visual-spatial abilities
- Limited knowledge of procedures
- Limited instruction

Possible Reasons for Low Math Reasoning

- Low basic math skills
- Low oral language
- Limited background knowledge
- Poor working memory
- Poor visual-spatial abilities
- Poor reasoning abilities
- Limited instruction

≡ *Rapid Reference 7.9*

Specific Behaviors Associated With Math Difficulties

Basic Math Skills

- Identifying the meaning of signs (e.g., ×, <, %)
- Recalling answers to basic math facts (e.g., $7 \times 6 =$)
- Using effective counting strategies to solve arithmetic problems
- Understanding the commutative property (e.g., $4 + 3 = 3 + 4$)
- Solving multidigit calculations that involve regrouping
- Misaligning numbers
- Ignoring decimal points

Math Reasoning

- Reading the problem
- Understanding the meaning of the sentences
- Understanding what the problem is asking
- Identifying and eliminating extraneous information
- Developing and implementing a plan for solving the problem
- Following multiple steps
- Using the correct calculations to solve problems

Source: Bryant, Smith, and Bryant (2008).

RESEARCH WITH THE WJ III and WJ IV AND SPECIFIC LEARNING DISABILITIES

Because the WJ IV has just been recently published, other than several validity studies presented in the technical manual, little research exists. Several studies were, however, conducted with the WJ III. Gregg and Hoy (McGrew & Woodcock, 2001) conducted a university study that included 200 students who were classified as being with and without learning disabilities. Mean score SLD/non-SLD comparisons were conducted on six WJ III ACH clusters and are reported in Table 7.1. These results indicate that the clusters reveal significant differences between the achievement of university students with and without SLDs. All but one of the six achievement clusters were significant at the .05 level, even after applying the Bonferroni adjustment procedure to control for overall error rate. This means that there is a 95% probability that the score differences are due to group status rather than mere chance. The students with SLDs scored significantly lower than the students without LDs on tasks requiring reading, writing, phoneme–grapheme knowledge, and academic fluency. Performance was not significantly different on the Oral Expression cluster. This finding provides support for the use of the WJ IV in the classification of individuals as having specific learning disabilities, as well as providing support for the provision of specific accommodations, such as documentation of the need for oral testing or extended time.

In addition, clinical validity data were analyzed and presented in the *Essentials of the WJ III Cognitive Abilities Assessment,* Second Edition (Schrank, Miller, Wendling, & Woodcock, 2010). For the clinical groups with academic disorders (i.e., reading disability, math disability, writing disability), those

Table 7.1 Mean Standard Scores for University Samples With and Without SLD

Cluster	SLD	Non-SLD	Significant
Broad Reading	86.5	102.4	Yes
Basic Reading Skills	84.3	98.2	Yes
Basic Writing Skills	86.5	104.3	Yes
Oral Expression	99.3	103.9	No
Phoneme–Grapheme	90.8	104.3	Yes
Academic Fluency	94.7	112.0	Yes

identified with a reading disability had the highest number of academic deficits, whereas those identified with a writing disorder had the fewest academic deficits. All three groups had difficulty with academic fluency measures.

Generalized Low or High Performance

Some students do not show discrepancies among achievement areas or variations among abilities and may have generally low or high performance. This is important information to consider when evaluating an individual for a possible learning disability. Typically, if the individual has generalized low or high performance, evaluators would usually rule out an SLD diagnosis because one or more domain-specific difficulties, when coupled with relative strengths, are important indicators of a specific learning disability.

Generalized Low Performance

Students with overall low performance may be several years below grade level in all academic subjects, as well as academic knowledge. These students require adaptations and adjustments in the curriculum. The difficulty level of the instructional materials has to be adapted to both the present performance levels and the level of knowledge.

Remember to consider extrinsic factors when a student has low academic performance and acquired knowledge. Some students come to school with very limited background knowledge, or their primary language is not English. The reasons that these students struggle in school are more related to a lack of educational opportunity than an intrinsic disability. These students have limited world knowledge, limited exposure, and, often, low vocabularies. Because vocabulary knowledge is needed for most academic tasks, the breadth and depth of an individual's vocabulary can affect school success. Although these students need help, they do not have disabilities. Rather than special instructional methods, these students often require a developmental curriculum that will provide language stimulation and enrichment within the general education setting. Rapid Reference 7.10 lists possible reasons or factors to consider when a student has generalized low academic performance.

Students with generalized low academic performance will also obtain low scores on the Academic Knowledge cluster. Rapid Reference 7.11 presents several factors that can affect performance on the Academic Knowledge cluster.

≡ Rapid Reference 7.10

Possible Reasons for Generalized Low Academic Performance

- Limited educational opportunity
- English is a second language
- Oral language impairments
- Cultural differences
- Poor reasoning abilities
- Intellectual disability
- Linguistic differences or delays
- Developmental delays
- Traumatic brain injury

Generalized High Performance

Other students have advanced academic knowledge and are above grade level in most academic subjects. Students with well established oral language and rich vocabularies tend to speak, read, and write more effectively than other students. Because they learn easily, these students often require an accelerated curriculum. They may take advanced courses, use higher-level textbooks, or complete special projects. In some cases, students with advanced academic performance participate in gifted and talented programs.

≡ Rapid Reference 7.11

Factors That Can Affect Academic Knowledge

Possible Reasons for Low Performance in Academic Knowledge

- Attention problems
- Lack of educational experiences and opportunities
- Difficulty with listening comprehension
- Cultural differences
- Poor word retrieval (difficulty recalling words that are known)
- Difficulty formulating ideas or organizing thoughts

Variation and Comparison Interpretation

Interpretation of WJ IV ACH variation and comparison information can aid in differentiating among specific learning disabilities (such as dyslexia) and generalized low academic performance. Chapter 4 provides details regarding the use and interpretation of the WJ IV ACH variation and comparison procedures.

Intra-Achievement Variation Procedure

The intra-achievement variation analysis can help you determine and document both strengths and weaknesses in academic performance. The relationship between achievement abilities in any particular domain can be explored in reference to other academic abilities. This type of analysis is often referred to as a *pattern of strengths and weaknesses* (PSW) approach. Although various methods are used by different districts in a PSW approach, the essential elements involve: (a) identifying an academic weakness in one of the eight IDEA areas, (b) determining if there are cognitive or linguistic processing problems that have an established link to the academic area (e.g., phonological awareness and basic reading skills, working memory and math computation), (c) establishing the intact abilities, and (d) determining whether the pattern seems related to an SLD (Schultz, Simpson, & Lynch, 2012). The PSW approach is not tantamount to merely listing an individual's unique strengths and weaknesses to determine the existence of an SLD, but rather to determining whether the particular PSW is indicative of an SLD, such as a child with dyslexia who has weaknesses in orthographic processing but strengths in listening comprehension and reasoning, or a child who has a specific mathematics disability with weaknesses in non-verbal reasoning or working memory but a strength in oral language.

> **DON'T FORGET**
> ....
> A PSW approach requires the identification of both strengths and weaknesses.

Oftentimes, a student's strengths can be used to justify the selection of accommodations. For example, a student with advanced academic knowledge but lower reading and writing skills would benefit from oral examinations in content-area classes, as well as the use of assistive technology. In addition, identification of an individual's overall pattern of cognitive strengths and weaknesses can increase self-understanding and is, in itself, therapeutic as it provides an explanation of why the person is struggling and what can be done about it (Pennington, 2009; Suhr, 2008). A diagnosis of an SLD using a PSW approach

Table 7.2 Intra-Achievement Variations for Sarah, a Fourth-Grade Student

	Standard Scores			Discrepancy		Interpretation at
Variations	Actual	Predicted	Difference	PR	SD	±1.50 SD (SEE)
Basic Reading Skills	78	112	−34	<0.1	−3.93	Weakness
Reading Comprehension	100	108	−8	19	−0.88	—
Math Calculation Skills	121	104	+17	91	+1.34	—
Math Problem Solving	128	104	+24	99	+2.33	Strength
Basic Writing Skills	80	111	−31	0.2	−2.87	Weakness
Written Expression	100	107	−7	26	−0.64	—
Academic Knowledge	134	103	+31	99.6	+2.70	Strength

results in the identification of the specific type of SLD that can have implications for both instruction and prognosis. The ultimate goal is to document a student's unique pattern of strengths and weaknesses so as to provide better services and more targeted interventions (Hooper, 1996; NJCLD, 2011; Norton & Wolf, 2012).

Useful information regarding strengths and weaknesses can be gained by analyzing the WJ IV intra-achievement variations. For example, Table 7.2 illustrates the intra-achievement variation results for Sarah, a fourth-grade student. With regard to academic performance, Sarah has significant weaknesses in basic reading skills and basic writing skills. In contrast, she has significant strengths in math problem solving and academic knowledge. Although more information is needed, these findings are suggestive of an SLD in reading and writing (significant weaknesses in domain-specific areas such as reading and writing skills with strengths in other domains such as math problem solving and academic knowledge).

After reviewing the intra-achievement variations, you can analyze the cluster and test results to reveal possible factors influencing performance. When using just the WJ IV ACH, it may be difficult to determine exactly why an individual is struggling within an academic area. Richer clinical information can be obtained when using the WJ IV COG and WJ IV OL in conjunction with the WJ IV ACH. However, within the WJ IV ACH, it is possible to consider the influence of academic knowledge, phoneme–grapheme knowledge, basic skills, rate and fluency, and reasoning abilities in general.

Table 7.3 illustrates a sampling of cluster and test results for Sarah. She is having particular difficulty with the acquisition of word identification and spelling skills,

Table 7.3 Exploring Underlying Differences in Test and Cluster Results for Sarah

Cluster/Test	Raw	GE	Easy	Diff	RPI	PR	SS (68% Band)
Phoneme–Grapheme Knowledge	—	1.8	1.5	2.3	41/90	11	82 (79–85)
Spelling of Sounds	17	1.7	1.2	2.8	64/90	13	83 (79–88)
Word Attack	7	1.8	1.6	2.1	21/90	13	83 (79–86)
Academic Skills	—	2.7	2.3	3.2	44/90	11	82 (79–84)
Academic Fluency	—	3.9	3.0	5.0	89/90	48	99 (97–102)
Academic Application	—	5.5	3.9	8.2	96/90	82	114 (110–118)

and as a result, she obtains low scores on the Phoneme–Grapheme Knowledge cluster. Her scores on both the Word Attack and Spelling of Sounds tests indicate a weakness in phonological and orthographic coding. In addition, her performances on the Academic Skills and Academic Fluency clusters are lower than her performance on the Academic Applications cluster. This means that her difficulties have a greater impact on basic skills and fluency than on the higher-level thinking skills, or application areas. Both poor knowledge of sounds and symbols and a weakness in phonological awareness appear to be underlying conditions influencing Sarah's performance and development in basic reading and writing skills.

DON'T FORGET

Questions to Ask
- Does a comparison of achievement areas highlight certain patterns in academic performance, such as math reasoning is higher than basic math skills?
- Does a comparison of achievement areas highlight certain weaknesses in performance, such as performance is significantly lower on all timed tests or tests of basic skills?
- Does a comparison of academic knowledge to achievement suggest that oral language and knowledge are more advanced than academic performance?

Academic Knowledge/Achievement Discrepancy

One important aspect of an SLD evaluation is to distinguish between children whose problems are specific to one or more cognitive domains from those whose problems result from a more pervasive impairment in language skills that may be more appropriately classified as an oral language disorder (Fletcher et al., 1998; Snowling & Hulme, 2012). Children who struggle in most aspects of language, as well as in many nonverbal domains, may be more appropriately classified as having some degree of intellectual disability (e.g., mild to severe).

The academic knowledge/achievement comparison procedure has particular relevance for helping evaluators distinguish between individuals with adequate academic knowledge but poor reading and writing abilities (i.e., specific reading disabilities) versus individuals whose levels of knowledge are commensurate with present levels of reading and writing performance. In the first case, when knowledge is higher than reading ability, instructional recommendations would focus on reading and writing development. In the second case, instructional recommendations would be directed to increasing knowledge and academic skills.

DON'T FORGET
....
Value of the Academic Knowledge/Achievement Comparison Procedure

The WJ IV ACH compares the Academic Knowledge cluster to the achievement clusters. This comparison helps differentiate between individuals with generalized low performance and individuals with specific strengths and weaknesses and/or domain-specific learning disabilities.

Table 7.4 illustrates the results for Josh, a fifth-grade student, using the academic knowledge/achievement comparison procedure. Josh obtained a standard score of 134 on the Academic Knowledge cluster, which is used as the ability score in this procedure. When using academic knowledge to predict academic performance, Josh demonstrated significant weaknesses in mathematics, whereas no significant strengths or weaknesses were noted in the reading and writing clusters. Josh is an individual who has superior knowledge and good reading and writing skills, but poor performance in mathematics. These results can help support the diagnosis that Josh has an SLD in mathematics.

Can the WJ IV ACH Diagnose the Problem?

Achievement tests are primarily designed to determine present levels of academic performance. When conducting a comprehensive evaluation, you will want to supplement any achievement test with other instruments designed to assess cognitive abilities, information processing, language, behavior, and so forth.

Table 7.4 Academic Knowledge/Achievement Comparisons for Josh, a Fifth-Grade Student

Comparisons	Standard Scores			Discrepancy		Significant at
	Actual	Predicted	Difference	PR	SD	+/− 1.50 SD
Reading	114	117	−3	41	−0.23	No
Basic Reading Skills	114	116	−2	44	−0.15	No
Reading Comprehension	117	113	4	61	+0.29	No
Mathematics	86	118	−32	0.5	−2.57	Yes (−)
Broad Mathematics	82	116	−34	0.4	−2.67	Yes (−)
Math Calculation Skills	81	114	−33	1	−2.38	Yes (−)
Math Problem Solving	84	119	−35	0.2	−2.88	Yes (−)
Written Language	117	117	0	52	+0.05	No
Basic Writing Skills	122	118	4	64	+0.36	No

Note. These comparisons are based on Academic Knowledge as the predictor.

Information from the WJ IV ACH can, however, be helpful in diagnosing certain reasons for academic difficulties. Although the most common type of SLD is a reading disability, some individuals have specific learning disabilities in writing or mathematics. In addition, some students have oral language impairments that contribute to difficulties with reading, writing, and mathematics. Although more information can be obtained from the WJ IV COG and WJ IV OL, for these types of cases, more in-depth testing is usually required, typically by a speech-language therapist. Throughout this chapter, we have identified the tests, clusters, and abilities most sensitive to the main clinical applications presented. Table 7.5 shows a summary of common profiles associated with academic learning disabilities.

CAUTION

Standard 3.18: In testing individuals for diagnostic and/or special program placement purposes, test users should not use test scores as the sole indicators to characterize an individual's functioning, competence, attitudes, and/or predispositions. Instead, multiple sources of information should be used, alternative explanations for test performance should be considered, and the professional judgment of someone familiar with the test should be brought to bear on the decision (AERA et al., 2014, p.71).

Table 7.5 Diagnostic Indicators of an Academic Learning Disability

Reading Disability	Writing Disability	Math Disability
Low performance on one or more of the following clusters: Reading, Broad Reading, Basic Reading Skills, Reading Fluency, Reading Comprehension, or Reading Rate	Low performance on one or more of the following clusters: Written Language, Broad Written Language, Basic Writing Skills, or Written Expression	Low performance on one or more of the following clusters: Mathematics, Broad Mathematics, Math Calculation Skills, or Math Problem Solving
Adequate oral language	Adequate oral language	Adequate oral language
Poor phonological or orthographic awareness resulting in poor decoding	Poor phonological or orthographic awareness resulting in poor spelling	Difficulty memorizing and recalling basic math facts
Low phoneme–grapheme knowledge	Low reading skills and/or comprehension	Strong concepts and weak basic skills
Slow reading rate	Poor handwriting and slow writing rate	Limited fluency with math
Slow processing speed	Difficulty copying	Low visual-spatial abilities
Higher scores in oral language and math than in reading	Organizational difficulties and difficulty formulating ideas in writing	Low working memory and reasoning ability
Presence of a significant intra-achievement variation in reading	Presence of a significant intra-achievement variation in writing	Presence of a significant intra-achievement variation in math

Use of the WJ IV ACH Across the Life Span

The wide age span covered by the WJ IV (ages 2-0 to 95+ years) makes it an ideal instrument for continuous measurement and longitudinal studies. The age span also provides evidence of developmental trends and differences in abilities measured by the test. For example, the WJ IV Technical Manual reports that abilities in reading, math, writing, and academic knowledge increase during the school years. Once individuals learn these abilities, they do not lose them in later years, but rather maintain them. Rapid Reference 7.12 provides information on the developmental trends noted when using cognitive abilities to predict achievement for various reading and mathematics tests and clusters from the WJ III (McGrew & Wendling, 2010). Most likely, these trends also apply to the WJ IV tests and clusters with the same composition.

≡ Rapid Reference 7.12

Developmental Trends in Reading and Mathematics

Reading

- The significance of skills required for developing basic reading skills tends to decline with age, whereas the significance of skills needed for comprehension increases with age.
- The influence of long-term retrieval (*Glr*) and processing speed (*Gs*) lessen after basic reading skills are acquired.
- The influence of comprehension-knowledge (*Gc*) and short-term working memory (*Gwm*) on reading comprehension increase with age.
- Perceptual speed, a narrow processing speed ability, has a significant relationship with both basic reading skills and reading comprehension across ages.
- Phonetic coding, a narrow auditory processing ability, has a significant relationship with basic reading skills.

Mathematics

- The significance of comprehension-knowledge (*Gc*) for math reasoning increases with age, which may be due to the increased linguistic demands of more complex math reasoning tasks.
- Fluid reasoning (*Gf*) and short-term working memory (*Gwm*) are strong predictors of basic math skills and math reasoning across ages.
- Processing speed (*Gs*) is important to both basic math skills and math reasoning.
- Phonetic coding, a narrow auditory processing ability, and several narrow long-term retrieval abilities are important to basic math skills, especially in the early school years.

TEST YOURSELF

1. **What two types of procedures on the WJ IV ACH may be helpful in documenting the presence of an SLD?**
2. **List the six SLD areas measured by WJ IV ACH clusters.**
3. **What is one possible criterion used for identifying an SLD?**
4. **The WJ IV ACH measures which key predictor of risk for reading failure?**
5. **If the WJ IV ACH results are being compared to the results on the WISC-V, the WJ IV ACH should be scored by age norms.** True or False?
6. **How can the academic knowledge/achievement comparison procedure help examiners differentiate between individuals with specific reading impairments and those with limited knowledge?**

7. **The Phoneme–Grapheme Knowledge cluster score is usually average or above average for an individual with dyslexia.**
   True or False?

8. **Typically, a domain-specific deficit is present for the identification of an SLD.**
   True or False?

9. **Which of these findings may be most inconsistent with a specific reading disability profile?**
   (a) Low academic knowledge
   (b) Low basic reading skills
   (c) Low phoneme–grapheme knowledge
   (d) Low basic writing skills

10. **Which of these statements is true if using a global IQ score to predict achievement?**
    (a) If the IQ is low, you should expect the achievement score to be as low or lower.
    (b) If the IQ is high, you should expect the achievement score to be as high or higher.
    (c) If the IQ score is high or low, you should expect the achievement score to be closer to the mean.

Answers: 1. Intra-ability variation and ability/achievement discrepancy; 2. Basic reading skills, reading fluency, reading comprehension, math calculation, math reasoning, and written expression; 3. A discrepancy between intellectual ability and achievement or intra-ability variations (a pattern of strengths and weaknesses) that are suggestive of an SLD; 4. letter–sound knowledge (Letter-Word Identification and Word Attack); 5. True; 6. Academic knowledge is higher than reading performance for those with a specific reading impairment, but it is commensurate with, or lower than, reading performance for those with limited knowledge; 7. False; 8. True; 9. a; 10. c

Eight

ILLUSTRATIVE CASE REPORTS

The purpose of this chapter is to illustrate the use of the WJ IV OL and ACH in evaluations. Although in most instances additional assessment data would be collected as part of a comprehensive evaluation, such as the results from group administered tests, additional standardized tests, informal measures, and so forth, the intent of this chapter is to demonstrate the type of information that you can derive from these two batteries when used together. Knowledge of the test content, administration, and scoring and interpretive options (presented in Chapters 1 through 7 of this book) is required to fully understand the information presented here. The types of scores selected for each report differ slightly to illustrate the use of standard scores, percentile ranks, and proficiency levels based on RPIs. Although these were real cases and the background information is true, the names of the cases, schools, and birthdates have been changed to protect confidentiality.

The first case report is a 9-year-old male, Bryan, who was referred due to concerns about his limited progress in reading. Even though Bryan is currently receiving help from both his parents and his school, more information was needed to make recommendations for increasing his academic success. Bryan was administered both the WJ IV OL and WJ IV ACH with a recommendation to also then administer the WJ IV COG. The second case is Jonas, an 11th-grade student who was referred for a reevaluation because of continued difficulties with handwriting and mathematics. The third case is Veronica, a recent college graduate who has been accepted to graduate school, who is seeking information about whether she has a learning disability and what she should do about her slow reading rate. Although in all three cases further documentation would be required to justify eligibility decisions, the reports illustrate the type of information that can be obtained through use of the WJ IV OL and ACH.

Each report includes the reason for referral, background information, information on prior evaluations, tests administered, behavioral observations, test

results, and recommendations. The focus of all three reports is on the characteristics and educational needs of the person, rather than on an in-depth description
of the scores. Each case includes the scores appended to the end of the report.
These may be used to provide additional practice with score interpretation.

CAUTION

Computer-generated reports are
strictly a beginning point. They can
report scores and describe tasks.
However, examiners are responsible
for interpreting the information and
making specific recommendations.

DON'T FORGET

Key Information to Include in a Case Report

- Identifying information
- Reason for referral
- Background information
- Tests administered
- Behavioral observations
- Test results
- Examples of specific strengths and
  weaknesses
- Conclusions and recommendations

As examiners attempt to resolve
referral questions and make appropriate recommendations, they must consider and integrate findings from
behavioral observations, error analysis, and test scores. The basic score
report generated by the WJ IV online
scoring program (free access included
with each Test Record) can serve as a
beginning point for the case report,
but it does not interpret the results.
Initially, the basic score report from
the online scoring program provides
only the score results and includes
observations (if entered). Future
releases will offer additional features,
some of which will be fee based. As
with any computer-generated report,
examiners are responsible for interpreting results, integrating information from various sources, drawing
conclusions, and making specific recommendations that address the referral concern.

EDUCATIONAL EVALUATION REPORT

Name: Bryan Anthony
Parents: Richard and Kathie Anthony
Date of Birth: 09/08/2004
Age: 9-8
Grade: 3.8
Test Dates: 5/6, 5/10, 5/12/2014
School: Harper Primary School

REASON FOR REFERRAL

Mrs. Kathie Anthony referred her son Bryan for an evaluation of his oral language and academic abilities. The purposes of this evaluation were to determine Bryan's current levels of academic performance, as well as what instructional methodologies would be most effective for addressing his educational needs.

BACKGROUND INFORMATION

Bryan will be entering the fourth grade in the fall. Mr. and Mrs. Anthony have been concerned about Bryan's limited progress in reading since the age of 5.

Current Situation

Bryan currently resides with his mother, father, and four sisters on a farm in Payson, Arizona. He has two younger sisters who are 3 and 6 years old, and two older sisters who are 10 and 13. Mrs. Anthony's brother and several of his children have been diagnosed with dyslexia and attention-deficit/hyperactivity disorder (ADHD). Mrs. Anthony reports that now as adults, "they have horrible spelling and spell words just the way they sound."

Bryan's parents reported that he loves information, enjoys figuring things out, and loves telling and hearing stories. In contrast, he is struggling with reading words, but not so much with comprehension. Once he figures out what something says, he understands the meaning. He often misreads simple words, such as *the, a, if,* and *of* and almost always asks for help when he has to pronounce longer words. If his parents sound out the word, he quickly gets it. If they try to point to syllables so that he has to figure it out, he gets frustrated and stops reading.

Bryan's grades are poor even though he studies before school, attends a math and reading reteach program after school until 5:30 p.m., and is pulled out of class to work with a reading teacher during school hours. His mother stated that his reading went from a 1.7 grade level in October, to a 2.4 level in December, to a 2.1 level in April. The school team advised that because he was working so hard and making no progress, they should pursue testing to find out what is hindering him. His third-grade teacher reported that just when she thinks that he has it down, he will forget what he has learned.

Mrs. Anthony reported that they spend their nights trying to get his homework done amidst the tears. He is frustrated that he has to study harder than others and is not improving. The Anthonys are frustrated because he is not making much improvement despite all of their efforts. When he is left to read on his own, he gets no more than 2 right out of 10 on his weekly comprehension worksheets. When his mother reads it to him, he can easily tell her all of the correct answers.

In spite of his struggles with reading, Bryan enjoys school. He likes to draw ice dragons, fire dragons, and Vikings with swords. He particularly enjoys classroom activities that involve projects.

Educational History and Prior Evaluations

Bryan began school at the age of 2. His mother taught a home preschool that Bryan was a part of from the time he could walk. When he was 2 he would often hop down from the table and show a 4-year-old child how to do the task on their worksheets without saying a word. Although he seemed bright in many ways, his mother observed that at the ages of 4 and 5, when the other kids in the class were grasping letter sounds and symbols, he was not.

Bryan's parents then took him to Head Start in New Mexico for an evaluation. He tested just under his age level and they were told it was developmental. Just before entering kindergarten, at the age of 5, his mother had him tested again through MECA in New Mexico. Mrs. Anthony reported that he scored well because he knew what a "quart Mason jar" was and used all three names, which none of the other kids did. When asked to tell about the picture of a penguin, he got excited and answered "icy cold penguins" and proceeded to tell how they play in the water. His scores were at 6 years in most areas and 4 years 6 months in a few others. His mother was told again that any concerns they had were just developmental.

Bryan attended Fuller Elementary in Eloy, Arizona, for the first semester of kindergarten. His mother developed a word wall and they constantly practiced his sight words. He struggled to retain them for very long. Bryan's teacher described him as "delightful and smart," but when she was asked how he was doing compared with the other kids, she said she was concerned about his speech and referred him for an evaluation. The family moved to Nevada and the testing was done at his new school. The results were similar to the prior assessments and his parents were told again that it was just developmental.

In first grade, the family moved back to New Mexico. When his mother asked the teacher at a conference how Bryan was doing, she replied that he was delightful, but behind in reading. For second grade, Bryan attended a project-based charter school; his teacher was sick the whole first semester and he had multiple substitutes. The principal tutored Bryan and other children who were struggling with reading, and Mrs. Anthony was told that he was a great kid and doing just fine.

The Anthonys then moved back to Arizona to run the family farm. Bryan began third grade at St. Paul Elementary. The third-grade teacher was brand new to teaching. In the first few months, her notes home changed from "he is a hard worker" to "wish he would pay more attention in class." His reading helper's notes also changed from "Bryan is a great kid trying hard" (first week) to "He is despondent and gets no support at home" (fourth week). The Anthonys felt that he was not getting the help he needed and that the situation was not going to change. They then moved Bryan to Harper Primary School down the road. He now likes learning again but is still struggling with reading.

TESTS ADMINISTERED

- Woodcock-Johnson IV Tests of Oral Language (WJ IV OL)
- Woodcock-Johnson IV Tests of Achievement (WJ IV ACH) Standard and Extended
- Interview with Mrs. Anthony

TESTING OBSERVATIONS

Testing was conducted in one 2-hour session and one 1-hour session. Although Bryan was engaged during all of the testing, his ability to sustain attention was quite variable. He was cooperative and pleasant throughout all testing.

On several occasions, directions had to be repeated, and Bryan had to be reminded about what he was supposed to be doing. Bryan also had a tendency to stop trying as soon as a question or problem became too challenging. When he had difficulty on one problem, he would then stop trying on the others and say that they were "too hard."

TEST RESULTS

The WJ IV OL and WJ IV ACH were scored according to grade norms. Because these two batteries are co-normed, direct comparisons can be made among his oral language and achievement scores. These comparisons can help determine the presence and significance of any strengths and weaknesses among his abilities. These tests provide measures of Bryan's specific oral language abilities, as well as his current levels of academic achievement.

Bryan's performance is compared to his grade peers using standard score (SS) ranges:

SS Range	<69	70–79	80–89	90–110	111–120	121–130	>130
Verbal label	Very low	Low	Low average	Average	High average	Superior	Very superior

Note. Standard scores (SS) have a mean of 100 and a standard deviation of 15.

His academic proficiency on specific tasks is described by the Relative Proficiency Index (RPI) levels:

RPI Range	0–3	3–24	24–67	67–82	82–95	95–98	98–100	100
Level of proficiency	Extremely limited	Very limited	Limited	Limited to average	Average	Average to advanced	Advanced	Very advanced

Note. The proficiency ranges (i.e., limited, average, advanced, etc.) are associated with RPI scores, not the standard scores. RPIs are presented as a fraction with the denominator fixed at 90, representing the 90% proficiency level of average age- or grademates on the task. The numerator (top number) fluctuates from 0 to 100 depending on the student's performance (e.g., 10/90 or 80/90). The RPI is interpreted as "when the typical student performs at 90% proficiency, this student can be expected to perform at 98%, 69%, or 45% proficiency or whatever the number on the top indicates." RPIs are indicators of functionality or proficiency on a task and predict how well the student will do on similar tasks. Sometimes there are differences between standard scores and RPIs. The best method is to consider both standard scores (relative standing compared to peers) and RPIs (proficiency compared to average age- or grademates with 90% proficiency).

A full set of scores is appended to the end of this report.

ORAL LANGUAGE ABILITIES AND ACADEMIC ACHIEVEMENT

Bryan's oral language abilities were assessed using the WJ IV OL, and his academic performance was assessed in reading, writing, and math using the WJ IV ACH. On the WJ IV ACH, only performance on the Broad clusters and a few of the individual tests are discussed because there were few significant differences in his performance among measures of basic skills, fluency, and comprehension.

Oral Language Abilities

Overall, Bryan's oral language abilities fell mostly in the average range. He demonstrated grade-appropriate vocabulary knowledge, listening comprehension, and phonological awareness. Bryan had average ability to blend together speech sounds, which is the basis for learning phonics, and to segment or break apart speech sounds, which is the basis for spelling. His lowest score was on the Rapid Picture Naming test, which required the rapid naming of pictures of common objects (SS = 86; 68% confidence band 81–92).

WJ IV OL Cluster/Tests	RPI	Proficiency	SS (± I SEM)
Sound Blending	85/90	Average	95 (89–102)
Segmentation	94/90	Average	104 (99–109)
Rapid Picture Naming	54/90	Limited	86 (81–92)
Broad Oral Language	92/90	Average	104 (92–109)
Picture Vocabulary	95/90	Average to advanced	108 (102–115)
Oral Comprehension	91/90	Average	102 (95–109)
Understanding Directions	89/90	Average	99 (94–104)

Reading

Bryan's proficiency was limited to very limited on all reading tests. On the timed Word Reading Fluency test, which required marking the two words in a row of four words that go together based on a semantic connection (e.g., horse yellow cab blue), Bryan had an RPI of 4/90. This indicates that when average grademates are having 90% success on tasks requiring quick word reading, Bryan will only have 4% success. On the Letter-Word Identification test, he had an RPI of 19/90, which indicates very limited proficiency in word recognition reading when compared to his average grade peers. He had difficulty applying phonic skills and recognizing common sight words with ease (e.g., *there* and *when*). As words increased in length, he tended to guess at their pronunciations by using the initial consonant, rather than examining the entire word (e.g., reading *sentence* as *science*). Bryan tended to give up on more difficult words rather than attempting to sound them out.

WJ IV ACH Cluster/Tests	RPI	Proficiency	SS (±1 SEM)
Word Reading Fluency	4/90	Very limited	81 (76–86)
Broad Reading	36/90	Limited	85 (82–88)
Letter-Word Identification	19/90	Very limited	81 (78–84)
Passage Comprehension	34/90	Limited	80 (75–84)
Sentence Reading Fluency	59/90	Limited	94 (89–98)

Written Language

Bryan's proficiency in writing was slightly more advanced than his reading proficiency. His lowest performance was on the Spelling test that measured his ability to spell simple to more complex words. Although he was able to represent the sounds in many of the words, he omitted salient sounds from several words and tended to spell words the way they sound, rather than the way they look (e.g., he spelled *from* as *frum*). Bryan found it easier to spell phonically regular nonsense words (made-up words that conform to common English sounds and spelling patterns; Spelling of Sounds, RPI = 83/90) than to spell real words that contained irregular elements (Spelling, RPI = 55/90).

On Writing Samples, a test that measures skill in formulating and writing sentences or phrases in response to a variety of demands, Bryan was able to write complete sentences. Although there is no penalty for misspelled words, he had several spelling errors on common words (e.g., *road* as *roud, hole* as *holl*).

WJ IV Cluster/Tests	RPI	Proficiency	SS (±1 SEM)
Spelling of Sounds	83/90	Average	94 (89–99)
Broad Written Language	80/90	Limited to average	93 (91–96)
Spelling	55/90	Limited	88 (85–91)
Writing Samples	86/90	Average	98 (94–101)
Sentence Writing Fluency	89/90	Average	99 (93–105)

Mathematics

Bryan also had some difficulty on tests of mathematics. He was able to add and subtract single digits by counting on his fingers. He was able to complete two-digit addition and subtraction problems without regrouping. He was able to count accurately with pictures, add and subtract using pictures, and identify the correct time on a clock. Although Bryan was able to identify the names of coins, he had difficulty adding up the value of coins. He was unable to complete multiplication problems involving more than single digits, and he was unable to solve simple division problems.

WJ IV Cluster/Tests	RPI	Proficiency	SS (±1 SEM)
Broad Mathematics	58/90	Limited	87 (83–90)
Applied Problems	40/90	Limited	80 (75–85)
Calculation	68/90	Limited to average	90 (86–94)
Math Facts Fluency	67/90	Limited to average	92 (87–97)

WJ IV VARIATION AND COMPARISON PROCEDURES

Variations

On the WJ IV, intra-individual variations are computed to show the likelihood of a person obtaining a particular score given the average of their other cognitive, oral language, or achievement cluster scores. Large variations indicate areas of significant strength or weakness. There were no significant variations among Bryan's oral language abilities or his achievement.

Comparisons

The WJ IV OL and ACH have several comparison procedures in which one composite ability is used to predict performance in other areas. When his Broad Oral Language score is compared to his achievement, all aspects of reading, as well as math problem solving, are lower than predicted. For example, when his predicted score based on the Broad Oral Language score (SS = 104) was compared to his actual score on the Reading cluster (SS = 79), only two out of 100 students would have a Reading cluster score as low or lower. When his predicted score based on his Broad Oral Language score (SS = 104) was compared to his Math Problem Solving score (SS = 80), only three out of 100 students would have a standard score of 80 or lower.

In addition, significant discrepancies were found when Bryan's Academic Knowledge (knowledge of humanities, science, and social studies) cluster score was compared to his overall reading achievement and math problem solving. These results indicate that Bryan's oral language abilities and academic knowledge are all significantly higher than his present performance in reading and math problem solving, and they suggest that he has the aptitude for a higher level of performance in both areas.

SUMMARY

Bryan will be entering fourth grade in the fall. He has a history of difficulty with reading, despite numerous interventions from both home and school. He was referred for an evaluation by his mother because of her concerns regarding his struggles with learning to read. Bryan's verbal ability (acquired knowledge and language comprehension) is average when compared to his grade peers, which suggests that he should be reading at grade level. Bryan appears to have some difficulty with the control of attention, rather than a weakness in memory per se. Although Bryan is cooperative and enjoys learning, he does not persist when he perceives that tasks have become too challenging for him. Instead, he just states that the problems are "too hard." Presently, Bryan needs targeted instruction that will increase his overall level of achievement and proficiency in word reading, spelling, and mathematics.

EDUCATIONAL RECOMMENDATIONS

School Programming

- Conduct further intellectual/cognitive assessment to help determine the specific factors that are inhibiting Bryan's performance in reading and math problem solving. Administer measures of associative memory and perceptual speed to see if these factors are contributing to reading difficulties; administer measures of reasoning ability, working memory, and visual-spatial thinking to determine if any of these abilities are affecting math performance. These findings should be integrated with the results from the present assessment.
- Ask the school to explore eligibility for learning disabilities (LD) services this summer or as soon as Bryan returns to school. Presently, Bryan has significant discrepancies between his oral language and reasoning abilities and his reading and math achievement; he has made insufficient reading progress in school even with additional assistance.

- As he enters fourth grade, Bryan will require specific accommodations in the classroom, such as extended time on assignments and shortened homework assignments. Until his reading and math performance improve, Bryan will need adjustments in the difficulty level in both school and homework assignments. Although he is entering fourth grade, his performance levels are below those of his grade peers.
- Bryan would benefit from sitting at the front of the classroom so as to maximize his attention.
- When possible, break Bryan's in-class assignments into smaller, more manageable chunks. Give him one part at a time with instructions to hand each in as it is completed and pick up the next. Each time he hands in a portion of the work, provide reinforcement for completed work. Using this technique, he will be more likely to stay on task and complete assignments.
- Bryan has average oral language skills, as well as a good foundation of world knowledge. Provide Bryan with opportunities, such as oral reports and science projects, so that he can demonstrate his strengths in certain school subjects.

Parents
- Have Bryan's third-grade teacher and his parents complete rating scales regarding his ability to control and sustain attention. Meet with Bryan's pediatrician to discuss the possibility of ADHD.
- Many of the behaviors that Bryan exhibits result from difficulties with attention. Keep in mind that these difficulties do not stem from a lack of effort or caring. Bryan wants to do well, but too often the expectations and academic demands are too high for his present skill levels.
- Bryan will feel frustrated by his attention and learning difficulties. Try to minimize his frustration by providing short periods of instruction (e.g., 10 to 15 minutes) that are followed by rewards or some type of engaging activity, such as a game. Alternatively, he may stay on task for longer periods of time if he receives feedback and rewards throughout the activity (e.g., chips, Monopoly money).
- Encourage Bryan to persist even when tasks become difficult. Show him that if he sticks with a problem and attempts alternative solutions, he will often be able to answer the problem correctly. When Bryan says that he cannot do a problem, say: "Let's take a closer look at that." Guide him in the steps to follow to solve the problem. As his confidence increases, he will need less support and encouragement.

INITIAL INSTRUCTIONAL GOALS

Reading and Spelling

- To make progress, Bryan requires specialized reading instruction. During the summer and ideally into the school year, he would benefit from enrollment in an online reading program: Virtual Reading Coach developed by Mindplay in Tucson, Arizona. The program begins with an initial reading assessment that determines exactly which skills he should use and then plans a prescriptive program based on the assessment results. He should spend 30 minutes a day, 5 days a week with this program, ideally for the next 6 months. A home version is available at www.myreadingteam.com and a school version is available at www.mindplay.com
- Bryan has mastered basic phonic skills, but needs to understand how to read multisyllabic words. Provide Bryan with instruction that increases his recognition of common letter patterns, builds his understanding of spelling rules, and shows him how to use structural analysis (breaking words apart into syllables). He needs to be taught common prefixes, suffixes, and roots. One program that would be beneficial is REWARDS, published by Sopris West (www.soprislearning.com). Reading and spelling instruction will be most effective if the patterns taught for reading are taught for spelling at the same time.
- In the classroom, use a systematic spelling program, such as Scholastic Spelling (Spelling Grade 4 Pupil Edition), that will provide Bryan with a solid foundation in common orthographic spelling patterns, as well as how to spell common high frequency words (www.scholastic.com). Another good program would be Spellography (www.soprislearning .com). This program addresses multisyllabic decoding skills, reading fluency, vocabulary using word roots, and spelling patterns and is appropriate as an intervention in grades 4 to 5.
- To build speed and accuracy in pronunciation of sight words and phonetically irregular words, use 1-minute speed drills. Time Bryan daily on reading lists of common, irregular words as quickly as he can but with accuracy as the primary goal. Record and display his daily performance on some type of graph. Also have him practice spelling these words.

Mathematics

- Teach Bryan basic math skills including the concept of place value, adding and subtracting multidigit numbers with and without regrouping, two-digit multiplication, and simple division. Introduce fractions and decimals.

- This summer have Bryan begin use of an online math program, such as ALEKS, to supplement math instruction (http://www.aleks.com). This program will design a math curriculum to address gaps in Bryan's knowledge.
- Provide practice in math facts and math using fun video games. Many of these can be found on www.coolmath.com
- Provide instruction in learning the value of coins, how to add them together, and how to make change.
- Provide daily review of different types of math problems. A good book to use would be *Math4Today* which provides daily 10-minute worksheets with a variety of math problems geared at a fourth-grade level.
- To maximize attention, alternate instruction in math skills with games to reinforce and develop those skills.

WOODCOCK-JOHNSON IV SCORE REPORT

Name: Anthony, Bryan   School: Harper
Date of Birth: 09/08/2004   Grade: 3.8
Age: 9 years, 8 months
Sex: Male
Dates of Testing:
  05/11/2014 (OL)
  05/12/2014 (ACH)

TESTS ADMINISTERED
Woodcock-Johnson IV Tests of Oral Language
Woodcock-Johnson IV Tests of Achievement Form A
Woodcock-Johnson Online Scoring and Reporting Program, Release 1.0

TABLE OF SCORES
Woodcock-Johnson IV Tests of Oral Language (Norms based on grade 3.8)

CLUSTER/Test	W	GE	RPI	Proficiency	SS (68% Band)
ORAL LANGUAGE	499	4.7	93/90	average	106 (101–112)
Picture Vocabulary	502	5.4	95/90	avg to advanced	108 (102–115)
Oral Comprehension	496	4.1	91/90	average	102 (95–109)

BROAD ORAL LANGUAGE	497	4.3	92/90	average	104 (99–108)
Picture Vocabulary	502	5.4	95/90	avg to advanced	108 (102–115)
Oral Comprehension	496	4.1	91/90	average	102 (95–109)
Understanding Directions	494	3.6	89/90	average	99 (94–104)
ORAL EXPRESSION	495	3.7	90/90	average	100 (95–104)
Picture Vocabulary	502	5.4	95/90	avg to advanced	108 (102–115)
Sentence Repetition	488	2.8	79/90	limited to avg	94 (89–99)
LISTENING COMP	495	3.8	90/90	average	100 (95–105)
Oral Comprehension	496	4.1	91/90	average	102 (95–109)
Understanding Directions	494	3.6	89/90	average	99 (94–104)
PHONETIC CODING	496	3.9	90/90	average	100 (96–105)
Segmentation	498	5.3	94/90	average	104 (99–109)
Sound Blending	494	2.3	85/90	average	95 (89–102)
SPEED of LEXICAL ACCESS	486	1.9	71/90	limited to avg	86 (81–91)
Rapid Picture Naming	480	1.6	54/90	limited	86 (81–92)
Retrieval Fluency	493	2.6	84/90	average	93 (86–99)
Sound Awareness	488	2.4	78/90	limited to avg	90 (84–95)

Woodcock-Johnson IV Tests of Achievement (Norms based on grade 3.8)

CLUSTER/Test	W	GE	RPI	Proficiency	SS (68% Band)
READING	462	1.9	26/90	limited	79 (77–82)
Letter-Word Identification	457	1.9	19/90	very limited	81 (78–84)
Passage Comprehension	467	1.9	34/90	limited	80 (75–84)
BROAD READING	463	2.3	36/90	limited	85 (82–88)
Letter-Word Identification	457	1.9	19/90	very limited	81 (78–84)
Passage Comprehension	467	1.9	34/90	limited	80 (75–84)
Sentence Reading Fluency	466	3.0	59/90	limited	94 (89–98)
BASIC READING SKILLS	468	2.0	42/90	limited	83 (81–86)
Letter-Word Identification	457	1.9	19/90	very limited	81 (78–84)
Word Attack	479	2.3	68/90	limited to avg	89 (84–93)
READING COMPREHENSION	477	2.1	61/90	limited	83 (79–86)
Passage Comprehension	467	1.9	34/90	limited	80 (75–84)
Reading Recall	488	2.7	83/90	average	93 (89–97)
READING COMP (Ext)	476	2.1	60/90	limited	82 (79–85)
Passage Comprehension	467	1.9	34/90	limited	80 (75–84)
Reading Recall	488	2.7	83/90	average	93 (89–97)
Reading Vocabulary	475	2.0	58/90	limited	83 (78–88)

READING FLUENCY	470	2.7	59/90	limited	90 (87–94)
Oral Reading	475	1.9	58/90	limited	86 (83–89)
Sentence Reading Fluency	466	3.0	59/90	limited	94 (89–98)
READING RATE	444	2.4	20/90	very limited	87 (83–90)
Sentence Reading Fluency	466	3.0	59/90	limited	94 (89–98)
Word Reading Fluency	422	1.8	4/90	very limited	81 (76–86)
MATHEMATICS	469	2.5	54/90	limited	85 (81–88)
Applied Problems	466	2.0	40/90	limited	80 (75–85)
Calculation	473	2.9	68/90	limited to avg	90 (86–94)
BROAD MATHEMATICS	471	2.7	58/90	limited	87 (83–90)
Applied Problems	466	2.0	40/90	limited	80 (75–85)
Calculation	473	2.9	68/90	limited to avg	90 (86–94)
Math Facts Fluency	475	2.9	67/90	limited	92 (87–97)
MATH CALCULATION SKILLS	474	2.9	67/90	limited to avg	91 (87–94)
Calculation	473	2.9	68/90	limited to avg	90 (86–94)
Math Facts Fluency	475	2.9	67/90	limited	92 (87–97)
MATH PROBLEM SOLVING	468	1.9	46/90	limited	80 (76–84)
Applied Problems	466	2.0	40/90	limited	80 (75–85)
Number Matrices	470	1.7	52/90	limited	84 (79–89)
WRITTEN LANGUAGE	480	2.8	73/90	limited to avg	92 (89–94)
Spelling	471	2.5	55/90	limited	88 (85–91)
Writing Samples	489	3.3	86/90	average	98 (94–101)
BROAD WRITTEN LANGUAGE	484	3.0	80/90	limited to avg	93 (91–96)
Spelling	471	2.5	55/90	limited	88 (85–91)
Writing Samples	489	3.3	86/90	average	98 (94–101)
Sentence Writing Fluency	492	3.7	89/90	average	99 (93–105)
BASIC WRITING SKILLS	475	2.6	66/90	limited	89 (87–92)
Spelling	471	2.5	55/90	limited	88 (85–91)
Editing	480	2.8	76/90	limited to avg	92 (87–97)
WRITTEN EXPRESSION	490	3.5	88/90	average	98 (95–101)
Writing Samples	489	3.3	86/90	average	98 (94–101)
Sentence Writing Fluency	492	3.7	89/90	average	99 (93–105)
ACADEMIC SKILLS	467	2.4	46/90	limited	84 (82–87)
Letter-Word Identification	457	1.9	19/90	very limited	81 (78–84)
Spelling	471	2.5	55/90	limited	88 (85–91)
Calculation	473	2.9	68/90	limited to avg	90 (86–94)
ACADEMIC APPLICATIONS	474	2.2	56/90	limited	84 (81–87)
Applied Problems	466	2.0	40/90	limited	80 (75–85)
Passage Comprehension	467	1.9	34/90	limited	80 (75–84)
Writing Samples	489	3.3	86/90	average	98 (94–101)

ACADEMIC FLUENCY	478	3.1	75/90	limited to avg	94 (90–97)
Sentence Reading Fluency	466	3.0	59/90	limited	94 (89–98)
Math Facts Fluency	475	2.9	67/90	limited	92 (87–97)
Sentence Writing Fluency	492	3.7	89/90	average	99 (93–105)
ACADEMIC KNOWLEDGE	494	3.6	89/90	average	99 (95–102)
Science	489	3.2	85/90	average	96 (91–102)
Social Studies	495	3.5	88/90	average	98 (93–103)
Humanities	497	4.2	92/90	average	102 (97–108)
PHONEME-GRAPHEME KNOWLEDGE	483	2.5	76/90	limited to avg	90 (86–94)
Word Attack	479	2.3	68/90	limited to avg	89 (84–93)
Spelling of Sounds	488	2.9	83/90	average	94 (89–99)
BRIEF ACHIEVEMENT	464	2.1	37/90	limited	82 (79–84)
Letter-Word Identification	457	1.9	19/90	very limited	81 (78–84)
Applied Problems	466	2.0	40/90	limited	80 (75–85)
Spelling	471	2.5	55/90	limited	88 (85–91)
BROAD ACHIEVEMENT	473	2.6	60/90	limited	87 (85–89)
Letter-Word Identification	457	1.9	19/90	very limited	81 (78–84)
Applied Problems	466	2.0	40/90	limited	80 (75–85)
Spelling	471	2.5	55/90	limited	88 (85–91)
Passage Comprehension	467	1.9	34/90	limited	80 (75–84)
Calculation	473	2.9	68/90	limited to avg	90 (86–94)
Writing Samples	489	3.3	86/90	average	98 (94–101)
Sentence Reading Fluency	466	3.0	59/90	limited	94 (89–98)
Math Facts Fluency	475	2.9	67/90	limited	92 (87–97)
Sentence Writing Fluency	492	3.7	89/90	average	99 (93–105)

VARIATIONS	STANDARD SCORES			DISCREPANCY		Interpretation
	Actual	Predicted	Difference	PR	SD	+ or – 1.50 SD
Intra-Oral Language (Extended) Variations						
ORAL EXPRESSION	100	98	2	57	+0.17	—
LISTENING COMP	100	100	0	53	+0.07	—
PHONETIC CODING	100	99	1	53	+0.06	—
SPEED of LEXICAL ACCESS	86	103	−17	11	−1.24	—
Picture Vocabulary^	108	98	10	82	+0.90	—
Oral Comprehension^	102	100	2	58	+0.19	—
Segmentation^	104	100	4	62	+0.30	—
Rapid Picture Naming^	86	102	−16	12	−1.17	—
Sentence Repetition	94	98	−4	37	−0.34	—
Understanding Directions	99	100	−1	46	−0.09	—
Sound Blending	95	99	−4	39	−0.28	—
Retrieval Fluency	93	103	−10	22	−0.76	—

^Core test for calculation of intra-oral language variations.

VARIATIONS	STANDARD SCORES			DISCREPANCY		Interpretation
	Actual	Predicted	Difference	PR	SD	+ or – 1.50
Intra-Achievement (Extended) Variations						
BASIC READING SKILLS	83	87	–4	31	–0.49	—
READING COMPREHENSION	83	87	–4	35	–0.39	—
READING COMP (Ext)	82	87	–5	29	–0.55	—
READING FLUENCY	90	88	2	57	+0.19	—
READING RATE	87	90	–3	40	–0.26	—
MATH CALCULATION SKILLS	91	86	5	68	+0.45	—
MATH PROBLEM SOLVING	80	89	–9	19	–0.88	—
BASIC WRITING SKILLS	89	86	3	66	+0.40	—
WRITTEN EXPRESSION	98	84	14	93	+1.48	—
Letter-Word Identification^	81	87	–6	22	–0.76	—
Applied Problems^	80	90	–10	18	–0.90	—
Spelling^	88	87	1	55	+0.12	—
Passage Comprehension^	80	87	–7	21	–0.80	—
Calculation^	90	86	4	64	+0.36	—
Writing Samples^	98	86	12	85	+1.03	—
Word Attack	89	89	0	48	–0.06	—
Oral Reading	86	90	–4	39	–0.28	—
Sentence Reading Fluency	94	88	6	69	+0.49	—
Math Facts Fluency	92	89	3	62	+0.31	—
Sentence Writing Fluency	99	85	14	90	+1.29	—
Reading Recall	93	90	3	60	+0.26	—
Number Matrices	84	92	–8	27	–0.62	—
Editing	92	87	5	67	+0.44	—
Word Reading Fluency	81	91	–10	18	–0.92	—
Spelling of Sounds	94	89	5	67	+0.44	—
Reading Vocabulary	83	89	–6	28	–0.58	—

^Core test for calculation of intra-achievement variations.

VARIATIONS	STANDARD SCORES			DISCREPANCY		Interpretation
	Actual	Predicted	Difference	PR	SD	+ or – 1.50 SD
Academic Skills/Academic Fluency/Academic Applications (Extended) Variations						
ACADEMIC SKILLS^	84	89	–5	24	–0.71	—
ACADEMIC FLUENCY^	94	87	7	76	+0.72	—
ACADEMIC APPLICATIONS^	84	91	–7	21	–0.80	—
READING RATE	87	89	–2	43	–0.17	—

^Core cluster for calculation of academic skills/fluency/applications variations.

| COMPARISONS | STANDARD SCORES | | | DISCREPANCY | | Significant at |
	Actual	Predicted	Difference	PR	SD	+ or – 1.50 SD
Oral Language/Achievement Comparisons*						
READING	79	102	–23	2	–1.98	Yes (–)
BROAD READING	85	102	–17	8	–1.42	No
BASIC READING SKILLS	83	102	–19	6	–1.60	Yes (–)
READING COMPREHENSION	83	103	–20	6	–1.55	Yes (–)
READING COMP (Ext)	82	103	–21	3	–1.84	Yes (–)
READING FLUENCY	90	102	–12	19	–0.88	No
READING RATE	87	102	–15	13	–1.11	No
MATHEMATICS	85	102	–17	8	–1.41	No
BROAD MATHEMATICS	87	102	–15	11	–1.24	No
MATH CALCULATION SKILLS	91	102	–11	20	–0.84	No
MATH PROBLEM SOLVING	80	102	–22	3	–1.83	Yes (–)
WRITTEN LANGUAGE	92	102	–10	22	–0.77	No
BROAD WRITTEN LANGUAGE	93	102	–9	27	–0.62	No
BASIC WRITING SKILLS	89	102	–13	15	–1.04	No
WRITTEN EXPRESSION	98	101	–3	41	–0.24	No
ACADEMIC SKILLS	84	102	–18	7	–1.45	No
ACADEMIC FLUENCY	94	102	–8	27	–0.61	No
ACADEMIC APPLICATIONS	84	103	–19	5	–1.63	Yes (–)
ACADEMIC KNOWLEDGE	99	103	–4	33	–0.44	No
PHONEME-GRAPHEME KNOWLEDGE	90	102	–12	18	–0.93	No
PHONETIC CODING	100	102	–2	46	–0.11	No
SPEED of LEXICAL ACCESS	86	102	–16	10	–1.27	No

* This procedure compares the WJ IV Broad Oral Language cluster score to selected achievement and cognitive-linguistic clusters.

| COMPARISONS | STANDARD SCORES | | | DISCREPANCY | | Significant at |
	Actual	Predicted	Difference	PR	SD	+ or – 1.50 SD
Academic Knowledge/Achievement Comparisons*						
BRIEF ACHIEVEMENT	82	99	–17	8	–1.43	No
BROAD ACHIEVEMENT	87	99	–12	18	–0.93	No
READING	79	99	–20	6	–1.53	Yes (–)
BROAD READING	85	99	–14	14	–1.09	No
BASIC READING SKILLS	83	99	–16	11	–1.24	No
READING COMPREHENSION	83	99	–16	12	–1.17	No

READING COMP (Ext)	82	99	−17	9	−1.36	No
READING FLUENCY	90	99	−9	26	−0.66	No
READING RATE	87	99	−12	19	−0.89	No
MATHEMATICS	85	99	−14	12	−1.20	No
BROAD MATHEMATICS	87	99	−12	16	−0.99	No
MATH CALCULATION SKILLS	91	99	−8	26	−0.63	No
MATH PROBLEM SOLVING	80	99	−19	5	−1.61	Yes (−)
WRITTEN LANGUAGE	92	99	−7	29	−0.56	No
BROAD WRITTEN LANGUAGE	93	99	−6	34	−0.41	No
BASIC WRITING SKILLS	89	99	−10	22	−0.77	No
WRITTEN EXPRESSION	98	99	−1	47	−0.08	No
ACADEMIC SKILLS	84	99	−15	12	−1.19	No
ACADEMIC FLUENCY	94	99	−5	34	−0.40	No
ACADEMIC APPLICATIONS	84	99	−15	11	−1.23	No
PHONETIC CODING	100	99	1	53	+0.08	No
SPEED of LEXICAL ACCESS	86	99	−13	17	−0.95	No

* This procedure compares the WJ IV Academic Knowledge cluster score to selected achievement and cognitive-linguistic clusters.

EDUCATIONAL EVALUATION REPORT

Student: Evan Ray
Parents: Roger and Jeanette Ray
Date of Birth: 07/07/1996
Grade: 11.9
Age: 17-11
School: Walnut Cove High
Dates of Testing: 6/7, 6/10/2014

REASON FOR REFERRAL

Evan was referred for his 3-year review of special education services. He has been receiving special education services under the category of learning disability since third grade. For the past 3 years, he has been receiving learning disability services in a resource setting at Walnut Cove High in Peoria, Wisconsin. The school team recommended an evaluation to help determine transition goals into postsecondary education. In addition, his parents expressed concerns to Ms. Elkins, the school psychologist, about Evan's continued difficulties in mathematics, his poor handwriting, and his general apathy about educational goals.

BACKGROUND INFORMATION

Evan is the adopted son of Roger and Jeanette Ray. He currently lives with his parents and an older brother, Jeremy, who is also adopted. The Rays adopted Evan at birth. His biological mother was 14 years old and smoked during the pregnancy. Although little is known about prenatal care, concerns were also raised about his biological mother's possible drug and/or alcohol abuse during pregnancy. Although little is known about his biological father, information from a court interview indicated that Evan's biological father had struggled throughout school with mathematics.

Evan attended preschool for two years and then entered Walnut Cove Elementary for kindergarten. Based upon parental and teacher concerns regarding motor development, Evan was referred for an occupational therapy evaluation in first grade. Results from the Peabody Developmental Motor Scale indicated delays of up to 17 months in fine-motor development and up to 26 months in gross-motor development. He demonstrated weakness in his flexor muscles, particularly abdominals and hip flexors, toe walking, and weaknesses in visual-motor planning. Evan was unable to hop on one foot without losing his balance. On the Gardner Test of Visual-Perceptual Skills (nonmotor), Evan obtained average scores on measures of visual discrimination and visual-spatial relations, and a below average score in visual memory. Recommendations were made for occupational therapy with the goals of improving fine- and gross-motor skills, visual-perceptual motor planning, and muscle weaknesses. In addition, Evan began to receive resource support for reading, writing, and math.

The Rays report that although Evan tried to participate in team sports throughout elementary school (baseball, soccer, swimming, and karate), the experiences were not positive. During baseball games, Evan would often sit down in the outfield. On the soccer field, Evan tried to stay away from the ball. His mother reported that on several occasions when she picked Evan up from practice, he would be crying. In swimming he was also 20 strokes behind the other children, and in karate he could not keep his balance.

Delays were also noted in gross-motor development. At the age of 9, Evan was unable to ride a bike or tie his shoes with ease. He walked with an awkward gait and often tripped. Because of continued toe walking, Evan had casts put on both legs to stretch his heel cords and position his feet flat on the ground. Results from a brain magnetic resonance imaging (MRI) indicated subtle cortical dysplasia involving the cerebellar hemispheres (the area of the brain involving motor development and balance).

Evan is currently in the 11th grade. Since third grade, he has received special education services in a resource setting under the category of specific learning disability. Currently, he is also receiving occupational therapy services 30 minutes per week, with the goal of teaching him how to use technology to compensate for his writing difficulties. He currently uses a laptop in all of his classes to assist with lengthy writing assignments. Presently, in high school, Evan is not involved in any extracurricular activities. He notes that he likes to play video games and spends most of his free time in this way. Evan's parents note that he is creative and has a good vocabulary and sense of humor. When asked to write what he likes to do on the weekends, Evan wrote: "Watch TV, play video games, and fall down the stairs."

CLASSROOM OBSERVATION

Evan was observed for the first 20 minutes in his algebra class. He was sitting in the back of the room. He looked at the floor and his shoes, glancing up only occasionally. He appeared to be listening. Fifteen minutes into the discussion, Evan began digging into the tread of his shoe with a pencil. He then removed his shoe and continued to run the tip of his pencil through the shoe treads, until a nearby student, then a teacher's aide, prompted him to put his shoe back on and listen. When independent seatwork began, Evan did not understand what he was supposed to do. The classroom aide came over and re-explained the assignment to Evan. Evan then began to work but had only attempted one problem after 5 minutes.

TESTS ADMINISTERED

Evan was administered the Woodcock-Johnson IV Tests of Achievement (WJ IV ACH) and the Woodcock-Johnson IV Tests of Oral Language (WJ IV OL). In addition, he was observed in his high school algebra class and a writing sample was collected.

BEHAVIOR DURING TESTING

Evan was tested through three sessions. In the first session, Evan complained of being tired, yawned, and kept his head down on the desk. He said that he did not get much sleep, then became teary-eyed and asked if he could please finish tomorrow. He completed two tests before he was dismissed to go back to class. Evan returned for testing the next morning and was once again mildly to moderately resistant. He complained that the examiner, while trying to get him engaged in the testing, was "annoying" him. When reminded that he agreed to come back to finish the test after being allowed to stop the day before, he became more cooperative. Nonetheless, he did not seem to have much stamina and struggled to maintain an adequate energy level. During oral language tests, he showed persistence and enthusiasm.

By the third session, Evan was cooperative. He was informed that he could earn coupons for "homework passes" by complying with requests and trying his hardest. He appeared at ease, comfortable, and attentive. He responded promptly but carefully to test questions and generally persisted with difficult tasks.

TEST RESULTS

The WJ IV OL and ACH were scored according to age norms. Because these two batteries are co-normed, direct comparisons can be made among his oral language and achievement scores. These comparisons can help determine the presence and significance of any strengths and weaknesses among his abilities. These tests provide measures of Evan's specific oral language abilities, as well as his current levels of academic achievement.

Evan's performance is compared to his age peers using percentile ranks (PR) and PR ranges:

PR Range	0.1–2	3–8	9–24	25–75	76–91	92–97	98–99.9
Verbal label	Very low	Low	Low average	Average	High average	Superior	Very superior

Note. Percentile ranks (PR) are scores that indicate rank order within the norm group and range from <0.1 to >99.9. They also indicate the percentage of the population that scored the same or lower.

His academic proficiency on specific tasks is described by the Relative Proficiency Index (RPI) levels:

RPI Range	0–3	3–24	24–67	67–82	82–95	95–98	98–100	100
Level of proficiency	Extremely limited	Very limited	Limited	Limited to average	Average	Average to advanced	Advanced	Very advanced

Note. An RPI is expressed as a fraction with the bottom number (denominator) fixed at 90. The 90 represents the 90% proficiency level of average agemates. The top number (numerator) ranges from 0 to 100 and reflects the student's proficiency on the task.

A full set of scores is appended to the end of this report.

ORAL LANGUAGE

Evan's proficiency was average to very advanced on all measures of oral language. His vocabulary knowledge, ability to repeat back orally presented sentences, and ability to blend speech sounds together and push them apart (segmentation) were all advanced to very advanced. Evan has a solid foundation in the oral language skills that underlie both reading and writing.

WJ IV OL Cluster/Tests	RPI	Proficiency	PR (±1 SEM)
Sentence Repetition	100/90	Very advanced	94 (86–98)
Phonetic Coding	100/90	Advanced	96 (93–98)
Sound Blending	100/90	Very advanced	98 (94–99)
Segmentation	99/90	Advanced	88 (81–94)
Broad Oral Language	97/90	Average to advanced	90 (82–95)
Picture Vocabulary	99/90	Advanced	94 (88–98)
Oral Comprehension	97/90	Average to advanced	81 (66–91)
Understanding Directions	95/90	Average	70 (48–86)

ACHIEVEMENT

Evan's proficiency ranged from very limited (e.g., Calculation) to very advanced (e.g., Writing Samples) on various measures of achievement. In general, his proficiency in reading and written language was average but his proficiency in mathematics was limited.

Reading

As with oral language, Evan's proficiency with reading was mostly average to advanced. He was able to pronounce both real words and nonsense words with ease. He had average proficiency on measures of reading rate and fluency. His lowest score was on the Passage Comprehension test. This was somewhat surprising given his high score on the Oral Comprehension test, a test of listening comprehension in the same format.

WJ IV Reading Cluster/Tests	RPI	Proficiency	PR (±1 SEM)
Word Attack	97/90	Average to advanced	83 (66–93)
Reading Vocabulary	98/90	Advanced	86 (76–93)
Reading Recall	85/90	Average	33 (24–43)

WJ IV Reading Cluster/Tests	RPI	Proficiency	PR (±I SEM)
Broad Reading	94/90	Average	63 (53–72)
Letter-Word Identification	99/90	Advanced	84 (75–91)
Passage Comprehension	76/90	Limited to average	30 (20–41)
Sentence Reading Fluency	93/90	Average	54 (42–66)
Phoneme–Grapheme Knowledge	97/90	Average to advanced	83 (72–91)

Written Language

Evan's responses on the Writing Samples test were highly sophisticated both in terms of writing style and use of vocabulary (see Figure 7.1 in Chapter 7). He wrote responses quickly and easily.

WJ IV Written Language Cluster/Tests	RPI	Proficiency	PR (±I SEM)
Broad Written Language	98/90	Advanced	91 (84–96)
Spelling	83/90	Average	39 (30–49)
Writing Samples	100/90	Very advanced	>99 (>99)
Sentence Writing Fluency	94/90	Average	68 (54–80)

Evan also provided the first page of his first draft of a short story he was writing for his English class (see Figure 8.1). Several aspects about his writing can be gleaned from this sample: He has an excellent vocabulary; his story is cohesive; he uses both simple and complex sentence structures; and his handwriting is difficult but not impossible to read.

Translation:

The earth shook violently and the ground parted to make way for the mighty titans rising from the depths. It was as if nature itself feared their presence. Mouth gaping wide Eric could only watch as they emerged. Thunderous footsteps tore through the countryside, why were they here? He rode on horseback in their shadows. Was this all a dream? Or some elaborate hoax? He wondered what their end goal was and could not help but envy how gracefully they traversed the land despite their daunting size. Unsure of where they were leading him the one thing he knew for sure was that by the end of all this, the world would never be the same.

Mathematics

On the WJ IV ACH, Evan's proficiency was limited on all aspects of math performance. His performance on the Calculation test, a measure of computational

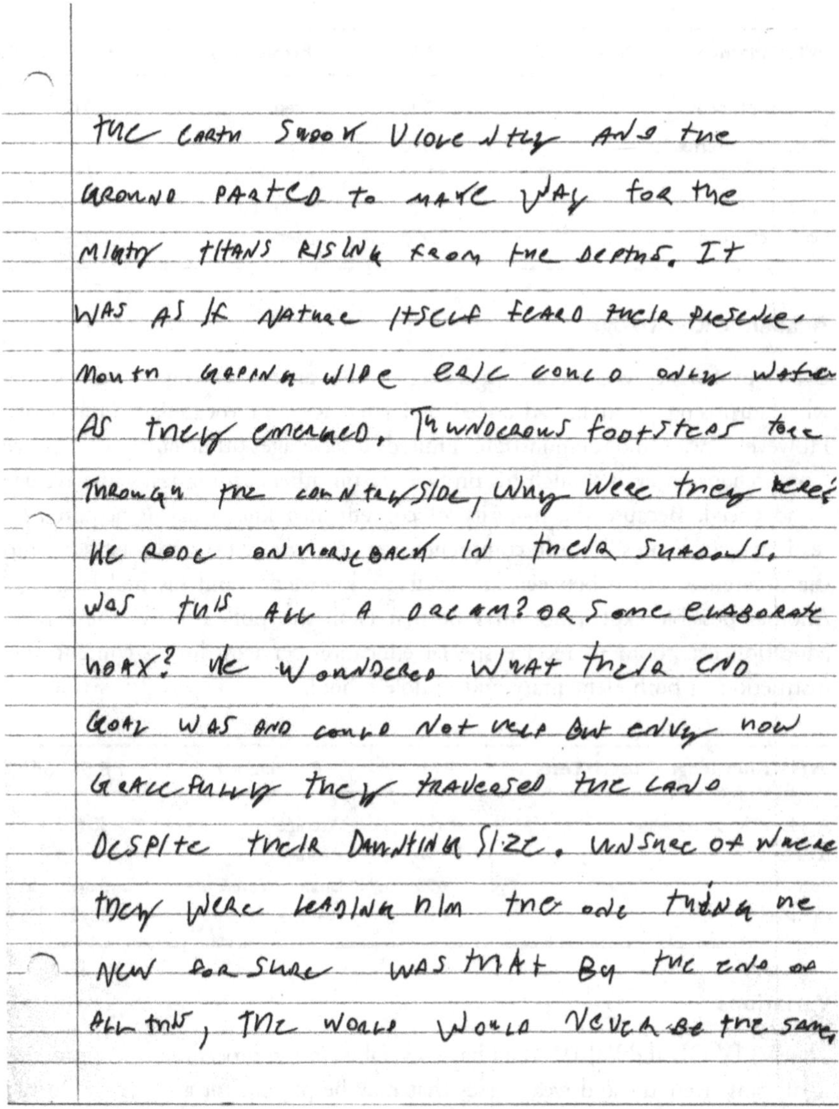

The earth shook violently and the ground parted to make way for the mighty titans rising from the depths. It was as if nature itself feared their presence. Mouth gaping wide each could only watch as they emerged. Thunderous footsteps tore through the countryside. Why were they here? He rode on horseback in their shadows. Was this all a dream? Or some elaborate hoax? He wondered what their end goal was and could not help but envy how gracefully they traversed the land despite their daunting size. Unsure of where they were leading him the one thing he new for sure was that by the end of all this, the world would never be the same.

Figure 8.1 Evan's Draft of a Short Story for English Class

skills, exceeded only 6% of his age peers. On the Calculation test, he was able to solve simple addition, subtraction, and multiplication problems but was unable to solve problems that involved division, addition and subtraction of fractions, or simple algebraic equations.

WJ IV Mathematics Cluster/Tests	RPI	Proficiency	PR (±1 SEM)
Number Matrices	59/90	Limited	20 (14–29)
Broad Mathematics	51/90	Limited	14 (10–19)
Applied Problems	77/90	Limited to average	31 (21–42)
Calculation	20/90	Very limited	6 (4–10)
Math Facts Fluency	59/90	Limited	70 (48–86)

Academic Knowledge

Evan's proficiency was average regarding content area knowledge. This is somewhat surprising given his advanced oral language and vocabulary knowledge. However, Evan did demonstrate limited to average proficiency on Passage Comprehension even though his proficiency on other reading tasks was average to advanced. Because the majority of content area knowledge is acquired by reading texts, Evan's limits in comprehension of connected text may be related to the differences noted between his academic knowledge and his oral language. Another possible explanation may be that Evan was pulled out of the general education classroom to receive special education services during content area instruction in both elementary and middle school.

WJ IV Knowledge Cluster/Tests	RPI	Proficiency	PR (±1 SEM)
Academic Knowledge	85/90	Average	38 (30–47)
Science	89/90	Average	48 (35–62)
Social Studies	79/90	Limited to average	32 (21–45)
Humanities	84/90	Average	38 (26–52)

Variations

The WJ IV OL and WJ IV ACH have several variation procedures to summarize significant strengths and weaknesses that may be present for a student. On the Intra-Oral Language Variation procedure, Evan had a significant relative strength on the Sound Blending test. On the Intra-Achievement Variation procedure, Evan had significant relative strengths on the Basic Reading Skills cluster, the Written Expression cluster, and the Writing Samples test. In fact, when his score on the Writing Samples test was compared to his other areas of achievement, less than one out of 1,000 students with the same predicted score (SS = 96) would have an actual standard score (SS = 147) as high or higher.

Evan had significant relative weaknesses on the Math Calculation Skills cluster, the Math Problem Solving cluster, and the Calculation test. On the Math Calculation Skills cluster, only one of 100 students with the same predicted score of 107 had an actual standard score of 77 or lower.

Comparisons

The WJ IV OL and WJ IV ACH have two ability/achievement comparison procedures in which one score (Broad Oral Language or Academic Knowledge) is used to predict performance in achievement. When Evan's Broad Oral Language cluster score is compared to his achievement clusters, his Written Expression is significantly higher than predicted. In contrast, the following clusters are significantly lower than predicted: Reading Comprehension, Mathematics, Broad Mathematics, Math Calculation Skills, Math Problem Solving, and Academic Knowledge. When Evan's Academic Knowledge (orally administered tests of Science, Social Studies, and Humanities) standard score is compared to his achievement, his Basic Reading Skills cluster, Written Language clusters (except for Basic Writing Skills), and Phonetic Coding cluster (pushing together and pulling apart speech sounds) are all significantly higher than predicted. The fact that Reading Comprehension and Academic Knowledge are both significantly lower than predicted by Evan's Broad Oral Language ability should be noted. His strong oral language predicts equally strong reading skills, which isn't the case, especially for comprehension of connected text as is measured by the Passage Comprehension test. Also, the content knowledge measured by Academic Knowledge, composed of Science, Social Studies, and Humanities, is typically acquired through reading of connected text. There may be other factors, such as attention/concentration, working memory, or processing speed impacting Evan's ability to comprehend what he reads at a level that is in line with his oral language abilities. Limits in these types of cognitive abilities also may explain Evan's ongoing difficulties in mathematics.

CONCLUSION

Evan is a student with dysgraphia who has advanced oral language and superior writing skills in terms of content. He uses a laptop in most of his classes. Evan has received services as a student with an SLD in mathematics since third grade, but he continues to struggle with most areas of mathematics. The multidisciplinary team will determine Evan's continued eligibility for special education services, as well as further develop a postsecondary transition plan.

RECOMMENDATIONS

Further Assessment and Educational Programming
- Conduct further intellectual/cognitive assessment to help determine the specific factors that are inhibiting math development and performance. Administer measures of reasoning ability, working memory, visual-spatial thinking, and processing speed to determine if any of these abilities are affecting Evan's mathematical performance. Integrate these findings with the results from the present evaluation.
- Schedule a multidisciplinary conference in the fall to consider Evan's continued eligibility for special education services for math remediation and his need for accommodations and support during his senior year.
- Administer the KeyMath3 or do informal testing to determine additional relevant instructional goals.
- Based on the findings of the more comprehensive report, Evan and his parents should explore modified entrance requirements to the state university, as well as procedures for applying to the program for students with learning disabilities.
- If possible in a postsecondary setting, consider waiving any credit requirements in the mathematical area due to his extreme difficulty with mathematical calculation skills and provide an acceptable substitution.
- For the first semester, consider a reduced course load so that Evan has enough time and energy to devote to his courses.
- Provide Evan with ongoing assistance in vocational planning.

Mathematics
Evan needs to continue receiving instruction in basic math skills.
- As part of math instruction, reteach and review procedures involved in computations with fractions, percentages, and decimals. Use manipulatives to demonstrate the meaning of fractions. Also review the concept of place value so that Evan can understand the meaning of a decimal point.
- Specifically teach strategies for translating word problems into computations. Help Evan learn to visualize what is happening in the problem.
- Encourage Evan to take a remedial class in functional mathematics. Review math skills needed for independent living, such as balancing a checkbook, figuring interest on a car loan, determining the amount of tip to leave at a restaurant, budgeting his salary, measuring for cooking, adjusting a recipe, and using map skills.

WOODCOCK-JOHNSON IV SCORE REPORT

Name: Ray, Evan
Date of Birth: 07/07/1996
Age: 17 years, 11 months
Sex: Male
Dates of Testing:
  06/07/2014 (OL)
  06/10/2014 (ACH)

Grade: 11.9

TESTS ADMINISTERED
Woodcock-Johnson IV Tests of Oral Language
Woodcock-Johnson IV Tests of Achievement Form A
Woodcock-Johnson Online Scoring and Reporting Program, Release 1.0

TABLE OF SCORES
Woodcock-Johnson IV Tests of Oral Language (Norms based on age 17-11)

CLUSTER/Test	W	AE	RPI	Proficiency	PR (68% Band)
ORAL LANGUAGE	533	>30	98/90	advanced	92 (85-96)
Picture Vocabulary	540	>30	99/90	advanced	94 (88-98)
Oral Comprehension	526	>30	97/90	avg to advanced	81 (66-91)
BROAD ORAL LANGUAGE	528	>30	98/90	avg to advanced	90 (82-95)
Picture Vocabulary	540	>30	99/90	advanced	94 (88-98)
Oral Comprehension	526	>30	97/90	avg to advanced	81 (66-91)
Understanding Directions	519	>25	95/90	average	70 (48-86)
ORAL EXPRESSION	550	>30	99/90	advanced	96 (92-99)
Picture Vocabulary	540	>30	99/90	advanced	94 (88-98)
Sentence Repetition	559	>30	100/90	very advanced	94 (86-98)
LISTENING COMP	522	>30	96/90	avg to advanced	81 (66-91)
Oral Comprehension	526	>30	97/90	avg to advanced	81 (66-91)
Understanding Directions	519	>25	95/90	average	70 (48-86)
PHONETIC CODING	539	>30	100/90	advanced	96 (93-98)
Segmentation	531	>30	99/90	advanced	88 (81-94)
Sound Blending	547	>28	100/90	very advanced	98 (94->99)
SPEED of LEXICAL ACCESS	521	>30	93/90	average	61 (50-71)
Rapid Picture Naming	535	>30	97/90	avg to advanced	70 (59-80)
Retrieval Fluency	508	13-11	86/90	average	36 (22-52)

Woodcock-Johnson IV Tests of Achievement (Norms based on age 17-11)

CLUSTER/Test	W	AE	RPI	Proficiency	PR (68% Band)
READING	534	24	94/90	average	63 (53-72)
Letter-Word Identification	553	>30	99/90	advanced	84 (75-91)
Passage Comprehension	515	14-0	76/90	limited to avg	30 (20-41)
BROAD READING	539	23	94/90	average	60 (51-68)
Letter-Word Identification	553	>30	99/90	advanced	84 (75-91)
Passage Comprehension	515	14-0	76/90	limited to avg	30 (20-41)
Sentence Reading Fluency	550	20	93/90	average	54 (42-66)
BASIC READING SKILLS	539	>30	98/90	advanced	86 (77-92)
Letter-Word Identification	553	>30	99/90	advanced	84 (75-91)
Word Attack	525	>30	97/90	avg to advanced	83 (66-93)
READING COMPREHENSION	508	13-5	81/90	limited to avg	28 (20-37)
Passage Comprehension	515	14-0	76/90	limited to avg	30 (20-41)
Reading Recall	502	12-0	85/90	average	33 (24-43)
READING COMP (Ext)	517	18-1	90/90	average	51 (42-59)
Passage Comprehension	515	14-0	76/90	limited to avg	30 (20-41)
Reading Recall	502	12-0	85/90	average	33 (24-43)
Reading Vocabulary	534	>30	98/90	advanced	86 (76-93)
READING FLUENCY	542	>30	95/90	avg to advanced	64 (53-74)
Oral Reading	534	>30	97/90	avg to advanced	77 (63-88)
Sentence Reading Fluency	550	20	93/90	average	54 (42-66)
READING RATE	542	17-8	90/90	average	49 (39-60)
Sentence Reading Fluency	550	20	93/90	average	54 (42-66)
Word Reading Fluency	533	15-9	85/90	average	45 (31-59)
MATHEMATICS	507	11-4	47/90	limited	12 (9-17)
Applied Problems	514	13-7	77/90	limited to avg	31 (21-42)
Calculation	499	10-5	20/90	very limited	6 (4-10)
BROAD MATHEMATICS	512	11-9	51/90	limited	14 (10-19)
Applied Problems	514	13-7	77/90	limited to avg	31 (21-42)
Calculation	499	10-5	20/90	very limited	6 (4-10)
Math Facts Fluency	523	12-7	59/90	limited	23 (15-33)
MATH CALCULATION SKILLS	511	11-5	37/90	limited	12 (8-16)
Calculation	499	10-5	20/90	very limited	6 (4-10)
Math Facts Fluency	523	12-7	59/90	limited	23 (15-33)
MATH PROBLEM SOLVING	509	12-1	69/90	limited to avg	23 (16-30)
Applied Problems	514	13-7	77/90	limited to avg	31 (21-42)
Number Matrices	503	11-2	59/90	limited	20 (14-29)
WRITTEN LANGUAGE	546	>30	99/90	advanced	93 (86-97)
Spelling	527	15-3	83/90	average	39 (30-49)
Writing Samples	565	>30	100/90	very advanced	>99 (>99->99)

BROAD WRITTEN LANGUAGE	537	>30	98/90	advanced	91 (84-96)
Spelling	527	15-3	83/90	average	39 (30-49)
Writing Samples	565	>30	100/90	very advanced	>99 (>99->99)
Sentence Writing Fluency	520	>30	94/90	average	68 (54-80)
BASIC WRITING SKILLS	521	14-10	82/90	limited to avg	35 (28-43)
Spelling	527	15-3	83/90	average	39 (30-49)
Editing	516	14-5	79/90	limited to avg	33 (23-45)
WRITTEN EXPRESSION	542	>30	99/90	advanced	>99 (97->99)
Writing Samples	565	>30	100/90	very advanced	>99 (>99->99)
Sentence Writing Fluency	520	>30	94/90	average	68 (54-80)
ACADEMIC SKILLS	526	14-10	82/90	average	38 (31-44)
Letter-Word Identification	553	>30	99/90	advanced	84 (75-91)
Spelling	527	15-3	83/90	average	39 (30-49)
Calculation	499	10-5	20/90	very limited	6 (4-10)
ACADEMIC APPLICATIONS	531	>30	96/90	avg to advanced	75 (65-84)
Applied Problems	514	13-7	77/90	limited to avg	31 (21-42)
Passage Comprehension	515	14-0	76/90	limited to avg	30 (20-41)
Writing Samples	565	>30	100/90	very advanced	>99 (>99->99)
ACADEMIC FLUENCY	531	15-10	87/90	average	44 (36-53)
Sentence Reading Fluency	550	20	93/90	average	54 (42-66)
Math Facts Fluency	523	12-7	59/90	limited	23 (15-33)
Sentence Writing Fluency	520	>30	94/90	average	68 (54-80)
ACADEMIC KNOWLEDGE	519	15-1	85/90	average	38 (30-47)
Science	517	17-1	89/90	average	48 (35-62)
Social Studies	521	14-3	79/90	limited to avg	32 (21-45)
Humanities	518	14-9	84/90	average	38 (26-52)
PHONEME-GRAPHEME KNOWLEDGE	522	>29	97/90	avg to advanced	83 (72-91)
Word Attack	525	>30	97/90	avg to advanced	83 (66-93)
Spelling of Sounds	519	>22	97/90	avg to advanced	80 (65-91)
BRIEF ACHIEVEMENT	531	20	92/90	average	55 (47-62)
Letter-Word Identification	553	>30	99/90	advanced	84 (75-91)
Applied Problems	514	13-7	77/90	limited to avg	31 (21-42)
Spelling	527	15-3	83/90	average	39 (30-49)
BROAD ACHIEVEMENT	530	18-3	90/90	average	51 (45-57)
Letter-Word Identification	553	>30	99/90	advanced	84 (75-91)
Applied Problems	514	13-7	77/90	limited to avg	31 (21-42)
Spelling	527	15-3	83/90	average	39 (30-49)
Passage Comprehension	515	14-0	76/90	limited to avg	30 (20-41)
Calculation	499	10-5	20/90	very limited	6 (4-10)
Writing Samples	565	>30	100/90	very advanced	>99 (>99->99)
Sentence Reading Fluency	550	20	93/90	average	54 (42-66)
Math Facts Fluency	523	12-7	59/90	limited	23 (15-33)
Sentence Writing Fluency	520	>30	94/90	average	68 (54-80)

VARIATIONS	STANDARD SCORES			DISCREPANCY		Interpretation
	Actual	Predicted	Difference	PR	SD	+ or – 1.50 SD
Intra-Oral Language (Extended) Variations						
ORAL EXPRESSION	127	111	16	91	+1.37	—
LISTENING COMP	113	115	–2	43	–0.17	—
PHONETIC CODING	127	107	20	92	+1.43	—
SPEED of LEXICAL ACCESS	104	111	–7	31	–0.50	—
Picture Vocabulary^	124	110	14	87	+1.10	—
Oral Comprehension^	113	114	–1	47	–0.08	—
Segmentation^	118	105	13	82	+0.93	—
Rapid Picture Naming^	108	109	–1	47	–0.08	—
Sentence Repetition	123	109	14	86	+1.08	—
Understanding Directions	108	112	–4	39	–0.29	—
Sound Blending	131	108	23	94	+1.58	Strength
Retrieval Fluency	95	111	–16	12	–1.18	—

^Core test for calculation of intra-oral language variations.

VARIATIONS	STANDARD SCORES			DISCREPANCY		Interpretation
	Actual	Predicted	Difference	PR	SD	+ or – 1.50 SD
Intra-Achievement (Extended) Variations						
BASIC READING SKILLS	116	101	15	95	+1.61	Strength
READING COMPREHENSION	91	105	–14	8	–1.43	—
READING COMP (Ext)	100	106	–6	27	–0.63	—
READING FLUENCY	106	101	5	68	+0.46	—
READING RATE	100	104	–4	37	–0.34	—
MATH CALCULATION SKILLS	82	107	–25	1	–2.38	Weakness
MATH PROBLEM SOLVING	89	105	–16	6	–1.54	Weakness
BASIC WRITING SKILLS	94	105	–11	14	–1.08	—
WRITTEN EXPRESSION	137	95	42	>99.9	+3.96	Strength
Letter-Word Identification^	115	101	14	93	+1.49	—
Applied Problems^	92	105	–13	12	–1.19	—
Spelling^	96	104	–8	21	–0.81	—
Passage Comprehension^	92	105	–13	8	–1.41	—
Calculation^	77	107	–30	<0.1	–3.10	Weakness
Writing Samples^	147	96	51	>99.9	+4.12	Strength

Word Attack	114	101	13	87	+1.14	—
Oral Reading	111	101	10	83	+0.94	—
Sentence Reading Fluency	101	104	−3	41	−0.22	—
Math Facts Fluency	89	106	−17	9	−1.37	—
Sentence Writing Fluency	107	96	11	81	+0.90	—
Reading Recall	93	104	−11	21	−0.81	—
Number Matrices	88	104	−16	9	−1.33	—
Editing	94	104	−10	15	−1.02	—
Word Reading Fluency	98	103	−5	35	−0.39	—
Spelling of Sounds	113	104	9	79	+0.81	—
Reading Vocabulary	116	105	11	86	+1.09	—

^Core test for calculation of intra-achievement variations.

VARIATIONS	STANDARD SCORES			DISCREPANCY		Interpretation
	Actual	Predicted	Difference	PR	SD	+ or − 1.50 SD
Academic Skills/Academic Fluency/Academic Applications (Extended) Variations						
ACADEMIC SKILLS^	95	104	−9	13	−1.14	—
ACADEMIC FLUENCY^	98	102	−4	35	−0.39	—
ACADEMIC APPLICATIONS^	110	97	13	92	+1.41	—
READING RATE	100	102	−2	44	−0.15	—

^Core cluster for calculation of academic skills/fluency/applications variations.

COMPARISONS	STANDARD SCORES			DISCREPANCY		Significant at
	Actual	Predicted	Difference	PR	SD	+ or − 1.50 SD
Oral Language/Achievement Comparisons*						
READING	105	113	−8	26	−0.65	No
BROAD READING	104	112	−8	26	−0.65	No
BASIC READING SKILLS	116	111	5	65	+0.38	No
READING COMPREHENSION	91	111	−20	6	−1.55	Yes (−)
READING COMP (Ext)	100	112	−12	15	−1.06	No
READING FLUENCY	106	109	−3	40	−0.26	No
READING RATE	100	109	−9	27	−0.62	No
MATHEMATICS	83	110	−27	2	−2.15	Yes (−)
BROAD MATHEMATICS	84	110	−26	2	−1.96	Yes (−)

MATH CALCULATION SKILLS	82	108	−26	3	−1.92	Yes (−)
MATH PROBLEM SOLVING	89	110	−21	3	−1.87	Yes (−)
WRITTEN LANGUAGE	122	111	11	82	+0.91	No
BROAD WRITTEN LANGUAGE	120	110	10	78	+0.78	No
BASIC WRITING SKILLS	94	111	−17	8	−1.40	No
WRITTEN EXPRESSION	137	108	29	98	+2.05	Yes (+)
ACADEMIC SKILLS	95	111	−16	10	−1.28	No
ACADEMIC FLUENCY	98	108	−10	22	−0.78	No
ACADEMIC APPLICATIONS	110	112	−2	43	−0.17	No
ACADEMIC KNOWLEDGE	96	115	−19	2	−2.05	Yes (−)
PHONEME-GRAPHEME KNOWLEDGE	114	109	5	65	+0.40	No
PHONETIC CODING	127	108	19	92	+1.41	No
SPEED of LEXICAL ACCESS	104	110	−6	33	−0.43	No

* This procedure compares the WJ IV Broad Oral Language cluster score to selected achievement and cognitive-linguistic clusters. _____

	STANDARD SCORES			DISCREPANCY		Significant at
COMPARISONS	Actual	Predicted	Difference	PR	SD	+ or − 1.50 SD
Academic Knowledge/Achievement Comparisons*						
BRIEF ACHIEVEMENT	102	97	5	67	+0.45	No
BROAD ACHIEVEMENT	100	97	3	63	+0.33	No
READING	105	97	8	74	+0.66	No
BROAD READING	104	97	7	70	+0.54	No
BASIC READING SKILLS	116	97	19	94	+1.55	Yes (+)
READING COMPREHENSION	91	97	−6	32	−0.46	No
READING COMP (Ext)	100	97	3	62	+0.30	No
READING FLUENCY	106	97	9	73	+0.62	No
READING RATE	100	98	2	56	+0.15	No
MATHEMATICS	83	97	−14	10	−1.26	No
BROAD MATHEMATICS	84	97	−13	14	−1.10	No
MATH CALCULATION SKILLS	82	98	−16	11	−1.21	No
MATH PROBLEM SOLVING	89	97	−8	23	−0.73	No

WRITTEN LANGUAGE	122	97	25	98	+2.00	Yes (+)
BROAD WRITTEN LANGUAGE	120	97	23	96	+1.80	Yes (+)
BASIC WRITING SKILLS	94	97	−3	42	−0.21	No
WRITTEN EXPRESSION	137	97	40	99.8	+2.92	Yes (+)
ACADEMIC SKILLS	95	97	−2	45	−0.12	No
ACADEMIC FLUENCY	98	97	1	52	+0.04	No
ACADEMIC APPLICATIONS	110	97	13	88	+1.18	No
PHONETIC CODING	127	98	29	98	+2.16	Yes (+)
SPEED of LEXICAL ACCESS	104	98	6	67	+0.43	No

* This procedure compares the WJ IV Academic Knowledge cluster score to selected achievement and cognitive-linguistic clusters.

EDUCATIONAL EVALUATION

Name: Veronica Jackson
Birth Date: 4/16/1992
Age: 22 Years, 3 Months
Grade: 16.9
School: University of Hampshire
Evaluation Dates: 7/27, 7/28/2014

REASON FOR REFERRAL

Veronica, a recent graduate from the University of Hampshire with a BS in biomedical engineering, referred herself for an evaluation because of difficulties with reading comprehension, reading rate, time management, test taking, and studying. Although she reports that she does very well on projects, she has trouble absorbing information when it is delivered in a lecture format, as well as on exams that require a great deal of memorization or a considerable amount of reading. Veronica wanted to gain a deeper understanding of her strengths and weaknesses, and explore whether she has a learning disability and if she will need specific accommodations in graduate school to help her compensate for her reading difficulties.

BACKGROUND INFORMATION

Veronica is currently living at her parents' home in Vermont with a roommate. For the next few years, both of her parents are residing in Sweden. Her father is an electrical engineer, and her mother is a research technician who does database/computer work from home. Veronica's younger brother Manuel, age 17, who is also in Sweden, has been diagnosed with dyslexia and ADHD.

Veronica attended elementary and middle school at Fountain Hills Academy, a private school. In first through third grade, Veronica was in the school's Gifted and Talented Education Program (GATE). In third grade, Veronica told her parents that she could not keep up with the other kids and it was too hard for her. Her parents then requested that she not attend the program anymore. From third to sixth grade, Veronica received private tutoring to help her build her reading skills. She completed all 12 steps of the Wilson Reading System with a Level II certified Wilson instructor.

Veronica attended Redfields High School, a private charter school in Sudbury, Vermont, and achieved high grades in all of her classes. Although she has never been evaluated for learning disabilities, she has received additional support at school throughout her educational career. Veronica noted that she has always had problems with her reading speed, and has always needed more time in her English and History classes. She felt that she didn't do well on the SATs because she did not have enough time to complete all of the items. Throughout her school years, she has always taken advantage of the extra help provided by teachers during their office hours or after school, and her teachers have always granted her additional time on tests when needed. She noted that she comprehends lectures much better when she has a copy of the notes or a study guide to take notes in as she listens.

As a student at the University of Hampshire, Veronica completed 13 credit hours a semester. In the fall of 2013, she had difficulty with Economics 214, a course that depended heavily on lecture notes and the textbook. She then applied for tutoring support and help with time management from the school's Alternative Learning Techniques (ALT) Center. In the spring of 2013, she started receiving tutorial help at the ALT Center and was then able to pass the class. Veronica graduated this summer, and has been accepted for graduate school at Gateway State to earn a master's degree in sustainability science, a program that focuses on ways to create a cleaner earth and a healthier environment. Presently, Veronica's main interests lie in mathematics, science, and art, particularly oil painting. She is a hard-working student who is willing to put in a great deal of effort to accomplish her goals. She is excited about beginning a graduate degree, but concerned that she will struggle with the requirements.

Tests Administered

- Woodcock-Johnson IV Tests of Cognitive Abilities (WJ IV COG)*
- Woodcock-Johnson IV Tests of Oral Language (WJ IV OL)
- Woodcock-Johnson IV Tests of Achievement (WJ IV ACH) Standard and Extended (scores are attached at the end of this report)
- Test of Word Reading Efficiency-2 (TOWRE-2)

The WJ IV tests were scored by both age (22-3) and grade norms (17.0). Grade norms were used to explore how her abilities would compare to students who are beginning their first year of graduate school. In almost every case, Veronica's relative standing (i.e., percentile rank) was lower when compared to grade peers than when compared to age peers. The age norm group includes individuals who did not attend college, whereas the grade norm group includes those who completed college and are in the first year of graduate school. It is this reference group that Veronica will be competing with when she attends graduate school.

Note. Veronica was also administered the WJ IV COG as part of a more complete evaluation. Because the focus of this book is on the use and interpretation of the WJ IV OL and WJ IV ACH, those results are not included here, although they were included and discussed in the final report. As an overview of the WJ IV COG results, many of her scores fell within the average range, but as with the WJ IV OL and WJ IVACH, a significant pattern of strengths and weaknesses was noted across the different types of abilities. Veronica excelled on tasks that required visual-spatial thinking, such as those involved in perceiving and recalling visual details and designs. She was able to quickly discern spatial relationships and visual patterns. Her score on the Visual Processing cluster exceeded 93% of her age peers. She also excelled on measures of reasoning ability. On the Fluid Reasoning cluster, her performance exceeded 83% of her age peers, and 77% of her grade peers. These findings suggest that Veronica is well suited for a career that involves visual-spatial thinking and reasoning abilities. In contrast, as with the WJ IV OL and the WJ IV ACH, Veronica had several significant weaknesses on timed measures. Her main area of weakness was perceptual speed, the ability to quickly complete symbolic tasks of a clerical nature. On this cluster, her performance exceeded only 27% of her age peers and 18% of her grade peers. These results were integrated to support the rationale for her need for extended time on tests.

TEST BEHAVIOR

Veronica was extremely cooperative during two 1.5-hour long testing sessions. In both sessions, she was attentive and maintained interest and effort throughout.

Oral Language

Veronica had both strengths and weaknesses on measures of oral language. For example, on a measure of vocabulary knowledge, Picture Vocabulary, her performance exceeded 98% of her age peers and 97% of her grade peers; on a listening comprehension measure, Oral Comprehension, her performance exceeded 83% of her age peers and 74% of her grade peers. Her performance was average on tests involving more memory (e.g., Understanding Directions and Sentence Repetition) as well as on the Segmentation test, in which she was asked to break words into sounds. Her performance on the Sound Blending test, the ability to push speech sounds together to form words, exceeded only 20% of her age peers, and 16% of her grade peers. This weakness in blending is somewhat unusual in light of the intensive reading tutoring she received.

Her weakest area was in speed of lexical access, which measures how quickly she could retrieve words. On the Rapid Picture Naming test, which required the quick naming of pictures of common nouns, her performance exceeded only 9% of age peers and only 6% of grade peers. Her performance on Retrieval Fluency, which required the rapid recall of words in a given category (such as types of transportation), exceeded 21% of age peers and 16% of grade peers. Thus, her performance on speeded oral language tasks was far below her levels of vocabulary knowledge, as were her listening abilities, which is a common finding among individuals with dyslexia.

ACHIEVEMENT

On the Woodcock-Johnson IV Tests of Achievement (WJ IV ACH), Veronica obtained scores in the average to high average range on most of the reading and written language tests with the exception of timed measures of reading and math computation. On untimed mathematical measures (Calculation and Applied Problems), Veronica worked carefully, but required a significant amount of time to complete computations and solve word problems.

Reading

On the Letter-Word Identification test, Veronica's ability to read real words exceeded 90% of age and grade peers; on the Word Attack test, a measure of her ability to use phonic skills to read nonsense words aloud, Veronica exceeded 52% of her age peers and 39% of her grade peers. On the Passage Comprehension test,

Veronica's performance exceeded 77% of her age peers and 71% of her grade peers. Veronica's lowest scores were on the timed reading tests. On the Sentence Reading Fluency test that requires the reading of simple sentences quickly and determining if the sentence is true or false (e.g., A cat has nine legs: yes or no), her performance exceeded only 15% of her age and grade peers. On the timed Word Reading Fluency test, which required reading rows of four words and marking the two that go together (e.g., apple can tree orange), her performance exceeded only 8% of her age peers and 5% of her grade peers.

TOWRE-2

On the Test of Word Reading Efficiency-2 (TOWRE-2), Veronica's score was in the average range for Sight Word Efficiency, a timed measure of real-word reading (her performance exceeded 47% of her peers), but in the below average range for Phonemic Decoding Efficiency, a timed measure that requires reading nonsense words aloud. Forms A and B were given to substantiate the results. On these measures, her performance exceeded only 19% and 14% of her age peers. These findings suggest that Veronica has difficulty applying the rules of phonics to pronounce unfamiliar words quickly. This difficulty with word pronunciation then affects her reading speed, as well as her comprehension.

TOWRE-2: Sight Word Efficiency

Age Equivalent	Grade Equivalent	Percentile Rank	Standard Score	Descriptive Rating
17-0	11.2	47	99	Average

TOWRE-2: Phonemic Decoding Efficiency, Forms A and B

Age Equivalent	Grade Equivalent	Percentile Rank	Standard Score	Descriptive Rating
Form A: 10-3	4.2	19	87	Below average
Form B: 9-6	3.8	14	84	Below average

Written Language

Overall, Veronica's written language scores fell in the average to high average range. Her performance on the Writing Samples test, which required writing responses to various prompts, exceeded 88% of her age peers and 84% of her grade peers. Her spelling skills were comparable to age and grade peers; her score on the Spelling test exceeded 51% of her age peers and 40% of her grade peers. A few of her misspellings were unusual for an adult, as the sounds in the word were out of order, such as spelling the word *garden* as *graden*. Although a longer sample, such as an essay, was not analyzed, Veronica commented that she has some difficulties with spelling, grammar, and organization when she writes longer papers.

Mathematics

Veronica's math calculation skills were in the average range, exceeding 43% of her age peers and 30% of her grade peers. A significant difference existed, however, between her scores on the Calculation test (a measure of computational skills) and her Math Facts Fluency test (a timed measure of simple addition, subtraction, and multiplication facts). On the Calculation test, although she worked very slowly, Veronica was able to complete more difficult problems involving fractions, decimals, negative numbers, and algebraic equations. Her performance exceeded 70% of her age peers and 60% of her grade peers. On the WJ IV Applied Problems test (untimed), Veronica's performance exceeded 68% of her age peers and 58% of her grade peers, and on the Number Matrices test, her score exceeded 67% of her age peers and 61% of her grade peers. In contrast, on the Math Facts Fluency test, her score exceeded only 20% of her age peers and 12% of her grade peers. As with oral language and reading, her rate of performance was also slower on a timed math test. Although Veronica showed good conceptual understanding of mathematics, she worked extremely slowly when solving all types of mathematical problems.

VARIATIONS AND COMPARISONS

The WJ IV OL and WJ IV ACH provide several variation procedures that evaluate a student's strengths and weaknesses among abilities and two comparison procedures in which two different abilities (oral language and academic knowledge) can be used to predict present achievement levels.

Variations

When Veronica's scores among the oral language measures were compared in the Intra-Oral Language-Extended Variation procedure, she had significant weaknesses on Rapid Picture Naming and Retrieval Fluency, both of which are timed measures. She had a significant strength in vocabulary. In fact, when her Picture Vocabulary test was compared to her predicted standard score of 100, only four out of 1,000 agemates with the same predicted score would obtain an actual standard score of 132 or higher.

When Veronica's achievement areas were compared in the Intra-Achievement-Extended Variation procedure, she had significant weaknesses on three timed tests (Sentence Reading Fluency, Math Facts Fluency, and Word Reading Fluency) and a significant strength on Letter-Word Identification.

When Veronica's Academic Skills, Academic Fluency, Academic Knowledge, and Reading Rate clusters were compared, she had a significant strength in Academic Skills and weaknesses in both Academic Fluency and Reading Rate (both containing timed measures). In fact, only one out of 100 agemates with a predicted standard score of 108 would obtain an actual standard score of 80 or lower on the Reading Rate cluster. Thus, her slow reading rate is quite unusual in light of her other abilities (e.g., superior vocabulary knowledge) but consistent with her low performance on timed measures.

Comparisons

When Veronica's Broad Oral Language cluster standard score (SS = 116) was compared to her obtained achievement scores, her oral language performance was significantly higher than her scores on the Reading Rate and Speed of Lexical Access clusters. When Veronica's Academic Knowledge score (SS = 126) was compared to her achievement scores, her knowledge was significantly higher than her scores on the Reading Rate, Academic Fluency, and Speed of Lexical Access clusters, all of which have timed measures.

CONCLUSIONS

Veronica is a hardworking, capable young woman who has a compromised reading rate despite 3 years of intensive reading tutoring. Although she has never been diagnosed with a specific learning disability, she exhibits a specific pattern of strengths and weaknesses that suggests the presence of a specific learning disability, primarily a rate disability. In regard to her strengths, her oral language and mathematical abilities (with the exception of speed) were comparable to or exceeded her age and grade peers. In contrast, her performances on all timed oral language, reading, and math measures were significant weaknesses. As a result of intensive tutoring, her word reading ability is exceptionally accurate, but her compromised reading rate has contributed to difficulties with reading comprehension. Veronica is very personable and responsible, and she wants to complete graduate school. With the proper support and accommodations, she should be able to succeed in her coursework at Gateway State.

DSM-5 Diagnosis

- 315.00 Impairment in reading rate or fluency
- Additional difficulties: fluent calculation

RECOMMENDATIONS

Post-Secondary

- Veronica should apply to receive supplemental tutorial support from the disability service center at Gateway State.
- Whenever possible, provide Veronica with visual supports, such as a copy of the PowerPoint lectures or a visual summary of class notes. In tutoring situations, drawings and concrete examples can help Veronica understand more complex concepts.
- Because of her slow reading rate in contrast to her more advanced oral language and mathematical abilities, Veronica will need extended time on all examinations, including courses involving mathematics; in most instances, double time should be a sufficient time extension. Although she has the conceptual knowledge, she works very slowly when solving mathematical problems. On examinations, Veronica will only be able to demonstrate her knowledge adequately when time is not a significant factor; thus, the emphasis should be placed on what Veronica knows and can do, rather than how fast she can take a test.
- Veronica should continue to work on her study skills, using available YouTube videos and other resources to support her learning.
- Veronica should provide a copy of this evaluation report to the Disability Resource Center at Gateway State so that she is able to receive extended time on all of her exams and support from the disability services office.

WOODCOCK-JOHNSON IV SCORE REPORT

Name: Jackson, Veronica
Date of Birth: 04/16/1992
Age: 22 years, 3 months
Sex: Female
Dates of Testing:
    07/27/2014 (OL)
    07/28/2014 (ACH)

TESTS ADMINISTERED
Woodcock-Johnson IV Tests of Oral Language
Woodcock-Johnson IV Tests of Achievement Form A
Woodcock-Johnson Online Scoring and Reporting Program, Release 1.0

TABLE OF SCORES
Woodcock-Johnson IV Tests of Oral Language (Norms based on age 22-3)

CLUSTER/Test	W	AE	RPI	SS (68% Band)	PR (68% Band)
ORAL LANGUAGE	542	>30	99/90	126 (120-131)	96 (91-98)
Picture Vocabulary	552	>30	100/90	132 (125-138)	98 (95->99)
Oral Comprehension	531	>30	98/90	114 (107-122)	83 (68-93)
BROAD ORAL LANGUAGE	529	>30	97/90	116 (112-121)	86 (78-92)
Picture Vocabulary	552	>30	100/90	132 (125-138)	98 (95->99)
Oral Comprehension	531	>30	98/90	114 (107-122)	83 (68-93)
Understanding Directions	505	12-1	79/90	91 (85-96)	27 (16-40)
ORAL EXPRESSION	542	>30	98/90	116 (110-121)	85 (75-92)
Picture Vocabulary	552	>30	100/90	132 (125-138)	98 (95->99)
Sentence Repetition	531	>30	92/90	101 (95-107)	54 (38-69)
LISTENING COMP	518	>30	92/90	104 (98-110)	60 (45-74)
Oral Comprehension	531	>30	98/90	114 (107-122)	83 (68-93)
Understanding Directions	505	12-1	79/90	91 (85-96)	27 (16-40)
PHONETIC CODING	510	16-10	88/90	98 (94-102)	45 (34-56)
Segmentation	518	>30	96/90	107 (103-111)	68 (57-78)
Sound Blending	502	10-8	68/90	87 (82-93)	20 (11-32)
SPEED of LEXICAL ACCESS	503	10-3	58/90	80 (75-84)	9 (5-15)
Rapid Picture Naming	499	9-4	32/90	80 (75-85)	9 (5-16)
Retrieval Fluency	506	12-4	80/90	88 (82-94)	21 (11-35)

Woodcock-Johnson IV Tests of Achievement (Norms based on age 22-3)

CLUSTER/Test	W	AE	RPI	SS (68% Band)	PR (68% Band)
READING	554	>30	99/90	119 (114-124)	90 (82-95
BROAD READING	543	>30	94/90	103 (99-107)	59 (48-69)
BASIC READING SKILLS	541	>30	98/90	114 (109-120)	83 (73-91)
READING COMPREHENSION	522	>30	94/90	106 (102-110)	65 (54-75)
READING COMP (Ext)	529	>30	96/90	112 (109-115)	79 (71-85)
READING FLUENCY	530	15-10	78/90	94 (90-99)	35 (25-46)
READING RATE	508	11-3	13/90	80 (75-85)	9 (5-15)
MATHEMATICS	539	>23	97/90	108 (105-111)	70 (63-77)
Applied Problems	534	>30	96/90	107 (103-111)	68 (57-78)
Calculation	544	>21	97/90	108 (104-112)	70 (61-78)
BROAD MATHEMATICS	534	>30	91/90	101 (98-103)	52 (44-59)
Applied Problems	534	>30	96/90	107 (103-111)	68 (57-78)
Calculation	544	>21	97/90	108 (104-112)	70 (61-78)
Math Facts Fluency	523	12-6	53/90	88 (83-92)	20 (13-30)
MATH CALCULATION SKILLS	534	15-7	86/90	97 (94-101)	43 (35-52)
Calculation	544	>21	97/90	108 (104-112)	70 (61-78)
Math Facts Fluency	523	12-6	53/90	88 (83-92)	20 (13-30)
MATH PROBLEM SOLVING	531	>27	96/90	107 (104-111)	69 (60-77)
Applied Problems	534	>30	96/90	107 (103-111)	68 (57-78)
Number Matrices	528	>24	95/90	107 (101-112)	67 (53-79)
WRITTEN LANGUAGE	535	>30	96/90	109 (105-113)	73 (64-81)
BROAD WRITTEN LANGUAGE	530	>30	95/90	109 (105-113)	73 (64-80)
BASIC WRITING SKILLS	537	>30	95/90	106 (102-109)	65 (56-73)
WRITTEN EXPRESSION	528	>30	97/90	115 (110-120)	84 (75-91)
ACADEMIC SKILLS	549	>30	98/90	112 (108-115)	78 (71-84)
Letter-Word Identification	567	>30	100/90	123 (115-130)	93 (84-98)
Spelling	535	23	90/90	100 (96-104)	51 (40-61)
Calculation	544	>21	97/90	108 (104-112)	70 (61-78)
ACADEMIC APPLICATIONS	537	>30	98/90	113 (110-117)	81 (75-87)
Applied Problems	534	>30	96/90	107 (103-111)	68 (57-78)
Passage Comprehension	542	>30	97/90	111 (106-117)	77 (66-87)
Writing Samples	535	>30	98/90	118 (112-123)	88 (78-94)
ACADEMIC FLUENCY	521	13-0	63/90	88 (85-92)	22 (16-29)
Sentence Reading Fluency	520	12-0	23/90	85 (80-90)	15 (9-25)
Math Facts Fluency	523	12-6	53/90	88 (83-92)	20 (13-30)
Sentence Writing Fluency	520	>30	93/90	106 (100-111)	65 (50-77)

ACADEMIC KNOWLEDGE	552	>30	99/90	126 (122-129)	96 (93-97)
Science	544	>30	99/90	120 (115-125)	91 (84-95)
Social Studies	560	>30	100/90	124 (119-130)	95 (90-98)
Humanities	553	>30	99/90	125 (119-131)	95 (89-98)
PHONEME-GRAPHEME KNOWLEDGE	514	>29	91/90	102 (97-106)	55 (42-66)
Word Attack	516	24	91/90	101 (95-107)	52 (36-68)
Spelling of Sounds	512	>22	92/90	102 (97-108)	56 (41-71)

VARIATIONS	STANDARD SCORES			DISCREPANCY		Interpretation
	Actual	Predicted	Difference	PR	SD	+ or – 1.50 SD
Intra-Oral Language (Extended) Variations						
ORAL EXPRESSION	116	100	16	91	+1.31	—
LISTENING COMP	104	106	-2	43	-0.18	—
PHONETIC CODING	98	104	-6	32	-0.47	—
SPEED of LEXICAL ACCESS	80	111	-31	1	-2.27	Weakness
Picture Vocabulary^	132	100	32	99.6	+2.64	Strength
Oral Comprehension^	114	106	8	77	+0.75	—
Segmentation^	107	103	4	62	+0.31	—
Rapid Picture Naming^	80	109	-29	2	-2.10	Weakness
Sentence Repetition	101	100	1	53	+0.08	—
Understanding Directions	91	104	-13	14	-1.08	—
Sound Blending	87	104	-17	12	-1.18	—
Retrieval Fluency	88	110	-22	5	-1.64	Weakness

^Core test for calculation of intra-oral language variations.

VARIATIONS	STANDARD SCORES			DISCREPANCY		Interpretation
	Actual	Predicted	Difference	PR	SD	+ or – 1.50 SD
Intra-Achievement (Extended) Variations						
BASIC READING SKILLS	114	109	5	75	+0.67	—
READING COMPREHENSION	106	110	-4	33	-0.44	—
READING COMP (Ext)	112	111	1	56	+0.14	—
READING FLUENCY	94	107	-13	10	-1.26	—
READING RATE	80	108	-28	1	-2.25	Weakness
MATH CALCULATION SKILLS	97	110	-13	11	-1.25	—
MATH PROBLEM SOLVING	107	110	-3	40	-0.26	—
BASIC WRITING SKILLS	106	113	-7	22	-0.77	—

WRITTEN EXPRESSION	115	109	6	74	+0.64	—
Letter-Word Identification^	123	109	14	94	+1.56	Strength
Applied Problems^	107	111	−4	35	−0.37	—
Spelling^	100	112	−12	13	−1.13	—
Passage Comprehension^	111	110	1	56	+0.14	—
Calculation^	108	110	−2	41	−0.23	—
Writing Samples^	118	107	11	80	+0.85	—
Word Attack	101	107	−6	27	−0.60	—
Oral Reading	112	107	5	67	+0.45	—
Sentence Reading Fluency	85	108	−23	2	−1.98	Weakness
Math Facts Fluency	88	108	−20	5	−1.69	Weakness
Sentence Writing Fluency	106	107	−1	46	−0.10	—
Reading Recall	95	108	−13	15	−1.05	—
Number Matrices	107	108	−1	46	−0.11	—
Editing	111	111	0	49	−0.02	—
Word Reading Fluency	78	107	−29	2	−2.15	Weakness
Spelling of Sounds	102	110	−8	24	−0.69	—
Reading Vocabulary	121	110	11	88	+1.18	—

^Core test for calculation of intra-achievement variations.

VARIATIONS	STANDARD SCORES Actual	Predicted	Difference	DISCREPANCY PR	SD	Interpretation + or − 1.50 SD
Academic Skills/Academic Fluency/Academic Applications (Extended) Variations						
ACADEMIC SKILLS^	112	101	11	94	+1.53	Strength
ACADEMIC FLUENCY^	88	109	−21	2	−2.00	Weakness
ACADEMIC APPLICATIONS^	113	100	13	93	+1.46	—
READING RATE	80	108	−28	1	−2.28	Weakness

^Core cluster for calculation of academic skills/fluency/applications variations.

COMPARISONS	STANDARD SCORES Actual	Predicted	Difference	DISCREPANCY PR	SD	Significant at + or − 1.50 SD
Oral Language/Achievement Comparisons*						
READING	119	111	8	77	+0.73	No
BROAD READING	103	110	−7	27	−0.61	No
BASIC READING SKILLS	114	110	4	65	+0.40	No
READING COMPREHENSION	106	109	−3	39	−0.27	No

READING COMP (Ext)	112	111	1	55	+0.14	No
READING FLUENCY	94	108	−14	15	−1.04	No
READING RATE	80	108	−28	2	−2.01	Yes (−)
MATHEMATICS	108	109	−1	48	−0.05	No
BROAD MATHEMATICS	101	108	−7	27	−0.62	No
MATH CALCULATION SKILLS	97	107	−10	24	−0.72	No
MATH PROBLEM SOLVING	107	109	−2	44	−0.14	No
WRITTEN LANGUAGE	109	109	0	51	+0.03	No
BROAD WRITTEN LANGUAGE	109	108	1	52	+0.04	No
BASIC WRITING SKILLS	106	110	−4	37	−0.34	No
WRITTEN EXPRESSION	115	107	8	73	+0.61	No
ACADEMIC SKILLS	112	109	3	58	+0.19	No
ACADEMIC FLUENCY	88	107	−19	7	−1.46	No
ACADEMIC APPLICATIONS	113	110	3	61	+0.28	No
ACADEMIC KNOWLEDGE	126	112	14	93	+1.45	No
PHONEME-GRAPHEME KNOWLEDGE	102	108	−6	30	−0.52	No
PHONETIC CODING	98	107	−9	25	−0.67	No
SPEED of LEXICAL ACCESS	80	109	−29	1	−2.22	Yes (−)

* This procedure compares the WJ IV Broad Oral Language cluster score to selected achievement and cognitive-linguistic clusters.

COMPARISONS	STANDARD SCORES			DISCREPANCY		Significant at
	Actual	Predicted	Difference	PR	SD	+ or − 1.50 SD
Academic Knowledge/Achievement Comparisons*						
BRIEF ACHIEVEMENT	112	116	−4	36	−0.37	No
BROAD ACHIEVEMENT	104	114	−10	19	−0.89	No
READING	119	115	4	63	+0.34	No
BROAD READING	103	113	−10	22	−0.76	No
BASIC READING SKILLS	114	113	1	54	+0.09	No
READING COMPREHENSION	106	111	−5	34	−0.40	No
READING COMP (Ext)	112	114	−2	44	−0.16	No
READING FLUENCY	94	109	−15	13	−1.14	No
READING RATE	80	108	−28	3	−1.96	Yes (−)

MATHEMATICS	108	115	−7	27	−0.62	No
BROAD MATHEMATICS	101	113	−12	14	−1.09	No
MATH CALCULATION SKILLS	97	112	−15	13	−1.13	No
MATH PROBLEM SOLVING	107	115	−8	25	−0.68	No
WRITTEN LANGUAGE	109	113	−4	38	−0.32	No
BROAD WRITTEN LANGUAGE	109	113	−4	38	−0.30	No
BASIC WRITING SKILLS	106	114	−8	22	−0.76	No
WRITTEN EXPRESSION	115	110	5	64	+0.37	No
ACADEMIC SKILLS	112	115	−3	39	−0.28	No
ACADEMIC FLUENCY	88	108	−20	7	−1.50	Yes (−)
ACADEMIC APPLICATIONS	113	115	−2	44	−0.14	No
PHONETIC CODING	98	109	−11	20	−0.85	No
SPEED of LEXICAL ACCESS	80	110	−30	1	−2.19	Yes (−)

* This procedure compares the WJ IV Academic Knowledge cluster score to selected achievement and cognitive-linguistic clusters.

WOODCOCK-JOHNSON IV SCORE REPORT
(Scored by grade norms, 17.0)

Name: Jackson, Veronica   Grade: 17.0
Date of Birth: 04/16/1992
Age: 22 years, 3 months
Sex: Female
Dates of Testing:
   07/27/2014 (OL)
   07/28/2014 (ACH)

TESTS ADMINISTERED
Woodcock-Johnson IV Tests of Oral Language
Woodcock-Johnson IV Tests of Achievement Form A
Woodcock-Johnson Online Scoring and Reporting Program, Release 1.0

TABLE OF SCORES
Woodcock-Johnson IV Tests of Oral Language (Norms based on grade 17.0
[4-year university])

CLUSTER/Test	W	GE	RPI	SS (68% Band)	PR (68% Band)
ORAL LANGUAGE	542	>18.0	98/90	124 (118-131)	95 (88-98)
Picture Vocabulary	552	>18.0	99/90	129 (121-136)	97 (92->99)
Oral Comprehension	531	>18.0	96/90	110 (102-117)	74 (55-88)
BROAD ORAL LANGUAGE	529	>18.0	95/90	113 (107-119)	81 (68-90)
Picture Vocabulary	552	>18.0	99/90	129 (121-136)	97 (92->99)
Oral Comprehension	531	>18.0	96/90	110 (102-117)	74 (55-88)
Understanding Directions	505	6.7	73/90	87 (82-93)	19 (11-31)
ORAL EXPRESSION	542	>18.0	96/90	111 (104-117)	76 (62-87)
Picture Vocabulary	552	>18.0	99/90	129 (121-136)	97 (92->99)
Sentence Repetition	531	13.0	86/90 98	(91-104)	44 (29-60)
LISTENING COMP	518	15.2	89/90	99 (93-105)	47 (32-63)
Oral Comprehension	531	>18.0	96/90	110 (102-117)	74 (55-88)
Understanding Directions	505	6.7	73/90	87 (82-93)	19 (11-31)
PHONETIC CODING	510	11.4	80/90	93 (90-97)	33 (25-42)
Segmentation	518	>18.0	94/90	105 (100-109)	62 (49-73)
Sound Blending	502	5.2	57/90	85 (80-90)	16 (9-25)
SPEED of LEXICAL ACCESS	503	4.8	51/90	74 (68-79)	4 (2-8)
Rapid Picture Naming	499	3.9	26/90	76 (71-82)	6 (3-11)
Retrieval Fluency	506	6.9	76/90	85 (79-91)	16 (8-28)

Woodcock-Johnson IV Tests of Achievement (Norms based on grade 17.0 [4-year university])

CLUSTER/Test	W	GE	RPI	SS (68% Band)	PR (68% Band)
READING	554	>18.0	98/90	118 (111-125)	88 (76-95)
BROAD READING	543	14.7	88/90	99 (95-102)	46 (37-56)
BASIC READING SKILLS	541	>18.0	96/90	111 (104-117)	76 (61-88)
READING COMPREHENSION	522	>18.0	90/90	101 (95-107)	52 (37-67)
READING COMP (Ext)	529	>18.0	95/90	112 (107-116)	78 (67-86)
READING FLUENCY	530	10.4	65/90	91 (87-95)	28 (20-37)
READING RATE	508	5.8	7/90	80 (76-84)	9 (5-14)
MATHEMATICS	539	>16.0	93/90	103 (100-107)	59 (49-68)
Applied Problems	534	>18.0	93/90	103 (98-108)	58 (45-70)
Calculation	544	>15.0	94/90	104 (99-109)	60 (48-72)
BROAD MATHEMATICS	534	13.0	82/90	94 (91-97)	35 (27-43)
Applied Problems	534	>18.0	93/90	103 (98-108)	58 (45-70)
Calculation	544	>15.0	94/90	104 (99-109)	60 (48-72)
Math Facts Fluency	523	7.1	36/90	83 (78-87)	12 (7-20)
MATH CALCULATION SKILLS	534	10.2	76/90	92 (88-96)	30 (22-39)
Calculation	544	>15.0	94/90	104 (99-109)	60 (48-72)
Math Facts Fluency	523	7.1	36/90	83 (78-87)	12 (7-20)

MATH PROBLEM SOLVING	531	>18.0	93/90	104 (100-109)	61 (49-72)
Applied Problems	534	>18.0	93/90	103 (98-108)	58 (45-70)
Number Matrices	528	>16.0	94/90	104 (98-110)	61 (46-74)
WRITTEN LANGUAGE	535	>18.0	94/90	106 (101-110)	65 (53-76)
BROAD WRITTEN LANGUAGE	530	>18.0	93/90	106 (102-110)	66 (54-76)
BASIC WRITING SKILLS	537	>18.0	91/90	101 (97-105)	53 (42-64)
WRITTEN EXPRESSION	528	>18.0	95/90	113 (107-119)	81 (68-90)
ACADEMIC SKILLS	549	>18.0	95/90	108 (103-112)	70 (59-79)
Letter-Word Identification	567	>18.0	99/90	120 (111-129)	90 (76-97)
Spelling	535	13.0	85/90	96 (91-101)	40 (28-52)
Calculation	544	>15.0	94/90	104 (99-109)	60 (48-72)
ACADEMIC APPLICATIONS	537	>18.0	96/90	110 (106-115)	76 (66-84)
Applied Problems	534	>18.0	93/90	103 (98-108)	58 (45-70)
Passage Comprehension	542	>18.0	95/90	108 (101-115)	71 (53-85)
Writing Samples	535	>18.0	98/90	115 (109-121)	84 (72-92)
ACADEMIC FLUENCY	521	7.5	51/90	86 (83-89)	18 (13-24)
Sentence Reading Fluency	520	6.6	11/90	84 (80-88)	15 (9-22)
Math Facts Fluency	523	7.1	36/90	83 (78-87)	12 (7-20)
Sentence Writing Fluency	520	>18.0	92/90	103 (96-110)	58 (40-74)
ACADEMIC KNOWLEDGE	552	>18.0	99/90	123 (119-127)	93 (89-96)
Science	544	>18.0	98/90	116 (111-122)	86 (77-93)
Social Studies	560	>18.0	99/90	120 (114-125)	91 (83-95)
Humanities	553	>18.0	99/90	121 (115-128)	92 (83-97)
PHONEME-GRAPHEME KNOWLEDGE	514	13.0	87/90	96 (91-102)	40 (27-54)
Word Attack	516	13.0	86/90	96 (89-102)	39 (24-56)
Spelling of Sounds	512	13.0	89/90	98 (92-105)	45 (29-63)

VARIATIONS	STANDARD SCORES Actual	Predicted	Difference	DISCREPANCY PR	SD	Interpretation + or – 1.50 SD
Intra-Oral Language (Extended) Variations						
ORAL EXPRESSION	111	98	13	84	+1.01	—
LISTENING COMP	99	103	−4	38	−0.31	—
PHONETIC CODING	93	102	−9	24	−0.69	—
SPEED of LEXICAL ACCESS	74	105	−31	2	−2.13	Weakness
Picture Vocabulary^	129	98	31	99	+2.27	Strength
Oral Comprehension^	110	102	8	71	+0.56	—
Segmentation^	105	103	2	54	+0.09	—
Rapid Picture Naming^	76	103	−27	4	−1.79	Weakness
Sentence Repetition	98	98	0	49	−0.03	—
Understanding Directions	87	102	−15	14	−1.06	—

Sound Blending	85	103	−18	9	−1.33	—
Retrieval Fluency	85	106	−21	7	−1.47	—

^Core test for calculation of intra-oral language variations.

VARIATIONS	STANDARD SCORES			DISCREPANCY		Interpretation
	Actual	Predicted	Difference	PR	SD	+ or − 1.50 SD
Intra-Achievement (Extended) Variations						
BASIC READING SKILLS	111	105	6	71	+0.54	—
READING COMPREHENSION	101	107	−6	29	−0.57	—
READING COMP (Ext)	112	108	4	63	+0.34	—
READING FLUENCY	91	105	−14	14	−1.08	—
READING RATE	80	106	−26	2	−2.00	Weakness
MATH CALCULATION SKILLS	92	107	−15	12	−1.15	—
MATH PROBLEM SOLVING	104	107	−3	40	−0.25	—
BASIC WRITING SKILLS	101	109	−8	24	−0.72	—
WRITTEN EXPRESSION	113	105	8	76	+0.70	—
Letter-Word Identification^	120	106	14	91	+1.35	—
Applied Problems^	103	107	−4	35	−0.38	—
Spelling^	96	108	−12	15	−1.02	—
Passage Comprehension^	108	107	1	56	+0.15	—
Calculation^	104	106	−2	43	−0.18	—
Writing Samples^	115	104	11	80	+0.83	—
Word Attack	96	104	−8	26	−0.65	—
Oral Reading	108	104	4	65	+0.38	—
Sentence Reading Fluency	84	108	−24	3	−1.83	Weakness
Math Facts Fluency	83	105	−22	5	−1.66	Weakness
Sentence Writing Fluency	103	104	−1	47	−0.08	—
Reading Recall	91	104	−13	17	−0.97	—
Number Matrices	104	105	−1	48	−0.04	—
Editing	109	108	1	53	+0.07	—
Word Reading Fluency	75	104	−29	2	−2.10	Weakness
Spelling of Sounds	98	107	−9	24	−0.72	—
Reading Vocabulary	119	107	12	86	+1.07	—

^Core test for calculation of intra-achievement variations.

VARIATIONS	STANDARD SCORES			DISCREPANCY		Interpretation
	Actual	Predicted	Difference	PR	SD	+ or – 1.50 SD
Academic Skills/Academic Fluency/Academic Applications (Extended) Variations						
ACADEMIC SKILLS^	108	98	10	85	+1.04	—
ACADEMIC FLUENCY^	86	106	–20	5	–1.69	Weakness
ACADEMIC APPLICATIONS^	110	98	12	88	+1.15	—
READING RATE	80	105	–25	3	–1.93	Weakness

^Core cluster for calculation of academic skills/fluency/applications variations.

COMPARISONS	STANDARD SCORES			DISCREPANCY		Significant at
	Actual	Predicted	Difference	PR	SD	+ or – 1.50 SD
Oral Language/Achievement Comparisons*						
READING	118	108	10	79	+0.81	No
BROAD READING	99	107	–8	27	–0.61	No
BASIC READING SKILLS	111	106	5	63	+0.34	No
READING COMPREHENSION	101	107	–6	32	–0.46	No
READING COMP (Ext)	112	108	4	63	+0.32	No
READING FLUENCY	91	105	–14	16	–1.00	No
READING RATE	80	104	–24	5	–1.64	Yes (–)
MATHEMATICS	103	105	–2	44	–0.15	No
BROAD MATHEMATICS	94	105	–11	22	–0.76	No
MATH CALCULATION SKILLS	92	104	–12	21	–0.81	No
MATH PROBLEM SOLVING	104	106	–2	46	–0.11	No
WRITTEN LANGUAGE	106	103	3	57	+0.17	No
BROAD WRITTEN LANGUAGE	106	106	0	51	+0.03	No
BASIC WRITING SKILLS	101	107	–6	33	–0.44	No
WRITTEN EXPRESSION	113	104	9	72	+0.59	No
ACADEMIC SKILLS	108	106	2	54	+0.10	No
ACADEMIC FLUENCY	86	104	–18	10	–1.26	No
ACADEMIC APPLICATIONS	110	107	3	60	+0.25	No
ACADEMIC KNOWLEDGE	123	109	14	90	+1.27	No
PHONEME-GRAPHEME KNOWLEDGE	96	106	–10	26	–0.65	No

PHONETIC CODING	93	105	−12	17	−0.97	No
SPEED of LEXICAL ACCESS	74	104	−30	1	−2.20	Yes (−)

* This procedure compares the WJ IV Broad Oral Language cluster score to selected achievement and cognitive-linguistic clusters.

COMPARISONS	STANDARD SCORES			DISCREPANCY		Significant at
	Actual	Predicted	Difference	PR	SD	+ or − 1.50 SD
Academic Knowledge/Achievement Comparisons*						
BRIEF ACHIEVEMENT	107	115	−8	29	−0.56	No
BROAD ACHIEVEMENT	100	111	−11	21	−0.82	No
READING	118	112	6	66	+0.40	No
BROAD READING	99	109	−10	23	−0.72	No
BASIC READING SKILLS	111	111	0	51	+0.02	No
READING COMPREHENSION	101	109	−8	30	−0.53	No
READING COMP (Ext)	112	112	0	48	−0.04	No
READING FLUENCY	91	105	−14	16	−0.99	No
READING RATE	80	104	−24	5	−1.62	Yes (−)
MATHEMATICS	103	112	−9	24	−0.69	No
BROAD MATHEMATICS	94	110	−16	13	−1.11	No

* This procedure compares the WJ IV Academic Knowledge cluster score to selected achievement and cognitive-linguistic clusters.

🪶 TEST YOURSELF 🪶

1. Write a descriptive statement about Bryan's RPI of 19/90 on the Letter-Word Identification test.

2. When Bryan's Broad Oral Language cluster score is compared to his Reading cluster score, the discrepancy percentile rank is 2. Write a sentence that describes this score.

3. Write a sentence to explain the meaning of Bryan's RPI of 92/90 on the Broad Oral Language cluster.

4. On the Intra-Achievement Variation procedure, explain the meaning of Evan's discrepancy percentile rank score of >99.9 in Written Expression.

5. On Evan's Broad Oral Language/Achievement comparison procedure, explain the meaning of his discrepancy percentile rank (6) on Reading Comprehension.

6. Why does Evan have a significant discrepancy between Broad Oral Language and Math Calculation Skills, but not between Academic Knowledge and Math Calculation Skills?

7. **On the Intra-Achievement Variation procedure (age norms), explain the meaning of Veronica's discrepancy percentile rank of I on the Reading Rate cluster.**

8. **Using age norms, explain Veronica's strength in Academic Skills on the Academic Skills/Academic Fluency/Academic Applications (Extended) Variation procedure?**

9. **When the Broad Oral Language cluster is used as the ability score to predict performance (age norms), what are Veronica's significant discrepancies (weaknesses)?**

10. **Why is it important to consider grade norms for Veronica?**

ANSWERS

1. Compared to average third-grade students with 90% proficiency on word recognition tasks, Bryan had only 19% proficiency, or very limited proficiency.

2. When Bryan's Broad Oral Language score is compared to his Reading cluster, only two out of 100 students with the same predicted score would have scored as low or lower on the Reading cluster (or only 2% of grademates with the same broad oral language score scored as low or lower on the Reading cluster).

3. Bryan's oral language proficiency is similar to that of average grademates. (Or: When average grademates have 90% success on oral language tasks, Bryan will have 92% success; his proficiency in oral language is average).

4. Evan scored significantly higher than predicted on the Written Expression cluster. Less than one out of 1,000 grademates with the same predicted score would have a score as high or higher on Written Expression.

5. Evan's Reading Comprehension score was significantly lower than predicted by his Broad Oral Language score. Only 6% of grademates with the same Broad Oral Language score would have scored as low as or lower than Evan on Reading Comprehension.

6. Evan's Broad Oral Language score (SS = 108) is higher than his score on Academic Knowledge (SS = 98), so his predicted performance on Math Calculation Skills also varied. The higher ability (Broad Oral Language) led to a higher predicted score that, when compared to his actual score on Math Calculation, resulted in a significant negative difference. The lower ability (Academic Knowledge) led to a lower predicted score that, when compared to his actual score on Math Calculation, did not yield a significant difference.

7. Veronica's performance on the Reading Rate cluster was significantly below the prediction. Only one out of 100 agemates with the same predicted score would have scored as low or lower on the Reading Rate cluster.

8. When Veronica's performance on Academic Skills is compared to her Academic Fluency and Academic Applications, only six out of 100 age peers with a predicted standard score of 101 would obtain a standard score of 112 (Discrepancy PR = 94) (or she scored as well as or better than 94 out of 100 age peers with the same predicted score).

9. Veronica has significant weaknesses on the Reading Rate cluster and the Speed of Lexical Access.

10. Veronica is planning to attend graduate school and will be competing with others who are in grade 17.0. This is the most relevant reference group to use in order to address Veronica's concerns about her ability to succeed in graduate school.

Appendix A

Fine Points of WJ IV ACH Administration and WJ IV OL Administration

APPENDIX A.1: FINE POINTS OF WJ IV ACH ADMINISTRATION

Standard Battery

Test 1: Letter-Word Identification
- Know the exact pronunciation of each word before administering the test.
- Use the suggested starting points.
- Ask the examinee to reread all the items on the page when a response is unclear; score only the item in question.
- Do not tell the examinee any letters or words during the test.
- Give the reminder to pronounce the word smoothly only once during test.
- Test by complete pages.
- Encourage the examinee to try the next word after 5 seconds unless the examinee is still actively engaged in trying to pronounce the word.
- Give credit for items below the basal.

Test 2: Applied Problems
- Use the worksheet in the Response Booklet.
- Use the suggested starting points.
- Read all of the items to the examinee.
- Provide the Response Booklet and a pencil at any time if the examinee requests it or appears to need it (e.g., uses finger to write on table).
- Give the examinee a pencil and the Response Booklet at Item 25.
- Repeat any question if requested by examinee.
- Query the response when needed.
- Do not require a unit label (e.g., cents) unless it is listed as required in the Test Book.
- Score the item incorrect if the response is wrong or if the examinee provides an incorrect unit label (required or not).
- Test by complete pages.
- Give credit for items below the basal.

Test 3: Spelling
- Use the Response Booklet.
- Use the suggested starting points.
- Know the correct pronunciation of all items.
- Do not penalize for poor handwriting or reversed letters as long as the letter does not become a new letter (e.g., a reversed *b* becomes a *d,* so it would be an error).
- Request that the examinee use printed (manuscript) responses, but accept cursive.
- Accept upper- or lowercase responses unless the case is specified, such as in the initial items.
- Give credit for items below the basal.

Test 4: Passage Comprehension
- Begin with the Introduction for examinees at a preschool or kindergarten level.
- Begin with Item 5 for all examinees at a grade 1 level.
- Begin with Sample Item B for all other examinees and then select an appropriate starting point.
- Do not insist on silent reading if the examinee persists in reading aloud.
- Do not tell the examinee any words.
- Accept only one-word responses unless otherwise noted in the key.
- Ask for the one word that goes in the blank if the examinee reads the item aloud and provides the answer in context.
- Score responses that differ in verb tense or number as correct, unless otherwise specified.
- Score responses that substitute different parts of speech as incorrect, unless otherwise specified.
- Test by complete pages.
- Give credit for items below the basal.

Test 5: Calculation
- Use the Response Booklet.
- Use the suggested starting points.
- Discontinue testing and record a score of 0 if the examinee responds incorrectly to both sample items.
- Accept poorly formed or reversed numbers.
- Score transposed numbers (e.g., 14 for 41) as incorrect.
- Score skipped items as incorrect.
- Complete any queries as listed in the Test Book.

- Do not point out or remind the examinee to look at the signs.
- Give credit for items below the basal.

Test 6: Writing Samples
- Use the Response Booklet.
- Use the suggested starting points.
- Administer the prescribed block of items.
- Read any word to examinee upon request.
- Do not penalize for spelling, punctuation, capitalization, or usage errors unless otherwise noted in the scoring guide.
- Ask examinee to write more neatly if responses are illegible or difficult to read.
- Consult the Adjusted Items Block chart to determine when additional items need to be administered (the score falls within a shaded area).
- Use the Scoring Guide in Appendix B of the Examiner's Manual to score items after testing.
- Score Items 1 through 6 as 1 or 0 points as indicated in Scoring Guide.
- Score Items 7 and higher 2, 1, or 0 points as indicated in Scoring Guide.
- Know that 0.5 and 1.5 can be used for scoring responses that fall between examples for 0 and 1 or 1 and 2.
- Do not penalize for spelling or handwriting errors unless the words are illegible.
- Score sentences that are illegible as 0.
- Do not ask examinee to read the response for the purpose of scoring the item.
- Alternate between higher and lower scores when unsure of how to score certain items.
- Score items based on examinee's interpretation of the picture.
- Select and score the one sentence that best satisfies the task demands if examinee writes more than one sentence for an item.
- Reduce the score by 1 point for severe grammatical or usage errors or if a significant word is illegible.
- Do not penalize for minor grammatical or usage errors.
- Round scores ending in .5 to the nearest even number, not always up.
- Enter the score for only one block of items (even if more than one block was administered) into the online scoring program.

Test 7: Word Attack
- Use the suggested starting points.
- Know the correct pronunciation of all items before administering the test.

- Say the most common sound (phoneme) for letters printed within slashes, such as /p/, not the letter name.
- If the examinee pronounces the nonword phoneme-by-phoneme or syllable-by-syllable, remind the examinee only once during the test to say the word smoothly.
- Ask the examinee to reread all the items on the page if a response is unclear; score only the item in question.
- Do not tell the examinee any letters or words during the test.
- Test by complete pages.
- Give credit for items below the basal.
- Record errors for further analysis.

Test 8: Oral Reading
- Use the suggested starting points.
- Follow the Continuation Instructions to determine what to administer or when to discontinue testing.
- Have the examinee read sentences aloud.
- Know the correct pronunciation of all words.
- Score as errors mispronunciations, omissions, insertions, substitutions, hesitations of 3 seconds, repetitions, transpositions, and ignoring punctuation.
- Count hyphenated words as one word.
- Mark a slash (/) at each point on the Test Record where an error occurs.
- After a hesitation of 3 seconds, mark the word as an error and tell the examinee to go on to the next word.
- Do not count self-corrections within 3 seconds as errors.
- Score each sentence as a 2 (no errors), 1 (one error), or 0 (two or more errors).
- Record the number of points earned on items administered.

Test 9: Sentence Reading Fluency
- Use a stopwatch or a watch with a second hand.
- Use the Response Booklet.
- Begin with the sample items for all examinees.
- Discontinue testing and record a score of 0 in the Test Record if the examinee has three or fewer correct on the Practice Exercises C through F.
- Adhere to the 3-minute time limit.
- Record the exact starting and stopping times if not using a stopwatch.
- Record the exact finishing time in minutes and seconds on the Test Record.

- Remind the examinee to read each sentence if he or she appears to be answering items without reading.
- Do not tell the examinee any letters or words.
- Remind the examinee to continue if he or she stops at the bottom of a page or column.
- Count the number of correct responses and the number of errors.
- Do not count skipped items as errors.
- Enter both the number correct and the number incorrect into the online scoring program.
- Subtract the number incorrect from the number correct when obtaining estimated AE/GE from the Test Record.
- Use the scoring-guide overlay to facilitate scoring.

Test 10: Math Facts Fluency
- Use a stopwatch or a watch with a second hand.
- Use the Response Booklet.
- Have all examinees begin with Item 1.
- Discontinue testing if the examinee has three or fewer correct after 1 minute, and then record a time of 1 minute and the number correct (0 to 3) in the Test Record.
- Adhere to the 3-minute time limit.
- Record the exact starting and stopping times if not using a stopwatch.
- Record the exact finishing time in minutes and seconds on the Test Record.
- Do not draw attention to the signs or remind the examinee to pay attention to signs during the test.
- Do not mark poorly formed or reversed numbers as errors.
- Remind the examinee to proceed across the page from left to right, row by row, if he or she starts skipping around.
- Remind the examinee to continue if he or she stops at the bottom of the first page.
- Use the scoring-guide overlay to facilitate scoring.

Test 11: Sentence Writing Fluency
- Use a stopwatch or a watch with a second hand.
- Use the Response Booklet.
- Begin with the sample items for all examinees.
- Discontinue testing if the examinee has a score of 0 on Sample Items B through D after error correction and record a score of 0 in the Test Record.

- Discontinue testing if the examinee has three or fewer correct after 2 minutes, and then record a time of 2 minutes and the number correct (0 to 3) in the Test Record.
- Adhere to the 5-minute time limit.
- Record exact starting and stopping times if not using a stopwatch.
- Record exact finishing time in minutes and seconds on the Test Record.
- Read a stimulus word to the examinee upon request.
- Remind the examinee to continue if he or she stops at the bottom of a page.
- Score responses that are complete, reasonable sentences using all target words as correct.
- Know that the target words may not be changed in any way (e.g., verb tense or nouns changed from singular to plural).
- Do not mark spelling, punctuation, or capitalization errors as incorrect.
- Do not penalize for poor handwriting unless the response is illegible.
- Score skipped items as incorrect.
- Score responses that omit critical words as incorrect.
- Score responses that omit less meaningful words (e.g., *the* or *a*) as correct if all other criteria are met.
- Accept abbreviations (e.g., w/ for *with*) or symbols (e.g., & for *and*) if all other criteria are met.

EXTENDED BATTERY

Test 12: Reading Recall
- Use the suggested starting points.
- Follow the Continuation Instructions to determine when to continue testing or when to stop.
- Do not tell the examinee any words.
- Allow the examinee to read each story silently only one time.
- Know the elements to be scored are listed on the Test Record.
- Score the element as correct if the key word or words (in bold) or a close synonym is used during retelling.
- Score elements as correct even if recalled in a different order.
- Do not penalize for mispronunciations due to articulation errors, dialect variations, or regional speech.
- Score a response correct if it differs from correct response listed only in possessive case, verb tense, or number (singular/plural), unless otherwise indicated in the scoring key.

- Know that any number that is a key word (in bold) must be recalled exactly.
- Score derivations of names as correct (e.g., Annie for Ann).

Test 13: Number Matrices
- Provide the worksheet in the Response Booklet and a pencil when directed.
- Use the suggested starting points.
- Provide corrective feedback as indicated for Samples A and B.
- Test by complete pages.
- After 30 seconds for Items 1–6 and 1 minute for Items 7–32, suggest that the examinee should move on to the next item; use a stopwatch or watch with a second hand to monitor response times. Allow more time if the examinee appears to be actively engaged in solving a problem.
- Give credit for items below the basal.

Test 14: Editing
- Begin with Sample Items A through D for all examinees and then use suggested starting points.
- Discontinue testing if an examinee has a score of 0 on the four sample items or Items 1 through 4, and record a score of 0 on the Test Record.
- Ensure that the examinee clearly indicates where the error is and how to correct it to receive credit.
- Do not read any words to the examinee after administering the sample items.
- Ask the examinee how to correct the error if he or she reads an item aloud and corrects the error in context.
- Ask the examinee how to correct the mistake if he or she indicates the error without explaining how to correct it.
- Test by complete pages.
- Give credit for items below the basal.

Test 15: Word Reading Fluency
- Use a stopwatch or a watch with a second hand.
- Use the Response Booklet.
- Administer the sample items and practice exercise to all examinees.
- Discontinue the test if an examinee has 1 or 0 correct on the Practice Exercise.
- Adhere to the 3-minute time limit.
- Record the exact starting and stopping times if not using a stopwatch.

- Record the exact finishing time in minutes and seconds on the Test Record.
- Do not tell the examinee any words during the test.
- Use the scoring guide overlay to facilitate scoring.

Test 16: Spelling of Sounds

- Follow the standardized procedures for audio-recorded tests.
- Use the Response Booklet.
- Use the suggested starting points.
- Present the Sample Items A through D and Items 1 through 5 orally and use the audio recording for all other items.
- Say the most common sound for letters printed within slashes, such as /m/, not the letter name.
- Know that responses listed in the Test Book are the only correct answers.
- Do not penalize for reversed letters as long as the letter does not become a new letter.
- Score the items 1 if spelled correctly or 0 if spelled incorrectly.
- Do not penalize the examinee if the stimulus word is not repeated or is pronounced incorrectly. Score only the written response.
- Pause or stop the audio recording if the examinee requires additional response time.
- Replay items upon examinee's request.
- Present items orally, if necessary.
- Give credit for items below the basal.

Test 17: Reading Vocabulary

- Administer both subtests (17A: Synonyms, 17B: Antonyms).
- Begin with the sample items for all examinees on each subtest.
- Use the suggested starting points for each subtest.
- Apply the basal and ceiling rules to each subtest.
- Know the correct pronunciation of all items.
- Do not read any words or items to the examinee after administering the sample items.
- Accept only one-word responses unless otherwise noted.
- Ask for a one-word answer if examinee provides a two-word or longer response.
- Score responses that differ in verb tense or number as correct, unless otherwise indicated in the key.
- Score responses that substitute a different part of speech as incorrect, unless otherwise indicated in the key.

- Do not penalize the examinee if the stimulus word is read incorrectly. Score only the synonym or antonym produced.
- Test by complete pages.
- Give credit for items below the basal on each subtest.
- Record errors for further analysis.
- Record the number correct for each subtest.
- Enter the number correct from each subtest into the online scoring program.
- Add together the scores from the two subtests when obtaining estimated AE/GE from the Test Record.

Test 18: Science; Test 19: Social Studies; Test 20: Humanities
- Use the suggested starting points.
- Apply the basal and ceiling rules correctly.
- Know the correct pronunciation of all words before administering the tests.
- Repeat any item upon request.
- Do not penalize for mispronunciations due to articulation errors, dialect variations, or regional speech patterns.
- Test by complete pages.
- Give credit for items below the basal.

APPENDIX A.2: FINE POINTS OF WJ IV ORAL LANGUAGE ADMINISTRATION

Test 1: Picture Vocabulary (Test 10: Vocabulario sobre dibujos)
- Use the suggested starting points.
- Point to the appropriate picture or part of the picture as directed.
- Complete any queries listed in the Test Book.
- Test by complete pages.
- Apply the basal and ceiling rules correctly.
- Give credit for items below the basal.
- Accept only words in English for Test 1 (Spanish on Test 10).
- Record errors for further analysis.

Test 2: Oral Comprehension (Test 11: Comprensión oral)
- Follow the standardized procedures for audio-recorded tests.
- Begin with Sample Items A and B for all examinees and then use the suggested starting points.

- Present Sample Items C and D and all test items from the audio recording.
- Pause or stop the recording if the examinee needs more time to respond.
- Do not repeat or replay any items unless an obvious noise (e.g., bell ringing) interferes.
- Accept only one-word answers unless otherwise indicated in the key.
- Ask for a one-word answer if the examinee provides a two-word or longer response.
- Accept responses that differ in tense or number unless otherwise indicated in the key.
- Score responses that use a different part of speech as incorrect, unless otherwise indicated in the key.
- Give credit for all items below the basal; do not include the sample items.
- Present items orally, if necessary.

Test 3: Segmentation
- Say the most common sound for letters printed within slashes, such as /s/, not the letter name.
- Use the suggested starting points.
- Repeat the items as needed; if unsure of what was said, re-administer the item.
- Follow the Continuation Instructions correctly.
- Do not penalize for mispronunciations due to articulation errors, dialect variations, or regional speech patterns.
- Accept words that are broken into acceptable segments as correct, even if the sounds are not pronounced perfectly.
- Give credit for all items below the starting point.
- Present test items orally, if necessary.

Test 4: Rapid Picture Naming
- Use a stopwatch or watch with a second hand.
- Adhere to the 2-minute time limit.
- Begin with the sample items for all examinees.
- Record the exact starting and stopping times if not using a stopwatch.
- Record the exact finishing time in minutes and seconds on the Test Record.
- Turn the page immediately after the last item on the page.
- Accept synonyms and words that are similar in meaning (e.g., *cat* or *kitty*).

Test 5: Sentence Repetition
- Follow the standardized procedures for audio-recorded tests.
- Present sample items orally to all examinees.
- Use the suggested starting points.
- Apply the basal and ceiling rules correctly.
- Accept words in exact order as correct.
- Score exact repetitions as correct (1) and sentences with any errors as incorrect (0).
- Do not repeat or replay any of the sentences.
- Give credit for items below the basal.
- Present the test items orally, if necessary.

Test 6: Understanding Directions (Test 12: Comprensión de indicaciones)
- Follow the standardized procedures for audio-recorded tests.
- Use the suggested starting points.
- Allow the examinee to review the picture for approximately 10 seconds before administering the items.
- Pause or stop the recording after the last item for each picture.
- Do not repeat or replay any item unless an obvious noise (e.g., bell ringing) interferes. In this case, finish the picture and then re-administer only the specific item.
- Give credit only if examinee completes all of the steps contained in the directions.
- Know the examinee can point in any order if the directions do not specify the sequence.
- Present the items orally, if necessary.
- Follow the Continuation Instructions correctly.
- Enter the number of points for each picture administered and an X for each picture not administered into the online scoring program.

Test 7: Sound Blending
- Follow the standardized procedures for audio-recorded tests.
- Begin with Sample Item A for all examinees.
- Present Sample Item A orally and Sample Item B and all test items using the audio recording.
- Choose the correct starting point based on examinee's estimated ability.
- Accept only words pronounced smoothly, not phoneme-by-phoneme, as correct.
- During the test provide only one reminder about saying the word smoothly.

- Do not repeat any items.
- Pause the audio recording to allow additional time for responses if needed.
- Present Items 1 through 16 orally, if necessary.
- Discontinue testing when a ceiling is reached.
- Give credit for items below the basal; do not include the sample items.

Test 8: Retrieval Fluency
- Administer all three items to each examinee.
- Allow only 1 minute for each item.
- Use a stopwatch or watch with a second hand.
- Use tally marks to record each correct response in the Test Record.
- Do not count duplicate answers as correct.
- During testing, do not ask the examinee to repeat a word.
- On Item 1, accept brand names of foods or drinks as correct (e.g., Coke or Spaghetti-O's).
- On Item 2, accept variations of the same name as correct (e.g., Bob, Bobby, and Robert), as well as formal names (e.g., Mrs. Smith).
- On Item 3, accept variations of the same animal (e.g., bear, polar bear).
- Record a maximum score of 99.

Test 9: Sound Awareness
- Administer both subtests (9A: Rhyming, 9B: Deletion).
- Follow the standardized procedures for audio-recorded tests.
- Begin with the sample items on each subtest for all examinees.
- Say the most common sound for letters printed within slashes, such as /s/, not the letter name.
- Apply the correct basal and ceiling rules to each subtest.
- Only score responses that are real words as correct.
- Administer 9A: Rhyming orally.
- Administer 9B: Deletion Sample Item A orally and administer all remaining items using the audio recording.
- Pause or stop the audio recording if the examinee requires additional response time.
- Replay or repeat items upon the examinee's request.
- Administer items orally, if necessary.
- Record errors for further analysis.

Appendix B

Frequently Asked Questions About the WJ IV ACH and the WJ IV OL

This section provides a summary of commonly asked questions about the WJ IV ACH and WJ IV OL. These questions and answers are organized into the categories of general administration, specific test administration and scoring, technical issues, and interpretation.

GENERAL ADMINISTRATION ISSUES

Selective Testing

Question: Do I need to administer all of the tests in the battery?

Answer: No, the WJ IV uses the principle of "selective testing." The WJ IV provides a comprehensive set of tests, but you do not need to administer all of the tests to all of the examinees. In the WJ IV ACH, Tests 1 through 6 serve as the core set of tests and offer a number of interpretive options. In the WJ IV OL, Tests 1 through 4 serve as the core set of tests. You can determine which tests to administer based on the referral questions or the information you are trying to obtain. A Selective Testing Table, designed to facilitate this process, is located in each Test Book and in the Examiner's Manual.

Age or Grade Norms

Question: Because the WJ IV offers both age norms and grade norms, how do I decide which one to use?

Answer: The norm group that you choose depends on your purpose for testing. For example, if a 30-year-old is starting college, you may want to use grade 13.0 to see how the person compares to beginning college students. If a person is age-appropriate for his or her grade, there will not be much difference between the scores from age or grade norms. However, if a person is old or young for a grade, differences will exist. For instructional purposes, grade norms might be best. For eligibility decisions, age norms may be preferred. Also, if you are comparing the WJ IV ACH results to the results of another test that only has age norms, such as the WISC-V, you must also use age norms. Sometimes in cases where a student has been retained, you may want to score the test both ways. (*Note:* Do not confuse age or grade norms with age and grade equivalents. Make sure you know the difference.)

Articulation Errors

Question: How do I score responses that appear to be errors, but I think they may be due to articulation problems?

Answer: Do not penalize an examinee for errors resulting from articulation problems or regional or dialectical speech differences. Be familiar with the speech patterns of any individuals you evaluate.

Timed Tests

Question: Why do I need to record the exact finishing time in minutes and seconds? Can't I just put in the time limit allowed?

Answer: Early finishers who do well will receive higher scores than those who work for the full time allowed. However, the examinee does not know this so do not tell them this information.

Basals

Question: If an individual doesn't attain a basal (e.g., doesn't get six correct in a row), can I use the raw score or is that test unusable?

Answer: When the examinee does not obtain a basal, test backward until either the basal is established or Item 1 has been administered. Item 1 is then used as the basal. Unless otherwise specified by the test directions (e.g., cutoff or discontinue rules), the test result is usable. If the examinee got one response correct, the raw score would be entered as 1. Any points earned by the examinee are counted as the raw score or the number correct. If the raw score is a zero, then you must determine the usability of that score (see "zero raw scores" question).

False Basals/False Ceilings

Question: What if the examinee appears to have two basals or two ceilings? Is the first one considered false and, therefore, should I ignore it?

Answer: The concept of false basals or ceilings does not apply to the WJ IV. In the event of two apparent basals, use the lowest-numbered one as the true basal. In the event of two apparent ceilings, use the highest-numbered one as the true ceiling.

Zero Raw Scores

Question: Can a zero raw score be used?

Answer: It depends on several factors (e.g., age of the examinee, task required, developmental appropriateness). You must decide about the usability of zero raw scores. The Examiner's Manual gives the following guidance:

> When an examinee receives a score of 0 on any test, the examiner needs to judge whether that score is a true assessment of the examinee's ability or whether it reflects the individual's inability to perform the task. If it is the latter, it may be more appropriate to assume that the examinee has no score for the test rather than using the score of 0 in further calculation and interpretation. For example, if a third-grade student had a score of 0 on Test 14: Editing, the score may be an accurate representation of the child's ability. However, if a kindergarten student obtained a 0 on Test 14: Editing, the score may indicate that the child has not yet learned to read. (p. 78)

Question: Why don't I get any standard scores for tests that have a zero raw score?

Answer: When an individual obtains a zero raw score, derived scores, other than AEs or GEs, are not available. A decision was made not to assign standard scores when an individual is unable to get at least one item correct. However, if the test with a zero raw score contributes to a cluster, all derived scores for the cluster are reported as long as at least one test in the cluster has a raw score higher than zero.

Hand-Scoring

Question: Because all scoring is done through a scoring program, does this mean I must use it to get scores? Is there any hand-scoring option?

Answer: You must use the scoring program to produce all derived scores. You can obtain estimated AEs and GEs for all tests by using the scoring tables in the Test Record. Other than raw scores, this is the only hand-scoring option available.

Cognitive Academic Language Proficiency (CALP)

Question: It appears from page 81 of the Examiner's Manual that you can derive a CALP score for Academic Knowledge and some of the reading and written language clusters. If so, which clusters yield a CALP score?

Answer: You can obtain a CALP level for the following clusters in the WJ IV ACH: Academic Knowledge, Reading, Basic Reading Skills, Reading Comprehension (and extended), Written Language, Basic Writing Skills, Written Expression, Academic Skills, Academic Fluency, and Academic Applications. In the WJ IV OL, you can obtain a CALP level for the following clusters: Broad Oral Language, Oral Language, Listening Comprehension, Oral Expression, Amplio oral lenguaje, Lenguaje oral, and Comprensión auditiva.

To display these levels, select to include the CALP level when using the scoring program. The CALP levels for all available clusters appear in a separate section of the report, titled "Cognitive Academic Language Proficiency (CALP) Scores and Interpretation." If using the CALP level as an indicator of proficiency, any of these clusters can be helpful. However, if trying to use the CALP level for eligibility (entrance/exit criteria), then use the broadest clusters available.

WJ IV ACH: TEST ADMINISTRATION AND SCORING

Test I: Letter-Word Identification, Form A, Form B, or Form C

Question: If the examinee "sounds out" the word first and then pronounces it as the correct, complete word, should I score it as a 1 or a 0?

Answer: Because you score the last response given, it would be scored a 1. As long as the examinee pronounces the stimulus word as a complete, blended word, score the response as 1. However, if an examinee reads the word syllable-by-syllable or sound-by-sound and does not pronounce the word as a whole on the last response, score the response as 0.

At the first occurrence of a sounded-out response that is not pronounced as a complete word by the examinee, remind the examinee to "first read the word silently and then say the word smoothly." You may only do this once during the test.

Remember, this is not a test of reading speed. Many readers need to use decoding strategies and should not be penalized for sounding out responses prior to pronouncing the complete word. An example is Item 43, Form C, *island*. If the examinee first reads "is-land" and then says, "Oh, that's *island*" (pronounced correctly), score the response as 1. However, if the examinee reads "is-land" and never blends the parts together, you would score the response as 0.

Question: I've been told that some examiners mark a response as incorrect if the examinee hasn't given a correct response within 5 seconds. Does the examinee only have 5 seconds to respond to each item, or should I allow the examinee more time?

Answer: Generally speaking, 5 seconds is enough time for most individuals to respond. However, this is a guideline, not a rule. If the examinee has not responded after 5 seconds, typically you would move on to the next item. However, if the examinee is still attempting to pronounce the word, you would allow more time.

Test 2: Applied Problems

Question: Some of the items seem to require a unit label and others do not. What happens if someone gives the correct numeric answer but fails to give the unit label or gives an incorrect label?

Answer: Some of the items do require a unit label and others do not. If it is required, there is a query asking for the unit label if only a correct numeric response was given. (Note: You would not query for a label if the numeric answer was incorrect. You would score the item 0 and move to the next item.) To receive credit for these items, both the numeric portion and the unit label must be correct. If an incorrect label is given at any time (required or not), the response is scored 0 even if the numeric portion of the answer was correct (e.g., the examinee says 16 cents instead of 16 dollars).

Test 5: Calculation

Question: Can I point out the signs to the examinee if it appears he or she is doing the wrong operation?

Answer: No, do not point out the signs. You would want to note in your assessment report that the examinee did not pay attention to the signs on certain problems.

Test 6: Writing Samples

Question: Should I penalize a response for poor spelling?

Answer: Do not penalize spelling errors with two exceptions. First, if spelling is part of the criteria for scoring that item, then score the response as directed. Second, if the misspelling makes the word unreadable, score the response and omit that word. If the word is critical to the sentence, then reduce the score by 1 point. If the word is a minor word, such as *the,* do not deduct a point. The Writing Samples test measures the quality of written expression, whereas the Spelling and Spelling of Sounds tests measure spelling ability.

Question: How do I score a run-on sentence?

Answer: Score the run-on sentence by selecting and scoring only the part of the sentence that best meets the task demands.

Question: What if the examinee writes more than one sentence in response to an item? How do I score that?

Answer: As with run-on sentences, select the one sentence that best meets the task demands and score it. Ignore the other sentences.

Question: Can I ask examinees to read their responses aloud if I'm having trouble reading them?

Answer: No, do not ask examinees to read their responses for the purpose of scoring. If the response is illegible, score it 0. This test helps you evaluate how well an examinee can communicate ideas in writing. It is not a test of oral language. Remember the ultimate criterion for scoring: If an adult without knowledge of the item content cannot read the response, score the response as 0.

Test 7: Word Attack

Question: How do I score a response that includes all the correct sounds but is not pronounced as a complete word?

Answer: Score responses that are not blended together and pronounced as a complete word as incorrect. On the first occasion that the examinee sounds out the word but does not blend it together, provide a reminder: "First read the word silently and then say the word smoothly." Give this reminder only once during the Word Attack test. Just as with Letter-Word Identification, score the last response the examinee provides.

Test 8: Oral Reading

Question: How do I score sentences if an examinee reads accurately but very slowly and in a monotone voice?

Answer: Review all the error types carefully and mark each one when it occurs. Some of the errors that are likely with this type of reader include hesitations of 3 or more seconds, repetitions, and ignoring punctuation. Completing the qualitative tally in the Test Record and recording your observations will be helpful for instructional planning. The Oral Reading test helps you evaluate accuracy, prosody, and rate, all of which are aspects of reading fluency.

Question: I am having difficulty catching all the errors when an examinee reads quickly. What can I do to ensure I am scoring the responses correctly?

Answer: When practicing administering and scoring this test, it might be helpful to record the examinee's reading. This allows you to become familiar with the process and to review your scoring and make any necessary corrections. It also allows more time for categorizing the types of errors the examinee makes. When conducting an actual evaluation, remind the examinee of the directions given at the start of the test: "Read as carefully as you can, not as fast as you can," or simply ask the examinee to pause after each sentence.

Question: When an examinee self-corrects and repeats the words around it, does that count as a repetition error?

Answer: If the examinee repeats while making a self-correction, do not count that repetition as an error.

Test 9: Sentence Reading Fluency

Question: Can I let the examinee skip around when taking the test?

Answer: No, do not allow the examinee to skip around. Examinees may skip an item they don't know, but they should work in sequence. The scoring is based on number correct and number incorrect within the range of attempted items. Items that fall beyond the last item attempted are not factored into the score. If an examinee skips around, it would be difficult to tell where the range of attempted items begins and ends.

Question: Why is the score based on number correct minus number incorrect? Isn't that unfair to the examinee?

Answer: Because Sentence Reading Fluency requires the individual to mark yes or no for each item, there is a 50% chance the individual will get each item correct without even reading the item. Therefore, evaluating correct and incorrect responses within the range of attempted items controls for guessing. The norms are based on this procedure (number correct – number incorrect), so the examinee is not being unfairly penalized. Remember to observe examinees during testing and remind them to read each item and continue working in sequence if it appears they are randomly circling or skipping around.

Question: Is the examinee supposed to read the sentences out loud or silently?

Answer: Although the directions don't specify, the examinee should read silently. It is a timed test so the examinee must read as quickly as he or she can. Therefore, silent reading is expected.

Test 10: Math Facts Fluency

Question: How should I present the Response Booklet to the examinee? Should I present it folded so that only one page is exposed, or should I present it open to both pages?

Answer: Although this is not specified in the test materials, it is preferable to present one page at a time. This is how the Response Booklet was presented during the standardization. When examinees reach the bottom of the page, make sure they turn to the next page quickly.

Test 11: Sentence Writing Fluency

Question: May I read any of these words to the examinee?

Answer: Yes, you may read any words upon request. However, do not spell any words for the examinee.

Question: Do I score the sentence 0 if the examinee misspells one of the stimulus words? It says the stimulus words cannot be changed in any way. Does spelling count?

Answer: Misspelling or incorrectly copying the stimulus words does not affect the scoring. As long as the examinee does not change the stimulus word to a different part of speech, tense, or number, a misspelling is acceptable. For example, if the person spelled the word *girl* as *gril,* this would not count as an error. If the person wrote *girls* instead of *girl,* this would count as an error.

Question: If the examinee's handwriting is so poor that I cannot read the response, may I ask him or her to read the response to me for scoring purposes?

Answer: No, do not ask the examinee to read the response aloud for scoring purposes. During the test, remind the examinee to write more neatly if the writing seems illegible.

Test 12: Reading Recall

Question: Can examinees earn a point for either bolded or paraphrased information? For example, on passage 5 the element is /invited her neighbors over/. Can a point be earned if the examinee simply recalls "neighbors" because that is bolded? Can a point be earned if the examinee does not say "neighbors" but does say a paraphrase of the element, such as "asked her next door friends to come over"?

Answer: To earn a point, the bolded information, or a close synonym, must be recalled. In your example, recalling only the bold word of "neighbors" earns a point, regardless if the person mentions they were "invited over." Recall of "asked her next door friends to come over" also earns a point because "next-door friends" is very similar in meaning to "neighbors." However, if the response was "asked some people over" this would not earn point for the bold element "neighbors." In addition, accept derivations of a proper name (e.g., Bill or Billy), or responses that differ in possessive case (e.g., Bill or Bill's), verb tense (e.g., run or ran), or number (singular or plural, e.g., car or cars).

Question: How do I score an element if the examinee recalls it out of order?

Answer: The order of the retelling does not matter. As long as the bold word or words in the element are recalled, it is given credit.

Test 14: Editing

Question: In the WJ III, we could read words upon request in this test. Why was that changed?

Answer: You are correct about the change in the directions for Editing. In the WJ IV, no reading assistance is permitted. Part of the proofreading process is the ability to read the text. Therefore, this change was made in the WJ IV to make the editing task more "real world."

Test 16: Spelling of Sounds

Question: To get examinees in my region to spell the nonsense words correctly, I would have to pronounce them as they "sound" in our part of the country. May I present the items orally, incorporating the regional dialect?

Answer: No. The audio recording presents the nonsense words using "standard" English pronunciation that everyone hears on the radio or television. The task is not just to spell the nonsense word as it sounds, but to spell it using the most common orthographic patterns for that sound. The standard English pronunciations lead to the common orthographic spelling patterns, which is essentially what this test is measuring. Dialect is an oral language issue. Spelling of Sounds is a written test requiring standard English pronunciations and spellings.

Question: What if the examinee does not repeat the word before writing it? Or what if they mispronounce the word? How do I score that?

Answer: Scoring is based on the written response only. If the examinee fails to repeat the word or mispronounces the word before writing, it does not affect the score of the written response. Asking the examinee to pronounce the word before writing not only helps focus the examinee, but it also provides important qualitative information to the examiner. For example, if the examinee mispronounces the word, that provides clues about auditory discrimination and processing. If the examinee repeats the word exactly and then writes it incorrectly, that provides clues about orthographic processing.

Test 17: Reading Vocabulary

Question: If examinees have difficulty reading the stimulus word, may I read it for them and see if they know the synonym or antonym?

Answer: No, do not read any words for examinees when administering a reading test. This test is measuring the examinee's reading abilities, not his or her oral language abilities. It is a good idea to evaluate the examinee's oral language abilities, but do not use the reading test for this purpose. Instead, administer Test 1: Oral Vocabulary from the WJ IV COG to compare oral performance on synonyms and antonyms to reading performance on those tasks.

Question: On 17A: Synonyms, what if the examinee misreads the stimulus word but provides a response that is a correct synonym for the misread word? For example, the stimulus word is *pal* but the examinee misreads it as *pail* and then gives the correct synonym, *bucket.* May I score that as correct?

Answer: No, you would score it as 0. This is a reading test, not an oral language measure. The examinee's misreading of the stimulus word does not affect scoring. The only correct answers are the synonym or synonyms for the actual stimulus word. For example, if the examinee misread *pal* as *pail* but then said *friend* as the synonym, you would score the response as correct. Record all errors for analysis.

TECHNICAL ISSUES

Special Education Students in the Norm Sample

Questions: Are special education students represented in the WJ IV norm sample? Are deaf students represented in the sample?

Answer: Special education students, including deaf students, are included in the WJ IV norm sample to the same extent to which they are represented in general education classrooms in the nation. Via random sampling of classroom rosters, a percentage of special education students that approximates the percentage of those special education students who spend the majority of their time in general education classes was obtained. Of course, separate validity studies are conducted on special populations to determine whether the test distinguishes among the various groups. For example, mean scores are expected to be lower for individuals with intellectual disabilities, reading scores are expected to be lower for individuals with reading disabilities, and so on.

Predicted Scores

Question: Regarding the use of the Academic Knowledge cluster in the ability/ achievement comparisons, why does the predicted score vary with each achievement area and not remain constant?

Answer: The predicted score is a function of the Academic Knowledge score and the correlation between it and each specific achievement cluster at that age or grade level. This is true for the other ability score options in the WJ IV COG as well (GIA, Scholastic Aptitudes, *Gf-Gc*) or the WJ IV OL (Broad Oral Language). The predicted scores change because the correlation varies between Academic Knowledge (or another ability measure) and different achievement clusters at a given age or grade. Because the correlation is the foundation for the predicted score, the scores will, therefore, vary.

If the correlation were perfect, the predicted score would be identical to the Academic Knowledge score. For example, if the Academic Knowledge score was 70 and the correlation is 1.00, then the predicted achievement score also would be 70. In addition, the closer to the mean the predictor is (e.g., SS = 99 or 100), the less change there will be in the predicted scores.

Because the correlations are not perfect, the predicted achievement score will fall closer to the mean (regression to the mean). For example, if the correlation is .70, the predicted score will be 70% of the distance away from the mean toward the ability score. In this case, if the Academic Knowledge score is 70. The predicted score would be 79.

There are two primary causes for confusion about the WJ IV predicted scores: (1) Examiners who do not correct for regression use the "ability" score as the predicted score, so they appear to be the same; or (2) examiners who do correct for regression use the same correlation for all areas at all ages or grades and get predicted scores that appear to be unchanging. (*Note:* Correlations are *not* the same across curriculum areas at the same age or grade.)

INTERPRETATION

Intra-Achievement Variation Procedure

Question: What is this procedure and how do I use it?

Answer: It is a procedure to determine if any significant strengths or weaknesses are present among an individual's achievement abilities. It requires a minimum of six tests (Tests 1–6), although additional tests and clusters can be included in the Extended procedure. This variation procedure helps identify an individual's pattern of strengths and weaknesses among achievement areas.

Question: Exactly what tests or clusters do I need to give to get an intra-achievement variation?

Answer: You will get an intra-achievement variation when a minimum of Tests 1 through 6 has been administered. You can add in additional tests to the procedure. Table 5.15 on page 102 of the Examiner's Manual lists the tests and clusters that you can include in the intra-achievement variation.

A second intra-achievement option is the Academic Skills/Academic Fluency/Academic Applications variation procedure. This requires a minimum of 9 tests, Tests 1 through 6 and Tests 9 through 11. Table 5.16 on page 103 of the Examiner's Manual lists the tests and clusters you can include in this procedure.

Question: Where do the predicted scores come from on the intra-achievement variation procedure?

Answer: First, the predictor (or ability) is derived by averaging five of the first six ACH tests. For example, if the Letter-Word Identification test were being compared to the other five tests, you would remove Test 1: Letter-Word Identification and then average the scores for Tests 2 through 6. Then the predictor is adjusted using correlations between it and the corresponding achievement area at the specific age or grade to create the "predicted" score. This procedure accounts for regression to the mean. All of the other reading tests and clusters will be compared to this same predictor from Tests 2 through 6. If Applied Problems was being compared to the other five tests, it would be removed and then the score adjusted. All of the other math tests and clusters would be then compared to this same predictor score.

z-Scores

Question: What is a z-score and how do I interpret it?

Answer: A z-score is a standard score with a mean of 0 and a standard deviation of 1. A z-score indicates how far above or below the mean the individual's score falls. A z-score of $+2.0$ indicates the individual scored 2 standard deviations above the mean. A z-score of -2.0 indicates the individual scored 2 standard deviations below the mean. In many cases, ± 1.5 SD is used as a cut point. The z-score is very helpful in these instances because a z of $+$ or -1.5

represents this criterion. Appendix C of this book presents a table that converts z-scores to PR and SS (M = 100, SD = 15).

RPIs

Question: What is an RPI and how do I interpret it?

Answer: An RPI (Relative Proficiency Index) is a criterion-referenced score that predicts level of success on a task and describes functionality. The denominator of the fraction is fixed at 90. The denominator represents 90% proficiency, or mastery, by average age or grade mates. The numerator changes based on the examinee's performance and ranges from 0 to 100. For example, if a seventh-grade boy obtains an RPI of 45/90 on Letter-Word Identification, interpret this to mean that when average seventh graders have 90% proficiency with this type of task, this student would have only 45% proficiency. Conversely, if an examinee has an RPI of 99/90, it means this examinee is far more proficient and advanced on this task than average grademates.

Instructional Zones

Question: What are instructional zones?

Answer: These zones represent the easy (independent) to difficult (frustration) range for a person on a task. The zones are created by adding and subtracting 10 W points from the obtained W score. The easy end of the range corresponds to an RPI of 96/90. The difficult end of the range corresponds to an RPI of 75/90. The person's obtained age or grade level (instructional or developmental level) is in the middle of the range. Instructional zones are usually discussed related to achievement tests, whereas developmental zones are usually related to cognitive or oral language tests.

Question: Why are some instructional zones so wide and some so narrow?

Answer: Since all instructional zones are 20 W points wide, the width of the instructional zones reflects the development of the underlying skill. If it is a period of rapid growth/change, the bands are narrow. If it is in a period of slow growth/little change, the bands are wide. Some abilities develop early and don't change much over time, whereas others have a steeper growth curve. When a person's ability falls in the steep part of a growth curve, the bands are narrow because the underlying ability is in a rapid period of change. When a person's ability falls in the flat part of the growth curve, the band is wide because the underlying ability is in a slow period of change.

Comparing WJ III Scores to WJ IV Scores

Question: How do WJ III scores compare to WJ IV scores?

Answer: The WJ IV test materials do not report the correlations between WJ III and WJ IV. Test and cluster composition is different between the batteries, making it impractical to compare scores directly. As a general rule, standard scores tend to be lower on tests with newer norms.

Testing Individuals Who Are Bilingual

Question: How do I determine if I should conduct a comprehensive evaluation for a bilingual individual in English or in Spanish?

Answer: The Comparative Language Index (CLI) available when using the parallel English and Spanish tests in the WJ IV OL will help you determine language dominance and proficiency in both languages. Because it would be best to have the broadest measure of language available, you would administer the three Spanish language tests and the three parallel English tests. After administering these six tests (three in each language), you will have the Broad Oral Language cluster and the Amplio lenguaje oral cluster. Each cluster reports a relative proficiency index (RPI). The numerators of each index are used to create the CLI. For example, if the person's RPI on Amplio lenguaje oral is 76/90 and his RPI on Broad Oral Language is 45/90, the CLI would be 76/45, indicating that the person is more proficient in Spanish than English. Consult Chapter 5 of the Examiner's Manual for the WJ IV OL for more information.

WJ IV OL: Test Administration and Scoring

Test 1: Picture Vocabulary

Question: What if the examinee provides a response that demonstrates knowledge of the item, but he or she does not say the correct answer? For example, for the picture of the whistle, the response is "you blow it." How do I score that?

Answer: When an examinee demonstrates knowledge of an item by describing an attribute or function but cannot retrieve the specific word, it can indicate some knowledge of the word or in some cases, a word-finding difficulty. The examinee may know something about a word but not know its exact name. For example, when looking at a picture of a toga, a second-grade student responded, "It was the kind of dress the Romans wore." Even though you would score the response as incorrect, it indicates rich knowledge. In other cases, the examinee knows the word, but cannot recall it at that instant. The examinee may say: "I know what that is, but I can't remember right now what it is called." In this case, you may repeat the question, providing additional response time to retrieve the word. If the correct response is still not retrieved, score the item 0 and record the incorrect responses for error analysis. If, however, at a later time during testing, the person says, "Oh, I remember, that was a stethoscope," you would return to the item and score it as correct. The goal is to determine if the errors are due to a lack of or incomplete knowledge of a word or the inability to retrieve a specific word.

Test 2: Oral Comprehension

Question: May I repeat an item if the examinee requests this?

Answer: No, do not repeat any items on this test because the construct being measured is listening comprehension.

Test 3: Segmentation

Question: May I repeat an item if the examinee requests this?

Answer: Yes, you may repeat any item in this test.

Question: I am not familiar with phonemes and can't really hear the different sounds. Can I administer and score this test?

Answer: Administration of this test is quite simple, but if you cannot distinguish the separate sounds yourself, you will not be able to score this test correctly. It is advisable to ask someone else to administer and score the test for you, such as a speech-language therapist or a reading teacher.

Test 4: Rapid Picture Naming

Question: When the person is naming the pictures, I cannot keep up writing 1s and 0s. What can I do?

Answer: It is difficult to keep up if someone is naming the pictures rapidly. There are two possible solutions: (1) Just write the 0s during the test and then go back and add the 1s later, or (2) make a continuous line through all the correctly named items. The Test Record is also designed to help you keep your place. Each group of five items (row of five pictures) is separated by extra space on the Test Record. Each page is separated by a solid line. As the examinee approaches the solid lines, make sure you are ready to turn the page.

Test 5: Sentence Repetition

Question: Didn't this used to be scored 2, 1, or 0 when it was called Memory for Sentences?

Answer: Yes. Scoring has been simplified. If the examinee repeats the sentence exactly, he or she receives 1 point. If any error is made, the sentence is scored 0.

Test 6: Understanding Directions

Question: Can the recording be stopped to allow for extended processing time after each item within a set?

Answer: You may pause any WJ IV audio-recorded test between items if the examinee needs more response time.

Test 8: Retrieval Fluency

Question: Why is there a maximum score of 99 for each item in this test?

Answer: It is set as an upper limit because no one in the norming sample had this many correct responses in one minute. In fact, very few people even had 60 correct responses, which was the upper limit to these items in WJ III. Increasing it to 99 virtually guarantees that no one will reach or exceed the upper limit. There is a maximum possible total of 297 for all three items.

Question: What if the examinee names many different types of cereal (e.g., Cheerios, oatmeal, Frosted Flakes) for the first item? Do I give credit for each one or just one point for the general category of cereal?

Answer: Award credit for each type mentioned. These types of responses demonstrate that the person is using a good strategy for naming things within a category.

Test 9: Sound Awareness

Question: I realize this test is intended to be a screening measure for younger children. However, can I use it for an older individual who I suspect is struggling with these basic phonological tasks?

Answer: Yes, you can administer it to older individuals.

Spanish Language Tests 10–12

Question: I don't speak Spanish but I can read it. Can I read the items to the examinee?

Answer: No, the examiner must be bilingual. If a bilingual examiner is not available, use the primary/ancillary examiner procedure that is described in Chapter 6 of the Examiner's Manual for the Tests of Oral Language. You could serve as the primary examiner and train a bilingual person to be your ancillary examiner.

Question: What tests do I have to administer if I'm trying to determine language dominance?

Answer: There are three parallel English and Spanish tests, so you would need to administer all six tests if you wish to get the broadest view of the person's performance in both languages. This includes Tests 1, 2, 6, 10, 11, and 12. Giving these six tests will yield three parallel clusters: three in English and three in Spanish. Those clusters can then be compared for relative proficiency in each language by using the Comparative Language Index (CLI).

Appendix C

Table for Converting z-Scores (z) to Percentile Ranks (PR) or Standard Scores (SS)

Z	PR	SS	Z	PR	SS
+2.33	99	135	0.00	50	100
+2.05	98	131	−0.02	49	100
+1.88	97	128	−0.05	48	99
+1.75	96	126	−0.08	47	99
+1.64	95	125	−0.10	46	98
+1.56	94	123	−0.13	45	98
+1.48	93	122	−0.15	44	98
+1.40	92	121	−0.18	43	97
+1.34	91	120	−0.20	42	97
+1.28	90	119	−0.23	41	97
+1.23	89	118	−0.25	40	96
+1.18	88	118	−0.28	39	96
+1.13	87	117	−0.31	38	95
+1.08	86	116	−0.33	37	95
+1.04	85	116	−0.36	36	95
+1.00	84	115	−0.39	35	94
+0.95	83	114	−0.41	34	94
+0.92	82	114	−0.44	33	93
+0.88	81	113	−0.47	32	93
+0.84	80	113	−0.50	31	92
+0.81	79	112	−0.52	30	92

(continued)

(*Continued*)

Z	PR	SS	Z	PR	SS
+0.77	78	112	−0.55	29	92
+0.74	77	111	−0.58	28	91
+0.71	76	111	−0.61	27	91
+0.68	75	110	−0.64	26	90
+0.64	74	110	−0.68	25	90
+0.61	73	109	−0.71	24	89
+0.58	72	109	−0.74	23	89
+0.55	71	108	−0.77	22	88
+0.52	70	108	−0.81	21	88
+0.50	69	108	−0.84	20	87
+0.47	68	107	−0.88	19	87
+0.44	67	107	−0.92	18	86
+0.41	66	106	−0.95	17	86
+0.39	65	106	−1.00	16	85
+0.36	64	105	−1.04	15	84
+0.33	63	105	−1.08	14	84
+0.31	62	105	−1.13	13	83
+0.28	61	104	−1.18	12	82
+0.25	60	104	−1.23	11	82
+0.23	59	103	−1.28	10	81
+0.20	58	103	−1.34	9	80
+0.18	57	103	−1.40	8	79
+0.15	56	102	−1.48	7	78
+0.13	55	102	−1.56	6	77
+0.10	54	102	−1.64	5	75
+0.08	53	101	−1.75	4	74
+0.05	52	101	−1.88	3	72
+0.02	51	100	−2.05	2	69
0.00	50	100	−2.33	1	65

References

American Educational Research Association, American Psychological Association, & National Council on Measurement in Education. (2014). *Standards for educational and psychological testing.* Washington, DC: American Educational Research Association.

Barbaresi, W. J., Katusic, S. K., Colligan, R. C., Weaver, A. L., & Jacobsen, S. J. (2005). Math learning disorder: Incidence in a population-based birth cohort, 1976–82, Rochester, MN. *Ambulatory Pediatrics, 5,* 281–289.

Berninger, V. W. (1990). Multiple orthographic codes: Key to alternative instructional methodologies for developing the orthographic-phonological connections underlying word identification. *School Psychology Review, 19,* 518–533.

Berninger, V. W., Abbott, R., Thomson, J., & Raskind, W. (2001). Language phenotype for reading and writing disability: A family approach. *Scientific Studies in Reading, 5,* 59–105.

Berninger, V. W., Abbott, R. D., Thomson, J., Wagner, R., Swanson, H. L., Wijsman, E., & Raskind, W. (2006). Modeling developmental phonological core deficits within a working-memory architecture in children and adults with developmental dyslexia. *Scientific Studies in Reading, 10,* 165–198.

Bryant, D. P., Smith, D. D., & Bryant, B. R. (2008). *Teaching students with special needs in inclusive classrooms.* Boston, MA: Allyn & Bacon.

Carroll, J. B. (1993). *Human cognitive abilities: A survey of factor-analytic studies.* Cambridge, England: Cambridge University Press.

Carrow-Woolfolk, E. (1996). *Oral and written language scales: Written expression.* Torrance, CA: Western Psychological Services.

Cattell, R. B. (1963). Theory for fluid and crystallized intelligence: A critical experiment. *Journal of Educational Psychology, 54,* 1–22.

Cooper, K. L. (2006). *A componential reading comprehension task for children* (Unpublished doctoral thesis). University of New England, Portland, Maine.

Cruickshank, W. M. (1977). Least-restrictive placement: Administrative wishful thinking. *Journal of Learning Disabilities, 10,* 193–194.

Cummins, J. (1984). *Bilingualism and special education: Issues in assessment and pedagogy.* Austin, TX: PRO-ED.

Cummins, J. (2003). BICS and CALP: Origins and rationale for the distinction. In C. B. Paulston & G. R. Tucker (Eds.), *Sociolinguistics: The essential readings* (pp. 322–328). London, England: Blackwell.

Dumont, R., & Willis, J. O. (2014). *Ten top problems with normed achievement tests for young children.* Retrieved from http://www.myschoolpsychology.com/wp-content/uploads/2014/02/Ten-Top-Problems.pdf

Ehri, L. C. (2006). Alphabetics instruction helps students learn to read. In R. M. Joshi & P. G. Aaron (Eds.), *Handbook of orthography and literacy* (pp. 649–677). Mahwah, NJ: Erlbaum.

Flanagan, D. P., Ortiz, S. O., & Alfonso, V. (2013). *Essentials of cross-battery assessment* (3rd ed.). Hoboken, NJ: Wiley.

Fleischner, J. E., Garnett, K., & Shepherd, M. J. (1982). Proficiency in arithmetic basic fact computation of learning disabled and nondisabled children. *Focus on Learning Problems in Mathematics 4,* 47–55.

Fletcher, J. M., Francis, D. J., Shaywitz, S. E., Lyon, G. R., Foorman, B. R., Stuebing, K. K., & Shaywitz, B. A. (1998). Intelligent testing and the discrepancy model for children with learning disabilities. *Learning Disabilities Research & Practice, 13*, 186–203.

Fletcher, J. M., Lyon, G. R., Fuchs, L. S., & Barnes, M. A. (2007). *Learning disabilities: From identification to intervention.* New York, NY: Guilford Press.

Floyd, R. G., McGrew, K. S., & Evans, J. J. (2008). The relative contributions of the Cattell–Horn–Carroll (CHC) cognitive abilities in explaining writing achievement during childhood and adolescence. *Psychology in the Schools, 45*, 132–144.

Fuchs, L. S., Fuchs, D., Schumacher, R. F., & Seethaler, P. M. (2013). Instructional intervention for students with mathematics learning difficulties. In H. L. Swanson, K. R. Harris, & S. E. Graham (Eds.), *Handbook on learning disabilities* (2nd ed., pp. 388–404). New York, NY: Guilford Press.

Fuchs, L. S., Fuchs, D., Stuebing, K., Fletcher, J. M., Hamlett, C. L., & Lambert, W. (2008). Problem solving and computational skill: Are they shared or distinct aspects of mathematical cognition? *Journal of Educational Psychology, 100*, 30–47.

Geary, D. C. (2013). Early foundations for mathematics learning and their relations to learning disabilities. *Current Directions in Psychological Science, 22*, 23–27.

Geary, D. C., Hamson, C. O., & Hoard, M. K. (2000). Numerical and arithmetical cognition: A longitudinal study of process and concept deficits in children with learning disability. *Journal of Experimental Child Psychology, 77*, 236–263.

Georgiou, G. K., & Parrila, R. (2013). Rapid automatized naming and reading. In H. L. Swanson, K. R. Harris, & S. Graham (Eds.), *Handbook of learning disabilities* (2nd ed., pp. 169–185). New York, NY: Guilford Press.

Goldman, R., Fristoe, M., & Woodcock, R. W. (1974). *The Goldman-Fristoe-Woodcock Auditory Skills Test Battery.* Circle Pines, MN: American Guidance Service.

Gregory, R. J. (1996). *Psychological testing: History, principles, and applications.* Needham Heights, MA: Allyn & Bacon.

Hale, J. B., & Fiorello, C. A. (2004). *School neuropsychology: A practitioner's handbook.* New York, NY: Guilford Press.

Hooper, S. R. (1996). Subtyping specific reading disabilities: Classification approaches, recent advances, and current status. *Mental Retardation and Developmental Disabilities, 2*, 14–20.

Horn, J. L. (1988). Thinking about human abilities. In J. R. Nesselroade & R. B. Cattell (Eds.), *Handbook of multivariate psychology* (2nd ed., pp. 645–865). New York, NY: Academic Press.

Horn, J. L. (1991). Measurement of intellectual capabilities: A review of theory. In K. S. McGrew, J. K. Werder, & R. W. Woodcock (Eds.), *WJ-R technical manual* (pp. 197–232). Itasca, IL: Riverside.

Horn, J. L., & Cattell, R. B. (1966). Refinement and test of the theory of fluid and crystallized intelligence. *Journal of Educational Psychology, 57*, 253–270.

Individuals with Disabilities Education Improvement Act (IDEA), Pub. L. No. 108–446, 20 USC 1400 (2004).

Kaufman, A. S., & Kaufman, N. L. (2004). *Kaufman Test of Educational Achievement* (2nd ed.). San Antonio, TX: Psychological Corporation.

Kintsch, W., & Rawson, K. A. (2005). Comprehension. In M. J. Snowling & C. Hulme (Eds.), *The science of reading: A handbook* (pp. 209–226). Oxford, England: Blackwell Publishing.

Lyon, G. R. (1996). State of research. In S. Cramer & W. Ellis (Eds.), *Learning disabilities: Lifelong issues* (pp. 3–61). Baltimore, MD: Paul H. Brookes.

Lyon, G. R. (1998). Why reading is not natural. *Educational Leadership, 3*, 14–18.

Martin, A. (2009). Circuits in mind: The neural foundations for object concepts. In M. S. Gazzaniga (Ed.), *The cognitive neurosciences* (4th ed., pp. 1031–1045). Cambridge, MA: MIT Press.

Mather, N., & Jaffe, L. (in press). *Woodcock-Johnson VI: Reports, recommendations, and strategies.* Hoboken, NJ: Wiley.

Mather, N., & Wendling, B. J. (2014a). Examiner's Manual. *Woodcock-Johnson IV Tests of Achievement.* Rolling Meadows, IL: Riverside.

Mather, N., & Wendling, B. J. (2014b). Examiner's Manual. *Woodcock-Johnson IV Tests of Cognitive Abilities.* Rolling Meadows, IL: Riverside.

McGrew, K. S. (2005). The Cattell–Horn–Carroll theory of cognitive abilities: Past, present, and future. In D. P. Flanagan & P. L. Harrison (Eds.), *Contemporary intellectual assessment: Theories, tests, and issues* (2nd ed., pp. 136–181). New York, NY: Guilford Press.

McGrew, K. S. (2009). Standing on the shoulders of the giants of psychometric intelligence research. *Intelligence, 37,* 1–10.

McGrew, K. S., LaForte, E. M., & Schrank, F. A. (2014). Technical Manual [CD]. *Woodcock-Johnson IV.* Rolling Meadows, IL: Riverside.

McGrew, K. S., & Wendling, B. J. (2010). Cattell–Horn–Carroll cognitive-achievement relations: What we have learned from the past 20 years of research. *Psychology in the Schools, 47,* 651–675.

McGrew, K. S., & Woodcock, R. W. (2001). Technical Manual. *Woodcock-Johnson III.* Itasca, IL: Riverside.

Meltzer, L. J. (1994). Assessment of learning disabilities: The challenge of evaluating cognitive strategies and processes underlying learning. In G. R. Lyon (Ed.), *Frames of reference for the assessment of learning disabilities: New views on measurement issues* (pp. 571–606). Baltimore, MD: Paul H. Brookes.

Morris, R. D., Stuebing, K. K., Fletcher, J. M., Shaywitz, S. E., Lyon, G. R., Shankweiler, D. P., . . . Shaywitz, B. A. (1998). Subtypes of reading disability: Variability around a phonological core. *Journal of Educational Psychology, 90,* 347–373.

Nation, K., Clarke, P., & Snowling, M. J. (2002). General cognitive ability in children with reading comprehension difficulties. *British Journal of Educational Psychology, 72,* 549–560.

Nation, K., Marshall, C. M., & Snowling, M. J. (2001). Phonological and semantic contributions to children's picture naming skill: Evidence from children with developmental reading disorders. *Language and Cognitive Processes, 16,* 241–259.

National Joint Committee on Learning Disabilities. (2011). Learning disabilities: Implications for policy regarding research and practice: A report by the National Joint Committee on Learning Disabilities March 2011. *Learning Disability Quarterly, 34,* 237–241.

National Reading Panel. (2000). *Teaching children to read: An evidence-based assessment of the scientific research literature on reading and its implications for reading instruction* (NIH Publication No. 00–4754). Washington, DC: National Institute of Child Health and Human Development.

Norton, E., & Wolf, M. (2012). Rapid automatized naming (RAN) and reading fluency: Implications for understanding and treatment of reading disabilities. *Annual Review of Psychology, 63,* 427–452.

Novick, B. Z., & Arnold, M. M. (1988). *Fundamentals of clinical child neuropsychology.* Philadelphia, PA: Grune & Stratton.

Pennington, B. F. (2009). *Diagnosing learning disorders: A neuropsychological framework* (2nd ed.). New York, NY: Guilford.

Pennington, B. F., Peterson, R. L., & McGrath, L. M. (2009). Dyslexia. In B. F. Pennington (Ed.), *Diagnosing learning disorders* (2nd ed., pp. 45–82). New York, NY: Guilford.

Perfetti, C. (2007). Reading ability: Lexical quality to comprehension. *Scientific Studies of Reading, 11*, 357–383.

Price, G. R., & Ansari, D. (2013). Dyscalculia: Characteristics, causes and treatments. *Numeracy, 6* (1), Article 2. Retrieved from http://scholarcommons.usf.edu/numeracy/vol6/iss1/art2

Rack, J. P., Snowling, M., & Olson, R. (1992). The nonword reading deficit in developmental dyslexia: A review. *Reading Research Quarterly, 27*, 28–53.

Rasch, G. (1960). *Probabilistic models for some intelligence and attainment tests.* Copenhagen, Denmark: Danish Institute for Educational Research.

Schneider, W. J., & McGrew, K. (2012). The Cattell–Horn–Carroll model of intelligence. In D. Flanagan & P. Harrison (Eds.), *Contemporary intellectual assessment: Theories, tests, and issues* (3rd ed., pp. 99–144). New York, NY: Guilford Press.

Schrank, F. A., & Dailey, D. (2014). *Woodcock-Johnson online scoring and reporting* [Online format]. Rolling Meadows, IL: Riverside.

Schrank, F. A., Mather, N., & McGrew, K. S. (2014a). *Woodcock-Johnson IV Tests of Achievement.* Rolling Meadows, IL: Riverside.

Schrank, F. A., Mather, N., & McGrew, K. S. (2014b). *Woodcock-Johnson IV Tests of Oral Language.* Rolling Meadows, IL: Riverside.

Schrank, F. A., McGrew, K. S., & Mather, N. (2014a). *Woodcock-Johnson IV.* Rolling Meadows, IL: Riverside.

Schrank, F. A., McGrew, K. S., & Mather, N. (2014b). *Woodcock-Johnson IV Tests of Cognitive Abilities.* Rolling Meadows, IL: Riverside.

Schrank, F. A., Miller, D. C., Wendling, B. J., & Woodcock, R. W. (2010). *Essentials of the WJ III cognitive abilities assessment* (2nd ed.). Hoboken, NJ: Wiley.

Schultz, E. K., Simpson, C. G., & Lynch, S. (2012). Specific learning disability identification: What constitutes a pattern of strengths and weaknesses? *Learning Disabilities, 18*, 87–97.

Shaywitz, S. (2003). *Overcoming dyslexia: A new and complete science-based program for overcoming reading problems at any level.* New York, NY: Knopf.

Shaywitz, S. E., Morris, R., & Shaywitz, B. A. (2008). The education of dyslexic children from childhood to young adulthood. *Annual Review of Psychology, 59*, 451–475.

Snowling, M. J., & Hulme, C. (2012). The nature and classification of reading disorders: A commentary on proposals for DSM-5. *Journal of Child Psychology and Psychiatry, 53*, 593–607.

Spencer, M., Quinn, J. M., & Wagner, R. K. (2014). Specific reading comprehension disability: Major problem, myth, or misnomer? *Learning Disabilities Research & Practice, 29*, 3–9.

Stanovich, K. E. (1988). Explaining the differences between the dyslexic and the garden-variety poor reader: The phonological-core variable-difference model. *Journal of Learning Disabilities, 21*, 590–604, 612.

Stanovich, K. E. (1991a). Conceptual and empirical problems with discrepancy definitions of reading disability. *Learning Disability Quarterly, 14*, 269–280.

Stanovich, K. E. (1991b). Discrepancy definitions of reading disability: Has intelligence led us astray? *Reading Research Quarterly, 26*, 7–29.

Stanovich, K. E. (1994). Are discrepancy-based definitions of dyslexia empirically defensible? In K. P. van den Bos, L. S. Siegel, D. J. Bakker, & D. L. Share (Eds.), *Current directions in dyslexia research* (pp. 15–30). Alblasserdam, Holland: Swets & Zeitlinger.

Stanovich, K. E., & Siegel, L. S. (1994). Phenotypic performance profile of children with reading disabilities: A regression-based test of the phonological–core variable–difference model. *Journal of Educational Psychology, 86*, 24–53.

Steeves, K. J. (1983). Memory as a factor in the computational efficiency of dyslexic children with high abstract reasoning ability. *Annals of Dyslexia, 33*, 141–152.

Suhr, J. A. (2008). Assessment versus testing and its importance in learning disability diagnosis. In E. Fletcher-Janzen & C. R. Reynolds (Eds.), *Neuropsychological perspectives on learning disabilities in the era of RTI: Recommendations for diagnosis and intervention* (pp. 99–114). Hoboken, NJ: Wiley.

Swanson, H. L., & Hoskyn, M. (1998). Experimental intervention research on students with learning disabilities: A meta-analysis of treatment outcomes. *Review of Educational Research, 68*, 277–321.

Torgesen, J. K. (2002). The prevention of reading difficulties. *Journal of School Psychology, 40* (1), 7–26.

Vygotsky, L. S. (1978). *Mind in society: The development of higher psychological processes.* Cambridge, MA: Harvard University Press.

Wagner, R. K., & Torgesen, J. K. (1987). The nature of phonological processing and its causal role in the acquisition of reading skills. *Psychological Bulletins, 101* (2), 192–212.

Wechsler, D. (2009). *Wechsler individual achievement test* (3rd ed.). San Antonio, TX: Pearson.

Willis, J. O., & Dumont, R. (2002). *Guide to identification of learning disabilities* (3rd ed.). Peterborough, NH: Authors.

Windsor, J., & Kohnert, K. (2008). Processing measures of cognitive-linguistic interactions for children with language impairment and reading disabilities. In M. Mody & E. Silliman (Eds.), *Language impairment and reading disability—Interactions among brain, behavior, and experience* (pp. 135–160). New York, NY: Guilford Press.

Wise, B. W., & Olson, R. K. (1991). Remediating reading disabilities. In J. E. Obrzut & G. W. Hynd (Eds.), *Neuropsychological foundations of learning disabilities: A handbook of issues, methods, and practice* (pp. 631–658). San Diego, CA: Academic Press.

Wolf, M. (1991). Naming-speed and reading: The contribution of the cognitive neurosciences. *Reading Research Quarterly, 26*, 123–141.

Wolf, M., Bowers, P. G., & Biddle, K. (2000). Naming-speed processes, timing, and reading: A conceptual review. *Journal of Learning Disabilities, 33*, 387–407.

Woodcock, R. W. (1978). *Development and standardization of the Woodcock-Johnson Psycho-Educational Battery.* Itasca, IL: Riverside Publishing.

Woodcock, R. W. (1987). *Woodcock Reading Mastery Tests—Revised.* Circle Pines, MN: American Guidance Service.

Woodcock, R. W. (1990). Theoretical foundations of the WJ-R measures of cognitive ability. *Journal of Psychoeducational Assessment, 8*, 231–258.

Woodcock, R. W. (1998). Extending *Gf-Gc* theory into practice. In J. J. McArdle & R. W. Woodcock (Eds.), *Human cognitive abilities in theory and practice* (pp. 137–156). Mahwah, NJ: Erlbaum.

Woodcock, R. W., & Dahl, M. N. (1971). *A common scale for the measurement of person ability and test item difficulty* (AGS Paper No. 10). Circle Pines, MN: American Guidance Service.

Woodcock, R. W., & Johnson, M. B. (1977). *Woodcock-Johnson Psycho-Educational Battery.* Itasca, IL: Riverside.

Woodcock, R. W., & Johnson, M. B. (1989). *Woodcock-Johnson Psycho-Educational Battery—Revised.* Itasca, IL: Riverside.

Woodcock, R. W., McGrew, K. S., & Mather, N. (2001). *Woodcock-Johnson III.* Itasca, IL: Riverside.

Woodcock, R. W., McGrew, K. S., & Mather, N. (2007). *Woodcock-Johnson III Normative Update.* Rolling Meadows, IL: Riverside.

Wright, B. D., & Stone, M. H. (1979). *Best test design.* Chicago, IL: MESA Press.

Annotated Bibliography

Flanagan, D. P., & Alfonso, V. C. (Eds.). (in press). *WJ IV clinical use and interpretation: Scientist-practitioner perspectives*. Manuscript in preparation.

This book is a comprehensive resource on the WJ IV and is divided into three parts. Part I provides information on how to interpret the WJ IV, including a description of the instructional implications that may be garnered from test performance by subtest and composite, as well as the use of online scoring and how to interpret the various discrepancy approaches that are available. Part II addresses the clinical and diagnostic utility of the WJ IV. Specifically, this part of the book addresses use of the WJ IV in identifying individuals with learning disabilities and intellectual disabilities, as well as individuals who are intellectually gifted. Part II also addresses use of the WJ IV with individuals from culturally and linguistically diverse backgrounds. Part III describes the use of the WJ IV in evidence-based assessment approaches, including neuropsychological assessment and cross-battery assessment, as well as in a response-to-intervention service delivery model.

Flanagan, D. P., Ortiz, S. O., & Alfonso, V. C. (2013). *Essentials of cross-battery assessment* (3rd ed.). Hoboken, NJ: Wiley.

This book describes a time-efficient approach to assessment and interpretation that allows for the integration of data from more than one battery to best address referral concerns. This approach, known as *cross-battery assessment* (or XBA), is based on rigorous psychometric principles and procedures and is grounded mainly in contemporary CHC theory, although its application to neuropsychological theory is discussed and demonstrated. In addition, this book shows how to use XBA within the context of a pattern of strengths and weaknesses method for identifying specific learning disabilities (SLD). Three software programs are included with this book to assist in interpreting XBA data, identifying a pattern of strengths and weaknesses consistent with SLD, and determining whether performance on ability tests is valid for individuals from diverse cultural and linguistic backgrounds.

Mascolo, J. T., Alfonso, V. C., & Flanagan, D. P. (Eds.). (2014). *Essentials of planning, selecting, and tailoring interventions for unique learners*. Hoboken, NJ: Wiley.

This book is intended to serve as a resource for practitioners who work with students with learning difficulties and disabilities. It provides guidelines and at times step-by-step procedures for identifying targets for intervention based on the available data. Numerous interventions are discussed and reviewed in this book, with particular emphasis on how they may be tailored to meet the student's unique learning needs. Practitioners will also learn how to intervene with students from underserved and misserved populations who are at risk for academic failure, including students from impoverished environments.

Mather, N., & Jaffe, L. (in press). *Woodcock-Johnson IV: Recommendations, reports, and strategies.* Hoboken, NJ: Wiley.

This book is intended to serve as a resource for evaluators using the WJ IV in educational and clinical settings. Its purpose is to assist examiners in interpreting the WJ IV and preparing and writing psychological and educational reports for individuals of all ages. It covers the WJ IV COG, WJ IV OL, and WJ IV ACH batteries and includes numerous recommendations and descriptions of research-based interventions that may be included in assessment reports. Case studies are included to illustrate the use and interpretation of the WJ IV.

Mather, N., & Wendling, B. J. (2014). Examiner's Manual. *Woodcock-Johnson IV Tests of Achievement.* Rolling Meadows, IL: Riverside.

The manual comes as part of the WJ IV ACH test kit. It provides a description of the tests and clusters in the WJ IV ACH, as well as information about administering, scoring, and interpreting the test. The Scoring Guide for Writing Samples and the reproducible Examiner Checklists are included in the manual's appendices.

Mather, N., & Wendling, B. J. (2014). Examiner's Manual. *Woodcock-Johnson IV Tests of Oral Language.* Rolling Meadows, IL: Riverside.

The manual comes as part of the WJ IV OL test kit. It provides a description of the tests and clusters in the WJ IV OL, as well as information about administering, scoring, and interpreting the test. The reproducible Examiner Checklists are included in the manual's appendices.

McGrew, K. S., LaForte, E. M., & Schrank, F. A. (2014). Technical Manual. *Woodcock-Johnson IV.* Rolling Meadows, IL: Riverside.

This manual comes as part of the WJ IV ACH test kit. It provides information about the design criteria for the complete WJ IV, development of the norms, and the standardization procedures. This manual presents reliability and validity studies and covers the cognitive, achievement, and oral language batteries. Numerous statistical tables are included for clinicians and researchers.

Index

Abilities:
  broad and narrow, 13–14, 102
    (see also individual tests)
  CHC (see CHC theory)
Ability/achievement comparison
    procedures, 18, 151–154, 219
  academic knowledge/achievement,
    18, 151–153, 239–241
  amplio lenguaje oral/achievement,
    193–194
  oral language/achievement, 18, 193–197
  other ability/achievement, 154
Academic Applications cluster, 137
Academic Fluency cluster, 136–137
Academic Knowledge cluster, 137
  factors that can affect performance,
    236
Academic Knowledge/achievement
    comparison procedure. See
    Ability/achievement comparison
    procedures
Academic Skills cluster, 136
Accommodations, 25–30
  for behavioral/attention disorders, 29
  for English language learners, 26–27,
    (see also Cognitive Academic
    Language Proficiency [CALP])
  for learning/reading disabilities,
    28–29
  for physical impairments, 28
  for preschoolers, 26
  for sensory impairments, 28
Achievement. See specific achievement
    area

ADHD. See Attention Deficit
    Hyperactivity Disorder
    (ADHD)
Administration, 21–68
  audio-recorded tests, 36–37, 165
  basal/ceiling rules, 33–35
  cautions, 25–30
  complete page, testing by, 33
  confidentiality, 30–31
  errors, common, 37
  modifying standardized procedures of,
    25–26, 29
  rapport, 24–25
  Response Booklet (RB), 23, 36
  selective testing, 21–22, 160
  and special needs individuals
    (see Accommodations)
  starting points, 32
  testing environment, 23
  testing materials, 23, 164
  testing order, 31–32, 164
  timed tests, 34, 36, 164–165
  time requirements, 32
  See also individual tests
Age-based norms. See Norms, age
Age equivalents. See Scores, age and
    grade equivalents (AE/GE)
Age profile. See Profiles, age/grade
Age range, 2, 15, 69, 87
Alternate forms of achievement.
    See Parallel forms of
    achievement
Amplio lenguaje oral cluster, 190, 194,
    197–198, 325

339